COMPUTERS AND INFORMATION PROCESSING

COMPUTERS AND INFORMATION PROCESSING

Gordon B. Davis

Professor, Management Information Systems
University of Minnesota

McGraw-Hill Book Company

New York   St. Louis   San Francisco   Auckland   Bogotá   Düsseldorf
Johannesburg   London   Madrid   Mexico   Montreal   New Delhi   Panama
Paris   São Paulo   Singapore   Sydney   Tokyo   Toronto

1 2 3 4 5 6 7 8 9 DODO 7 8 3 2 1 0 9 8 7

This book was set in Plantin by York Graphic Services, Inc.
The editors were Peter D. Nalle and Annette Hall;
the cover was designed by John Hite;
the production supervisor was Joe Campanella.
R. R. Donnelley & Sons Company was printer and binder.

Library of Congress Cataloging in Publication Data

Davis, Gordon Bitter.
    Computers and information processing.

    Condensation of the author's Introduction to computers, 3d ed., with additional material.
    Bibliography: p.
    Includes index.
    1. Electronic digital computers. 2. Electronic data processing. 3. Programming languages (Electronic computers) I. Davis, Gordon Bitter. Introduction to computers. II. Title.
QA76.5.D292   001.6′4   77-11613
ISBN 0-07-015564-X

CONTENTS

APPENDIXES

PREFACE

The computer is a central force in changes occurring in many fields: production, management, accounting, mathematics, and information retrieval to name a few. It has been and will continue to be a dominant influence in information processing in organizations. As such, it is a topic of interest for anyone having contact with organizational information processing—as an employee, customer, manager, etc. A knowledge of computers is a necessity for students who expect to understand modern organizational practices.

This text represents a condensation of a larger text, *Introduction to Computers,* Third Edition, McGraw-Hill Book Company, 1977. The longer book includes seven chapters which are omitted from this shorter version. The omitted chapters are:

>Computer Arithmetic and Data Representation
>Machine-oriented Symbolic Assembly Language
>The BASIC Programming Language
>FORTRAN—Elementary Features
>FORTRAN—Additional Features
>Elementary COBOL
>Additional Features of COBOL

In other words, the difference between the two texts is primarily in the omission of the detailed language chapters for assembly language and the three high-level languages.

This text can be used very effectively as a general introduction to computers and information processing in two types of courses:

1 A general course which includes a survey of programming languages but without specific programming problems.

2 A general, introductory course which is accompanied by the study of a specific language, such as BASIC, COBOL, FORTRAN, or PL/I, etc.

There are two programming language texts which make excellent companion volumes for implementing the second type of course with either the COBOL or the FORTRAN language. The language texts implement the approach to programming discipline described in this text.

Davis, Olson, and Litecky: *Elementary Structured COBOL*, McGraw-Hill Book Company, 1977.

Davis and Hoffmann: *FORTRAN—A Structured, Disciplined Style*, McGraw-Hill Book Company, 1978.

Recent emphasis in information processing systems has been upon the development of a master plan for the organizational information system, the use of programming discipline in the design and coding of computer programs, and the use of structured programming concepts. There is also an emphasis on terminal-based systems and remote data entry. All these developments are emphasized in the text. The text also covers in some depth the necessity for adequate information and adequate controls in information processing. Some major features of the text are:

1 Material on the development life cycle for both data processing applications and mathematical-statistical-modeling applications (Chapter 3).

2 Discussion of alternative processing methodology (Chapter 3).

3 A chapter on computer program structure and design, emphasizing programming discipline, structured design, and top-down development (Chapter 5).

4 Arrangement of chapters to place the chapters on development of computer applications and computer programs early in the text (Chapters 3–5).

5 A chapter which describes the concept of high-level languages and surveys alternatives in language selection, including packages (Chapter 6).

6 A discussion of data preparation methods and alternatives for data preparation in systems designs (Chapter 8).

7 Coverage of the data processing service center alternative to an in-house computer (Chapter 10).

8 Explanation of quality control in computer processing (Chapter 11).

9 Material on selecting application hardware and software (Chapter 12).

10 Reference appendixes on the CDP examination and computer organizations and a glossary of terms.

The technology of computer hardware continues to change very rapidly, and no textbook can be completely current. The student of computers in information processing is urged to read selections from journals in the field. A list of journals and suggestions for the beginning student are contained in Appendix 2. An *Instructor's Manual* is available.

Gordon B. Davis

COMPUTERS AND INFORMATION PROCESSING

1

INTRODUCTION

The chapters in Part 1 provide an introduction to the study of computers. The first chapter gives an historical overview and surveys the equipment and other elements to be found in computer systems. Chapter 2 describes some of the uses for computers. The variety of uses provides a background for the study of computer application development, computer technology, computer operations, and programming languages.

Chapter

1

An
Overview
of Computers

The modern computer represents a fundamental advance in computation on a par with other advances such as the development of the zero or the discovery of calculus. The computer is a result of, and a major contributor to, the current technological explosion. No one can escape some contact with computers. This contact may result from such mundane computer applications as the preparation of payroll checks and department store charge account billings, or it may be from such esoteric activities as predictions of the outcome of elections or analysis of the probable authorship of ancient documents. Since the present and the future are often best understood in terms of the past, it will be valuable to an understanding of computers to briefly review their history.

Definition of a Computer

Strictly speaking, a computer is any calculating device. The name is derived from the Latin *computare,* meaning "to reckon" or "to compute," and can be applied as properly to an abacus or an adding machine as to the modern computer. However, the term "computer" has come to mean a special type of calculating device having certain definite characteristics.

There are basically two types of computers—analog and digital. *Analog computers* use electronic circuitry to represent physical processes, with changes in electric current representing the behavior of the system being studied. *Digital computers,* on the other hand, are based essentially on counting operations. A *hybrid computer* is a combination of an analog and a digital computer. Most modern computers are digital computers, and usually digital computers are meant when the word "computer" is used. For this reason, the explanations in the chapters to follow apply only to digital computers.

Several characteristics typically found in digital computers differentiate them from mechanical and electronic calculators. These features are speed, internal memory, and stored program. The speed of the electronic computer is the result of electronic circuitry. Mechanical counters are severely limited by the speed with which mechanical devices can start, move, and stop, while the speed of electronic circuitry is limited only by the speed at which electricity is transmitted (which is the speed of light). Electronic computers can hold data and instructions in an electronic representation in an internal memory unit. This feature not only adds to the speed of processing but also forms the basis for a stored program. In contrast to a mechanical or electronic calculator, which requires human direction at each step in a computational routine, the computer is automatic in the sense that the stored program will direct the performance of a long and complicated sequence of operations without operator intervention. For this reason, early writers often spoke of the automatic computer as contrasted to the existing nonautomatic calculating devices. The stored program usually includes logical tests to determine which of many possible program steps should be taken at important junctures in the program. Thus, the stored program is not just a sequence of steps to be followed in computation but typically includes all possible paths that computation might take within the scope of the problem.

Historical Events in the Development of Computers

While modern computers were not developed until the late 1940s, some important prior developments were the algebra of logic by George Boole, the punched card by Herman Hollerith, and the calculator built by George Aiken. Also important historically is Charles Babbage. His work did not directly influence the design of the first modern computer, but certain basic ideas of the stored computer program can be traced to this remarkable nineteenth-century inventor.

Babbage and the Analytic Engine

In 1812, Charles Babbage, professor of mathematics at Cambridge University, devised a machine called a "difference engine" to automatically perform simple computations needed for trigonometric and logarithmic tables. Babbage's difference engine carried out a set sequence of operations one at a time, but Babbage also conceived of an analytic engine which would execute an arbitrary sequence of operations and would have internal storage for data. Babbage's description of the analytic engine's stored program is remarkably close to the concept of the stored program of modern computers.

Boolean Algebra

The switching networks in a computer can be very complex, and the logic of a complicated program can be very difficult to analyze. Boolean algebra provides a systematic method of representation and analysis. It is named after the English mathematician George Boole, who pioneered in the field of symbolic logic. His book *The Laws of Thought,* published in 1854, represents logic in mathematical symbols and provides rules for calculating the truth or falsity of statements.

A simple illustration will show why mathematical logic is important in the design of computers. If an electronic switch is open, we shall assign the value 0, and if it is closed, we shall assign the value 1. These two states of the switch will correspond to the values of false (0) and true (1) in the symbolic logic of Boolean algebra. Two switches which operate independently such that there is current at the output line C only if both switches A and B are closed can be described by the Boolean statement A AND B (written symbolically as A $\land$ B). A circuit in which there will be current at C if either A or B is closed is described by the Boolean statement A OR B (A $\lor$ B). The results from these circuits can be described by examining all possible combinations of open and closed states for switches A and B and determining the effect on output C. The resulting tables (Table 1-1) are identical to the truth tables derived from symbolic logic. The work of Boole and others in the mathematics of symbolic logic thus provided an analytical basis for computer design.

TABLE 1-1 ANALYSIS OF SWITCHING CIRCUITS

GIVEN THESE COMBINATIONS OF SWITCH POSITIONS		AND CIRCUIT DESIGN DESCRIBED BY A ∧ B		AND CIRCUIT DESIGN DESCRIBED BY A ∨ B	
A	B	Diagram	Output at C	Diagram	Output at C
Closed	Closed		On		On
Closed	Open		Off		On
Open	Closed		Off		On
Open	Open		Off		Off

The Machine-readable Punched Card

Although not a component of the electronic computer, the punched card has become an integral part of input to data processing using electronic computers, and as such, it should be mentioned in a history of electronic computers. The use of punched cards began in 1745 when a Frenchman, Joseph M. Jacquard, designed a method for using holes in cards to control the selection of threads in weaving designs. Babbage also proposed cards with holes as input for data into the analytic engine.

The originator of the modern machine-readable punched card was Herman Hollerith. The need for mechanical tabulating equipment was seen by Hollerith while working with the 1880 United States census. During the 1880s, he developed the idea of the punched card and designed a *census machine*. The Hollerith method was chosen for tabulating the 1890 census, and the tabulation was done quickly and at a substantial savings in cost over the previous hand method. In 1896, Hollerith organized the Tabulating Machine Company to manufacture and market the machines and cards. This company merged with others to eventually become International Business Machines Corporation (IBM). James Powers, also connected with the Bureau of the Census, designed some card-processing equipment with slightly different features. This equipment was used to tabulate the 1910 census. In 1911, Powers formed the Powers Accounting Machine Company, subsequently acquired by Remington Rand (now a division of Sperry Rand Corporation). The cards designed by Hollerith used 80 columns and rectangular punches, while those designed by Powers used 90 columns and round punches. Sperry Rand has discontinued the 90-column card, and the field is dominated by the 80-column Hollerith card (Figure 1-1). A 96-column small card is used primarily in connection with the IBM System/3 computer introduced in 1969 (Figure 1-2). The small size is made possible by use of very small holes and a more compact coding scheme.

It is helpful to understand how data is encoded in punched cards. In the 80-column card there are 80 columns, and each column has 12 rows or punching positions numbered (from top to bottom) 12, 11, 0, 1, . . . , 9. A numeric digit 0 to 9 is encoded in a column by punching the corresponding row position (see Figure 1-1). An alphabetic character is encoded by a combination of a zone punch

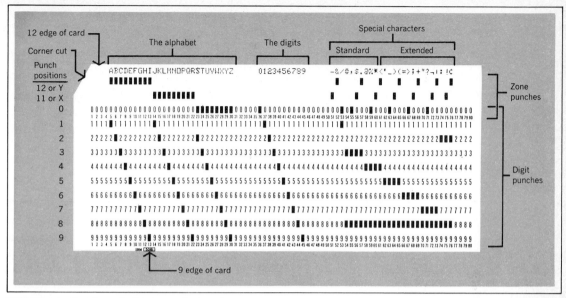

FIGURE 1-1 80-column Hollerith punched card.

in row 12, 11, or 0, and a numeric punch in rows 1 through 9. For example, the letter A is a 12 punch plus a 1 punch; the letter Z is a 0 punch plus a 9 punch. Special characters such as # and $ are encoded by a zone punch and one or more numeric punches. The 96-column card is divided into three separate areas each of

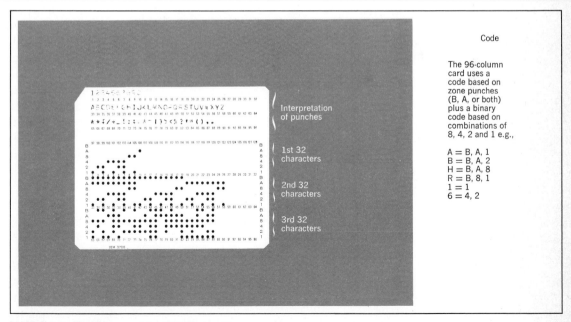

FIGURE 1-2 96-column card for IBM System/3.

which encodes 32 characters using two zone positions (named B and A) and four numeric positions having a value of 8, 4, 2, and 1. The three sets of codes are interpreted in three lines across the top. For example, the code for 3 is a 2 and a 1 punch; the code for an A is an A and a B punch and a 1 punch; the code for D is an A and a B punch plus a 4 punch.

There are several variations in the design of 80-column punched cards:

1   *Rounded corners versus square corners*   Corners of cards are prone to bending and then becoming jammed in the equipment; rounding the corners reduces this problem (Figure 1-3). The corner cut is used to keep all the cards in a deck with the top edge up. The cut may be on the left or right corner.

2   *Color*   Cards come in a variety of colors. Coloring a card or printing a colored stripe on the top edge is often used to differentiate the uses of cards.

3   *Printing*   The card may have nothing printed on it except the column numbers, or it may be printed with a design which shows the type of data in each column (Figure 1-3).

4   *Printing of card contents on the card itself*   It is customary, when punching data into cards with a keypunch, to print the contents of the card across the top, each character being printed above the punch which represents it. The contents of the card may be printed elsewhere on the card by the use of an interpreter.

FIGURE 1-3 Punched card with rounded corners and printed format to show card column contents.

5 *Hole codes* There are two different hole codes for some of the special characters. Older style punches use one code; newer punches tend to use an expanded code.

The Automatic Sequence Controlled Calculator—Mark I

In 1937, Howard Aiken of Harvard University designed a machine that would automatically perform a sequence of arithmetic operations. Completed in 1944, the Mark I was essentially a huge mechanical calculator. It contained 72 adding accumulators and 60 sets of switches for setting constants and was instructed by means of switches, buttons, wire plugboards, and punched tape. Information was represented by patterns of open and closed mechanical relays. The Harvard Mark I was the immediate predecessor of automatic electronic computers. The ENIAC (described below), although lacking some features associated with computers, is the machine which bridges the gap between mechanical calculating machines and electronic devices.

The First Generation of Automatic Computers

ENIAC[1] (Electronic Numerical Integrator and Calculator)

The ENIAC was designed by J. Presper Eckert and John W. Mauchly of the Moore School of Engineering of the University of Pennsylvania, and was much faster than the Mark I. It did not have an internally stored memory, but was programmed instead by means of switches and plug-in connections. Completed in 1947, the ENIAC was used mainly for calculating tables. It is often identified as the first electronic computer. Eckert and Mauchly can therefore be identified as the originators of the electronic computer. As with many inventions it is difficult to identify the originator of the idea. For example, in a lawsuit relating to validity of early patents by Eckert and Mauchly, some of the key concepts for an electronic computer were traced to I. V. Atanasoff, a theoretical physicist whose ideas and computing devices were known to Eckert and Mauchly.

EDVAC, EDSAC, and IAS

During the work on the ENIAC, Eckert, Mauchly, and others working with them designed a larger machine called the EDVAC, which was different from the ENIAC in two fundamental ways. These differences were in the use of binary numbers for electronic arithmetic operations and in the internal storage of instructions written in digital form. The completion of the EDVAC was delayed until 1952, but the EDVAC design can be considered the prototype of serial computers. Another computer using internal storage, called EDSAC, which was completed in 1949 at the University of Manchester (England), is identified as the first stored program computer.

[1] The student of computers will find a frequent use of acronyms, i.e., words formed from the initial letter or letters of the words describing some item. Examples are ENIAC and EDVAC. The "AC" ending of names for many early computers usually stands for "automatic computer."

John von Neumann, a noted mathematician, had become acquainted with the computer work of Eckert and Mauchly during a stay at the Moore School. He became interested in the use of computers for numerical analysis and also in the design of the computer itself. The writings of von Neumann are significant because they contain a description of the computer logic being developed by Eckert and others at the Moore School. The IAS computer, which began as a joint project of Princeton's Institute for Advanced Study and the Moore School, was first described in a report prepared for the U.S. Army Ordnance Department.[1] The paper describes the features which should be incorporated into a computer. Of note is the suggestion that the proposed computer be a parallel machine rather than a serial machine. The IAS computer, not actually completed until 1952, used the binary system, a one-address command structure (explained in a later chapter), and parallel arithmetic. The EDVAC and the IAS thus introduced the basic designs for two important types of computers—serial and parallel. The differences between the two types are in the methods of moving information from one part of the machine to another and of performing addition. The parallel machine moves all the digits in a number at the same time, the serial machine moves them a digit at a time. When the parallel concept is used for addition, all corresponding pairs of digits are added simultaneously. In a serial machine, pairs of digits are added a pair at a time, in much the same fashion as in manual arithmetic.

UNIVAC (UNIVersal Automatic Computer)

The UNIVAC I is important because it was the first commercially available computer. It was built as a commercial venture by the Eckert-Mauchly Computer Company, founded in 1946 by Eckert and Mauchly and purchased in 1949 by Remington Rand (later Sperry Rand). The UNIVAC I followed the EDVAC design but used the one-address structure of the IAS.

The first UNIVAC computer went into operation at the Bureau of the Census in April 1951. The first UNIVAC installation for business use was at General Electric Appliance Park in Louisville, Kentucky, in 1954. The name UNIVAC was synonymous with "computer" for a few years until IBM, which initially showed only a limited interest in computers, changed directions and entered the computer field.

The computers discussed above are significant because they represented important new concepts in computer design. However, many other computers were developed during this period. First in operation was the ENIAC in 1947, then the EDSAC and BINAC in 1949, four separate machines in 1950, and six machines in 1951. The first year in which computers were commercially available was 1951, with two UNIVAC Is being installed.

In 1953, IBM installed its first computer, the IBM 701. Late in 1954, IBM installed the first IBM 650 computer. The IBM 650 computer was the most

---

[1] This report, entitled "Preliminary Discussion of the Logical Design of an Electronic Computing Instrument," was never issued to the public. However, it has been reprinted in two parts in *Datamation,* pp. 24-31, September 1962, and pp. 36-41, October 1962.

popular computer during the next 5 years. The computers of this period are often referred to as the "first-generation computers." They generally used vacuum tubes, were large, required much air conditioning, had little internal storage, and were relatively slow.

Computers since the First Generation

A transistor performs the same function as a vacuum tube but is smaller, less expensive, generates little heat, and requires little power. The change from tubes to transistors began with military computers in 1956 and with commercial computers in 1959 (Figure 1-4). The computers of the period 1959 to 1965 are referred to as "second-generation computers." The most widely used second-generation computers were:

Model	Size and orientation
IBM 1620	Small scientific computer
IBM 1401	Small to medium commercial computer
IBM 7094	Large scientific computer

The third generation of computers is generally dated from 1965 when IBM introduced a family of computers. The family was termed System/360 with each

FIGURE 1-4 Transistor circuit card for a computer (about 1960). (*Courtesy of UNIVAC Division of Sperry Rand Corporation.*)

size or model having a unique number. For example, System/360 model 30 was a small computer; System/360 model 65 was a fairly large computer. The System/360 continued the trend toward miniaturization. IBM chose a hybrid technique termed "solid logic technology" in which tiny chip transistors and diodes were mounted on a ceramic base (Figure 1-5). The elements were interconnected by a printed circuit. The completed module, about $\frac{1}{2}$ in. square, was enclosed in plastic. Other vendors during the period used integrated circuitry in which the entire circuit is formed from the controlled growth of a crystal structure.

The computers in the third generation from about 1965 to 1970 were characterized by hybrid or integrated circuits, by the integration of hardware with software (programming and operating aids), by an orientation to data communications, and by the handling of more than one processing program simultaneously. The third-generation idea of a compatible family of computers which allows a user to move from a smaller to a larger model without reprogramming was an important concept fully implemented by many computer vendors. The dominant third-generation computer was the IBM System/360. A small scientific computer, the IBM 1130, also received substantial use. The System/3, a family of small computers for business data processing and other uses, was introduced in 1969. It had become by 1975 the most common computer (over 30,000 in use).

The idea of computer generations having about a 5-year life can be seen from the active marketing periods for the first-, second-, and third-generation equipment just described. Although some vendors have used the term "fourth generation," there appears to be a trend away from the revolutionary changes of the three generations and a more gradual upgrading and improvement. This is illustrated by the IBM System/370 introduced in 1970. The equipment is compatible in design and concept with the predecessor IBM System/360 but uses improved, faster hardware features and more advanced storage organization and operating systems.

FIGURE 1-5 Chip transistor assembled onto ceramic base with printed circuit (left) and encased in plastic (right). Compare the size of this module (1965) with 1960 circuit card in Figure 1-4. (*Courtesy of International Business Machines Corporation.*)

The circuitry advances were primarily in the use of integrated circuits containing hundreds of circuits or memory elements (say, 1024 to 2048) on a single chip $\frac{1}{8}$ in. square (Figure 1-6). These circuits provide lower cost, improved speed, reduced failures, etc. Other improvements have been introduced in input and output devices and in data communications facilities.

Elements of a Computer Processing System

There are five basic elements in a system which uses a computer for processing data, performing computations, etc. These are hardware, system software, application software, procedures, and personnel. Each of these is defined in this chapter and receives further explanation in subsequent chapters.

Hardware Hardware for computer processing involves equipment which can perform the following functions: data preparation, input to the computer, processing, secondary

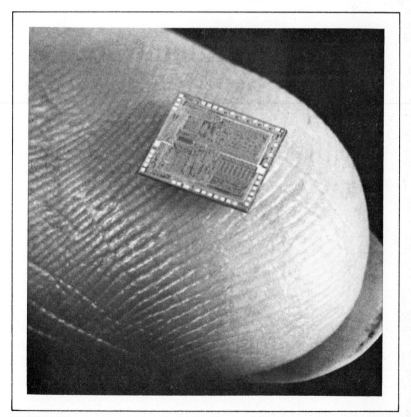

FIGURE 1-6 Integrated circuit of type used with 1970s computers. (*Courtesy of Intel Corporation.*)

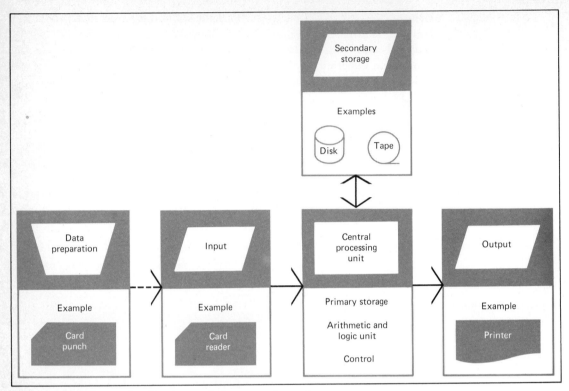

FIGURE 1-7 Equipment functions in a computer processing system.

or auxiliary storage, and output from the computer. Equipment may be online, i.e., connected directly to the computer, or offline. The relationship of the different equipment functions is shown in Figure 1-7.

System Software   System software consists of nonhardware aids, namely, computer programs and computer routines which facilitate the operation of the computer by the user installation. These aids consist of computer programs for standard tasks such as sorting data records, organizing and maintaining files, translating programs written in a symbolic language into machine-language instructions, and scheduling jobs through the computer. Perhaps the most important system software is the operating system, a set of programs which directs and manages the execution of jobs by the computer. System software is as vital to effective use of a computer as the hardware.

Application Software   Application software consists of programs for performing specific processing applications. A program consists of a set of instructions to the computer to perform a set of operations. Each user, whether organization or individual, normally writes some programs for unique applications; however, generalized applications programs can be purchased or leased from software organizations. The terms "routine" and "program" are somewhat synonymous. *Routine* refers to a set of instructions to perform a particular process. A *program* may consist of one or more routines—for example, an input routine, a processing routine, and an output routine. The process by which an application program is developed and placed into use may vary depending on the type of application. Figure 1-8 describes the activities to develop and use a computer program for a simple application. The cycle of activities for such development is explained in greater detail in Chapter 3.

Procedures The operation of a data processing system requires procedures for obtaining and preparing data, operating the computer, distributing output from processing, initiating new programs, etc. These procedures include control steps such as actions to be taken by users in the event they detect errors or actions by operators if the equipment malfunctions.

Personnel Computer processing requires new skills. Three major classes of positions are required in computer processing installations: systems analyst, programmer, and computer operator. Additional positions are explained in Chapter 11. Of these jobs, that of systems analyst requires the broadest background in terms of education and understanding of organizations. The position of programmer requires a skill in coding (writing computer instructions). The computer operator function involves fairly well-defined tasks which do not require high technical skill, and therefore this job requires less training than the others.

Job title	Job description
Systems analyst	Study information and processing requirements. Design the flow of operations and prepare specifications for the processing system.
Programmer	Code computer programs based on specifications prepared by the systems analyst.
Computer operator	Operate the computer.

Processing Methods

Computer processing may be performed periodically in batch mode or immediately in online mode. A computer system may be dedicated to regularly scheduled jobs, or it may be shared by many unscheduled users simultaneously. The latter is termed "time sharing."

In batch processing, data to be processed is accumulated over a period of time.

Steps		Comments
1 Analysis of a problem and preparation of requirements for application	Proposed report	Collect information and decide what information is needed, frequency of processing, etc.
2 Design of a system to perform processing and provide required output		Plan the system of processing using a system flowchart plus layouts (diagrams) of reports, documents, records, files, etc.
3 Planning the computer program		Plan the program logic using a program flowchart and other methods of describing a program.
4 Program coding and testing	READ DATA. ADD A AND B GIVING C.	Write the program of instructions and debug it to remove all textual or logical errors. Translate it into machine language. Prepare program documentation. Prepare operator and user procedures.
5 Input data preparation	Document — Key-punching → Punched card	Prepare input data by collecting or transcribing data into machine-readable form such as punched cards.
6 Running of program	Program — Input → Computer → Output	Put program into computer memory. Computer program reads data, processes it, and outputs the result.
7 Use of the output	Report	

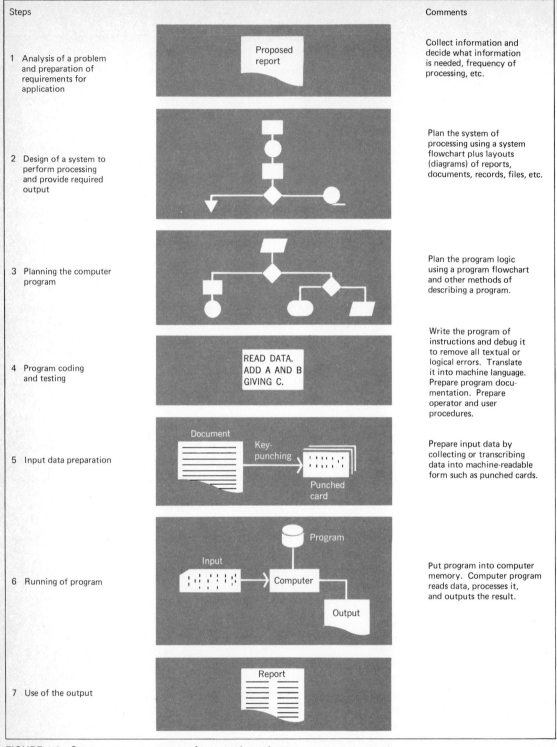

FIGURE 1-8 Steps in using a computer for a simple application.

The accumulated batch of transactions is processed periodically. This method is very efficient, but its use means that there is always a processing delay.

In online processing (also referred to as online realtime processing), each transaction is processed as soon as it is received. There is no waiting to accumulate a batch of transactions. Online realtime processing is used especially in situations such as a computerized reservation system where an immediate response is useful.

Time sharing is the concurrent use of a single computer system by many users, each of which has an input/output device and can access the same computer at the same time. The computer gives each user a small, but frequently repeated, slice of the time, so that each user gets almost immediate response.

The Equipment in a Computer Installation

The equipment that is found in a specific computer installation will depend on the amount and type of processing being performed and on the types of equipment available for that model of computer. In general, a computer system will have a central processing unit, plus one or more units of equipment for the functions of secondary storage, data preparation, input, and output.

The Central Processing Unit The central processing unit (CPU) is the "computer" part of the system. It contains an arithmetic unit for computation, a control unit, and the primary storage (also called the "main" or "internal memory"). The primary storage usually contains a part of the operating system software, one or more application programs being executed, and the data required by the programs. The control unit fetches instructions from the storage, decodes them, and directs the various equipment units to perform the specified functions. The arithmetic unit performs all arithmetic, comparisons, and data manipulation. There is a control console or control panel for operator use. Figure 1-9 shows a central processor with an attached console.

FIGURE 1-9 Central processing unit with attached console (IBM System/370 model 158). Console has visual display unit with keyboard and light pen for input. (*Courtesy of International Business Machines Corporation.*)

Secondary Storage   Also called "auxiliary storage," secondary storage is supplementary to the primary storage associated with the central processing unit. It is used to hold system software and application programs not currently required in primary storage plus data files. It has large-capacity storage relative to the primary storage. When a data record or program is to be used in processing, it is copied from the secondary storage into the primary storage. After processing, the updated record is stored back in its storage position in the auxiliary storage. Punched cards can be used for secondary storage, but magnetically encoded storage media are usually more desirable. Data can be written on a magnetic surface and read as many times as necessary. The storage may be used again by writing new records in place of the old records. The concept is identical to that of a home tape recorder—once recorded, the tape may be played as often as desired, and the tape may be reused by recording on it again. The most popular magnetic storage media, magnetic tape and magnetic disk, are illustrated in Figure 1-10.

Data Preparation   Data and programs must be in a machine-readable form in order to be read into the
Equipment   computer for processing or for recording on secondary storage for subsequent use. The most common machine-readable input medium is the punched card. The most common device to prepare punched cards is the card punch. Data may also be keyed directly onto a magnetic disk using a keydisk system. The data on the disk is transferred to magnetic tape for input. The keydisk system has substantial use because of several operating advances over the card punch.

FIGURE 1-10   Examples of commonly used secondary storage devices.

Both the card punch and the keydisk systems convert data that has been captured on a document. This process is expensive, time-consuming, and error-prone. There is a trend toward eliminating manual data conversion by creating a machine-readable by-product while recording the transaction or entering data directly into the computer via a terminal device such as a typewriter or visual display unit. Some common data preparation equipment is shown in Figure 1-11; additional explanation is given in Chapter 8.

Input Devices The machine-readable input medium prepared by data preparation equipment is read by an input device (Figure 1-12) and stored in internal memory for processing, writing onto secondary storage, or output. The most commonly used input device is the punched card reader. Paper tape readers are used when input data has been placed on punched paper tape. Magnetic character readers are used mainly in banks for check processing. Optical scanners are becoming more popular. They are used for reading ticket-type data, such as gasoline charge tickets and airline tickets, and for reading typed and handwritten documents.

Output Devices Figure 1-13 illustrates output devices. The printer is the most commonly used output device. Terminals such as typewriters and visual display devices are receiving substantial use especially in systems which require persons at various locations to input data for immediate processing and then receive a fast response or to interrogate the computer files. Output may be on paper or microfilm, it may be on a display tube, it may be in the form of a graph drawn by a graph plotter, or it may be in machine-readable form, such as punched cards or punched tape.

The Computer Industry

Except for the UNIVAC computers in the early 1950s, IBM has dominated the computer industry. In the United States, IBM has furnished about 70 percent of computers (by value) to organizations other than the military. There is a vigorous non-IBM industry which has frequently been innovative in hardware and software, but it has not been able to match IBM's marketing strength or profitability. The dominance of IBM in the United States market has resulted in frequent antitrust investigations and in a major court case, begun in 1975, to decide whether IBM should be restructured to provide more balanced competition.

Other than IBM, the major computer companies based in the United States marketing a full line of computers are Honeywell, UNIVAC (division of Sperry Rand), Burroughs, NCR, and Control Data. Several large, diversified companies have dropped out of the computer business. Major examples are General Electric, RCA, Xerox, and Singer. There are a number of somewhat specialized companies. For example, Digital Equipment Company is the dominant manufacturer of small, specialized computers called "minicomputers."

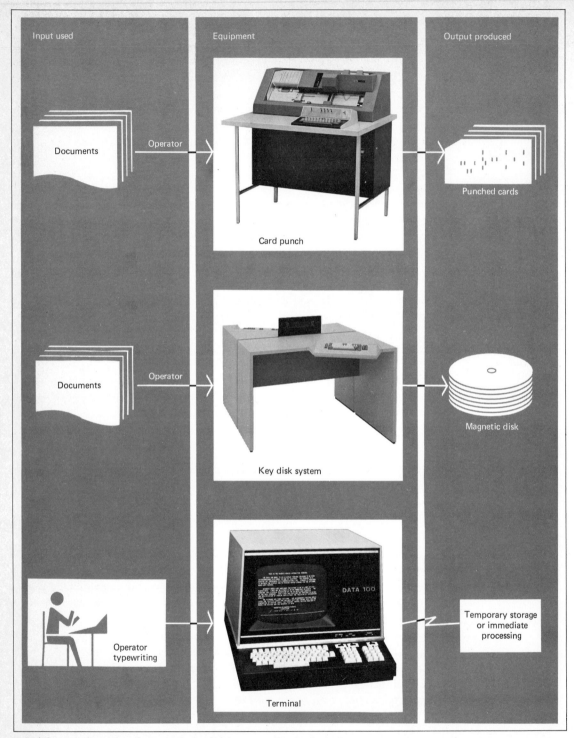

FIGURE 1-11 Examples of commonly used data preparation equipment.

FIGURE 1-11 (*Continued*)

Although some of the earliest work in computers was performed in Europe, the United States adopted computer technology at a considerably faster rate during the 1960s. But the European growth rate in computer use exceeds the United States in the 1970s. The United States–based computer companies are active worldwide. IBM, for example, has about 50 percent of the European market. There are a number of well-established computer manufacturers in most industrialized countries. The more significant vendors are based in Europe or Japan. The U.S.S.R. has a computer industry serving primarily the Eastern European countries. Some of the major European and Japanese manufacturers providing a comprehensive line of computers are shown below.

Manufacturer	Country of origin
CII (Compagnie Internationale pour L'Informatique)—Honeywell Bull	France
Nippon Electric Co.	Japan
Hitachi	Japan

Fujitsu	Japan
ICL (International Computers Limited)	Great Britain
Siemens	Germany

FIGURE 1-12 Examples of commonly used input devices.

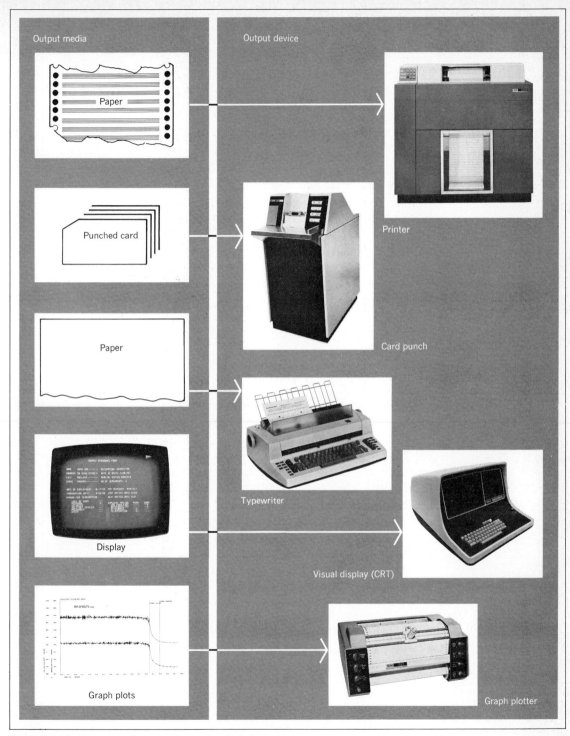

FIGURE 1-13 Examples of commonly used output devices.

The two largest of the European manufacturers are CII-HB and ICL. The European manufacturers have received considerable government subsidy and governmental direction to merge, cooperate, etc., with other vendors. For example, a European company called Unidata was formed in 1974 by Phillips, CII, and Siemens as a method of pooling design and marketing resources, but this effort was a failure. There is also some trend for the European companies to form arrangements with the United States computer companies. For example, CII purchased a majority interest in Honeywell-Bull (the European subsidiary of Honeywell computers); ICL, Control Data, and NCR have a joint venture to produce and market peripheral devices.

The computer manufacturers sell, rent, or lease equipment. Software may be furnished as part of the hardware price or may be priced separately (unbundled). A computer user may obtain the central processing unit from one vendor and peripheral devices (printer, tape and disk drives, etc.) from other vendors. These industry practices are the basis for a number of independent companies which provide software, peripherals, and computer leasing.

Computer System Configurations

Computer systems may range in price from simple minicomputer systems selling for less than $1000 to large-scale computing systems selling for several million dollars (renting for over $100,000 monthly). The cost of a computer configuration depends on the basic model plus the various options such as size of storage and number and type of devices. Figure 1-14 provides a rough idea of the range of costs for the computers of one manufacturer. Five configurations are described briefly in order to provide some idea of the type and cost of equipment a computer installation might contain. The large, medium, and small-scale systems are general purpose. The small-business computers and minicomputers are somewhat restricted in scope. Data preparation equipment is not included. Although not a computer system in the same sense as the four configurations, the microcomputer is also explained in this section.

One of the factors affecting computer system configurations is a trend toward distributed processing in which an organization having computer processing needs at several locations will use a network of computers interconnected by data communications. Each remote location has a small computer or minicomputer for input, output, communication with a central computer, and some local processing. A central location has a medium-to-large computer which does major processing tasks for the remote locations.

Large-Scale Computer   The costs of renting a large-scale computer system may range from about $50,000 to over $200,000 monthly (purchase prices ranging from $2 million to over $10 million). A large-scale system may have one or more central processing units for computation, perform operations such as an addition in less than one-millionth of a

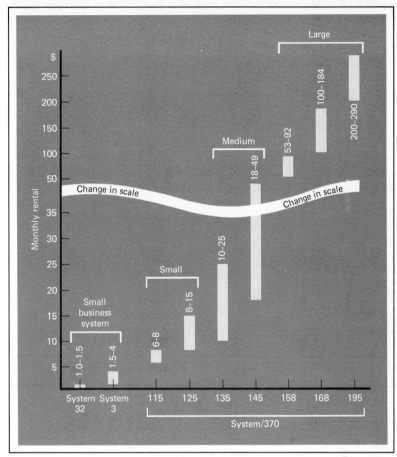

FIGURE 1-14 Monthly rental for typical configurations of IBM computers (adapted from data in DATAPRO).

second, have main storage hardware capability of storing several million characters, and include a large complement of input, output, and storage devices. Secondary storage directly accessible by the computer will range in billions of characters. The system can typically be working on a number of different programs or processing tasks at the same time, with at least some of the tasks involving input and output via data communications to remote terminals. Figure 1-15 shows the central processors in an IBM 370/168 multiprocessor system containing two processors. The input, output, and secondary storage devices are not shown.

Medium-Scale Computer   A medium-scale computer system has reduced capacity and performance compared with a large-scale system. Monthly rental for typical medium-scale systems is in the range of $15,000 to $45,000. Operating speeds are perhaps one-tenth to

FIGURE 1-15 Large-scale computer system—two central processors in an IBM 370/168 multiprocessor system. The input, output, and secondary storage devices are not shown. (*Courtesy of International Business Machines Corporation.*)

one-twentieth as fast as the large system. Main storage has a capacity of several hundred thousand characters (perhaps up to 1 million). Peripheral devices will include a card reader, card punch, high-speed printer, several magnetic tape drives (say, four), and several disk drives (say, four to six). It can process more than one program at a time.

Small-Scale Computer A small-scale general-purpose configuration (relative to the large- and medium-scale systems) will have the same type of equipment but will be much slower—it may take 3 to 10 times longer to perform operations. Internal storage will be smaller—say, 65,000 up to 260,000 characters of storage capacity. There will be fewer input, output, and storage devices. Figure 1-16 shows a small-scale computer system.

Small-Business Computer A number of small computer systems have been designed for the data processing requirements of small businesses. The configurations are generally more costly than the minicomputer (although they are similar in basic capabilities), and there are more available input and output devices and more vendor support for the use of the system in data processing. The systems may also be used as part of a large-scale configuration (say, as remote devices—doing limited functions at distant sites). The most common small-business computers are the IBM System/3 (over 30,000

FIGURE 1-16 Small-scale computer system—IBM System 370/115. (*Courtesy of International Business Machines Corporation.*)

installed) and the IBM System/32, but a large number of alternatives are available. The System/3 ($1000 to $4000 monthly rental) represents a small but somewhat traditional computer configuration, whereas the System/32 (less than $1000 per month rental) has a compact integrated design that makes it suitable for an office environment. Compared with the small-scale systems, the small-business computers are about as fast but less versatile. Internal storage tends to be small—say, 16,000 to 65,000 characters, and the storage, input, and output devices tend to be slower or of lower capacity. Figure 1-17 shows two small-business computer systems.

Minicomputer Systems

A minicomputer is a small computer, but there is no clear definition of how small a computer must be to be classified as a "mini." As a rough guide, a minicomputer costs less than $50,000 and probably costs less than $20,000. Several systems at the low end of the spectrum cost less than $5000. The typical minicomputer is small in size (mounted on a rack or put on a table), weighs less than 50 pounds, and uses a standard electrical outlet. It is fast in basic operations but has a limited set of instructions. Main memory is small (say, 8000 to 32,000 characters of storage), and the number of input and output devices is very limited. The minicomputer is frequently dedicated to a specific function such as control of a manufacturing process, management of data communications, and management of access to a database. Some of the larger minicomputers provide a low-cost (but limited capability) time-sharing system. Figure 1-18 shows a typical minicomputer system. An example of how minicomputer technology may be used for limited-purpose

FIGURE 1-17 Two small business computers—IBM System/3 and System/32. (*Courtesy of International Business Machines Corporation.*)

computers is the IBM 5100 desk-top computer. The basic system (about $9000 for purchase) has 16,000 characters of main memory, a built-in visual display for input and output, a built-in tape cartridge for auxiliary storage, and a built-in programming language interpreter. This computer is aimed at individual users who need the capabilities of a computer for small analytical, mathematical, and statistical problems.

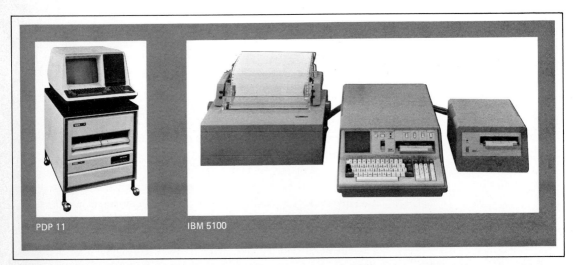

FIGURE 1-18 Two minicomputers—PDP 11 (*courtesy of Digital Equipment Corporation*) and IBM 5100 (*courtesy of International Business Machines Corporation*).

Microprocessors   A microprocessor is the "computing" part of a computer—on a chip. The microprocessor contains all the elements necessary to manipulate data. The chip is produced by etching and other processes which make and interconnect transistors, diodes, and resisters to make tiny but complete circuitry on a silicon wafer. A large number of circuits can be placed on a single chip costing less than $10 (Figure 1-19). Several chips may be combined to form a multichip processor. A power source and memory are required, as is some form of input and output to make an operational microcomputer.

The microprocessors are being used in a variety of applications. They form the computing logic for hand-held electronic calculators and desk computers. They provide a logic capability for directing the operation of machines of all types. They can add "intelligent" capabilities to data entry terminals, display devices, automobile carburetors, large household appliances, etc. For example, by using programmed logic in a microprocessor, a piece of equipment can automatically adjust itself to a variety of conditions affecting performance. Microprocessors are, therefore, likely to have a major impact on automobiles, household appliances, industrial equipment, etc.

SUMMARY   This chapter has provided an overview of the history of computers and has described the elements in a computer processing system, processing methods, the equipment found in a computer system, and typical system configurations. A computer was defined as a computational device having electronic construction, internal storage (for the program and the data being operated on), a stored program, and program modification capabilities. The history of computers starts in the 1940s with Aiken's automatic sequence controlled calculator, but the Hollerith

Microprocessor—16-bit CPU chip (actual size)

Microprocessor in a ceramic package with connections

Microcomputer—computer on a board ($7\frac{1}{2} \times 9\frac{1}{2}$ in.) with 4K words of memory

FIGURE 1-19   Microprocessor or CPU on a chip, microprocessor in a ceramic package, and microcomputer. (*Courtesy of Data General Corporation.*)

punched card was an important development preceding Aiken's machine. Babbage and Boole are also historically significant: Babbage for his idea of the computer, long before it was feasible to build one, and Boole for his mathematical logic, which is useful in designing computer circuits. In a fast-moving technological field, computer hardware is well past the first three generations—the first using vacuum tubes, the second using transistors, and the third using integrated circuits. During this period of development and change, increases in speed have been great and reductions in cost very significant.

The elements in a computer processing system were surveyed: hardware, system software, application software, procedures, and personnel. Each is explained in more detail in subsequent chapters. The hardware functions of data preparation, processing, secondary storage, input, and output were described briefly and illustrated. Methods of processing—periodic batch, online realtime, and time sharing—were defined. The computer industry in the United States and elsewhere was identified with the role of IBM noted. Computer configurations were described and illustrated.

EXERCISES

1 What was contributed to the development of computers by:
   (a) George Boole   (e) John von Neumann
   (b) Herman Hollerith   (f) J. Presper Eckert
   (c) Charles Babbage   (g) John W. Mauchly
   (d) Howard Aiken

2 What were the important features of:
   (a) ENIAC   (c) EDVAC   (e) UNIVAC I
   (b) MARK I   (d) IAS

3 Match the computer systems on the left with descriptions on the right.
   (a) IBM System/360   (1) Most popular first-generation computer
   (b) IBM 1401   (2) Most popular small scientific computer of second generation
   (c) IBM 1620   (3) Most popular large-scale second-generation computer
   (d) IBM 1130   (4) Most popular small-to-medium commercial computer of second generation
   (e) IBM 7094   (5) First commercially available computer
   (f) IBM System/3   (6) Popular small system using new-size punched cards
   (g) IBM 650   (7) Compatible successor to the System/360
   (h) UNIVAC I   (8) Most popular small scientific third-generation computer
   (i) System/370   (9) Most popular third-generation computer family

4 What are the essential functions of the equipment in a computer center?

5 List the equipment in your computer center, classifying it by function.

6 Define the following terms:
   (a) First-generation computer   (d) Integrated circuit
   (b) Second-generation computer   (e) Transistor
   (c) Third-generation computer   (f) Analog computer

(g) Analytic engine
(h) Boolean algebra
(i) Hollerith card
(j) Batch processing

(k) Acronym
(l) Time sharing
(m) Unbundled
(n) Operating system

7 Name and define the duties of the three major classes of positions in a computer processing installation.

8 What is the difference between a minicomputer and a microprocessor?

9 Identify the major European and Japanese manufacturers and country of origin:
(a) ICL   (c) Siemens   (e) Hitachi
(b) CII-HB   (d) Fujitsu

10 Describe the two main shapes for punched cards and the variations in 80-column cards.

11 Explain the difference between system software and application software.

12 Prepare a short report on one of the following topics (see the selected references at the end of the text plus general business reference sources):
(a) The difference between IBM and UNIVAC leading to the differing market shares.
(b) The IBM decision for the System/360.
(c) The rise and fall of Unidata.
(d) The decision to drop out of the computer business by General Electric, RCA, Xerox, and Singer.

13 Despite the companies which have dropped out of the computer business, new companies enter. Write a short report on the Amdahl Corporation.

Chapter

2

The Uses
of Computers

Capabilities of Computers
Advantages Possessed by the Computer
Advantages Possessed by Humans

Recordkeeping
Inventory Accounting—Periodic Batch Processing
Inventory Accounting—Immediate Processing

Customer Service
Airline Reservations
Savings Bank Transactions
Grocery Store Checkout

Computer-based Analysis and Processing
Linear Programming
Critical Path Analysis (PERT/CPM)
Systems Simulation
Information Retrieval

Education
Computer-assisted Programmed Learning
Decision Simulations

Guidance and Control
Missile and Submarine Guidance
Process Control
Message Switching

Management Information Systems

Other Interesting Uses of Computers
Prediction of Elections
Medical Diagnosis
Computer Art

Summary

Exercises

The computer is perhaps the most important technological element affecting society in the 1960s and 1970s. The computer is an important technological advance because it extends and expands human capabilities. Unaided, a human is rather puny. A person can lift perhaps 150 to 175 pounds, can move at 5 to 10 miles per hour, and can perform on the order of 10 to 15 additions of five-digit numbers per minute. Aided by equipment which extends their ability, humans may lift thousands of pounds, move themselves about at speeds of thousands of miles per hour, and perform millions of computations per minute. The computer is not only an extension of humans' ability to compute; it also expands their ability to store and retrieve data, to manipulate data, and to make decisions.

This chapter provides background for the chapters to follow by surveying the capabilities of computers and by describing a few representative ways in which computers are being used.

Capabilities of Computers

As illustrated by Table 2-1, a computer cannot perform any operation which cannot also be performed by a human, but the computer executes operations with such speed that it is in a different class. This speed also opens new approaches to problem solving and data processing. The speed of execution by computers ranges from several hundred million operations per second for a very large computer to tens of thousands of operations per second for a rather slow computer.

Although Table 2-1 indicates the ability of a human to do anything a computer

TABLE 2-1 WHAT A COMPUTER CAN DO

Operation performed by a computer	Corresponding action performed by a human
1 Hold program of instructions in internal storage.	1 Remember a set of instructions.
2 Read data in machine-readable form and store in internal memory or in secondary storage.	2 Read data in written or printed form and memorize it or file it.
3 Perform arithmetic computations.	3 Perform arithmetic computations.
4 Manipulate symbols (such as alphabetic characters or words).	4 Manipulate symbols.
5 Make comparisons.	5 Make comparisons.
6 Choose a path of instruction based on a comparison or an examination of the results to that point.	6 Make a decision as to further processing based on results to that point.
7 Retrieve any data from internal memory or secondary storage.	7 Remember data or retrieve data from a file.
8 Output the results on an output device.	8 Write or speak the results.

can do, the reverse is not true—a computer cannot do everything a human can do. Some people have characterized the computer as a very fast but somewhat moronic assistant. The computer does only what it is instructed, and these instructions must take into account every possible set of conditions relating to the action. Although a computer exceeds human capability in some activities, a human has some inherent advantages over a computer. The capabilities of computers and human clerks in performing data processing tasks are summarized in Table 2-2.

Advantages Possessed by the Computer

As seen from Table 2-2, the computer is extremely fast and almost perfect in reliability and accuracy. Once provided with a program of instructions, it will accurately retrieve information and will follow the set of directions perfectly. In substance, then, the computer is suited to any task that involves large amounts of retrieval, computation, manipulation, and comparison, so long as the procedures can be completely described in advance by a set of instructions.

Advantages Possessed by Humans

Humans are rather poor data processors. They are slow and not completely accurate. But they have two advantages—they can innovate or adapt, and they can reason heuristically. The ability to innovate and adapt means that a human's set of instructions does not have to anticipate everything that could happen because he or she can relate the new situation to old ones and make and execute a new procedure immediately.

Humans can reason heuristically. This means that they can learn by trial-and-error discovery. We do not usually reason in a simple step-by-step manner, but, in some fashion, we reach a conclusion based on trial and error, taking into account incomplete information and the effect of past experiences. A computer does not learn from past experience; a human does. Humans are aware of their environment and have their entire past experience always available; a computer has

TABLE 2-2 COMPARISON OF COMPUTERS AND CLERKS IN PERFORMING DATA PROCESSING TASKS

Basis for comparison	Clerk	Computer
Speed of execution	Relatively slow	Extremely fast
Ability to continue processing over an extended period	Poor	Very good
Ability to remember or retrieve information	Relatively inaccurate	Accurate
Accuracy of work	Makes errors	Makes virtually no errors
Ability to consistently follow instructions	Imperfect	Perfect
Ability to innovate in new situation	Fairly good	Lacking
Ability to learn by trial and error	Fairly good	Lacking

only the information which the program of instructions has made available. A human is best suited to think, reason, and discover; a computer is best adapted to calculate, manipulate, and compare.

The computer can thus extend the power of the human by performing tasks perfectly which humans perform imperfectly and by providing the raw material (data, results of processing, etc.) with which we may reason and discover. This suggests that information processing systems should be designed as human-machine systems in which each is assigned the part for which it is best suited. The applications to be described in the following sections illustrate the ways in which the computer has been used to replace, extend, or enhance human processing.

Recordkeeping

Recordkeeping requirements are an important element in the expenses of almost any organization. These requirements have increased in recent years until about $1 out of every $8 spent for wages and salaries in the United States is used for clerical work. Although the first computers were not intended for the recordkeeping function, the potential in this area was soon recognized, and today recordkeeping applications take up considerably more computer time than any other type of application. Recordkeeping applications are characterized by large numbers of items to be processed with only a small amount of processing required for each item. Some typical examples of recordkeeping applications are payroll, customer accounts, inventory accounting, and production scheduling. A very simple inventory accounting will be described as an example of the recordkeeping use of the computer. Two computer-based approaches to inventory processing will be described—the first is periodic batch processing and the second is immediate processing of each transaction.

Inventory Accounting— Periodic Batch Processing

In inventory accounting, a record is usually kept for each stockkeeping unit (SKU) in inventory, showing the number of units on hand and the cost associated with these units. When there is a receipt or a disbursement, an updating of the SKU record is necessary. Even for a fairly small business, the number of different inventory SKUs will run into the thousands. In the simplest inventory record-keeping system, the record of the past balance on hand for an SKU is read in the computer from a file of SKU records together with the records of transactions affecting the stockkeeping unit, and a new balance is calculated and stored. As part of the updating of the balances, a listing of the current number on hand may be prepared for all stockkeeping units, or the listing may show only items for which there was a transaction (i.e., changes since last listing). The documents, records, and files used are illustrated in Figure 2-1. The illustration is for a simple system of periodic batch processing using magnetic tape for file storage. The flow of processing is diagrammed in Figure 2-2. The general flow is to prepare input (say on punched cards) for all transactions, sort the transactions into the same order as the inventory file, and update each record for which there are transactions. If there are

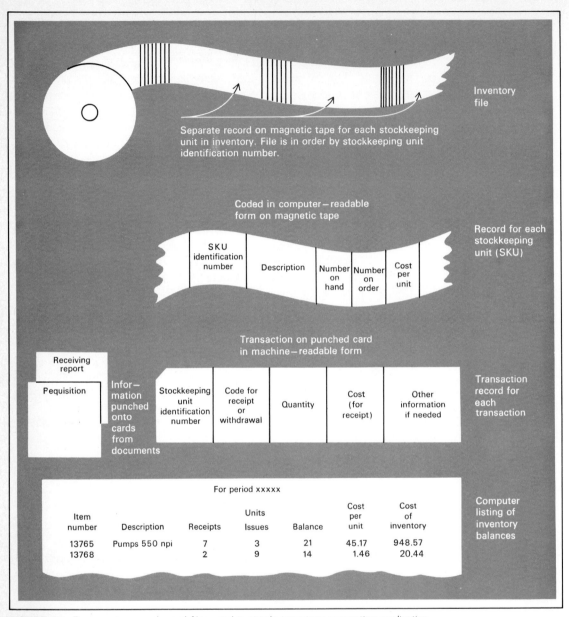

FIGURE 2-1 Documents, records, and files used in simple inventory accounting application.

no transactions, the record is written on the updated file without change. Most inventory applications which make use of computers are much more complex than this and can include the preparation of a forecast of usage for the item, the calculation of a safety stock requirement, the calculation of an optimal order quantity, and an analysis to detect obsolete and slow-moving items.

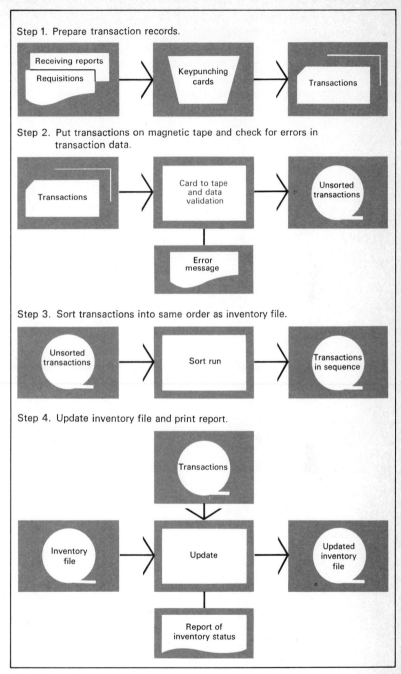

FIGURE 2-2 Steps in simple computer processing procedure for inventory accounting.

Inventory Accounting— Immediate Processing

Most clerical recordkeeping is performed in a periodic processing mode: transactions are accumulated and processed as a batch. This is very satisfactory for some applications, but other applications require or can benefit from immediate processing. An immediate or fast-response system, also referred to as an online-realtime (OLRT) system, consists of a central computer and terminals for input of transactions to the computer and for receiving responses back from the computer. The terminals are provided for every person or machine in the organization having a requirement to originate, retrieve, or utilize information from the computer. A system is described as "realtime" if a request for information is sent to the computer and the result received back very quickly within the time allowed for acting on the information. In other words, processing is performed immediately as each transaction occurs rather than periodically with batches of transactions. The term "online" refers to the fact that the data files, input/output devices, etc., are all connected to the computer either directly or over data communications.

An inventory application may profit from immediate processing of inventory transactions so that the status of inventory records is up-to-date with very little processing delay. In such a system, the receiving department immediately enters via a terminal the record for receipt of items to be placed into inventory. When a customer order is received (say, via the telephone), an order clerk enters the requested order into a terminal. The computer checks the inventory status to determine whether the order can be filled. If inventory is available, the order is confirmed through the terminal to the clerk and by the clerk to the customer (Figure 2-3). The computer reduces the onhand balance because it is sold (even though not yet shipped). The maintenance of the inventory balances by such immediate processing probably is part of an online order entry application which performs other tasks related to entry of customer orders. Note that there must still be an inventory record for each stockkeeping unit, but each record must be accessible very quickly (within a few thousandths of a second). The record is therefore on a direct access storage medium such as a magnetic disk (rather than magnetic tape). Since the computer may be interrogated to obtain the balance on hand for any SKU, there is no need for a listing of balances or transactions except for backup in case of computer failure and for historical analysis.

Customer Service

The use of online terminals and fast-response processing means that many customer transactions can be processed while the customer is being served. This may not only improve the response time for the transaction; it may also improve the amount and quality of the data provided for the customer to make a decision. Three examples will illustrate terminal-based processing to aid customer service—airline reservations, savings bank transactions, and grocery store checkout.

Airline Reservations

In an airline reservation system a central computer maintains a record of all scheduled flights for several weeks into the future. Each reservation agent has a

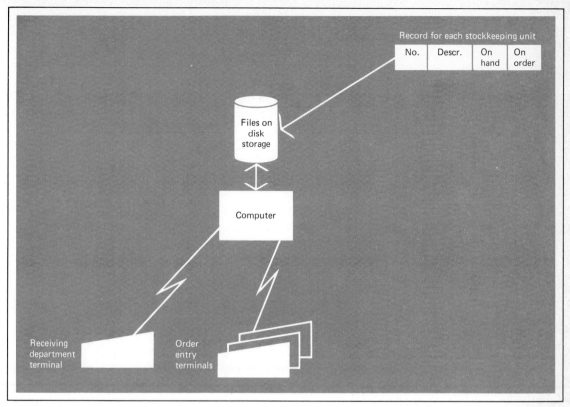

Record for each stockkeeping unit

No.	Descr.	On hand	On order

Files on disk storage

Computer

Receiving department terminal

Order entry terminals

FIGURE 2-3 Immediate processing of inventory transactions.

device for interrogating the computer to determine whether the space that a customer is requesting is available (Figure 2-4). The terminal device is usually a keyboard input and a visual display like a small television screen for output.

If a customer makes a reservation, the computer records this fact in memory and reduces the number of seats available for the flight. The interrogation of the computer and the recording of the reservation occur in a few seconds. If a reservation is not available, alternative flights are displayed on the terminal screen. In many cases, the computer for one airline can interrogate the computer of another airline to make connecting flight reservations.

Savings Bank Transactions

In an installation in a savings bank, customer records are maintained on a central computer, and input/output devices are set up at each branch of the institution. Thus, every deposit, withdrawal, payment, etc., is recorded at the time of the transaction, and current customer balances are available at all times at all branches. Savings institutions have an unusually high rate of transactions at pay periods, end of the month, and at interest-earned dates. The online processing allows these peak

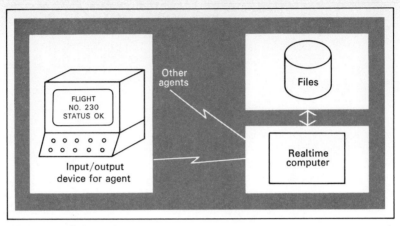

FIGURE 2-4 Online airline reservation system.

loads to be handled with much less delay than when manual retrieval of customer records is required. The system also allows customer-service terminals to be installed in locations such as grocery stores.

Grocery Store Checkout

The supermarket is a very efficient, low-cost method of selling and distributing grocery items. It has a few simple functions: order merchandise (based on rate of sale), price the individual boxes, cans, etc., place items on the shelf, add up the customer order, and bag the order for the customer to carry (or to be placed in the customer's car). The supermarket can be made more efficient if up-to-date rate of sales is available for ordering purposes, if individual items do not have to be marked with price, and if checkout can be speeded up (and be made more accurate). Computer-based checkout systems are now in use. Each item in the store is marked with a bar code which identifies the product by a unique number—the Universal Product Code (Figure 2-5). The price is shown on the shelf for all items, but no individual item is marked for price. At checkout, the product code on each item is in turn placed over a slot containing a beam of light which reads the code. A minicomputer then looks up the current price for the item in computer storage and causes the checkout terminal to print a description of the item, the unit price, the number of items, and the total for the items. An item can be placed on sale (and taken off) merely by changing the price in the computer and the price on the shelf sign. The computer keeps a record of sales by item for reorder purposes.

The advantage to the store is improved inventory control, reduced price-marking expense, reduced checkout expense, and elimination of checkout errors. The advantages to the customer may be lower prices (presumably stores doing this will pass on part of their savings in the form of lower prices), more descriptive data on the checkout listing, and elimination of checkout pricing errors. The disadvantage is the lack of a price on each item.

FIGURE 2-5 Universal Product Code for supermarket checkout—example on a package of gum.

Computer-based Analysis and Processing

The computer can perform any computations that have, in the past, been made by hand or by mechanical calculator. In addition, the stored program used by a computer permits complex-solution procedures to be programmed, and the electronic speed of the computations means that problems which could not be solved because of the time required for manual computation can now be solved in minutes by the computer. Not only the time, but also the cost of computation have been dramatically reduced. A popular large computer system can do computations in 1 minute that would take 100 to 200 years to do manually. Yet the commercial rental cost for using such a system is only about $10 a minute. A man-year of computation, on this basis, costs about 5¢ to 10¢.

The speed and low cost of computations make it possible to provide traditional mathematical and statistical computation at very low cost. These have also resulted in new computer-oriented techniques and in applications not previously feasible. Examples are linear programming, critical path analysis, system simulation, and information retrieval.

Linear Programming Linear programming is a mathematical method for allocating the resources of a firm to achieve some optimum result (for example, to minimize cost or to maximize profit). The solution to a linear programming problem of any size and complexity involves hundreds of thousands of simple repetitive calculations which would be impractical without a computer. In fact, linear programming methods were developed specifically to take advantage of computer technology. The concepts underlying these methods were known previously but could not be economically utilized because of the volume of calculations involved. Linear programming is used by business firms to find the optimum solution to such problems as the least-cost blend of ingredients for feed (Figure 2-6), the most profitable combination of oil refinery production, and the most economical shipping schedules.

Critical Path Analysis (PERT/CPM)   The scheduling of projects with interdependent activities can become quite complex. Computer programs have been written which analyze activities in order to calculate which are critical to the timely completion of a project and which can take longer than expected without delaying the completion date (have slack). This technique is called PERT, CPM, or critical path scheduling (Figure 2-7).

Systems Simulation   The term "systems simulation" refers to duplicating the essence of a system in a way that allows an investigator to study and work with it. The mathematical or symbolic representation of a system is called the "model." This approach to problem solving is not new. Investigators have frequently made models or representations of reality in order to learn, to test ideas, and to predict the effect of introducing changes. However, the computer has made possible systems studies that heretofore were impractical. Even a modestly scaled systems simulation usually requires more computations than can be efficiently performed by hand.

The sciences use simulation for both physical processes, such as airplane engine performance, and human behavior; business uses it for commercial systems.

FIGURE 2-6   Linear programming (for least-cost feed formula).

FIGURE 2-7 Critical path analysis by computer.

The simulation approach requires a quantitative description of the system and the programming of the model for computers. The model allows those using it to compress realtime, so that years of operation can be studied in a few minutes. Or the process may be slowed down to study problem areas in detail. Simulation can thus offer a basis for decisions about a new system without the disruptions and the costs associated with trying a system which may fail. To illustrate simulation, consider a business selling hot-water heaters which forecasts its sales as a percentage of new home construction plus a percentage of old homes (some of which need replacement heaters). This could be expressed mathematically as

$$s_1 = ph + gr$$

$$s_2 = s_1 m$$

where s_1 = sales in units, p = percentage of new homes, h = new homes, g = percentage of old homes, r = old homes, s_2 = sales in dollars, and m = average sales price per unit. These simple equations coupled with many others which describe the operation of the business can be programmed on the computer, and the effect on the company of various alternatives can then be studied using this program to perform the necessary computations. There are special languages to assist in writing such planning simulations using either periodic batch processing mode or the interaction at a terminal available with time sharing.

**Information
Retrieval**

Advances in technology have been accompanied by an almost overwhelming increase in information. It is becoming more and more difficult for a person to keep up with developments in even a narrow field. Persons doing research find it very time-consuming and sometimes impossible to make an adequate search of the literature bearing on the subject they are investigating. Millions of dollars are spent each year in duplicating research which has already been completed and reported in the scientific journals. The computer offers a fruitful approach to information retrieval. There are a number of available retrieval systems, especially for technical information. Most of the systems use a key-word approach.

In the approach of the technical information retrieval using key words, the contents of each technical paper are identified by key words. For example, an article about the effect of radiation on metals in the Van Allen belt might be identified by metals, radiation, Van Allen belt, and space. In addition to the key-word identifiers, a short abstract is prepared and stored on secondary storage medium. A person wishing information on a topic chooses a set of identifiers which best describes the topic. The computer is programmed to compare this set of identifiers with the list of all identifiers and to select papers having sets of identifiers containing one or more identifiers common to the topic identifiers. The abstracts for these papers are then printed out, together with an identifying number through which the reference may be located. The retrieval service may use either periodic batch input and output or interactive terminal processing. There are over a hundred retrieval systems which an organization may access for a fee. Examples are psychological abstracts, research in education, United States government research reports issued through the National Technical Information Service (NTIS), and chemistry and chemical engineering abstracts.[1]

Education

The computer has become a key factor in research and analysis by students and faculty. In addition, the computer is being used in the education process itself. Although progress has been slow and costly, the computer will almost certainly be a significant factor in altering the teaching process. Two examples of use of the computer in teaching are computer-assisted programmed learning and decision simulations.

**Computer-assisted
Programmed
Learning**

There are many variations of the concept of programmed learning, but all of them involve short, simple instructional steps and continuous testing. The instruction may be implemented by a book which is arranged into a series of short explanations followed by a quiz question to reinforce the points being made. Or the instruction

---

[1] For a list of 80 such services, see Beatrice Marron, Elizabeth Fong, and Dennis Fife: *A Mechanized Information Systems Catalog*, National Bureau of Standards Technical Note 814, U.S. Government Printing Office, February 1974.

may use a machine which exposes one instructional frame at a time. Both of these methods are single-path instruction methods. The computer allows the use of variable paths. Not all students, in a computer-assisted method, study the same sequence. If a student has grasped a concept (as evidenced by a correct response), he or she proceeds in a direct path to the next step in the material. If a mistake is made at some point, the student is given additional material to explain the topic again. On the basis of the responses, the computer selects the material to be presented. Grading of questions is done instantaneously (Figure 2-8).

The use of computer-assisted instruction (CAI) has tended to be experimental because of the high costs of development of programs and the cost of operating CAI applications. The cost of students using the terminals in CAI has generally been more than $1 per hour. A very competitive price (compared with the lecture method) is less than 50¢ per hour. The use of CAI has, in some applications, been very successful, and therefore this use of computers can be expected to increase.

Decision Simulations   Students in business and economics may gain a good understanding of such topical areas as accounting, finance, and insurance but not have any grasp of the interrelationship of these topical areas and the problems of top management. The decision simulation or management game is a tool for teaching students to integrate what they have learned into a top-management viewpoint. Decision simulations that are complex enough to be effective require a computer for making the necessary computations.

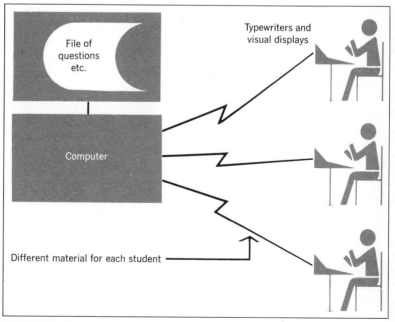

FIGURE 2-8 Computer-aided instruction.

In a decision simulation, several teams represent the management of different companies. Each team must make such management decisions as what to charge for a product, how much to produce, etc. The results of these decisions are calculated by the computer and translated into financial and operating statements which are the basis for evaluation and the making of more decisions.

Guidance and Control

Computers are used in guidance and control systems. In such systems, the computer is connected to measuring devices and controls. The measuring devices furnish data on the process being regulated. The computer then provides data to set or adjust the controls. Since the calculations necessary for these adjustments occur with electronic speed, the measurement and adjustment process is almost continuous. Some examples of computer guidance are missile and nuclear submarine guidance. Examples of computer control are manufacturing process control and message switching. Minicomputers are frequently used for these purposes.

Missile and Submarine Guidance

The large, complex intercontinental missile has a miniaturized but powerful computer inside its guidance portion. The computer accepts information on speed, velocity, etc., and produces data for altering the speed and direction of flight.

Since a nuclear submarine can remain underwater for extended periods, it needs a method for determining its position accurately without the aid of an external reference point, such as a star. The guidance system for the nuclear submarine contains a computer which continuously calculates the position of the submarine by keeping track of the distance it has moved in any direction.

Process Control

Continuous manufacturing processes such as oil refining and chemical production have measuring and regulating devices at various points in the process. When the measurements indicate that the process is deviating from the desired norm by more than an allowable limit, the regulating devices are adjusted (Figure 2-9). Computers are programmed to run a plant in the sense that the measurement devices are connected to the computer for continuous comparison. Necessary changes in controls are made directly by the computer. The measurements and the setting of the controls are carried out faster and more accurately than when performed by human operators.

Message Switching

Any large organization with geographically dispersed units has a problem in the control of messages which are transmitted from one location to another via a communication system (such as the ones provided by telephone companies or by Western Union). This problem can be solved by a communications system in which each location is equipped with a transmitting and receiving terminal linked to a

FIGURE 2-9 Diagram of computer process control.

central switching center. The switching center makes the connections between the receiving and sending terminals. Computers are being used to perform the switching function. They also make a record of all messages for reference and do statistical analysis.

Management Information Systems

The early use of computers in organizations tends to concentrate on clerical functions such as payroll accounting and processing of customer accounts. As organizations mature in the use of computers, they emphasize applications which provide information processing support for managerial functions. A system built around this emphasis is often termed a "management information system" or MIS. An MIS utilizes computer hardware and software, manual procedures, management and decision models, and a database to provide information in support of operations management, and decision-making functions in an organization. In terms of the type of information and information processing provided by an MIS, the system may be described as a pyramid structure (Figure 2-10) in which the bottom layer consists of the information for transaction processing, status inquiries, etc.; the next level consists of information resources in support of the day-to-day operations management; the third level consists of information system resources to aid in tactical planning and decision making for management control; and the top

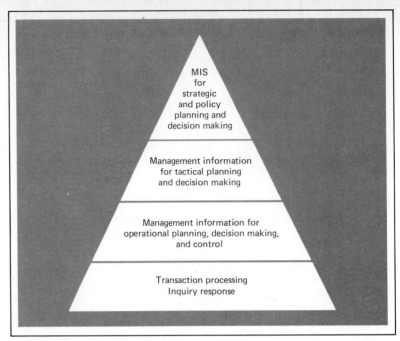

FIGURE 2-10 Management information system. (*Adapted from Robert V. Head, "Management Information Systems: A Critical Appraisal,"* Datamation, *May 1967, p. 23.*)

level consists of information resources in support of the planning and policy making by higher levels of management.

Another way to describe an MIS is the way in which major users of the system will utilize the capabilities provided, as shown below:

User	Uses
Clerical personnel	Handle transactions, process data, and answer inquiries.
First-level managers	Obtain operations data. Assistance with planning, scheduling, identifying out-of-control situations, and making decisions.
Staff specialists	Information for analysis. Assistance with analysis, planning, and reporting.
Management	Regular reports. Special retrieval requests. Special analyses. Special reports. Assistance in identifying problems and opportunities. Assistance in decision-making analysis.

The concept of a management information system is a design objective; implementation will vary considerably among organizations on the basis of the organizational function being served, the information resources available, and the organizational commitment to an MIS.

Other Interesting Uses of Computers

Prediction of Elections
Predictions are based on discovering causal or predictive relationships between variables which can be measured sufficiently in advance of an event or activity to make possible a prediction of the outcome. Computer analysis of election results is possible because the computer can be programmed to carry out complex computations to discover predictive relationships from past election returns and then to apply these predictive formulations to the early returns in an election in order to predict the final outcome. Conceptually, the computer is programmed to do what the shrewd observer does. However, it can do it much more precisely and much faster. The accuracy of the predictions has been excellent. Accurate predictions have been made with as little as 1 percent of the total vote counted. In fact, they have been so accurate that it has been suggested the television networks should delay giving out the results of the computer predictions for national elections for the United States presidency until the polls have closed on the West Coast to avoid influencing the vote there through the prediction of the final outcome.

Medical Diagnosis
Although currently in a very experimental state, computer-assisted medical diagnosis has great potential. In the diagnosis of illness, the physician must note the patient's symptoms and then compare them with the symptoms associated with different illnesses. From this comparison, the physician selects the illness which appears to best explain the patient's condition. The physician may or may not be able to confirm the diagnosis by laboratory tests. This procedure may result in imperfect diagnosis since the matching process which is the basis for the diagnosis depends on the memory of the physician both in detecting all relevant symptoms and in considering all possible illnesses which have such symptoms. The computer application involves having the initial symptoms which were detected by the physician input to a computer, where they are compared with the symptoms and indications associated with all illnesses. The computer can make these comparisons because the specific and detailed information is stored in its memory. The computer memory is then searched to arrive at all possibilities for the diagnosis, together with a description of indicators which should be searched for in order to make a final decision.

Computer Art
There have been two approaches to computer art—one using the symbols of the printer and the other using a graph plotter. For printer art, a program is written to print a series of lines which in total provide a desired visual effect. A graph plotter

is an output device which is programmed to draw lines. A stylus with ink is moved over the page under computer control. The pens can be filled with different colored inks to achieve some very interesting effects. Figure 2-11 illustrates the type of computer art that has been produced.

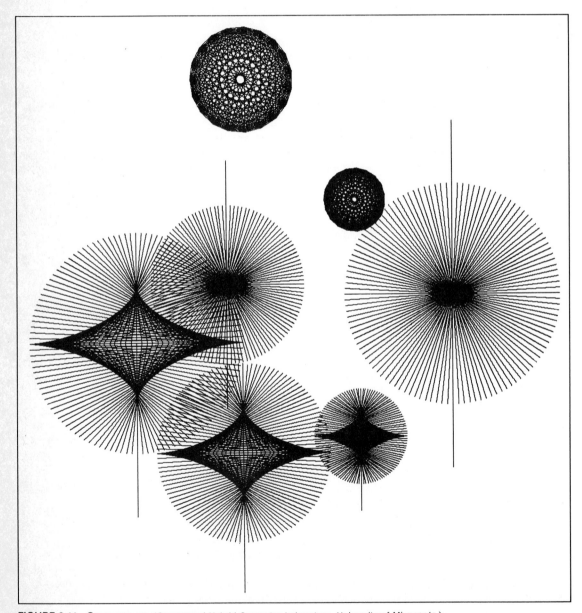

FIGURE 2-11 Computer art. (*Courtesy of Hybrid Computer Laboratory, University of Minnesota.*)

SUMMARY The computer represents a breakthrough in computation. It extends the capability of humans through its superior speed, accuracy, retrieval capability, confirmability, and ability to follow directions. Humans have unique abilities not found in computers—the ability to innovate and to reason heuristically.

Although originally thought of as being primarily for scientific applications, most computers now in use are in commercial organizations. Routine data processing, such as payroll, sales analysis, inventory control, billing, and accounts receivable, dominates the commercial machines, but new applications are ingenious and exciting. The changes from traditional business information processing systems to customer service online processing and to the concept of a management information system represent a revolution in business systems. The computer has made feasible new techniques such as linear programming, critical path analysis, systems simulation, and information retrieval. Without the computer, these techniques were impractical. Computers are being used as part of the educational process, and guidance and control computers have made possible space exploration and automated factories. This brief description of computer uses has not been exhaustive; rather, it has indicated the types of uses to which computers are being put.

EXERCISES

1 Of what advantage are the unique features (speed, stored program, memory) of the electronic computer in the following uses:
   (*a*) Payroll
   (*b*) Inventory accounting
   (*c*) A management information system
   (*d*) Systems simulation
   (*e*) Information retrieval
   (*f*) Process control

2 Outline the logic of accounting for the following recordkeeping applications. What records must be maintained, what transactions recorded, what analyses conducted, and what decisions made?
   (*a*) Customer accounts receivable
   (*b*) Payroll
   (*c*) Sales analysis

3 What are the features associated with:
   (*a*) Periodic batch processing?
   (*b*) An online, realtime processing application?
   (*c*) A management information system?

4 A small businessman has trouble with his cash planning, even though he seems to have a good grasp of his business. He is in constant difficulty with his bank. He has asked you to design a cash model of his business which will inform him of the need for loans under various sales conditions. He gives you the following data as a starter:
   (*a*) Cash sales are 40 percent of total sales. Credit sales are collected in total during the following month.
   (*b*) Sales are increasing at a rate of 1 percent per month.
   (*c*) Cost of sales is 70 percent of selling price. Payment for the goods is made in the month of the sales.
   (*d*) Fixed administrative expenses (executive salaries, rent, etc.) are $2000 per month.
   Write mathematical equations that describe this information. (These equations are only part of the mathematical model.)

5 In manipulating symbols, a computer often needs to make comparisons and order a list of words, numbers, etc. Assume that the computer interprets a blank as less than any other digit. Special characters are the next highest, then numbers, and finally the alphabetic characters are highest. This is called the collating sequence, and it may vary among different models of computers. Sequence the following list of terms into ascending order (smallest first). A small "b" means a blank.

(a) $15370
(b) 453700
(c) b15370
(d) DOGGIE
(e) DOGbIE
(f) bCLASS
(g) CLASSb

6 Forecasting models on a computer can be much more complex than those using manual computation. Exponential smoothing is a computer-oriented forecasting method similar to a moving average in which unequal weights are given to the data for each past period. The formula is: New forecast = old forecast + alpha (actual for prior period — old forecast for prior period). Alpha is a smoothing constant that can vary from 0 to 1.0, but is usually in the range of from .1 to .2. For computational purposes, the formula can be rearranged as: New forecast = alpha (actual) + (1 — alpha) (old forecast).

(a) Compare exponential smoothing to traditional moving-average methods of forecasting with respect to storage requirements and processing time.

(b) In order to evaluate the simplicity and versatility of exponential smoothing, compute forecasts (rounded to the nearest tenth) using a 6-month moving-average method and using exponential smoothing with an alpha of .2.

Actual data	Six-month moving-average forecast	Exponential smoothing forecast
29		
16		
40	6-month	
36	total = 180	30.5
31		30.6
28	30.0	30.1
32	30.5	30.5
23		
34		
25		

7 Identify a realtime application such as a savings and loan association or airline reservation system. If possible, visit an office where an online terminal is being used for the application. Evaluate the advantages of the realtime processing.

8 What are the characteristics of a processing problem that is suitable and economically justified for computer processing?

9 What are the characteristics of problems that are not suitable for computer processing?

10 What are the general characteristics of a human-machine system using the best capabilities of both human and computer?

2

THE DEVELOPMENT OF COMPUTER APPLICATIONS AND COMPUTER PROGRAMS

There is a process which has proved effective in the design and development of computer applications and computer programs. Chapter 3 describes this process for both organizational data processing applications and mathematical applications. Chapter 4 explains tools such as layouts, flowcharts, and decision tables that are used in design and development activities. Chapter 5 considers the design of understandable and maintainable computer programs. Chapter 6 covers considerations in selecting a high-level language for use in programming, and surveys the major high-level languages.

Chapter

3

The Development of a Computer Application

The Master Plan for Organizational Information System Applications

Information System Application Development Life Cycle
Overview of the Life Cycle
Definition Stage
Physical Design Stage
Implementation Stage

The Development of a Computer-based Application for Mathematics, Statistics, or Modeling

The Selection of a Processing Methodology
The Basic Processing Cycle
Alternative Processing Methods

The Development of a Computer Program
Characteristics of a Computer Program
Steps in Preparing a Computer Program

Coding Computer Instructions
Machine-Language Coding
Symbolic Assembly-Language Coding
Macro Instructions
High-Level Languages

Aids to Programming
Library Routines
Program Library Software
Utility Programs
Program Generators
File and Database Management Systems
Application Packages
Conversion Programs

Approaches to Program Job Submission

Summary

Exercises

A computer application is the use of the computer for a specific task such as processing a payroll or performing statistical computations. Applications can be categorized in a variety of ways. A useful classification of applications is:

Organizational information processing (data processing and MIS)
Mathematical, statistical, and modeling
Information retrieval
Computer-assisted instruction
Data communications
Process control

The basic approach to development and implementation of a computer application is very similar for all types of applications. There are, however, some differences. This chapter describes the development of two major categories—organizational information processing and mathematical, statistical, and modeling applications. Although they have special characteristics, the other four categories of applications named above tend to follow the pattern of development described for organizational information processing.

Organizational information processing applications (often termed "data processing") are characterized by large volumes of transactions and repeated operation over a number of years. Frequently a number of different persons prepare input data and use output from the application. Those who use the output typically do not prepare the input. The format of the documents and reports produced by the data processing application must satisfy a variety of uses and must meet the requirements of internal as well as external recipients (customers, vendors, governmental agencies). The storage requirements for the data files associated with these applications are frequently very large (from a few million to several billion characters). The organizational information processing applications are generally interrelated because of common use of data and the interrelationship of the organizational uses of the output.

Mathematical, statistical, and modeling applications are frequently single jobs or jobs that are repeated somewhat infrequently. The number of transactions to be processed is usually not large (when compared with data processing applications). The user of the application is likely to be involved in preparing (or deciding on) the input. The output is probably used by a few people, and the format of the output is not important so long as it contains the necessary data. Storage requirements are generally fairly small, although there are exceptions. The different applications of this type are generally independent.

The Master Plan for Organizational Information System Applications

Information processing applications in an organization are not usually independent—they are part of an information processing system which processes transactions (such as sales, shipments of goods, etc.) to produce transaction documents and records and provides reports and analyses for management and decision-making purposes. Even though the applications are interrelated, not all applications can be developed at the same time. Priorities must be set. There is therefore a need for a plan which defines an orderly development of the applications needed to meet the organization information processing needs. Such a plan is termed a "master plan" or "master development plan." The master plan defines the processing environment and the development timing for each application. Consideration of development for an organizational application therefore begins with the master plan.

The master plan for an organization's information system is developed by a planning group which is given this responsibility. The work of the planning group will usually be supervised by an information systems steering committee composed of executives whose departments are affected by information processing. When the plan is prepared and approved by the steering/review committee, it is presented to the chief executive or the overall planning committee for the organization (Figure 3-1). The master plan, when approved, becomes part of the overall organizational plan. The master plan generally contains the plan for the next 3 to 5 years, with the current year having the most detail. The plan is updated periodically to reflect changes in the organization, experience with applications in use, and developments in technology. A complete review and updating are performed as part of the organization's planning and budgeting process.

The contents of the information system master development plan will vary among organizations; it is useful for the plan to contain four major sections:

Section of master plan	Contents of section
1 Information system goals and objectives	(a) Organizational objectives affecting the information system (b) External environment affecting the information system (c) Internal organization constraints on information system development (d) Overall objectives for the information system (e) Overall structure of the information system (how the applications fit together to form an information system)
2 Inventory of current capabilities	(a) Inventory of equipment, generalized software, applications, and personnel (b) Analysis of expenses and facilities utilization (c) Status of projects in process (d) Assessment of capabilities
3 Forecast of developments affecting the master plan	(a) Technology forecast relevant to plan (b) Other developments
4 The specific plan	(a) Hardware and software acquisition schedule (b) New application development schedule (c) Old application maintenance (revision) schedule (d) Personnel requirements schedule (e) Financial resources schedule

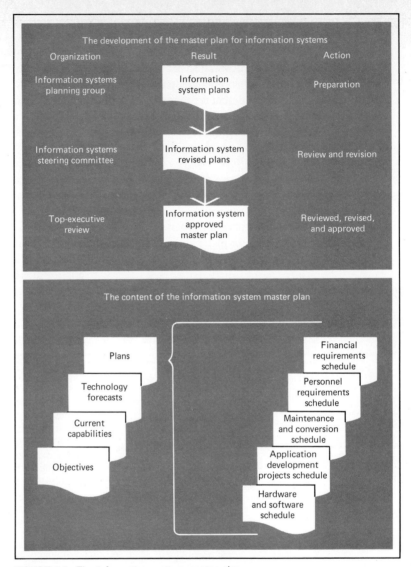

FIGURE 3-1 The information system master plan.

The master plan provides the basis for deciding which application to work on next. It also provides the information system context in which the application will fit. It contains only a general description of the application. The detailed development and implementation of the application follows a sequence of application development procedures (also termed a "development life cycle").

Information System Application Development Life Cycle

The basic idea of the development life cycle is that every application needs to go through essentially the same process to be conceived, developed, and implemented. Information system development involves considerable creativity; the use of the life cycle is the means for obtaining more disciplined creativity by giving structure to a creative process.

The life cycle is important in the planning, management, and control of information system application development. The use of the life cycle concept provides a framework for planning the individual development activities. In order to manage and control the development effort, it is necessary to know what should have been done, what has been done, and what has yet to be accomplished. The phases in the development life cycle provide a basis for this management and control because they define segments of the flow of work which can be identified for managerial purposes and specify the documents to be produced by each phase.

Overview of the Life Cycle

The steps or phases in the life cycle for information system development are described differently by different writers, but the differences are primarily in amount of detail and manner of categorization. There is general agreement on the flow of development steps.

The information system application development cycle has three major stages:

Definition of the application
Physical design
Implementation

In other words, first there is the process which defines the requirements for a feasible cost/effective system. The requirements are then translated into a physical system of forms, procedures, programs, etc., by system design, computer programming, and procedure development. The resulting system is tested and put into operation. No system is perfect, so there is always a need for maintenance changes. To complete the cycle, there should be an audit of the system to evaluate how well it performs and how well it meets cost and performance specifications. The three stages of definition, physical design, and implementation can therefore be divided into smaller steps or phases as follows:

Stage	Phases in development cycle	Comments
Definition	Feasibility assessment	Evaluation of feasibility and cost/benefit of proposed application
	Information analysis	Determination of information needed
Physical design	System design	Design of processing system and preparation of program specifications

	Program development	Coding and debugging of computer programs
	Procedure development	Design of procedures and writing of user instructions
Implementation	Conversion	Final test and conversion
	Operation and maintenance	Day-to-day operation, modification, and maintenance
	Postaudit	Evaluation of results

The information system development cycle is not followed in 1, 2, 3 fashion (Figure 3-2). The process is iterative so that, for example, the review after the system design phase may result in cancellation or continuation, but it may also result in going back to the beginning to prepare a new design.

Each phase in the development cycle results in documentation. The sum of the documentation for the phases is the documentation for the application. The amount of detailed analysis and documentation in each phase will depend on the type of application. For example, a large, complex application will require considerable analysis and documentation at each phase; a report requested by a manager will require little analysis and documentation, but all phases are still present.

Note that the information system development life cycle does not include the equipment selection and procurement cycle. The reason is that the selection and procurement of equipment (except for some specialized equipment) are generally related to many systems rather than a single application. If an application requires equipment selection, this will generally take place during the physical design development stage.

The following percentages provide a rough idea of the allocation of effort (say, man-hours) in the information system development life cycle from inception until the system is operating properly (i.e., excluding operation and maintenance). These percentages will, of course, vary with each project. The ranges shown are indicative of the variations to be expected.

Stage in life cycle	Phase in life cycle	Rough percentage of effort*	Range in percentage of effort*
Definition	Feasibility assessment	10	5–15
	Information analysis	15	10–20
Physical design	System design	20	10–30
	Program development	25	20–40
	Procedure development	10	5–15
Implementation	Conversion	15	10–20
	Operation and maintenance	(not applicable)	
	Postaudit	5	2–6
		100	

*Source: Author's estimates.

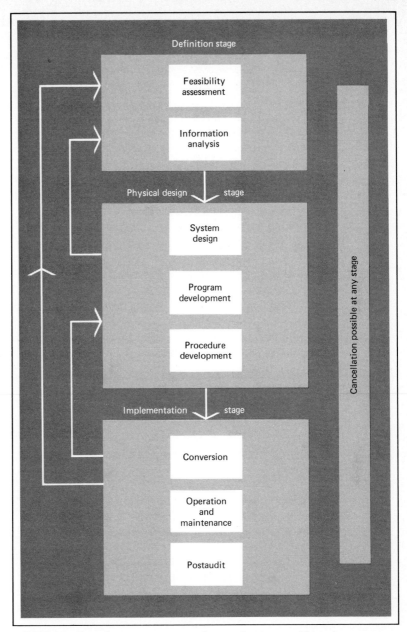

FIGURE 3-2 The information system application development life cycle.

It is instructive to note that upon completion of coding of computer programs (about halfway through program development), the application is probably only about 60 percent complete. For complex systems involving much testing, completion of program instruction coding may mark about the halfway point.

Definition Stage After the project or problem is proposed, the first step is to define the problem. An analyst is assigned to work with the potential users and prepare a report describing:

The need for the project (a problem, opportunity for savings, improved performance, etc.)

The expected benefits (in very rough form)

The outlines of a feasibility study (objective, time required, and resources required)

The proposal report is reviewed by the department proposing the project, the information system executive, and the information systems planning committee. If the project definition is approved, the feasibility study is begun.

One or more analysts conduct the feasibility study which is to assess three types of feasibility:

1 *Technical feasibility* Is it possible with existing technology?
2 *Economic feasibility* Will the system provide benefits greater than the cost?
3 *Operational feasibility* Will it work when installed?

The objectives of the system are amplified from the rough objectives in the feasibility study proposal and the following are prepared:

Rough outline of the system
Development work plan
Schedule of resources required for development
Schedule of expected benefits
Project budget

The feasibility report is reviewed by the management of information systems and by the requesting department. If it is not part of the master plan (and of significant impact), the project will need to be reviewed by the information systems planning committee. If the project is approved, the next phase is information analysis.

One or more information analysts (or systems analysts if no distinction is made between information analysts and system designers) are assigned to the project. The analysts work with users to define the information requirements in detail and to define the information flow. The results of the information analysis phase are:

1 Layouts of the outputs (reports, transaction documents, terminal output, etc.)

2 Layouts of inputs (transaction input forms, terminal input, etc.)

3 Data definitions for required data items

4 Specifications regarding information such as processing response time, accuracy, frequency of updating, and volume

These specifications complete the definition of what the system is to do; the next step is to design the processing system to produce the results as defined.

Physical Design Stage The design of the processing system for an application is divided into three phases—system design, program development, and procedure development. Upon completion of this stage of the life cycle, the processing system will be ready for implementation.

The physical design stage begins with the system design. This is the design of the processing procedure (computer and noncomputer) that will produce the reports specified in the information analysis. It designs the equipment usage, the files to be maintained, the processing method, the file access method, and flow of processing. The results of the system design phase are:

1 System flowcharts showing, for example, use of equipment and flow of processing

2 File organization and design

3 A file-building or file-conversion plan

4 Control flowchart showing controls to be implemented at each stage of processing

5 Backup and security provisions

6 A system test plan

7 A hardware/software selection schedule (if required)

The programming and procedure development phases can proceed concurrently. Programmers will be assigned to do the programming; analysts will normally prepare the procedures. The programming phase uses the system specifications from the analysis and system design phases to define the programming tasks. The programs may be obtained by writing and testing new programs or by selecting generalized application programs that are offered for purchase or lease. The result of the programming phase is a set of tested programs that are fully documented.

Procedure development involves the preparation of instructions for users, clerical personnel providing input, control personnel, and operating personnel. The procedure development phase can also include the preparation of training material to be used in implementation.

Implementation Stage When the programs and procedures are prepared, the conversion phase can begin. Data is collected, files built, and the overall system tested. There are various methods of testing. One is to test the system under simulated conditions; another is to test under actual conditions, operating in parallel with the existing systems and procedures. It is generally considered not good practice to implement a complex system without one of these full system tests.

After all errors and problems that have been detected in the system test are corrected, the system is put into actual operation. Any subsequent errors or minor modifications are handled as maintenance. This is not a trivial activity—about one-third of the analyst/programmer effort is devoted to maintenance of existing programs.

The last phase of the implementation stage is a postaudit. This is a review by an audit task force (composed, for example, of a user representative, an internal auditor, and a data processing representative). The audit group reviews the objectives and cost/benefit representations made in behalf of the project and compares these with actual performance and actual cost/value. It also reviews the operational characteristics of the system to determine if they are satisfactory. The postaudit report is intended to assist in improved management of future projects, improvements in the application under review, or cancellation of the application if it is not functioning properly.

The Development of a Computer-based Application for Mathematics, Statistics, or Modeling

Applications which perform mathematical, statistical, and model processing form a large class of computer usage. This class of usage has sometimes been termed "scientific use." The mathematical applications use the computer to perform computations required by mathematical solution procedures, as for example in the solution of equations. Statistical applications perform the computations to arrive at statistical measures such as mean, standard deviation, and correlation coefficient. Models to be processed by the computer are sets of computer program statements which describe the essential properties of a problem or a process being investigated. For example, a planning model is a set of program statements which compute the values in the various planning equations. A user can change the input data to a model and then rerun the program to investigate the effect of the altered conditions.

Although some of the mathematical, statistical, and model applications may be part of the organizational information system and be specified as applications in the information system master plan, most of these types of applications are in response to the needs of a single user or a class of independent users rather than being required by the information system of an organization. The steps in the application of computer processing to the mathematical, statistical, or modeling problem can be described by the same general life cycle flow as for organizational processing applications, but there are differences in the activities carried on in each phase:

Life cycle phase	Mathematical, statistical, or modeling application
Feasibility assessment	1 Problem identification (and assessment of feasibility of use of computer)
Information analysis	2 Problem (information) analysis to describe input, output, and processing requirements

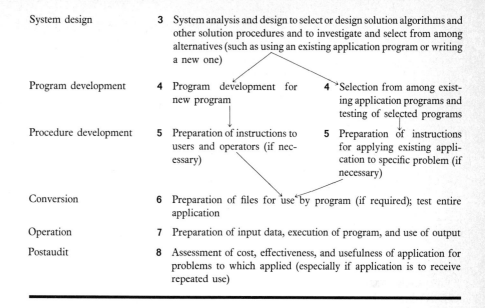

System design	3	System analysis and design to select or design solution algorithms and other solution procedures and to investigate and select from among alternatives (such as using an existing application program or writing a new one)		
Program development	4	Program development for new program	4	Selection from among existing application programs and testing of selected programs
Procedure development	5	Preparation of instructions to users and operators (if necessary)	5	Preparation of instructions for applying existing application to specific problem (if necessary)
Conversion	6	Preparation of files for use by program (if required); test entire application		
Operation	7	Preparation of input data, execution of program, and use of output		
Postaudit	8	Assessment of cost, effectiveness, and usefulness of application for problems to which applied (especially if application is to receive repeated use)		

Major differences between the life cycle for the data processing applications and the life cycle of the mathematical, statistical, and modeling applications are the reduced emphasis on procedure development, conversion, and postaudit activities for the mathematical, statistical, and modeling applications. In a large percentage of these applications, the life cycle might be described as:

Problem identification
Problem analysis
Solution procedure (algorithm)
Program development (or selection)
Operation

The reduction or elimination of emphasis on procedure development, conversion, and postaudit is a result of the difference between the data processing applications and the scientific applications. The data processing applications require instructions and training for a large number of persons involved with the operation and use of the application. This instruction is required not only when the application is installed but is also used for the training of new and replacement personnel as existing personnel change positions or leave the organization. By way of contrast there may be only one user of the scientific application. If there is repeated use by a variety of users, there will be an increased need for instructions to users. Conversion is generally a small or nonexistent problem for the scientific applications because they do not involve the complex interaction of a number of programs, large data files, and a variety of clerical personnel doing input and making use of the output. Postaudit is a useful practice if there is extensive use of an application.

If it receives a single use or infrequent use, questions of efficiency or effectiveness may be less significant than the cost of new development.

The system analysis phase of the data processing application must devote considerable attention to the design of input, the layout of reports, the structure of files, and the processing approach to be followed. By way of contrast, the system design activity for the scientific applications concentrates on the identification or design of solution procedures.

Program development for a data processing application almost always requires professional programmers. Scientific applications are frequently programmed by the users themselves using programming languages designed for users. The steps in programming are essentially the same for both types of applications.

The Selection of a Processing Methodology

Two processing methods are described in Chapter 2—periodic batch processing and immediate online processing. In the development of a computer application, a decision must be made as to the processing method to be employed.

The Basic Processing Cycle An application in operation will generally require the performance of six functions (Figure 3-3). These functions will be the basis for the functions in the program design to be explained in Chapter 4.

1 *Data preparation* Activities which capture data and prepare it for input.

2 *Data validation* Checking of data for correctness (also called input-editing). This may occur during data preparation and prior to or during input.

3 *Input* Reading of data from input storage medium or accepting of data from input/output terminal.

4 *Processing* Manipulation of data and performing computational processes.

5 *Normal output* Writing of reports and lists or writing data onto storage for subsequent processing.

6 *Error output* Printing of error messages or writing of error data onto storage for subsequent processing. The error output can occur during data validation, input, or processing.

Alternative Processing Methods There are two major elements in the different processing methods—time and method of updating the records that are being maintained. The timing is either periodic or immediate; the methods of record updating in files is either serial rewriting of the entire file of records or an updating of each record to be updated in the place in storage occupied by that record. The method of updating of records is related to file organizations. Records may be organized sequentially on the basis of some record key (an identification for a record) or organized nonsequentially.

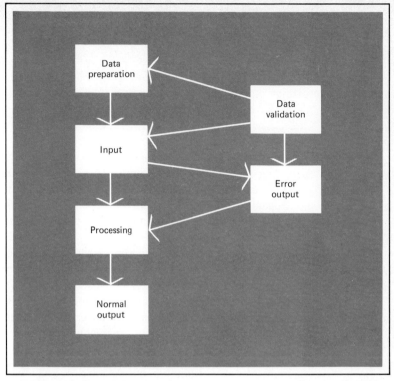

FIGURE 3-3 Basic processing cycle.

The functions associated with an application need not occur in the same time mode. Historically, it has been common to refer to batch (periodic) processing and online (immediate) processing as the two alternatives, but each of the six functions in the flow of processing may be periodic or immediate.

Function	Timing alternatives
Data preparation	The data can be prepared in batches for periodic data entry, or data can be entered immediately via a terminal.
Data validation	Data may be validated immediately at the terminal or by the computer if the terminal is doing direct input.
Input	Input can be individual transactions as they occur, or it can be batches of data at periodic processing intervals.
Processing	The processing can be performed on individual transactions as they occur or on batches of data processed periodically.

Normal output	The normal output can be printed immediately or displayed immediately at a terminal, or output may be written onto storage for later output.
Error output	Error messages may be produced immediately on the printer or at a terminal during processing or may be accumulated for a special error analysis output.

Although each function may be periodic, using batched data, or immediate, using single sets of data items (transactions), some combinations are not feasible. In order to have immediate processing, there must be immediate data preparation, immediate input, immediate data validation, and immediate error output. Three combinations will illustrate common data processing methods.

1   All processing periodic based on batched data. In this traditional batch processing mode (see Chapter 2 for an example), data preparation produces batches of data that are input as a batch, validated as a batch, processed as a batch, and output in an output batch run. Error outputs are accumulated and prepared periodically as a batch. This mode is very efficient for processing which needs to be performed periodically, such as payroll.

2   Immediate data preparation activities with data entry via a terminal and immediate data validation, but data is then accumulated as a batch on storage for periodic processing. In other words, data entry and validation are immediate in order to get validated data in machine-readable form as quickly as possible. This reduces the problems of detecting and correcting data errors but allows the remaining processing to proceed in an efficient batch mode. A variation on this processing approach is inquiry-only processing. Inquiries from user terminals requesting display of data from a file are processed immediately, with the result provided at the user terminal. However, transactions that update or change data in a file are held for periodic batch processing.

3   All functions are immediate for online processing. This is desirable when immediate response is needed using records that are kept up-to-date for each transaction. This is often termed "interactive" processing.

The Development of a Computer Program

A computer is directed by a set of instructions called a program. This section explains the characteristics of a program and describes the steps in preparing a computer program. Subsequent sections summarize the ways an instruction can be coded and identify some important aids to the preparation of computer programs. It is useful to differentiate clearly between system software and application programs. System software consists of programs which facilitate the operation and use of the computer by the application programs. Both types are computer programs and both require the same program development procedure, but the development of system software is an exacting activity generally carried out by specialists. Most system software is developed by the computer manufacturers or by vendors of system software. The emphasis of this text is on the development of application programs rather than system software.

Characteristics of a Computer Program

A program consisting of machine-language steps for directing a computer has three salient features:

1   Each computer instruction specifies the execution of an elementary step or operation in data processing.

2   The sequences of instruction specify what shall be done under all possible conditions during data processing.

3   Instructions can be altered by other instructions as the program is run.

Some examples of program instruction are:

Read a card and store the contents in memory.
Move the contents of one memory location to another memory location.
Add the contents of one memory location to the contents of another.
Print one line of output.

As can be seen by these examples, the computer instructions specify the execution of small, well-defined steps or operations. A program must specify what the computer is to do under all possible conditions. If there is only one possible condition or decision, the program will be a single-path program. If there are alternatives, different program paths must be provided for each of the conditions or alternatives, and a test must be made to determine which condition or alternative is true. This can be illustrated by the conduct of two individuals, Mr. Cautious and Mr. Ordinary, regarding the taking of an umbrella when leaving for work. Mr. Cautious always takes his umbrella just in case it rains. Mr. Ordinary takes his umbrella only if it is raining or cloudy (Figure 3-4).

The decision process of Mr. Ordinary creates two possible sequences of events, whereas the routine of Mr. Cautious is fixed. A computer program may contain both types of sequences. Since the program is a preplanned sequence of instructions to be followed for any and all sets of data relevant to a given problem, all possible conditions must be anticipated, and the sequence of instructions prepared for each. This preplanning of all possible program paths allows the computer to process data at high speed without human intervention. For example, a consumer survey of customer tastes may ask a question, "Do you like the XYZ brand?", and the customer is given three choices—"Yes," "No," and "Not acquainted with XYZ brand." When programming to tally the responses, it is

FIGURE 3-4 Short sequence in morning routine of two individuals.

necessary to decide in advance not only how to tally the standard responses, but also what instructions will be followed if the question is not answered or if some other answer is written in.

Steps in Preparing a Computer Program

The preparation of a computer program should have been preceded by system design (solution procedure design). The system design should have provided specifications such as the following:

Reports or analyses to be prepared

Algorithms or solution procedures to be used

Source documents for data collection

Method by which data on source documents will be transcribed to machine-readable form

Computer files to be maintained

Type of file media and file organization to be used

Layout of source document, computer record, computer file, and report

Processing, computer and noncomputer, required

Frequency of processing

Processing approach

Distribution and use of output

The programming of the computer for an application using computer processing follows system design and generally involves five steps.

1	Program planning	Outlining the procedures and logic for the computer processing required for the application
2	Coding	Writing detailed computer instructions using a coding language
3	Assembly or compilation	Translating the computer instruction from the coding language into actual machine language
4	Debugging	Testing the computer instructions to eliminate errors in procedure, logic, and coding
5	Documentation	Preparing and assembling documents which describe the program and its operation

Planning the Program   A program of even modest complexity can rarely be written without preplanning. This planning breaks the program (if complex) into smaller modules. A chart may be used to show module relationships. The planning of program flow and logic frequently takes the form of a programming flowchart. In some cases, a decision table is used as an alternative. A set of program flowcharts typically begins with flowcharts showing the overall flow of program steps. This macro or overall flowchart is then supported by one or more levels of detail (micro) program flowcharts. The macro flowchart allows the reader and programmer to keep in mind the overall flow of work, while the micro flowchart has sufficient detail to be useful as a guide in the coding of the computer instructions. The program planning and design tools are described in Chapter 4.

Coding   The writing of the actual computer instructions is known as *coding*. Although the computer will accept only instructions written in the absolute or machine-language form, the programmer typically codes in a symbolic coding language more suitable for human use. The symbolic instructions must follow rather rigid rules with respect to format, punctuation, etc. The translation of the symbolic coding to machine-language instructions accepted by the computer is done by the assembly or compilation process.

Assembly or Compilation

Assembly is the translation of a program written in symbolic machine-oriented instructions into machine-language instructions. *Compilation* is the term given to the translation or preparation of a machine-language program based on a higher-level procedure-oriented language. The terms are sometimes used interchangeably although they do have slightly different meanings. One *assembles* a program written in BAL (name of a symbolic assembly language), whereas one *compiles* a program written in FORTRAN or COBOL (names of procedure-oriented languages). In both cases, the assembly or compilation process is carried out by a special computer program generally furnished by the manufacturer. The result is a machine-language program which performs the steps represented by the symbolic coding.

Debugging

Rarely does a program run perfectly the first time. There are usually errors in it. The removing of these errors ("bugs") is known as "debugging." Errors in programming can occur from mistakes both in writing the symbolic language and in the logic. Checking for errors should be performed at several stages as follows:

Debugging stage	Description
1 Desk checking	The programmer (and supervisor) review the program before it is released for assembly or compilation. The program is stepped through manually using sample data.
2 Assembly or compilation checking	The translator routine checks to see that all coding rules have been followed. Diagnostic messages are printed out.
3 Program testing using test data	The program is run using data which tests the actions of the program. The test results are compared with precomputed results.
4 Diagnostic procedures	Various procedures are available. For example, a program trace provides a step-by-step printout of the actions of the program, and a memory dump allows the programmer to look at the program and data at a given point in the program.
5 Running during a test period	A program generally needs to run under actual operating conditions for a test period before being accepted.

Documentation

The documentation phase consists of pulling together all the documents associated with the program and assembling them into a run manual and operating instructions. The run manual contains the complete set of documentation for the program. A typical run manual might contain the following: problem description; system flowcharts, layouts of records, files, reports, etc.; program flowcharts and/or decision tables; copy of the symbolic coding; test data used in debugging; program approvals; and record of program changes. The operating instructions used by the computer operator contain all information necessary for the operator.

Coding Computer Instructions

Coding of computer instructions can use different levels of instruction code, ranging from machine-language code to code which is procedure- or problem-oriented, not machine-oriented. These different levels are:

Machine language (absolute)
Symbolic assembly language
Symbolic assembly language with macro instructions
High-level language (procedure- and problem-oriented)

Machine-Language Coding

The computer operates with absolute machine-level instructions, and all coding in other languages must be converted to this form. At execution, each machine-level instruction is stored in a set of computer main memory locations. (Data to be used by the program may also be stored in the main storage or may be obtained from secondary storage.) Each computer has its own repertoire of instructions based on the circuitry of the computer. Basically, all digital computers are very similar, but the instructions for one computer will not usually work on another computer of a dissimilar design.

A machine-level computer instruction contains at least two parts—the operation code and the operand. The *operation code* specifies what is to be done, and the *operand* specifies what is to be used to perform the operation. The particular operation code determines how the operand code is to be interpreted. The operand can be:

1 A memory address where a data word is to be stored or retrieved.

2 An addressable register (used in processing).

3 The location of an instruction in memory.

4 A unit of the computer system such as the card reader, a tape unit, or the printer.

5 Literal numbers to be used by the program.

The computer stores instructions and data using an internal code based on the two conditions or states of electronic circuitry (to be explained in Chapter 6). The equivalent arithmetic notation is binary (using 0 and 1 to represent the two computer states). Machine-language code is printed using some form of notation in place of binary, such as hexadecimal (also to be explained in Chapter 6).

The machine-language instruction typically contains one or two digits (or the equivalent in binary) for the operation code and four or five digits to identify an operand. Thus, a machine-language instruction may look like 563603, where 56 is, for example, the operation code for addition and 3603 is the address of the memory location where the number to be added is stored. The instruction is, or course, stored in a memory location in a binary representation. Using the hexadecimal operator notation, a machine-level instruction (to add contents of location 1E9 to location 1EF) for the IBM System/370 would appear as follows:

FA6541EF41E9

The corresponding binary representation stored in the computer would be:

111110100110010101000001111011110100000111101001

Symbolic Assembly-Language Coding

The machine-language form necessary for machine operation is not well suited to the person who must code the instructions. The reason for this is the problem of keeping track of where everything is stored. Since each instruction and each data word must be given a unique address, writing instructions in absolute code necessitates keeping track of all memory locations. In addition, the numeric memory location identifiers and numeric operation codes are difficult to remember.

Computer manufacturers have met this problem by the use of coding which is symbolic rather than absolute. Mnemonic combinations which suggest the nature of the operation are used in place of numeric operation codes. For example, ADD or A is used as a symbolic operation code for addition instead of a numeric code (such as 12). Each symbolic system has a more or less unique set of mnemonic operation codes. The programmer may also use symbolic addresses for identifying the memory locations used for storage of instructions. The programmer chooses his or her own symbolic addresses, subject only to the naming restrictions of the particular symbolic system. For example, a programmer writing a program to compute a payroll might refer to the memory location by using mnemonics which suggests the nature of the contents of the locations.

Contents	Symbolic address
Gross pay	GROSS
FICA tax rate	FICAR
Cumulative FICA tax	FICAC
Net pay	NET

The symbolic coding might look like the following:

Instruction stored at	INSTRUCTION	
	Operation code	Operand
PAY	ADD	GROSS
	MUL	FICAR

Coding of instructions is usually done on coding paper which assists the programmer in following the correct format. Figure 3-5 illustrates symbolic coding in assembly language.

Since the computer will not operate using mnemonic codes and symbolic addresses, these must be translated into absolute codes and absolute addresses. The translation is done by a set of computer programs referred to as an "assembly system" or assembler. The assembly routine reads the symbolic program from input (say, from punched cards), translates the mnemonic operation codes to machine operation codes, and assigns memory locations for storing instructions and data. The assembly system outputs a machine-language program. The translation from symbolic is one for one; that is, one symbolic instruction results in one machine-language instruction. The assembly routine keeps track of all memory locations used and of all symbolic tags associated with the memory locations. Once

FIGURE 3-5 Sample page of symbolic assembly-language coding.

a memory location is assigned to a particular symbolic address, the same memory location will be assigned to all subsequent uses of that symbolic tag. The process of using a symbolic assembly system is illustrated in Figure 3-6. The translation process includes error diagnostics to detect certain types of coding errors.

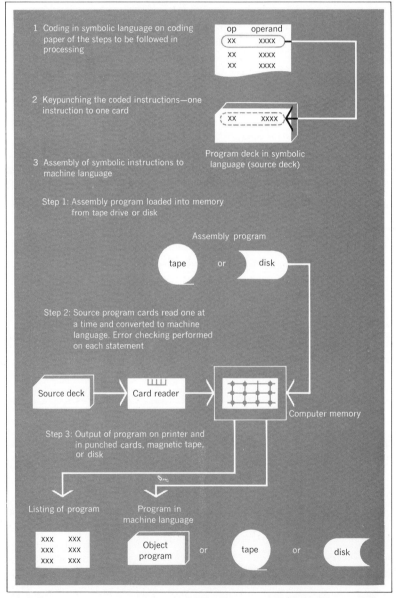

FIGURE 3-6 Preparing a program using a symbolic assembly system.

The advantages of the symbolic coding and assembly program compared with coding directly in machine coding are:

1   Coding is easier, since the programmer can use easy-to-remember mnemonics and symbolic address tags.

2   If a program is changed later or if two programs are combined, machine-language programming would require extensive checking to prevent incompatible memory location use. Programs written in symbolic code are merely reassembled to provide a reassignment of memory locations.

3   The assembly routine provides diagnostic routines to detect errors.

Assembly-language coding is generally used only when the program must be very machine-oriented.

Macro Instructions   The use of a symbolic assembly system does not reduce the amount of coding. There is still one symbolic instruction for each machine-language instruction. But many programs have small segments in common. Examples are the steps in reading and writing records, error checking, and scaling values. Since these operations are common to many different programs, it is possible to write short program segments to be included in any program which calls for performing these operations. To accomplish this, an instruction is added to the symbolic system which indicates that the program segment is to be added. When this instruction is used, the assembly system inserts the instruction segment in the machine-language program. An instruction of this type is called a "macro instruction" because one symbolic instruction results in many computer instructions. The macro instruction relieves the programmer of writing repetitious, standard routines and thereby lessens the chance of coding errors. Macros are quite commonly used for programming input and output operations.

High-Level Languages   The logic of using macro instructions can be carried one step further to build a coding language which is machine-independent. The coding language, being machine-independent, can be oriented toward the problem of procedure for which the language will be used. These problem-oriented or procedure-oriented languages are frequently referred to as "high-level languages." There must be a separate compiler for each computer on which the high-level language is to be used. The compiler consists of the translator program and other programs necessary to convert the high-level statements into a machine-language program.

Of the many procedure-oriented languages, the most popular are BASIC, FORTRAN, and COBOL. These three high-level languages are surveyed in Chapter 6. The nature of the high-level languages is illustrated by sample lines of coding from FORTRAN and COBOL.

Description of a problem	Language	Coding
$X = \sqrt{\dfrac{A^2 + Y}{2B}}$	FORTRAN	X = SQRT ((A ** 2 + Y)/(2. * B))
Compute net pay by subtracting the total deductions (income tax, FICA tax, etc.) which have already been calculated	COBOL	SUBTRACT DEDUCTIONS FROM GROSS-PAY GIVING NET-PAY.

A high-level language such as FORTRAN or COBOL thus consists of a set of simple rules for writing steps to solve a problem. The compiler program translates these statements and creates a machine-language program (Figure 3-7). The creation of a machine-language (object) computer program by a compiler is a result of translating the high-level coding into program instructions and then combining these instructions with prewritten sets of instructions from a library of such routines provided by the compiler. The compiler thus puts together (compiles) a program from a number of parts and links all the parts together. The high-level language is problem- or procedure-oriented rather than computer-oriented and is therefore much easier to use than symbolic or machine language. Reasonable proficiency in FORTRAN or COBOL can be attained in a small fraction of the time required to develop proficiency in symbolic or machine coding. The advantages of the macro-instruction languages would seem to be so overwhelming as to preclude the use of absolute or symbolic coding, and the trend is for most programming to be in the high-level languages. On the other hand, the translation routine to convert from the language coding to absolute coding must be general enough to handle all possible cases, and, therefore, the resulting program is not so efficient in terms of running time as one which is programmed specifically for the particular problem. The disparity in running time may not be important for one-time scientific problems but may become significant for commercial problems that are run day in and day out. If the inventory-updating run takes 3 hours per day using machine-oriented programming and 4 hours using a high-level language, the difference in running time may preclude the use of the high-level language. Compilers have become so efficient, however, that disparity in running time is frequently not significant.

Aids to Programming

As may be apparent, the success of programming efforts depends not only on the hardware on which the application is to be run, but also on the software aids to programming. Programming aids generally available to users include (in addition to the symbolic assembly systems and compilers already discussed) library routines, program library software, utility programs, program generators, file and database management systems, applications programs, and conversion routines.

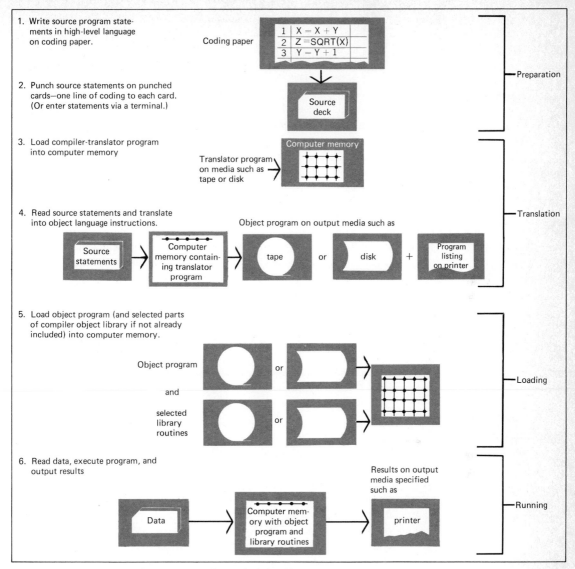

1. Write source program statements in high-level language
   on coding paper.

2. Punch source statements on punched
   cards—one line of coding to each card.
   (Or enter statements via a terminal.)

3. Load compiler-translator program
   into computer memory

4. Read source statements and translate
   into object language instructions.

5. Load object program (and selected parts
   of compiler object library if not already
   included) into computer memory.

6. Read data, execute program, and
   output results

FIGURE 3-7   Preparing an object program from a high-level language program.

Library Routines   *Library routines* are program sections which solve a common computational problem. They are written to be spliced into any program being written by a user. Library routines generally include a wide range of mathematical and statistical routines. For example, a routine to calculate the square root of a number is prepared once by the manufacturer or by the user installation and then inserted in a user's program where needed. When the routine is spliced directly into the main program, it is termed an "open subroutine"; when it is attached to the main program, but remains a separate program, it is termed a "closed subroutine." The technique of using closed subroutines is very important in programming and is discussed in Chapter 5.

Program Library Software

An installation may have hundreds or thousands of programs. At any time, several of the programs may be in the process of correction or other modification. The various versions of a program must be controlled because only the latest, tested version of a program should be used. New programs can often make use of parts (modules) from existing programs, and such modules need to be available for inclusion. Programs are available (often called "librarian programs") that keep track of the program copies and keep a catalogue of program modules that can be copied into a new program.

Utility Programs

Utility programs are programs for performing operating and testing functions frequently used in the operations of a particular computer. Examples are:

Program to load a program into memory

Program to duplicate magnetic tapes

Program to dump memory (output the entire contents of storage, using printer or other output device)

Program to trace the operation of a program (print the results of each step)

Program to sort data

Program Generators

A *program generator* is a routine that will write a simple program based on the specifications for a particular type of problem. For example, a report generator (often called RPG) will write a complete program for producing a report from a description of the desired report. RPG routines allow the user to specify simple manipulation of the data as well as the printing of a report. For many small computers, RPG may be the most important aid to coding of programs.

Another type of program generator (often termed a "preprocessor") is a program which expands a program written in a shorthand notation into a fully coded program. For example, a COBOL program generally uses long, descriptive operation and data names for documentation purposes. A programmer may write shortened names and use a preprocessor to expand the coding to the full names.

File and Database Management Systems

A major segment of a program deals with the management of data files. Software termed "file management systems" or "database management systems" is available for file management, relieving the application programmer of many tasks. These file management systems often also contain facilities for easily programming the selection and retrieval of records and preparation of outputs.

Application Packages These are complete programs which solve problems common to many users. The applications programs are typically ready to use, requiring only a set of data prepared according to the specifications. Examples are linear programming, critical path (PERT) analysis, sales analysis, and inventory simulation. There is also a trend to applications programs that are suitable for a whole industry, such as a complete billing program for electric and gas utilities or an analysis program for brokerage firms.

Conversion Programs Manufacturers of computers typically provide users with considerable assistance. For customers changing to a new computer from an old one, conversion routines have been written to assist in the process. Since a major problem in conversion is the rewriting of old programs for the new computer, a major difficulty is removed by using a program for the new machine that will accept instructions written for the old. This is done by having the new computer simulate the operation of the old. The simulation program approach to conversion is in contrast to the use of a routine called an "emulator" which interprets instructions for the old computer and executes the corresponding set of instructions on the new computer.

Approaches to Program Job Submission

The contrast between immediate input via terminals and periodic batch input described earlier in the chapter in relation to the timing of processing flow is reflected in two different approaches to the submission of programs. (1) Batch coding and submission and (2) online coding and submission from a terminal.

In batch coding and job submission, a program is coded and punched into cards, job control cards are added to the deck, and the program job deck is left at the computer center to be run along with other jobs of this type. After being run, the output is printed and distributed. Turnaround time between submission can range from less than an hour to several hours.

A terminal may be used to enter the lines of program code and to call for compilation and/or execution. Error messages to the terminal allow immediate correction of errors, resubmission via the terminal, etc. The advantages are quick turnaround and reduced time to make corrections. The disadvantage is the inefficiency of programmers entering coding via a terminal.

A mixed strategy may be used in which programs are first submitted as a batch job (to avoid the entry of large programs via the terminal). The programmer uses a terminal to debug and to make minor changes. When this is completed, a regular batch output is specified, and a program listing is produced on the printer.

SUMMARY The steps in the development of a computer application follow a similar pattern for all types of applications, but there are differences in emphasis between major application areas such as organizational information processing (data processing) applications and scientific (mathematical, statistical, and modeling) applications. The data processing applications should be defined by a master plan for the information processing system of the organization. Such a plan is developed as part of the planning and budgeting process of the organization. Within the context of the master development plan, each information processing application development follows a development life cycle consisting of a definition stage, a physical design stage, and an implementation stage. These three stages can be further described by eight phases: feasibility assessment, information analysis, system design, program development, procedure development, conversion, operation and maintenance, and postaudit. The organizational use of the applications means there is much emphasis in the life cycle on the design of the input, output, and files and on the preparation of procedures for users.

The scientific applications to perform processing for mathematical, statistical, and modeling problems are not generally part of a master plan. They are most likely to be developed in response to the needs of a researcher or group of researchers. The emphasis of the application development shifts from the design of input, output, and files to the design of processing procedures and solution algorithms. The life cycle for the development of these applications is generally reduced in scope to problem identification, problem analysis, solution procedure design, program selection or development, and operation.

Processing methodology is generally defined as batch or online, but there are a number of variations in the timing of the basic functions of data preparation, data validation, input, processing, normal output, and error output.

A computer program consists of a set of instructions which specify what the computer is to do under all possible conditions. Program development follows the general steps of program planning, coding, assembly or compilation, debugging, and assembly of documentation. The coding of instructions may take several forms—absolute machine-language coding, symbolic assembly-language coding, symbolic coding with macro instructions, and high-level problem- or procedure-oriented language coding. In addition to the coding languages and related translators, the manufacturers of computers and software vendors usually make available software packages which reduce programming effort. Programs may be submitted in batch mode or through a terminal with immediate response.

EXERCISES

1 Why is the master plan important in the development of most organizational information processing applications but not significant for scientific applications?
2 How does programming fit into the development of a data processing application?
3 What parts are logically contained in a master plan?
4 The life cycle for data processing applications has been described differently by different authors. Explain the difference between the life cycle in the chapter and the following two life cycles:

(a) Problem definition   Programming
     Preliminary survey   Programming tests
     Detailed business systems   System tests
     Detailed computer systems   Installation
     Programming specifications

(*b*) Survey   Filemaking
      Systems investigation   Clerical procedures
      Systems design   Systems testing
      Programming   Parallel running

5   What is the life cycle for a scientific application? Show the relationship of this life cycle to the information system application development life cycle.

6   An organization decides to develop a planning model for use by all its 345 branch managers. Which development life cycle is most appropriate? Explain.

7   What is the difference between the following:
(*a*) Assembly and compilation
(*b*) FORTRAN and COBOL
(*c*) Machine-level code and symbolic assembly-language code
(*d*) Emulator and simulator
(*e*) Library routine and applications program

8   Define the following terms:

(*a*) RPG   (*e*) Debugging
(*b*) Macro instruction   (*f*) Desk checking
(*c*) Operand   (*g*) Assembly system
(*d*) Utility routine   (*h*) Library routine

9   How might a programmer use a code-expanding COBOL generator? What would be its value?

10   Why is not all programming done in high-level languages?

Chapter

4

Tools for Use in Design of Computer Applications and Computer Programs

This chapter describes some of the tools used by systems analysts and computer programmers in analyzing, planning, and designing computer applications and computer programs. The tools are layout charts, grid charts, flowcharts, and decision tables. These tools assist the analysts and programmers in organizing their thinking, describing what must be done, and communicating the design to others. When the application is completed, the various charts are included with the documentation.

Layout Charts

A *layout* is a drawing which shows the format of an input/output record or the placement of data in storage. Preprinted forms are generally used for this purpose. Computer manufacturers make these forms available as part of their service to users of their equipment. They are also available from vendors of forms. The major layout forms in use are card (or terminal input) layout, tape or disk layout, and printer layout. Each of these is described and illustrated.

Each type of input or output card is described by the use of a card layout form (Figure 4-1). The fields on the card are marked off and described by noting the

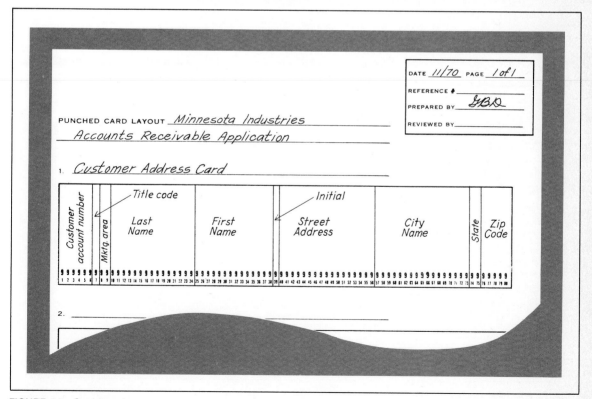

FIGURE 4-1 Card layout.

name of the field, the type of characters (alphabetic, numeric, or alphanumeric), and the location of the decimal point where appropriate. If input is from a terminal, each line of terminal input can be described by a layout form similar to the card layout but containing a larger number of columns.

The *tape layout* shows the format of records written on magnetic tape. It is similar to the card layout except that a card is limited to 80 characters, and a tape record can be as many characters as desired, limited primarily by the main storage space available for holding a tape block during processing (Figure 4-2). A tape layout may also specify tape characteristics such as density and number of records in a block. A disk layout is similar.

The *printer* or *visual display screen layout* assists the programmer in planning the exact placement of data for a printed or displayed output. Headings are shown on the form as well as X's or other notation indicating the data field locations. The vertical spacing of printer paper is often (but not always) controlled by holes in a short paper or plastic tape which is mounted on the printer. When used, this carriage control tape is planned with a form along the side of the printer layout sheet (Figure 4-3).

FIGURE 4-2 Magnetic tape layout.

FIGURE 4-3 Printer layout.

Grid Charts

Grid charts are a tabular method of summarizing the connections or relationships between two sets of factors in a matrix format. For example, in planning the organization of a set of interrelated programs which use the same set of data, it may be necessary to summarize which programs use which data items. A grid-chart form is useful for this and similar purposes (Figure 4-4).

A grid-chart analysis is often useful in eliminating unnecessary reports or simplifying reports by eliminating redundant data items. All the data items are listed on the side of the chart; the reports are listed across the top (Figure 4-4). An entry of 1 indicates that the data item appears on the report. By analyzing the redundancies, the systems analyst may be able to reduce the number or complexity of reports.

A grid chart may be applied to the documentation of user procedures. For example, an input procedure which requires different data item input depending on

FIGURE 4-4 Grid charts.

the transaction type may use a grid-chart format to summarize these inputs for the user (see Exercise 3).

Flowcharts

Flowcharts are symbolic diagrams of operation sequence, data flow, control flow, and processing logic in information processing. Flowcharts are used both in the design of data processing applications as a means of recording the proposed system design and also as part of the documentation of the completed application. Flow-charts are also useful to those who must review systems (such as auditors) as a concise method to document understanding of an application being reviewed.

The communication function of flowcharts is enhanced if standard symbols are used in drawing the charts. Standard flowchart symbols have been adopted by the American National Standards Institute (ANSI).[1] The symbols have also been adopted internationally by the International Organization for Standardization (ISO).[2] The use of these flowchart standards is voluntary, but they have been widely adopted and their use is therefore encouraged for data processing personnel and others who prepare flowcharts.

Even though the same set of symbols is used for both, it is convenient to distinguish between two types of flowcharts:

1 *System flowchart* This chart describes the sequence of major processing operations (both manual and computer), data flow from and to the files used in processing, and the flow of processing controls.

2 *Program flowchart* This type describes the sequence of operations and logic for a computer program. It is sometimes referred to as a block or logic diagram.

Flowcharts are normally prepared using a flowchart template which is available from computer manufacturers and from independent suppliers of drawing templates. A template is not necessary but does add to the neatness and speed with which a good flowchart can be drawn. Special forms are available to aid in drawing flowcharts. The forms contain predrawn areas in which symbols can be drawn neatly. These forms are a convenience but not absolute requirements.

Various software packages are available to prepare flowcharts from a source program code (computer instructions written in the COBOL, FORTRAN, or assembly languages). The flowcharts prepared by this software tend to be some-what more detailed than a programmer or an analyst might draw. However, the software provides a useful method of developing a flowchart for those cases in which there is no documentation or documentation is inadequate.

Explanation of Symbols Figure 4-5 summarizes the 30 standard flowchart symbols; Figure 4-6 provides an example of the use of each of the symbols. There seem to be a large number of symbols to learn. However, there are four basic symbols which are sufficient to describe a data processing system or a program. All other symbols provide additional specificity and clarity.

The general I/O symbol can be used in place of all I/O and storage symbols (except communication link). However, the specialized symbols provide a clearer

[1] The complete American National Standard, X3.5-1970, *Flowchart Symbols and Their Usage in Information Processing*, is available from the American National Standards Institute, Inc., 1430 Broadway, New York, N.Y. 10018.

[2] ISO/R 1028-1969.

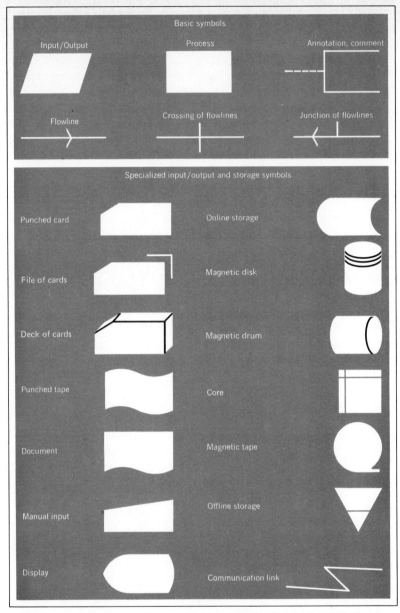

FIGURE 4-5 International (ISO) and American National Standard (ANSI) flowchart symbols for information processing.

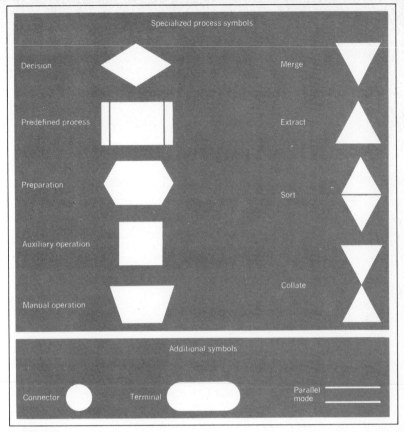

FIGURE 4-5   (*Continued*)

picture of the system. If there is to be output but the exact medium has not been decided, the system is flowcharted with the general I/O symbol; when the output has been decided as printer, then the flowchart is made more specific by drawing the output using the printer symbol. A short description of the document, file, or process is usually written inside the symbol. If additional description or explanatory notes are required, the annotation symbol is used.

Flowchart Usage Conventions   The standard is to draw flowcharts so that they read from left to right and top to bottom. If the flow goes in a reverse direction, arrowheads are used. Arrowheads can, of course, be used in normal flow to increase clarity or readability.

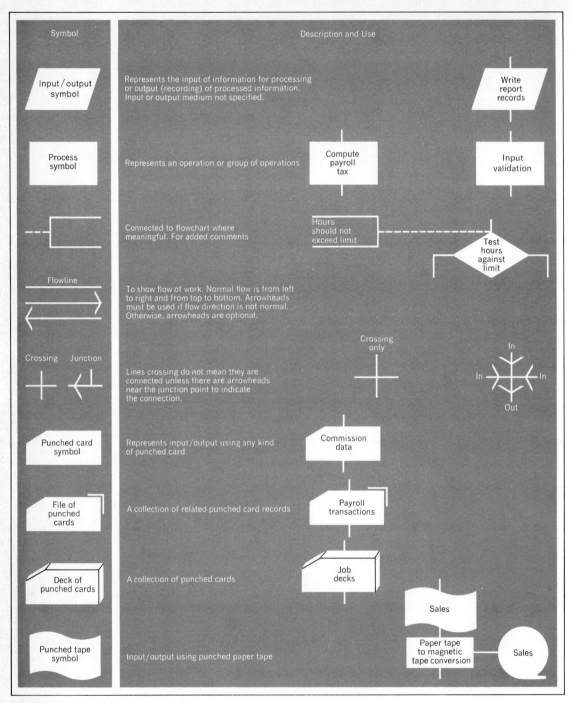

FIGURE 4-6 Use of flowchart symbols.

FIGURE 4-6 (*Continued*)

FIGURE 4-6 (Continued)

FIGURE 4-6   (*Continued*)

FIGURE 4-6 *(Continued)*

When it is desirable to identify a symbol for the purpose of referencing it, a notation is placed above the symbol to the right or left of the vertical bisector or inside the symbol separated by a stripe. American National Standards for the use of the flowcharts specify a standard use for each. The symbol identifier and striping code can be constituted so as to reflect other information important for the reader, e.g., department involved.

Overlay patterns may be used to show multiple input or output media or files. The front symbol is drawn in full and the other patterns offset behind it (right or left). There may be multiple copies of the same output or different inputs and outputs which are part of a set.

Guidelines for System Flowcharting

Drawing flowcharts is sufficiently creative that no two people will draw them exactly alike. However, following the guidelines for system flowcharting in this section and program flowcharting in the next section will enhance the effective use of flowcharting as an aid to design and documentation.

In the design of a data processing application, it is useful to use system flowcharts to show the flow of data and controls in an application. Figure 4-7 shows a simple system flowchart for one of the major functions in an accounts receivable application—the run which updates the accounts receivable master file. In drawing

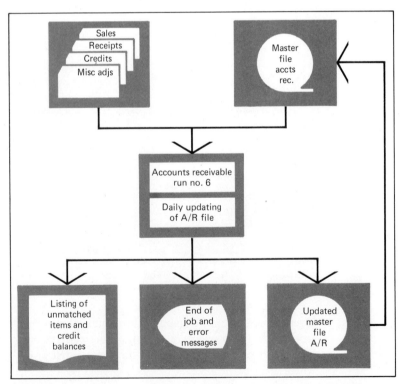

FIGURE 4-7 Simple system flowchart for updating of accounts receivable file.

the system flowchart, the sandwich principle[1] is useful—to have one or more inputs and one or more outputs from a process. The output from one process may be the input to another process (Figure 4-8). When a system flowchart is too large for a single page, it may be divided into a macro chart and several micro charts (one for each process on the macro flowchart). When a system chart must be continued on another page, a clear method of breaking it is to identify the output which will be

[1]The term was coined by Chapin. See Ned Chapin, "Flowcharting with the ANSI Standard: A Tutorial," *Computing Surveys*, June 1970, pp. 119–146.

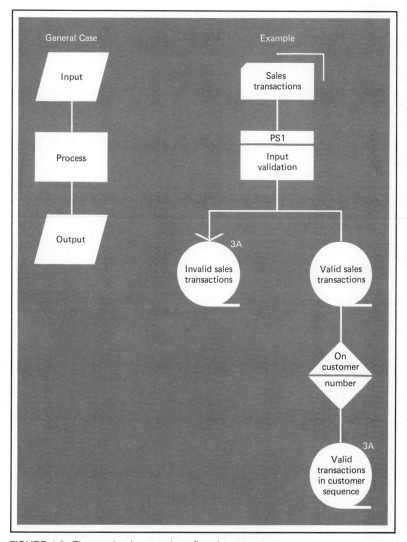

FIGURE 4-8 The sandwich principle in flowcharting.

the input on the next chart with a page and symbol number. Repeat the symbol as an input on the continuation chart with a page and symbol reference back to the flowchart page from which it came. For example, the system flowchart output invalid transactions on page 1 shown in Figure 4-9 is continued on page 2 of the system flowcharts. The flowcharting would repeat the invalid transaction file with a reference.

It is frequently impossible to write suitable explanations in the symbols. One alternative is the use of the annotation symbol. Another alternative is to use an annotation column to the right of the flowchart. Additional comments may be written opposite each symbol (Figure 4-10).

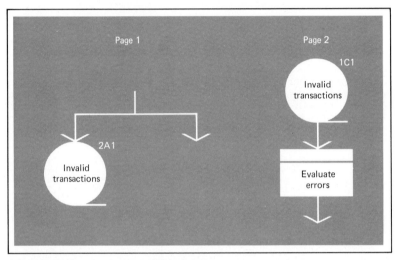

FIGURE 4-9 Breaking a system flowchart.

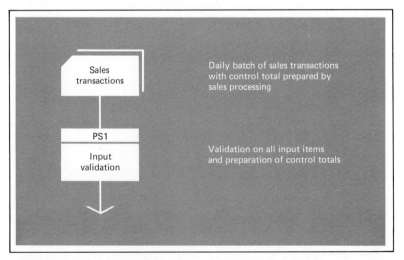

FIGURE 4-10 Use of annotation column.

System charts can be used to show manual processing such as manual procedures to prepare data for computer processing and the manual use of output. For example, the preparation of sales transaction input (shown as input in Figure 4-8) can be diagrammed by a manual procedure system flowchart (Figure 4-11).

Effective error and quality control of a processing application is an important consideration in the design. Although both purposes can be shown on a single system flowchart, it is often useful to draw a separate system control flowchart[1] to identify the flow of controls in an application. Such a control flowchart which

[1] Robert I. Benjamin, *Control of the Information System Development Cycle*, New York, John Wiley & Sons, 1971, pp. 52–53.

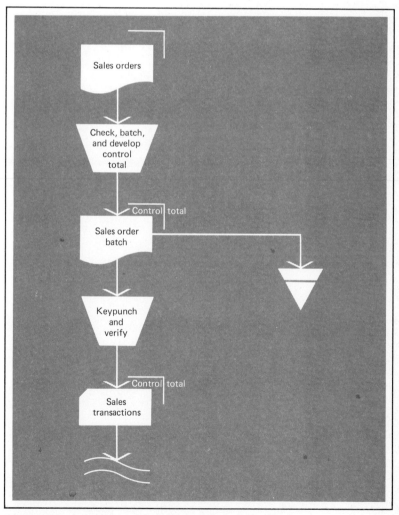

FIGURE 4-11 Flowcharting of manual processes.

accompanies the data flowchart is very useful for reviewers of system design. A copy of the system flowchart for the data flow without any notation is utilized for drawing the control flowchart. The controls associated with each input, transformation, and output of data are written in each box of the control flowchart (Figure 4-12).

Guidelines for Program Flowcharting

The program flowchart (also called a flow diagram or logic diagram) shows the details of the operations or algorithm which transforms the input to the output. A program flowchart may detail the logic of a process symbol in a system flowchart or may detail the logic of a module charted in a higher-level program flowchart by a striped processing symbol (Figure 4-13).

The program flowchart begins and ends with a terminal symbol. The beginning terminal symbol should show the routine name or other identification. The end or exit from the routine is a terminal symbol that identifies the end of the processing or a return to the routine to which the charted module belongs.

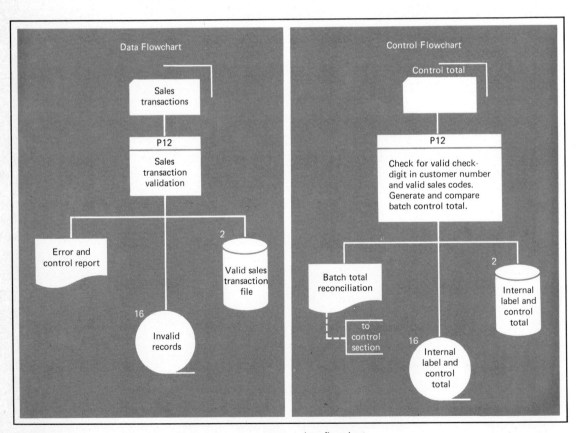

FIGURE 4-12 System control flowchart to accompany system data flowchart.

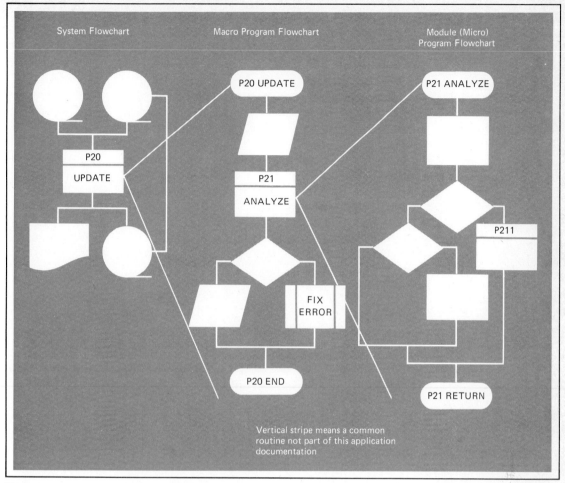

FIGURE 4-13 Relationship of system flowchart, macro program flowchart, and module (micro) program flowchart.

Striping is used in program flowcharts (and system flowcharts as well) to identify processing described in another flowchart. Horizontal striping is used to reference a more detailed flowchart of a module that is described in the same set of flowcharts. In other words, the highest level of flowchart references detailed flowcharts for each major process. Some of the processes at the second level of detail may reference more detailed flowcharts (Figure 4-14). This process is consistent with the modular approach to system and program design explained in Chapter 5. Vertical striping references a routine common to many programs. It is in the routine library, and its flowchart, etc., is found in the library routine documentation. For example, in Figure 4-13, the routine to fix error may be a common routine for all programs.

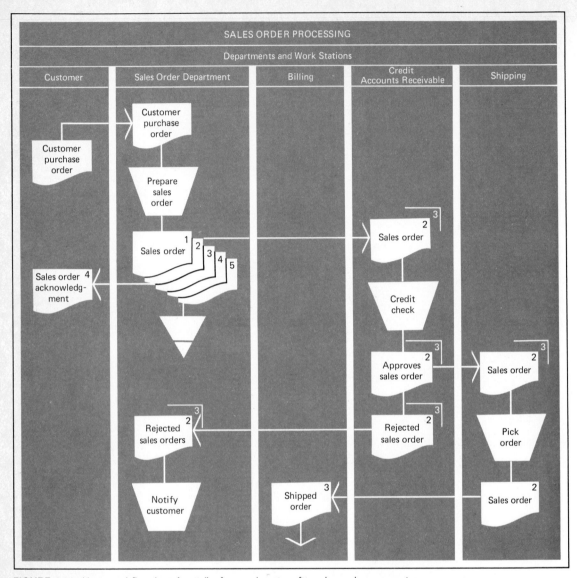

FIGURE 4-14 Horizontal flowchart (partial) of manual system for sales order processing.

Horizontal Flowcharts The ANSI standard for flowcharts has the flow going from top to bottom and from left to right. Another type of flowchart useful in describing an organizational application is a horizontal flowchart which shows the different organizational units involved in processing (manual and computer) for an application. The flow is between organizational units. The flow described may be documents only or may show operations as well (Figure 4-14).

Decision Tables

Decision tables are a graphic method for describing the logic of decisions. In a tabular format, the decision table lists a set of conditions plus a set of actions and identifies different combinations of decisions which lead to different combinations of actions. These different combinations are termed "rules." The decision table in Figure 4-15 illustrates this tabular format. It is a decision table for use by clerks making a decision on granting of credit at a department store. Rule 2 says to grant credit for an applicant who has not held his or her present job more than 1 year if the applicant has lived in his or her present residence more than 2 years and has a yearly income of more than $7500.

A decision table may be used in place of a flowchart or narrative, or it may be used as a supplement. When applicable, it is a very powerful graphic tool for describing the logic of processing and should be part of the tools of every systems analyst and programmer. A decision table may be used in conjunction with a flowchart. For example, the flowchart may have a section that is more clearly represented by a decision table. As shown below,

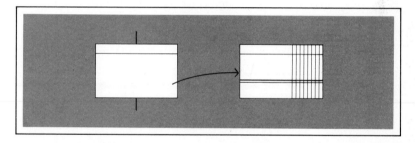

this section is represented by a striped process box in the flowchart which references the decision table. The decision table may be used both for manual procedures and for computer program logic. The decision table can be very useful when collecting data from users on the logic they wish to have applied to a problem

	Credit granting table	1	2	3	4	5	6
Conditions	Held present job more than 1 year	T	F	T	F	F	T
	Lived at present residence more than 2 years	–	T	F	T	F	T
	Yearly income greater than 7,500	T	T	F	F	–	F
Actions	Grant credit	X	X				
	Refuse credit			X	X	X	X
	Refer to credit manager						X

Rule 2

FIGURE 4-15 Example of decision table.

to organize it into a decision table. It helps to bring out any undefined rules (conditions without specified actions) and is often more understandable to the users than a flowchart. One of the useful applications of decision tables is in the analysis of rules, regulations, and procedures. For example, using decision tables to analyze governmental regulations, French officials discovered 44 classes of persons the regulations excluded from entering France who were supposed to be admissible.

Format of Tables The decision table is a tabular form divided into four areas (Figure 4-16):

1	Condition stub	**3**	Action stub
2	Condition entries	**4**	Action entries

Conditions and actions are connected by an "if . . . then . . ." relationship. The rule can be read, "If the specified set of conditions exists, then perform the indicated actions." The condition stub lists all conditions; the condition entries note the fact that the condition must be met (Y), must not be met (N), or can be either because the answer does not affect the actions (—). Tables with Y, N, and — for condition entries are termed "limited entry" tables. An "extended entry" table may use values or relationships in the condition entries:

Type of table	Condition	Condition entries	
Limited entry	Pay greater than $5000	Y	N
Extended entry	Pay compared with $5000	$>$	$\leq$

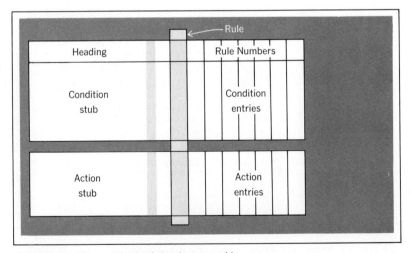

FIGURE 4-16 General form of the decision table.

Since an extended entry table is an extension of a limited entry table, the explanation will concentrate on the latter.

The action stub lists all actions which can follow from the stated conditions. The action entries identify with an X those actions to be taken for a rule. A blank or 0 means the action is not to be taken for that rule.

One of the powerful analytical features of a limited entry decision table is that for a given set of conditions and actions, one can analyze whether or not all the rules have been stated. There are theoretically 2^n rules for n separate conditions. This follows from the number of combinations of the two conditions Y and N. In other words, four conditions would result in 2^4 or 16 rules. A set of eight conditions would require 256 results, which gives a large table. However, in practice the table need not be so large, because many of the rules are redundant. Part of the procedure for developing a decision table should therefore be elimination of unnecessary conditions, testing for completeness, and elimination of redundant (unnecessary) rules.

Steps in Preparing a Decision Table

The steps in preparing a limited entry decision table are:

1 List conditions and actions.
2 Combine conditions which describe both of only two possibilities.
3 Make "yes" or "no" responses (Y or N).
4 Mark actions to be taken for each rule with X.
5 Check for completeness.
6 Combine redundant rules to simplify table.
7 Reorder table for most understandable order of rules.

The explanation will emphasize a systematic procedure for developing a decision table. As analysts or programmers develop some skill, they may be able to arrive more directly at the final table. The beginner should proceed carefully and systematically.

An example will be used to explain and illustrate the procedures. A university has the following criteria for deciding whether to admit students to its graduate school:

> Admit a student who has undergraduate grades of B or better, has test scores on the admission test of over 550, and has a grade average of B or better for the past 2 years. Also admit if the overall grade average is less than B but the last 2 years' average is B or better and the test score is over 550. Admit on probation if the overall and 2-year grade averages are B or better but test score is 550 or less. Admit on probation if overall grades are B or better and test score is above 550 but grades during the last 2 years are below B. Also admit on probation if overall grades are less than B average and test score is 550 or less, but grades for past 2 years are B or better. Refuse to admit all others.

The first step is to write down all the conditions and actions.

Conditions **1** Undergraduate grades of B or better
2 Test scores of over 550
3 Grade average of B or better during the past 2 years
4 Test score of 550 or less
5 Grades less than B during the last 2 years
6 Overall grade average less than B

Actions **1** Admit
2 Admit on probation
3 Do not admit

The second step is to combine conditions which describe the only two possibilities of a single condition. In this case "test scores over 550" and "test scores of 550 or less" can be combined. A single condition "test scores over 550" can represent both because a "no" answer means test score 550 or below. The same reasoning allows the combination of conditions 1 and 6 and also 3 and 5. There are thus only three conditions:

1 Undergraduate grades of B or better
2 Test scores of over 550
3 Grade average of B or better during the past 2 years

Step three is to prepare the "yes" and "no" responses using Y and N for all possible combinations of conditions. Then for each set of conditions mark the action(s) to be taken with an X. The number of rules to be handled in the step is 2^n where n is the number of conditions. In the example, there are three conditions, so there will be 2^3 or 8 rules. The Y's and N's can be inserted in any order, but a systematic method will reduce the effort of filling in the table and reduce the chance of error. Start with the bottom row of the condition entries, and fill in the row starting with Y and then alternating between N and Y. The row above this is filled in by writing two Y's, two N's, two Y's, two N's, etc. The third row from the bottom uses sets of four Y's and four N's. This doubling of the sets of Y's and N's continues until the table is complete. Then analyze each rule and fill in the action entries. Figure 4-17 shows the completed table at this stage.

The next action is to combine rules where there are redundancies. Two rules can be combined into a single rule if all the conditions except one have the same Y and N (or —) condition entries *and* the actions are the same for both. Combine the two rules into one and replace the condition entry of Y and N with a dash (—), which means the condition does not affect the actions below. By use of this procedure, rules 1 and 5 can be combined, as shown. In other words, if grades are B or better in the past 2 years, the student is admitted without regard to overall average. Rules 3 and 7 can be combined, as can 4 and 8 (or alternatively 6 and 8). The resulting table with redundancies removed is shown in Figure 4-17.

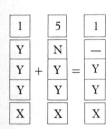

Graduate school admission	1	2	3	4	5	6	7	8
Conditions Undergraduate grades of B or better	Y	Y	Y	Y	N	N	N	N
Test score over 550	Y	Y	N	N	Y	Y	N	N
Grades of B or better past 2 years	Y	N	Y	N	Y	N	Y	N
Actions Admit to graduate school	X				X			
Admit on probation		X	X				X	
Do not admit				X		X		X

Graduate school admission	1	2	3	4	5
Conditions Undergraduate grades of B or better	–	Y	–	–	N
Test score over 550	Y	Y	N	N	Y
Grades of B or better past 2 years	Y	N	Y	N	N
Actions Admit to graduate school	X				
Admit on probation		X	X		
Do not admit				X	X

FIGURE 4-17 Decision table for example. Top table is complete table before redundancies. Bottom table is final table with redundancies removed.

The completed table with only five rules must represent the eight possible rules. To check for completeness of the rules, analyze the completed table as follows:

1 Count number of dashes in the condition entries for each rule. The number of rules "represented" by each rule are 2^m where m is the number of dashes. Where there are no dashes, the number represented is 2^0, or 1. A single dash means two rules have been combined ($2^1 = 2$), etc.

2 Sum the number of rules represented by the different rules as computed above.

3 Compare the number of rules represented by the table with the number to be accounted for, which is 2^n ($n =$ number of conditions). If they are equal (and all other features are correct), the table is complete.

In the example, rules 1, 3, and 4 have one dash (2^1 for each, or 6), and rules 2 and 5 have no dashes (2^0 for each, or 2). The sum of 6 plus 2 is equal to 2^3, or 8, rules required by the three conditions. The final table could be rearranged for easier use, but this is not necessary.

**Using a Set
of Tables**   If a problem has many conditions, the decision table may become quite large and
difficult to follow. Since the objective of the table is to show the logic of the
procedure as clearly and as simply as possible, a large, complex table should be
avoided. In most cases a large problem with many conditions can be subdivided
into two or more tables. One or more of the actions of the first table will specify
that the user should proceed to another table to complete the logic. An action to
GO TO another table implies no return; an action to PERFORM another table is
used to perform the named table and then return to the next action in the calling
table. An example will illustrate this use of more than one table.

A sales organization is seeking to hire some salesmen and saleswomen having special
characteristics. Only unmarried personnel between the ages of 25 and 35 are needed. If
male, the salesman is to be over 6 ft in height but less than 200 lb in weight, and not
bald. If female, the saleswoman is to be less than 5 ft 4 in. in height and less than
120 lb in weight and is to have shoulder-length hair.

This problem has nine conditions, which would mean a table with 512 rules before
reduction. But the problem fits logically into three parts—the overall criteria, male
criteria, and female criteria. This suggests that three decision tables should be
used—initial screening, male selection, and female selection. The result of this use
of three tables is shown in Figure 4-18. All tables have had redundancies removed.
Note the third line of the condition stub of the initial screening table. There could
have been two conditions, "male" and "female," but, as described previously, there
are only two sexes, so naming one is sufficient; a "no" to "male" means female just
as clearly as "yes" to "female."

**Decision Table
Processors**   The analysis of the decision tables has followed fairly simple steps, suggesting that
the computer might be used in table analysis and that the computer might write
instructions to carry out the logic of the rules. This is exactly what has been done.
There are decision table processors which will generate computer code from a
decision table. The processors also analyze the tables for redundancies, completeness, etc. The processors are used in connection with a programming language such
as COBOL, so that part of the program is written in the regular way and part is
generated from the decision table.

**Evaluation
of Decision Tables**   The decision table has a number of advantages as a tool for analysis and communication.

1   The table provides a framework for a complete and accurate statement of
processing or decision logic.

2   The table is compact and easily understood, thus being very effective for
communication between analysts or programmers and others.

3   The table allows mechanization of some programming tasks.

Initial screening	1	2	3	4
Conditions Unmarried	Y	Y	Y	N
25 to 35 yrs. in age	Y	Y	N	–
Male = Y; female = N	Y	N	–	–
Actions Reject			X	X
Go to male selection table	X			
Go to female selection table		X		

Male selection	1	2	3	4
Conditions Over 6 ft. in height	Y	Y	Y	N
Less than 200 lbs. in weight	Y	Y	N	–
Not bald	Y	N	–	–
Actions Reject		X	X	X
Accept	X			

Female selection	1	2	3	4
Conditions Under 5 ft. 4 in. in height	Y	Y	Y	N
Less than 120 lbs. in weight	Y	Y	N	–
Shoulder length hair	Y	N	–	–
Actions Reject		X	X	X
Accept	X			

FIGURE 4-18 Use of a set of decision tables.

The decision table is best for presenting a problem with many conditions; it is not well suited to show the flow of processing where there are few decisions. Decision tables have been used much less frequently than flowcharting. One reason for this is the fact that many applications do not lend themselves to decision tables, but another is the lack of training in their use. On balance, then, the decision table is a very helpful tool for some applications and should therefore be one of the methods that the analyst or programmer can use when appropriate.

SUMMARY When a computer application is being designed, it is necessary to define explicitly the form and content of input/output documents and files and to describe both the overall flow of work and the processing logic. The tools which are used have been described. These are layout charts, grid charts, flowcharts, and decision tables.

Layout charts are used to describe the form and content of input, files, storage, and output. Examples are card, magnetic tape, and printer layouts. The layouts are usually drawn on printed forms prepared for this purpose.

Flowcharting is the most common method of planning the logic and flow of a computer application. Two types of flowcharts are used—the system flowchart, which describes the flow of documents and major processing tasks, and the program flowchart, which describes the logic of a computer program.

The solution to a problem may be flowcharted in many different ways. There are individual differences in the way a flowchart is prepared in much the same way that there are individual differences in the way different individuals will write a description. The main objective of the flowchart is to communicate the logic and flow of processing in such a way that it is as understandable as possible to the reader. Clarity is enhanced by using standard symbols which have an agreed-upon meaning. Therefore, it is recommended that the ISO or ANSI symbols presented in the chapter be used.

The decision table is used as a supplement or in place of a flowchart, especially for problems with complex sets of conditions and actions. A systematic approach to the development of a limited entry decision table was presented. Although not as widely used as flowcharting, decision tables are a very useful tool for the analyst and programmer.

EXERCISES

1 What is the difference between planning of the application and planning of the program for the application?

2 Using only a knowledge of the meaning of the flowchart symbols, explain what is probably being described by the flowchart segments, which have no description in them, on page 113.

3 Which technique described in the chapter would be used to provide a check in the design process by showing the relationship between data items required for an output document and data items obtained from input documents or storage records?

4 What is the purpose of the card, tape, and printer layouts?

5 Tell in words the contents of a card described by the following card layout.

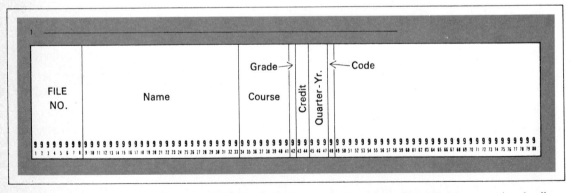

6 Flowchart the following using system flowcharts. Do not show excessive detail.

(a) A computer run to read cards, write the data on magnetic tape, accumulate a count, and write the count and any error messages on the printer.

(b) An updating run to update a file on magnetic disk with transactions on punched cards. Error and control messages are written on the printer.

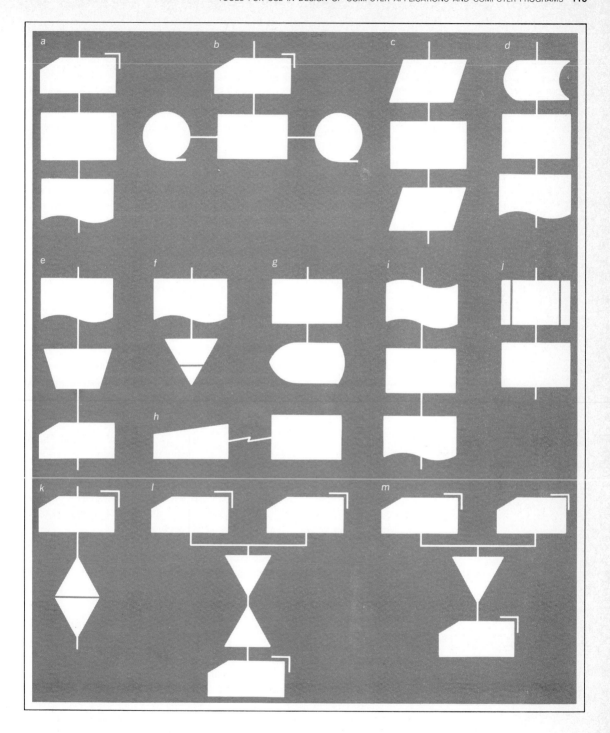

(*c*) A computer run to print customer statements from a file on magnetic tape. Records in error are copied onto an error file on a magnetic disk. Control totals are written on the printer.

(*d*) A three-part invoice is prepared. One part is filed, one is accumulated into batches, a batch total is prepared, and the batch is sent to the keypunching and verifying section. The batch is then filed. The punched cards are sent to the computer department for processing.

(*e*) The accounts-payable department receives a copy of the purchase order (PO) from the purchasing department and a copy of the receiving report (RR) from the receiving department. When invoices are received from vendors, the invoice is matched with the purchase order and the receiving report by a clerk. The clerk prepares a voucher. The accounts-payable supervisor reviews the document and prepares a check. The check is signed and mailed by the office manager, who cancels the documents. The documents are filed.

(*f*) The cash receipts section of the company opens the mail and prepares remittance advice (a small form for each remittance describing the customer and amount received). The batch of remittance advices for the day are totaled on an adding machine, the total is attached to the batch of remittance advices. These are sent to keypunching where they are keypunched and verified, after which they are filed by batch in a file. The payment cards headed by a batch card with the control total are input to a computer run in which they are sorted by account number, and the control total is checked. The results of the run are:

(1) An audit and control report listing the amount received plus any exceptions found on the input editing. This goes to the accounting department to be used for a general ledger entry and for review of any errors.

(2) A cash receipts journal listing each remittance. This also goes to accounting.

(3) The payment cards which were the input to the run are stored in a temporary file pending the weekly update run, after which time they are destroyed.

(4) A magnetic tape of the receipts is produced as a result of the run. This is held for input to a weekly accounts receivable updating run.

7 Flowchart the following using a program flowchart.

(*a*) The logic of a computer dating service that matches couples on the basis of similarity of interests with regard to music, art, and sports (a match on one or more of the three), plus same religion and age difference not greater than 5 years older for men and not greater than 1 year older for women.

(*b*) The logic of computing gross pay. Forty hours or less are at standard pay. Hours over 40 are $1\frac{1}{2}$ times standard pay except Sunday and holiday work, which is at 2 times standard. Sunday and holiday hours are coded separately on the payroll input.

(*c*) Determine which of four quantities A, B, C, and D is the largest.

(*d*) $\sum\limits_{i=1}^{100} x_i$ i.e., sum one hundred quantities referred to as $x_1, x_2, \ldots, x_{100}$

Hint: Obtain the sum by adding the x_i's one at a time to an accumulated sum. Set up a test to stop accumulating when you reach 100.

(*e*) Read a student's numerical score on an exam from a punched card and determine if the grade is to be A, B, C, D, or F. (Set your own limits for each grade.)

(*f*) Calculate the number of each type of coin (penny, nickel, dime, quarter, or half-dollar) a newsstand vendor should give in change when a person makes a purchase and gives a sum of money as payment. To simplify the problem, assume no purchase or payment amount is in excess of $1.

(g) The logic of selecting charge accounts for audit examination. A positive confirmation form requesting the customer to check the balance as reported against his records and report whether or not it is correct will be sent to all accounts which are over $300 and over 60 days old, and to all accounts showing a credit balance greater than $10. A negative confirmation requesting an answer only if there is an error will be sent to all accounts owing less than $300 and over 60 days old, to every tenth account for accounts not over 60 days old, but greater than $200 owing, and to every fiftieth account which is not over 60 days old and has a balance not greater than $200.

(h) Hire a prospective employee if he or she is between 21 and 35 years old, does not have long hair, is married male or unmarried female, and has experience in selling or has a grade point average of 3.5 or better.

8 Prepare a decision table for problem 7(b), 7(c), and 7(h).

9 Prepare a set of two decision tables for problem 7(a).

10 Fill in the following table, simplify, and analyze completeness:

Reservation procedure	1	2	3	4	5	6	7	8	9	10	11	12	13	14	15	16
Conditions Request for 1st class																
Requested space available																
Alternate class available																
Alternate class acceptable																
Actions Make 1st class reservation																
Make tourist reservation																
Name on 1st class wait list																
Name on tourist wait list																

11 Draw a flowchart to detail the logic shown in the following decision table. The table covers the deductibility of educational expenses on the federal income-tax return.

Educational expenses	1	2	3	4
Conditions				
Education to qualify for employment	Y	N	N	N
Education to maintain or improve skills required in your employment	—	N	Y	N
Education required by your employer or by regulations to retain current employment	—	N	—	Y
Actions				
Educational expenses deductible			X	X
Educational expenses not deductible	X	X		

Chapter

5

Computer Program Structure and Design

The purpose of this chapter is to provide insight into the design and structure of computer programs. The chapter describes the modular design of a program, coding structures, types of instructions, and some fundamental coding techniques. These topics are presented within the framework of a disciplined, structured approach to program design and development.

Objectives of a Structured, Disciplined Approach to Programming

During the 5-year period 1970 to 1975, the costs of hardware dropped dramatically—close to one-half as much at the end of the period compared with the beginning. During the same period, the costs of developing programs increased significantly. Control of software performance has become a more important factor than control of hardware performance. The major problems of software performance have been that computer programs frequently:

Do not meet user requirements
Are not produced on time
Cost considerably more than estimated
Contain errors
Are difficult to maintain (to correct or change to meet new requirements)

These difficulties have been observed with such frequency that many organizations have attempted to change the practice of programming to improve software performance. The revised approach can be termed "programming discipline"— well-defined practices, procedures, and control processes. This approach to program design and development has the following objectives:

1 Meeting user needs
2 Development on time within budget
3 Error-free set of instructions
4 Error-resistant operation
5 Maintainable code
6 Portable code

The techniques for achieving these objectives are presented later in the chapter.

Meeting User Needs A program has a purpose, such as to produce a report, prepare a sales invoice, or compute a set of statistics. A program may be elegant, but if it is not used because the potential users find it too complex or too difficult, then it is a failure. A disciplined approach to program design includes a careful analysis of user needs and user involvement in key decisions affecting the practicality of the application.

Development on Time within Budget Estimates of time and cost for programming projects have frequently been substantially in error. Programmer productivity has generally been lower than expected. One objective of a structured, disciplined approach to programming is more accurate estimates, greater productivity, and closer control of the actual time and cost required.

Average productivity in the industry (in 1975) was about eight lines of tested code per day for a programmer using a high-level language such as FORTRAN or COBOL (about 2000 lines per year). Using a more structured approach, installations have achieved dramatic improvements in productivity. One installation boosted productivity to 5000 lines per year, and another expects to achieve an average of 10,000 lines of tested code per programmer per year.

Error-free Instructions

It is generally conceded that all large-scale computer programs contain errors, and it may be impossible to remove every single error from a large set of programs. However, programs may be designed and developed in a way which facilitates detection and correction of errors and thereby achieves virtually error-free instruction coding. There are two approaches to error-free programs. One is a mathematical approach for proving the correctness of a computer program. While promising, the mathematical method is still experimental and not operationally useful. The second approach to error-free instructions is the use of a program structure and programming discipline which supports error-free program design and production. Programming groups with strong quality control procedures have been able to reduce errors in completed, tested programs to an average of one undetected error in 10,000 lines of instructions. This contrasts with a rate of perhaps one error per 100 lines of delivered, tested instructions by programming groups without a disciplined approach to error-free code.

Error-resistant Operation

The erroneous results of a program may be due to program errors or to incorrect input. The program should be designed so that errors will, insofar as possible, be detected during execution of the program. The design features to assist in detecting errors (described further in Chapter 10) are:

1 Input validation
2 Tests of correctness during processing

Input validation is a testing of all input data items to determine whether or not they meet the criteria set for them. For example, data input may be tested for:

Existence of necessary input data items

Data item values within acceptable range

Illogical relationships among input items

Incorrect class of data (e.g., alphabetic characters in a data item field which should be numeric)

Every computer application should perform input validation. This may be accomplished by a separate input validation program (also termed "input editing") or by a separate section of a program, depending on the design of the application and its programs. The input validation will detect all errors which can be found by logic tests; additional errors can be detected by human review of the input data. This human review may be part of the input process, or the input data may be included with the output, and human review for errors can be performed as part of the use of the output.

Tests of correctness during processing generally take the form of reasonableness tests on results and checking the logical relationship of results. For example, the results of payroll processing (say, gross pay for each employee) may be tested for reasonableness, and data items may be tested by crossfooting (e.g., sum of gross pay amounts minus sum of all deductions should equal sum of net pay amounts).

When errors are detected, error messages should be output which clearly identify both the nature of the error and the user responsibility for error correction. The detailed steps in error correction and re-input of the data may be described in the error message or in user documentation for the application.

Maintainable Code   Computer programs change, especially when first placed into use. Programs should be written with the maintenance activity in mind. The structure, coding, and documentation of the program should allow another programmer to understand the logic of the program and to make a change in one part of a program without unknowingly introducing an error in another part of the same program.

Portable Code   A tested program, written in a high-level language, should be transferrable without substantial change to another computer having a compiler for that language. This means that programming which takes advantage of unique machine features should be avoided as should all nonstandard instructions. Straightforward, well-documented instructions are portable with little difficulty; programs with intricate or poorly documented logic are not.

The Structure of a Computer Program

The set of instructions in a computer program will be executed sequentially as written unless an instruction transfers control backward or forward in the programmed sequence. Such transfers are common, and so a computer program can become quite complex (Figure 5-1). The structure presented in this section provides a method for simplifying the design of programs.

Modular Design   Most programs in operational use are too large (in numbers of instructions) to be easily understood if coded as a single sequence of instructions. The method of simplification is to design the program as a set of units often referred to as "blocks"

FIGURE 5-1 Impact of forward and backward transfers of control on complexity of programs. (Horizontal lines indicate instructions; vertical lines show processing sequence.)

or "modules." A program module is defined as a part of the program which performs a separate function such as input, input validation, or processing one type of input. A program function may be quite large (in terms of logic and instructions required), so that the function may be further subdivided into logical subfunctions, each of which is defined as a program module. This process of subdivision continues until all modules are of manageable size in terms of complexity of logic and numbers of instructions. A module may therefore consist of only a few instructions; many programmers feel a module should not be more than 50 lines of instruction code (which means it will be contained on one page of printer output). Modular design is useful in managing a large programming project because modules may be assigned to different programmers for coding.

A simple computer program using the modular approach consists of a control module and a number of processing modules. The control module directs the execution of the processing modules (Figure 5-2). A more complex program contains a main control module and a hierarchy of processing modules. The main control module directs the execution of the processing modules. The processing modules invoke other lower-level modules. The control routine can be programmed in a very straightforward manner with no (or few) forward or backward transfers of control. The flow of processing logic is therefore quite clear. This

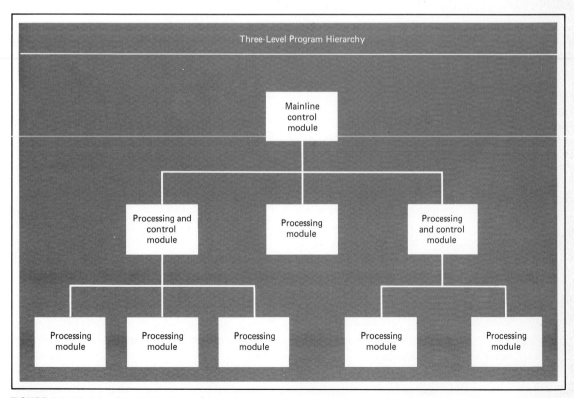

FIGURE 5-2 Modular (block) structure of a program.

enhances the clarity of the original design and improves debugging; it also makes program maintenance easier to accomplish.

Basic Modules in a Program

Although computer programs differ greatly in purpose and processing, it is possible to identify functional modules which will appear in most programs because they tend to be necessary functions.

Function (module)	Description
Main line control	Performs all tests to determine order of processing and directs execution of processing modules.
Initialization	Performs program tasks to open files, set variables to initial values, set program switches to initial conditions, print headings, etc.
Input	Performs input of data required by the program.
Input data validation	Performs validation of input data to detect errors or omissions in input. Edits input.
Processing	Performs computation or data manipulation.
Output	Performs output of data to be provided by the program.
Error handling	Performs analysis of error condition and outputs error messages.
Closing procedure	Performs procedures to end the execution of the program such as rewind and close files, print summary data, and print end-of-program message.

These modules form a logical flow in a program (Figure 5-3). A program begins with initialization after which the control module directs execution of processing. The processing proceeds logically with input, input validation, various processing modules, and output. Error handling may be required during any of the modules. At the conclusion of processing, various closing procedures are performed to complete the program execution.

Basic Coding Structures

All computer programs can be coded using only three logic structures (or patterns) or combinations of these structures.[1]

[1] The proof of this statement is presented in C. Bohm and G. Jacopini, "Flow Diagrams, Turing Machines and Languages with Only Two Formation Rules," *Communications of the ACM,* May 1966, pp. 366–371.

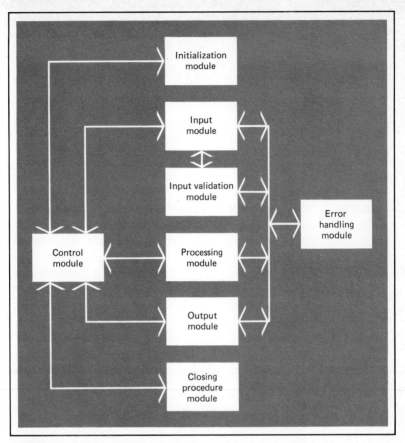

FIGURE 5-3 Basic modules in a computer program.

1   Simple sequence
2   Selection
3   Repetition

The three structures are useful in a disciplined approach to programming because:

1   The program is simplified. Only the three building blocks are used, and there is a single point of entry into the structure and a single point for exit.

2   The three coding structures allow a program to be read from top to bottom making the logic of the program more visible for checking and for maintenance. There is no backtracking.

The ease of coding of programs using the three basic structures and a modular program design depends somewhat on the programming language being applied. Some languages have excellent facilities for this approach; others are somewhat cumbersome. But the technique can be applied with all languages. A fourth structure, the multiple-case selection, is sometimes included as a basic structure, although it is attainable using the sequence, selection, and repetition structures.

Simple Sequence

The simple sequence consists of one action followed by another. Logically, it can be termed an AND structure because the first operation is always followed by the second. In other words, the flow of control is to first perform operation A (Figure 5-4) AND then perform operation B. A simple sequence is flowcharted as two process symbols connected by a flowline.

Selection

The selection structure consists of a test for a condition followed by two alternative paths for the program to follow. The program selects one of the program control paths depending on the test of the condition. After performing one of the two paths, the program control returns to a single point. This pattern has been termed IF THEN ELSE because the logic can be stated (for condition P and operations C and D): IF P (is true) THEN perform C ELSE perform D (Figure 5-4). A flowchart for the selection structure consists of a decision symbol followed by two paths, each with a process symbol, coming together following the operation symbols. In terms of symbolic logic, the selection structure is an OR pattern because C OR D is executed (but not both).

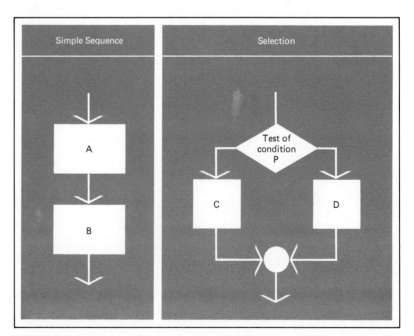

FIGURE 5-4 Flowchart of simple sequence and selection program structures.

Repetition   The repetition structure is also termed a "loop." In a loop, an operation (or set of operations) is repeated until some condition is satisfied. The basic form of repetition is termed DO WHILE (Figure 5-5). In the DO WHILE pattern, the program logic tests a condition; if it is true, the program executes operation E and loops back for another test. If the condition is not true, the repetition ceases. A variation of this same basic pattern is the DO UNTIL. The operation F is performed until the condition is true. The major differences between the loop logic for DO WHILE and DO UNTIL is the location of the test. In DO WHILE, the test occurs before the first execution of the operations; in DO UNTIL, the test occurs after the first execution. In reference to Figure 5-5, if the condition P is not true, the operation E will not be executed for the DO WHILE structure; operation F will be executed once in either case with the DO UNTIL pattern.

Multiple-Case   There are fairly frequent situations in writing programs in which a code or other
Selection   condition having several values will be tested. Each value of the code or condition results in a specified processing path. This can be coded by nested sets of the basic

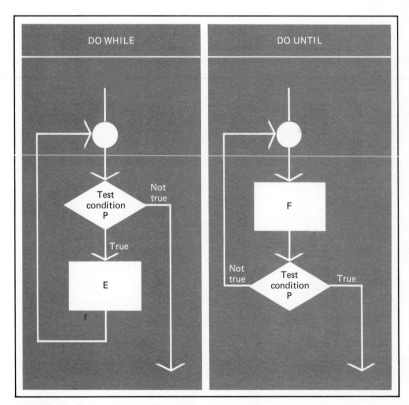

FIGURE 5-5   The two forms of repetition structure.

sequence structure. However, it is often useful to use instructions which provide for a multiple selection. These instructions have names such as CASE, GO TO DEPENDING ON, or COMPUTED GO TO (Figure 5-6).

Combinations of the Basic Structures

One of the objectives of using the three basic structures is to make programs more understandable to those concerned with design, review, and maintenance. It is possible to nest the three simple structures to produce more complex coding while maintaining the simplicity inherent in the three patterns. For example, the logic of the program may involve a selection between two program paths. If one path is chosen, there should be a repetition or loop; if the other is selected, there is a simple sequence. The nesting of the structures is illustrated in Figure 5-7. Note that there is still a single entry/single exit for each structure.

Formatting Programs to Show Coding Structure

The major programming languages provide language facilities for coding the basic logic patterns. Some languages provide better facilities than others, but the basic coding concepts can be used in all programming. Chapter 6 will illustrate these concepts in the examples of language coding.

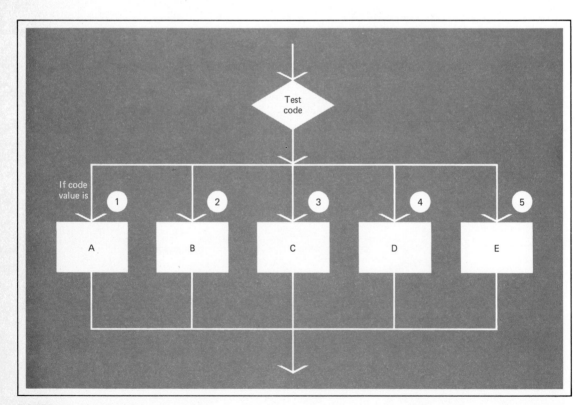

FIGURE 5-6 Multiple selection structure.

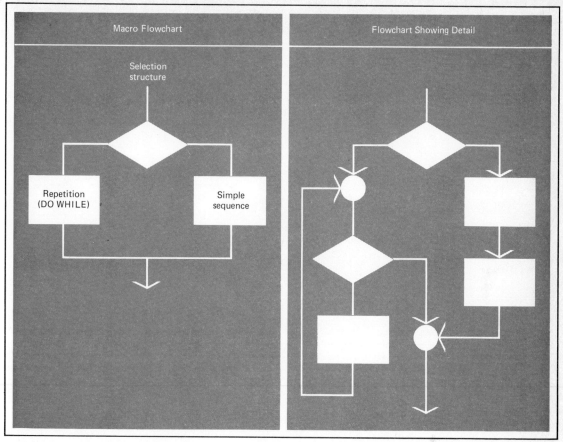

FIGURE 5-7 Nesting of coding structures.

A major factor in writing clear, understandable programs is the use of names, comments, or indentation as a method of showing the program structure. Some guidelines for formatting instruction code are:

1 Each module is identified by a descriptive name. Some programmers also use a code in a module name which shows its relationship to other modules (Figure 5-8). As an example of one possible naming approach, a hierarchical prefix is used to define module relationship. If the main module is identified with A-MAIN-MODULE, the name for an error-handling module might be AE-ERROR-HANDLING; if three submodules are called upon by the error module, these might be labeled AEA, AEB, AEC followed by a descriptive name, e.g., AEA-ERROR-CODE-ANALYSIS.

2 Comments are used in the program to document the logic. Comments are (*a*) at the beginning of the program to explain the purpose, structure, and flow of the program; (*b*) at the beginning of each module to explain the purpose of the

FIGURE 5-8 Use of code at front of module name to show relationship among modules. (Suggested at workshop given by H. Blair Burner, Boeing Computer Services.)

module; and (*c*) in among the program coding lines to explain coding which may not be clear. Some programmers suggest that well-documented programs will have a ratio of comment lines to instruction lines of about one comment line to five instruction lines.

One suggestion for comments is to consider the program as a book.[1] The program starts with a table of contents listing each module and a very short description of its purpose. Each module (like a chapter in a book) begins with a description of the purpose of the module and the processing logic utilized.

3 Lines of coding are indented to identify logical blocks of code and to show the range of code belonging to program structures. For example, coding might be indented as shown in Figure 5-9. The concept of indentation for clarity of coding receives further illustration in Chapter 6.

Elementary Computer Instructions

The instructions available for coding a computer program will depend, in part, on the language being used. However, the nature of a computer program suggests that all languages must have certain instructions. These elementary computer instruc-

[1] Knut Bulow, "Programming in Book Format," *Datamation,* October 1974, pp. 85–86.

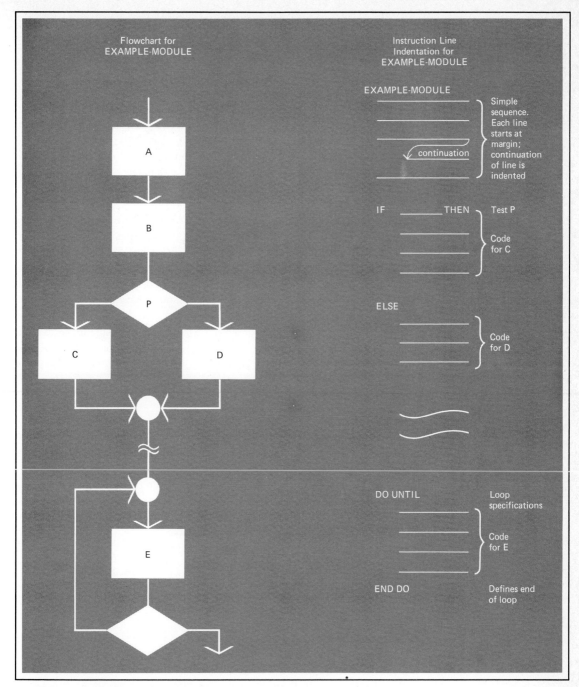

FIGURE 5-9 Indentation of instruction lines to show code structures.

tions may be classified as move, edit, arithmetic, transfer of control, looping, input/output, and compiler/assembler instructions. This general introduction will assist in understanding the instruction set for a specific language.

Move Instructions

The move instructions transfer data from one location in storage to another. Moving might also be termed "copying" because the sending storage locations are not changed; the data codes are copied into the receiving locations. The receiving locations are altered, the former contents being replaced with the new data.

Since the data transfer of the move instruction results in the data being found in identical form in two storage locations, why is it necessary to move data? The major reasons are:

1 The data in the original location may be destroyed by subsequent operations. The move preserves the data. Examples of this situation are:

   (*a*) Data from an input operation is brought into a specified area of memory (sometimes termed an "input buffer area"). Each input operation will bring additional data to occupy the same storage location. Data from an input must therefore be moved prior to the next input operation in order to retain it for subsequent use.

   (*b*) Some arithmetic operations store the results in the storage location occupied by one of the operands. For example, an instruction such as ADD A TO B stores the sum in location B replacing the value of the addend stored there. If the value of the addend (B in this case) is to be preserved, it must be moved prior to the arithmetic.

2 Data may need to be in specified storage locations for operations to be executed using the data. For example, output will generally use a set of storage locations designated as an output area. Data to be output (printed, etc.) is moved to the output area.

3 Data may need to be rearranged before processing or output.

4 In machine-language coding, data may need to be moved from storage into a register which holds data while operations take place.

Edit Instructions

When read into the computer, data may not be in a proper form for computational use. After computation, the data may not be in the form desired for output. Decimal points, commas, etc., need to be inserted. Editing instructions change the form of the data. Examples are:

Changing data coding for a data item
Inserting characters for the output format

Arithmetic Instructions

A computer will have instructions for addition, subtraction, division, and multiplication. In low-level languages, the programmer must provide instructions which scale the operands properly; in high-level languages, scaling is automatic. There are two basic approaches to arithmetic scaling. The first is for the programmer to keep track of the scale factor associated with each number and to write instructions to "line up" the digits in numbers having different scale factors. The other approach is for the computer to keep track of the scale factor and make all necessary adjustments. This is termed "floating point arithmetic."

Computer arithmetic is generally performed using a fixed number of digits (represented by a fixed number of bits, as explained in Chapter 6). The number of digits that can be encoded determines the number of significant digits in the result (the precision). In performing addition, subtraction, and division, it is possible to have overflow or truncation in which some digits are lost because the digits in the result exceed the space for the result. The digits lost through overflow are the leftmost digits in the result; these digits are significant, and therefore it is important for the programmer to detect overflow and to correct for it. Truncation occurs if the rightmost digits cannot all be stored in the space for the fractional result.

Truncation is less serious than overflow, but programs should normally perform rounding prior to truncating any righthand digits. Some high-level languages do the overflow testing and adjustment or rounding automatically; others require specific coding.

Transfer-of-Control Instructions

The sequence of instructions in a computer program will be executed one after another unless a transfer-of-control instruction breaks the sequence. There are few general types of transfer-of-control instructions.

1 Unconditional transfer
2 Transfer and return
3 Conditional transfer based on comparison
4 Conditional transfer based on absence or existence of a condition

The unconditional transfer of control is called a BRANCH, JUMP, or GO TO instruction. The instruction may be used to branch forward around code not to be executed or backward to a prior instruction. Unconditional transfer-of-control instructions which branch back in a program complicate the program logic; therefore branching backward is generally avoided, where possible.

The transfer and return instructions are used in connection with program modules. The instruction transfers control to call or perform another module. When the called module has been executed, control returns to the instruction in the calling module following the instruction to call or perform.

Conditional transfers are required for the selection coding structure. Comparison is between two data items with the test being for an equality, greater than, or less than condition. Alternative forms such as not equal, greater than, or equal may be used. In some languages, comparisons may be made quite complex by the use of more than one condition in the comparison, for example, IF A IS GREATER THAN B AND A EQUALS D . . . .

Transfer of control based on an absence or existence of a hardware or data condition is required in programming because the existence or absence of a number of conditions is used to decide on the processing path. Examples of such hardware or data conditions are:

1 An interrupt caused by a read, busy, or error condition of processing units or communications units. The interrupt is a hardware feature which causes processing to halt. The program can test the reason for the interrupt in order to decide on the actions to be taken.

2 Arithmetic overflow (an interrupt may occur).

3 The "on" or "off" condition of a computer operator console switch (in computers which have them).

4 Data condition, such as negative, zero, or nonnumeric.

5 End of data file condition.

Some of these condition tests are handled by the operating system and are therefore not the responsibility of the individual program. In some situations, failure to test for a condition may lead to an undetected error. For example, when some languages are used, a failure to program a test for arithmetic overflow may allow undetected overflow to occur with incorrect data resulting.

Looping Instructions

Repetition or looping is a fundamental programming structure. The objective is to use the same set of instructions over and over again rather than to write and store many instructions. Programming languages generally have instructions to code a loop. A loop is generally controlled by a variable which has been or is set to an initial condition. As the loop is executed, the loop control variable may be altered as part of the procedures being executed in the loop, or it may be incremented or decremented by a separate modification. The loop variable is tested to determine whether or not the loop should terminate. The two logic patterns presented earlier are reflected in two alternative arrangements of the loop elements, the loop elements being (Figure 5-10):

1 Initialization of loop control variable
2 Test loop variable for termination of loop
3 If no termination, execute sequence of instructions
4 Modify loop control variable

The instructions for loops provide for setting the initial value of the loop control variable, the modification of the loop control variable, and the test for termination.

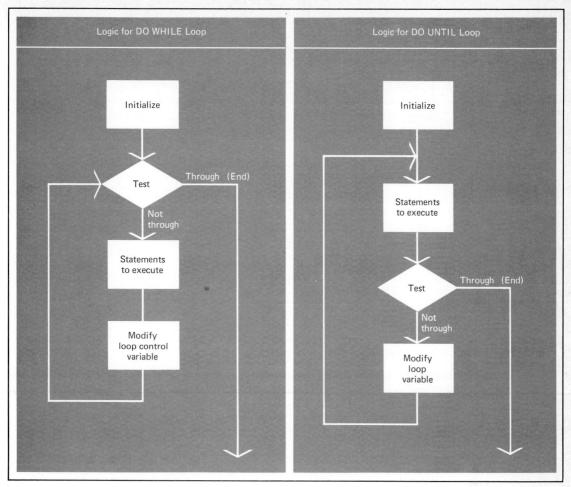

FIGURE 5-10 Detailed logic for two forms of loop.

There is also a program coding method for indicating the range of instructions included in the loop.

Input/Output Instructions The processing instructions typically operate upon data that is input (read) during processing. When processing is complete, the results are output. There are three major sources of input and three objects for output:

Source	Example for input	Example for output
External storage medium	Punched card	Printed lines Punched cards
A terminal	Typewriter keyboard	Visual display cathode-ray tube (CRT) screen

| Online storage | Magnetic tape | Magnetic tape |
| | Magnetic disk | Magnetic disk |

Data is originally prepared for input via some keying operation which places the data on a machine-readable storage medium, such as punched cards, punched tape, or magnetic tape. A processing program reads the data from this medium and may also read data previously stored on an online storage medium (such as magnetic tape or magnetic disk). The output from the processing may be written on an external medium (using a device such as a printer, typewriter, or display device) or may be written on an online storage medium for subsequent processing by the same or other programs.

The devices used for input and output are connected to the computer by an input/output path called a "channel." The instruction for input and output must therefore specify (or imply):

1 The input or output operation
   (*a*) The device
   (*b*) The channel
   (*c*) Read or write
   (*d*) Internal storage locations in which input data is to be put or from which output data is to be copied

2 Control operations such as backspace, rewind, or position

3 Sensing for errors or unusual conditions and error routine to which control should go if detected

The form of input and output construction depends upon the language being used. In business data processing languages, it is usual for the program coding to include a set of specifications for the file to be input and output, instructions to open and close the file for use, and simple instructions to read or write a record from or to the file. The flow of typical instructions for data processing input and output is therefore:

File definition entries	Definitions at beginning of program
OPEN file-name	Open before file is used
GET or READ file-name	Repeated for each record to be read or written
PUT or WRITE file-name or record-name	
CLOSE file-name	Close after last use of file

In the case of some scientific processing languages, the only file definition is a description of the record format. The instructions to read or write specify the device, the data to be input or output, and the format to be used.

Compiler/Assembler Instructions A program written in a symbolic language must be translated into machine-language instructions. The program may contain some instructions that are instructions to the assembler or compiler which performs the translation. COBOL, for example, provides for compiler instructions which causes the compiler to insert debugging statements. Other instructions will be contained in the job control instructions required for each program to be assembled or compiled.

Additional Programming Techniques

In programming, certain techniques have proved useful. Three of these techniques will be described: programmed switches, table look-up, and subroutines.

Programmed Switches In programming, a condition may occur in one part of the program which will determine the path the program should take at a later time. In other words, there is a need to program a delayed transfer of control. This can be handled by a programmed switch (also called a "flag"). A switch may be programmed in a number of ways. In high-level languages, a common approach is to set a variable to one of two conditions for the switch to be "on"; the variable is set to a second condition for the switch to be "off." For example, a code of "1" or a literal OFF may be stored in a location to indicate that the switch is off; a code of "2" or the literal ON may be moved to the location to indicate that the switch is on. The switch is tested by a selection coding structure.

Table Look-up There are many processing situations in which a data item or other factor to be used in a processing must be obtained from a table in storage. In fact, it is considered good programming practice to store tax rates, pay rates, etc., as separate tables rather than including them directly in the program coding. The method of coding should efficiently locate the correct entry in the table for program use. There are many methods of table look-up, but the essence of the methods is to operate upon a given input data item in order to establish a correspondence between the data and the table entry needed. For example, a payroll computation may use a shift-pay differential for the different shifts. The gross pay before shift differential is multiplied by the shift differential factor to give a shift-adjusted gross pay. The shift differentials for five different shifts are stored as five entries in a table. The shift number is used as an index for locating the entry in the table. In many cases, the data is not in suitable form for use as a table index, so that it must be processed further to yield table index numbers.

Subroutines Even though subroutines were mentioned in connection with program design, the importance of subroutines in programming justifies further discussion. The design of programs as modules or blocks means that a program consists of modules, each defined as performing a separate function. A module may be sections of code within the program and identified only by name as being a separate module, or a module may be a subroutine.

Subroutines are sometimes classed as open or closed. Open subroutines are prewritten sections of code inserted into and made part of the main program. A closed subroutine (the type usually meant by the term) is written so that it may be used independently by any part of the main program or by any program. The subroutine is essentially a program used by another program and can be coded, translated, and debugged independently of the program using it. The usual program procedure is for the main program to CALL the subroutine. The CALL statement describes all data items to be used by the subroutine—data items to be used as input and data items for holding the results to be provided by the subroutine. At the completion of the subroutine processing, control is passed back to the calling program, exiting or returning to the statement following the CALL instruction (Figure 5-11).

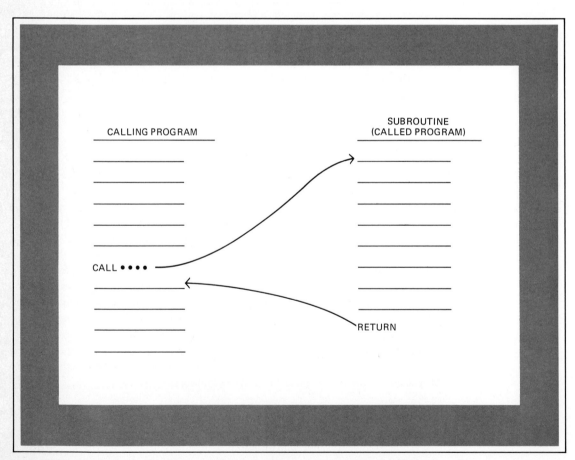

FIGURE 5-11 The use of a subroutine.

A Structured, Disciplined Approach to Program Development

Many of the concepts and approaches presented in this chapter are based on a structured, disciplined approach to program development. Some additional elements have not yet been presented. This section summarizes the elements of an approach to programming that has proved very successful in producing low-error, maintainable programs.

The approach to program development to be described has evolved over 25 years of computer programming. It is sometimes termed "structured programming," but that represents only one element. Although the major software producers have used many of the techniques, IBM pioneered in the synthesis of the elements. The approach was tested during 1970 and 1971 with outstanding success by an IBM team which programmed an online information retrieval system to access data published in *The New York Times*. The system was large (83,000 lines of high-level instruction code). It was developed online over 22 months during 1970 and 1971. Productivity was about five times greater than industry average, and the resulting programs were virtually error-free.

The organizational and structural elements that have produced the improved results for program development are:

1 Top-down program development
2 Structured programming
3 Chief programmer teams
4 Structured walk-throughs
5 Development support libraries
6 Hierarchy plus input-process-output (HIPO) charts

Top-down Program Development

As explained earlier in the chapter, it is useful (and a common practice in programming) to write a program as a set of modules. A hierarchy of modules is normally used with first-level modules controlling the use of second-level modules, second-level modules controlling the execution of third-level modules, etc. Top-down program development is a different approach to the order in which modules are coded and tested.

In a common approach to program development, sometimes termed a "bottom-up procedure," the lowest-level (say level 3) modules are defined, coded, and individually (unit) tested. When all the modules controlled by a higher-level module are ready, the next higher level (say level 2) module is coded and tested. This process continues until the highest-level module (the main routine) is coded. The program can then be tested in total with all interactions among modules being exercised by the testing. The problems in this approach are the lack of integrated testing until the end of the development and the necessity for redesign to correct problems resulting from interfaces (connections) among modules.

An alternative method of program development is a top-down approach. In top-down development, the program is planned as a hierarchy of modules, but programming and testing begins with the top (main) module. When the main module is programmed and tested, second-level modules are then programmed and tested. The testing utilizes both the first- and second-level modules already completed. In other words, at each test the entire program developed to that point is tested. A program unit is coded only after the unit that calls for it to be performed has been coded and tested. How can a module be tested if part of or all its instructions are calls to perform lower-level units (subprogram or subroutine modules) which have not been coded? The answer is the use of a dummy module or stub which contains only one or two statements to identify that the unit is to have been executed by the unit above it. For example, the stub may print the name of the routine. This procedure tests the logic of the next higher level unit.

With Figure 5-12 as a basis for explanation, the steps in top-down development are:

1   Design program. Define a hierarchy of modules or units.

2   The highest-level module (A) is coded completely, and the next level modules (AA, AB, and AC) are coded as dummy modules with only a stub. The highest-level module is tested.

3   Lower-level modules (AA and AB) are coded and stubs inserted for units which they invoke (AAA and AAB for AA and ABA, and ABB for AB). The entire program to that point is tested.

4   Units at a lower level are coded and then tested along with the higher-level modules already coded and tested. The process continues until all units are programmed, integrated, and tested.

The coding and testing of modules proceeds from top to bottom, but it does not have to proceed in parallel for all levels. Some branches of the structure will be developed earlier than others. For example, in Figure 5-12, the module AC remains a stub while AA and AB are coded and tested.

Data for testing the program is developed in an incremental manner. The test data for the highest-level test exercises the main module logic; test data is added at the next level to test the logic of that level, etc. Data-base definitions are written, and data records prepared before the modules requiring the record are coded.

The top-down development approach therefore ensures that the program units are integrated properly. As each lower-level unit is coded and added, the entire, integrated program, as developed to that point, is tested. The higher-level modules which control the logic of the program thus receive the most testing.

Structured Programming

Structured programming is a term applied to a structured approach to the coding of a computer program. The approach generally assumes top-down development and modular hierarchy for a program. Elements generally considered part of structured programming are:

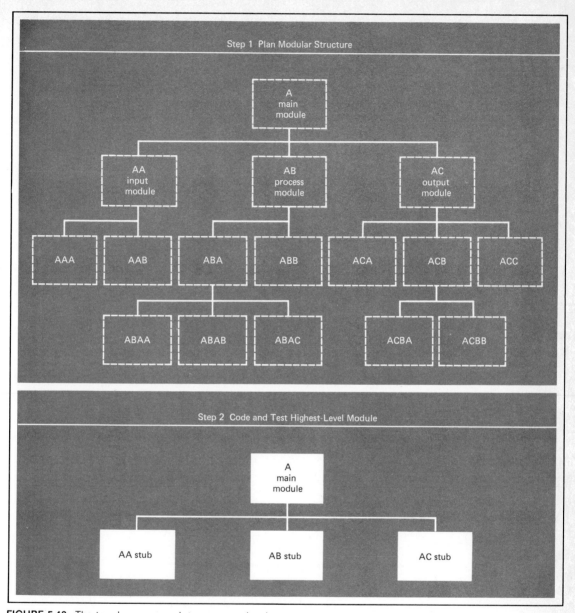

FIGURE 5-12 The top-down approach to program development.

1   Program code uses only the three coding structures of sequence, selection, and repetition (plus the case structure). Forward or backward transfer of control (instructions such as GO TO . . . , BRANCH, . . . , etc.) are not used, or used very sparingly. Structured programming, for this reason, is sometimes referred to as GOTOLESS programming.

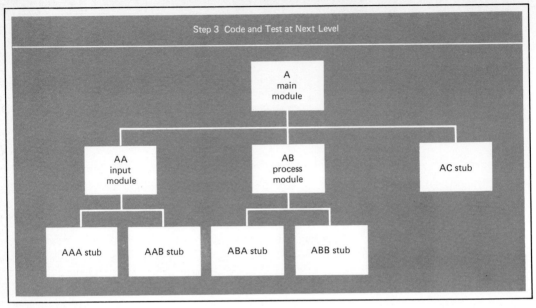

FIGURE 5-12 *(Continued)*

2 Instruction code is indented to reflect the logic of the coding structure. The indentations indicate the beginning and end of coding structures by the same indentation level; functions within the structure are indented further.

3 No module (or unit) of the program shall exceed a stated limit in size. This limit is generally 50 lines of instructions.

Chief-Programmer Teams

The chief-programmer team is a method of organizing and managing the programming of an application. Each programming project is assigned to a team consisting of the following:

Position	Description
Chief programmer	Senior-level professional programmer. Responsible for program design. Has complete technical responsibility for the project. Defines modules to be coded by programmers on the teams and reviews the code written by them. Writes main control routines and other critical code.
Backup programmer	Senior-level programmer. Provides backup for chief programmer and may be given assignment of developing test data for project.

Programmers	Programmers are added to the project as needed. Each is assigned the coding of specific modules which have been defined by the chief programmer.
Librarian	Responsible for semitechnical duties in support of the project such as maintaining the records of the project—documentation, program compilation printouts, test data. Arranges all compilation and testing runs for the programmers on the team.
Others	Specialists may be assigned to the team, as appropriate, for assisting in application design, special coding, etc.

The chief-programmer team concept is a recognition of the need for technical expertise in the leadership of a project, the need for a support function to relieve programmers of clerical duties, and the need for a review of all code by a senior programmer. The leadership and review function of the chief programmer assists in training the programmers in good practice.

Structured Walk-throughs

A structured walk-through is a review of the work of members of a programming team. The review may encompass program design, program instruction code, and documentation. The review is conducted by reviewers (other designers, other members of the team, etc.) selected and invited by the person whose work is being reviewed. The reviewers receive documentation prior to the review meeting. At the meeting, the reviewers comment on the completeness, accuracy, and quality of the work. The developer of the work being reviewed then goes through step by step (walks through) the logic of the work (design, program, documentation, etc.). The walk-through may include a discussion of test data. The reviewers note errors in logic, problems in the design, etc.

The structured walk-through provides a quality control mechanism utilizing the resources of the developer's colleagues. If a proper, open environment is maintained, the structured walk-through not only improves the quality of the product, but also is a method for work improvement by those being reviewed. It is recommended that the review be used only for improving the product, not for management review of individual performance.

Development Support Libraries

The development support library function maintains the records, documents, coded modules, and test data produced by a programming team. Four elements make up the library support function:

Element	Description
A program library stored on the	All modules already developed and latest versions of modules under de-

computer	velopment are stored on a computer file, along with sets of job control statements required for the application.
Software support for library on computer files	The library support software will provide for creating and updating a library for a programming project, retrieving modules for compilation, storing results, and producing listings.
External project documentation	A library of documentation is maintained by the librarian function. It consists of project notebooks containing current listings of all modules, all superseded listings (in order of assembly or compilation), project notes, project documents and reports, etc. Current documentation is thus always available to the project members.
Librarian procedures	The librarian accepts coding or code changes prepared by the programmers; arranges for keypunching, adding of job control cards, and submission for compilation; and updates the computer library and external library for the project.

The librarian support function frees the programmer from many clerical tasks, handling of program decks, submitting jobs, and maintaining the internal and external libraries. It provides for up-to-date, complete records of the project and a complete set of finished and in-progress code at all times.

HIPO Charts HIPO (hierarchy plus input-process-output) charts are a method of planning and documentation of program logic and structure developed by IBM. Often identified with structured programming, the method is useful but not necessary for structured programming. Some programming groups have found HIPO useful, but others have not. A set of HIPO documentation consists of a visual table of contents plus one or more overview diagrams and detail diagrams.

HIPO documentation	Description
Visual table of contents (Figure 5-13)	The visual table of contents is a block diagram showing the hierarchial relationship of program modules. Each module is

further described by HIPO overview and detail diagrams.

Overview diagram (Figure 5-14)

An overview diagram consists of three major blocks:

1 *Input.* All input requirements are listed (generally files of transactions, master files, and tables).
2 *Process.* The major functions to be performed are listed. Each process will be shown either in another lower-level overview or in a detail diagram.
3 *Output.* All intermediate or final outputs are listed. Examples are files, updated files, reports, and error messages.

Detail diagram (Figure 5-15)

The detail diagram is the lowest level of the hierarchy. In format, it is the same as an overview diagram except for an extended description section which gives a verbal description of each process shown in the detail diagram and identifies the module name to be used in programming the module.

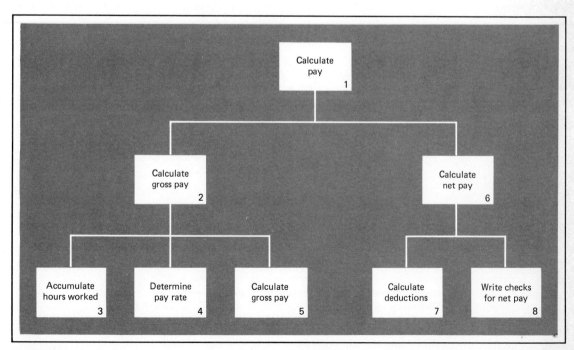

FIGURE 5-13 Visual table of contents. Each block refers to a diagram. (*Courtesy of International Business Machines Corporation.*)

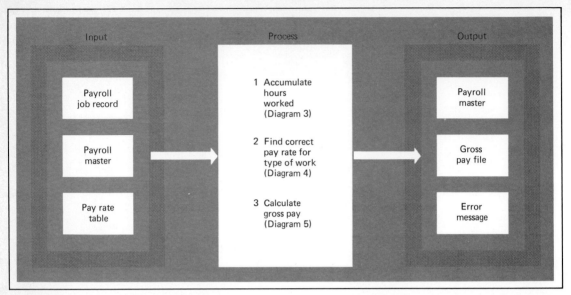

FIGURE 5-14 Overview diagram for block 2 of table of contents (Figure 5-13). (*Courtesy of International Business Machines Corporation.*)

In this approach, the HIPO charts are produced during the development cycle. The initial design uses only overview diagrams; as the development proceeds to detail design, lower-level overview and detail diagrams are added. Regular flowcharts of the type described in Chapter 4 may be used in defining the logic of a program module, but such program logic flowcharts are no included in the final documentation. The modules are small in size and clear in structure so that the program instruction code is sufficient module documentation.

Documentation of Programs

There are essentially two purposes for documentation—the first is to assist in the development process; the second is to assist in program maintenance. Since program maintenance generally involves changes and corrections by programmers other than the developers, the documentation which accompanies a completed, tested program should be clear and complete. The scope of satisfactory documentation may vary considerably depending on the type of application, length and complexity, and language used in coding. However, a minimum documentation for a program should provide for the following:

Documentation element	Description
Purpose and scope of program	A short narrative summary of the purpose and scope of the program.

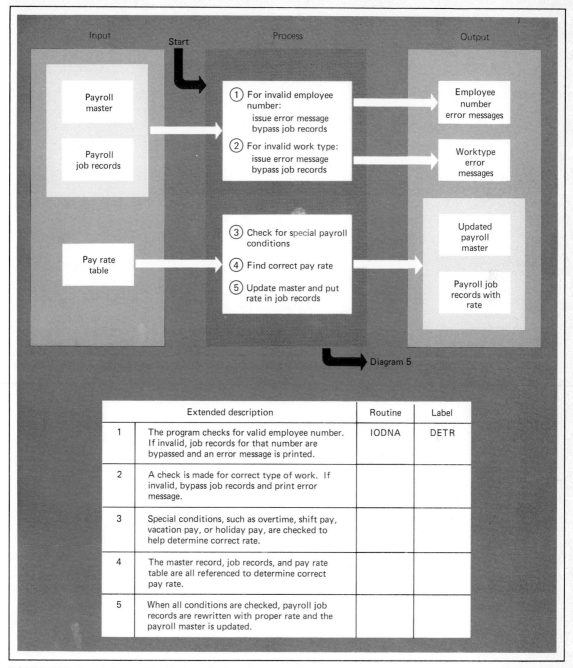

FIGURE 5-15 Detail diagram for block 4 of table of contents (Figure 5-13). (*Courtesy of International Business Machines Corporation.*)

Description of input and output	Layouts or other descriptions of input and output documents. In cases of some files, the program description of the file is sufficient.
Description of structure of program	A diagram of hierarchial listing showing the relationship of program modules or blocks plus a description of each module.
Overall flow of program	Macro flowchart or narrative describing the overall flow of logic for the program.
Detailed logic of program	If small modules are coded in structured format, with ample notes in the program, the computer code will suffice for detailed logic. In some cases, however, the code will need to be supplemented by detailed logic flowcharts.
Test data	A description of data which was used in testing the program (and can be used in future testing).
Operating instructions	Instructions to the operators when running the program. Includes program error messages relevant to operators.
User instructions	Instructions on how to prepare input, to prepare corrections, and to use the output (if appropriate). List of error messages with meaning and corrective action to be taken in each case.
Change record	A record of all changes made to the program—who authorized, performed, tested, and approved them.

SUMMARY   The emphasis of the chapter has been on a structured, disciplined approach to computer program structure, design, and development. The objectives of such an approach are programs which meet user needs, development on time within budget, error-free instructions, error-resistant operations, maintainable instruction code, and portable instruction code.

The structure of a program was defined as a hierarchy of modules, each module invoking and controlling the modules below it in the hierarchy. The basic modules found in most programs are main line control, initialization, input, input validation, processing, output, error handling, and closing procedures.

There are three basic coding structures that can be used to code a program. By using these three structures, the coding is more disciplined and clearer to review and maintain. The structures are simple sequence, selection, and repetition. An additional structure, multiple case selection, is often used. Programs should be formatted to show coding structure. There should be a descriptive name (and comments) at the beginning of each module. Comments are included in the coding where necessary to explain the flow of logic. Lines of coding are indented to identify logical blocks and to show the range of coding structures.

A basic set of computer instructions is found in all languages. These are move, edit, arithmetic, transfer of control, looping, input/output, and compiler/assembler instructions.

Additional programming techniques (over the basic structures) that have proved useful are programmed switches, table look-up, and subroutines. The general ideas are presented in this chapter; the implementation may vary depending on the characteristics of the language being used.

A structured, disciplined approach to program development was presented. The elements, which may be used singly or in groups, are top-down program development, structured programming, chief-programmer teams, structured walk-throughs, development support libraries, and HIPO charts. The chapter concludes with a discussion of program documentation.

EXERCISES

1 Define:
   (a) Error-resistant operations
   (b) Maintainable code
   (c) Portable code

2 (a) Explain modular design.
   (b) Draw a chart showing the modular hierarchy for a computer program with the following modules:

A	Main line control	AC	Compute pay
AA	Initialize	ACA	Compute regular pay
AB	Read input	ACB	Compute overtime pay
ABA	Validate input data	AD	Report output
ABB	Input error messages	AE	Closing procedures

3 What are the differences in meaning among each set of terms:
   (a) Module, block, or program unit   (c) Branching or transfer of control
   (b) Repetition or looping   (d) Switch or flag

4 Draw a flowchart for a selection structure which performs actions on the IF THEN condition but not on the ELSE condition. Does this still fit the basic structure?

5 (a) Flowchart nested selection structures to select procedures as follows:

Code equal to	Perform procedure
1	ONE
2	TWO
3	THREE
>3	ERROR

(*b*) Show an indentation format for the coding of the above logic.

6 What difference does it make if the structure is DO WHILE or DO UNTIL?

(*a*) Assuming the procedure is to be executed 10 times;

(*b*) Assuming the procedure is to be executed until N > 10 but N is already 15 when the repetition structure is reached.

7 Combine, using a flowchart, a sequence, a selection, and a repetition (DO WHILE) for each branch following the selection.

8 Explain the need for and purpose of each type of elementary computer instructions.

9 Explain for arithmetic:

(*a*) Overflow　　(*b*) Precision

10 Flowchart problem 5(*a*) using a case selection structure.

11 How is a programmed switch set, tested, and reset?

12 Why is it better to use a separate tax table that a program can refer to than coding the table in the tax computation program? How is a table accessed using table look-up techniques?

13 How does a closed subroutine differ from prewritten segments of code inserted in a program?

14 A subroutine is coded separately from the programs that will use it. How does the subroutine know what data is to be used when it is invoked by the calling program?

15 Explain the difference between top-down and bottom-up program development. How does it affect the amount of testing for the higher-level modules?

16 How can a module be tested if the modules which it invokes are not yet coded? Explain the use of the stub.

17 Explain structured programming. Why is it called GOTOLESS programming?

18 Define the different job functions in the chief-programmer team method.

19 What might be the responses of a programmer to a structured walk-through?

20 Describe the elements of a development support library.

21 Describe the structure of HIPO charting.

22 Compare the use of macro and micro program flowcharts with HIPO flowcharts.

23 Describe a complete set of documentation for:

(*a*) A small program to calculate the rate of return for an investment. The program will be used by all investment analysts.

(*b*) A large program to do online reservations.

24 A company with a large programming staff reported that they had decided to use three of the six techniques for disciplined program development. Which three do you feel would be most valuable for them?

25 A small company with one programmer asks your advice on introducing the elements of programming discipline. What might they do?

Chapter

6

Selecting a High-level Language for Computer Programming

Given a specific algorithm or procedure to be processed by a computer, how shall the processing or solution procedures be programmed? There are many possibilities. The time and effort for programming may vary considerably depending on the language used. Beginning students frequently do not appreciate the variety of languages and programming aids that can be used. The purpose of this chapter is to describe the types of languages and software packages that are generally available. The discussion covers only high-level languages and software packages. Three major languages—BASIC, FORTRAN, and COBOL—are surveyed; other languages are described in less detail.

Considerations in Selecting a Language

In selecting a language, there are a large number of considerations. Some of the major ones are noted below along with comments.

Selection consideration	Comments
Type of problem	There are languages especially designed for specific types of problems. These are described later in the chapter.
Skill level of programmer	Certain languages are designed for the occasional programmer; others are for the professional programmer.
Terminal or offline program entry	Some languages are well suited for entry via a terminal.
Complexity of problem	Some languages are designed for simple problems; other are better able to handle complex problems (but the languages are more complex). Some languages have versions which optimize coding to reduce either compiling time or execution time.
Portability	If a program is to be used at more than one installation and perhaps on more than one computer, a standard language in common use should be selected.
Availability	A language that is available and well supported by an installation is preferred to a language that must be purchased or is not well supported.
Availability of consulting	There will usually be a need for consultation regarding a program if the programmer is unfamiliar or inexperienced in the language. The availability of such support for use of a language is a significant plus factor for a language.
General purpose versus specialized	Languages may be general purpose and very versatile or specific and restricted. The general-purpose language, when learned, has wide applicability. The specialized package, while more applicable to one problem, has little transferability to other problems.

Language versus package	A language is generally used to describe procedures, a package (such as a statistical package) is generally programmed by specifications and procedural statements.

In general, the beginning user should select well-supported, widely used languages and packages in preference to little-used but specialized languages. Simple languages with high consulting support are favored over complex languages rich in esoteric features. The beginner should not fail to consider alternatives such as statistical packages and callable subroutines.

The Operation of a Compiler

As explained in Chapter 3, a high-level language is a language that is designed to describe the problem, the desired results, or the procedures of problem solution to be followed. The program written in a high-level language must be translated into machine-language statements. The software to do this is termed a "compiler."

There are two types of high-level languages to be described in this chapter. The first group are procedure-oriented. They are used to describe the procedures to be followed to solve a problem or perform processing. Examples are BASIC, FORTRAN, and COBOL (the languages described later in the chapter). Other software packages for solving problems are programmed by the use of specifications which describe the data and the result to be obtained. They are more problem-oriented than procedure-oriented. Examples are the statistical packages. The explanation of translation procedures and operation of a compiler will emphasize use of the procedure-oriented language, but the principles of translation are similar.

Development of High-Level Languages

The idea of high-level languages is attributed to Grace Hopper, head of programming for UNIVAC. Her work led to two early languages—FLOWMATIC and MATHMATIC, which reflect the development of the two major types of languages—algebraic and commercial. Since high-level languages are oriented toward the procedures by which problems are solved, it is logical to have one language which is designed for problems formulated in mathematical terms and another designed for commercial data processing problems. The development of high-level languages has been rapid and has led to a proliferation of languages. Each language consists of a set of words and symbols, plus a set of rules for using this vocabulary to define problem-solving procedures. The words, symbols, and rules are intended to allow the computer user to clearly state the procedures needed to solve a problem. The vocabulary of the language is therefore similar to the language used in mathematics and/or data processing.

If each computer manufacturer or large user were to develop a separate high-level language, an important benefit available with problem-oriented languages would not be realized. This advantage is a standard language which can be translated by all computers. With such standardization of high-level languages, a program written by persons having access to one computer can be used by persons having the use of an entirely different computer. This portability is possible because the language itself is designed for expressing solutions to problems and is essentially independent of the particular computer on which the problem will be run. Each computer must, however, have its own individual programs to do translation of the high-level coding into a machine-level program.

The use of a common, standardized language has developed in two ways—first, by the prior establishment of specifications for a common language (examples are COBOL and ALGOL), and second, by the evolution of a widely used language to a standard form (such as FORTRAN). The three major high-level languages, FORTRAN, COBOL, and BASIC, have been standardized by the American National Standards Institute (ANSI). The use of these three languages in this text is based on ANSI standards.

Translation Procedure

To implement a high-level language using the compiler concept requires three elements—specifications for the language; a translator routine to interpret statements written in the language and convert them to appropriate machine-language instructions; and a library of subroutines which can be compiled into the machine-language program.

The source program, written in a specific language, must follow the rules for that language. These rules specify the form, structure, and terms used in writing instructions. Certain words, sometimes called "reserved words," have precisely defined operational meanings when used in source program statements. The specifications essentially describe a limited-purpose language. One has to learn both operation words and symbols, which are like a foreign-language vocabulary, rules of grammar for using the vocabulary, and punctuation symbols to produce statements. In addition to words and symbols, the language provides for names chosen by the programmer to designate the storage locations where input data items, results obtained during processing, etc., are stored.

The use of language specifications is illustrated by the following statements using two common procedure-oriented languages to specify the computation $x = a - b - c$.

Language	Statement
FORTRAN	X = A − B − C
COBOL	SUBTRACT B AND C FROM A GIVING X.

In both cases, X, A, B, and C are names assigned by the programmer. In the FORTRAN statements, the minus sign is interpreted by the translator program as meaning subtraction. In the COBOL statement, the words SUBTRACT, AND,

FROM, and GIVING have specified meanings the same or similar to those associated with the terms in ordinary English.

The translator, sometimes called the "processor," is a computer program which reads the source language statements one at a time and prepares a number of machine-language instructions to perform the operations specified or implied by each source statement. Typically, the preparation of a set of instructions does not involve the compiler writing all the required machine-level steps. In many cases, the compiler merely writes linkage instructions so that the object program can make use of subroutines provided by the compiler library of subroutines. For example, a FORTRAN statement to solve the problem $x = \sqrt{y}$ is written as X = SQRT(Y). The translator interprets the different symbols and letters and then generates instructions to obtain the value of a variable designated as Y from a storage location, to transfer this value to a prewritten library subroutine which calculates the square root, to return control back to the main program, and to store the results of the square-root computation in a memory location associated with the variable name X.

The prewritten subroutines are contained in the compiler library. The object language statements generated by the computer are an incomplete program until they are combined with the appropriate routines from the library. Two approaches are used. In one method, all subroutines needed by the object program are written out with the rest of the object program. In the other approach, the library routines are added when the object program which includes the subroutine linkages is loaded for execution.

The process of translating a source statement so as to compile a program requires that the computer program identify:

1 The memory location associated with each quantity used in the program
2 The operations to be performed
3 The proper order for processing

The translator keeps a table for identifying names that refer to data items (and related storage locations) and a table of words and symbols that describe operations. The computer can compare each symbol, name, or other word in a source statement with those in the tables and thereby identify its meaning. The proper order of processing is specified by the rules of the language.

The design of a translator routine will vary with the computer on which it will be used. A typical sequence of actions a translator routine might follow are:

1 The source statement is read character by character until a complete variable name, operation word, or operation symbol has been detected.

2 A comparison is made of the variable name, operation word, or operation symbol with tables of these symbols until an identification is made.

3 The combination of variable names and operation identifiers is translated into an ordered sequence of actions based on the order rules of the language and form of the statement.

4 The translator writes the machine-language statements onto the output medium to be used. The instructions are either operating instructions or linkages to subroutines.

As an example, suppose that the translator reads a statement such as $X = A + B - 3.5$. It compares X with a list of identifiers, and finds that X has been assigned to a location such as 3407, so it sets up the final instruction as "store result in location 3407." The locations for A and B are found from the same list as being perhaps 3804 and 3812. A value of 3.5 is stored in a table of constants to be used by the program, say, in location 2412. The translator also identifies the plus and minus by comparing these characters with a list in storage. The compiler now constructs a sequence of instructions to:

1 Add contents of locations 3804 and 3812 and hold results in a temporary location.

2 Subtract contents of location 2412 from temporary location used to store $A + B$.

3 Store results of step 2 in location 3407.

These three steps may involve many instructions because of arithmetic scaling considerations, error checking, etc.

Types of High-Level Programming Languages

There are a large number of high-level languages. Some are fairly specialized; others are quite general in scope. Some are primarily for use by those doing their own programming; others are for use by trained programmers. A useful categorization for this chapter is by the orientation of the language.

1 Algebraic formula-type processing
2 Business data processing
3 String and list processing
4 Multipurpose processing
5 Simulation
6 Specialized applications

Each of these categories is discussed in order to provide a general understanding of the types of languages available.

Algebraic Languages The algebraic languages are oriented toward the computational procedures for solving mathematical and statistical problems or problems which can be expressed in terms of formulas or numerical solution procedures (called algorithms). These problems are often termed "scientific" as opposed to data processing problems. Examples of problems for which this type of language is suited are statistical analysis of data, solution of sets of equations, and cash flow analysis for a firm.

The algebraic languages have good facilities for expressing formulas, for describing computational procedures, and for doing common mathematical functions. These facilities are illustrated here together with some examples of statements in an algebraic language which execute solution procedures. On the other hand, the algebraic languages have rather poor facilities for describing complex input or output, for manipulation of nonnumeric data, and for handling of files, because these capabilities are not generally important in scientific processing.

EXAMPLES

Language Facility	Sample Algebraic Language Statements
Express formulas.	
Solve formula for x	
where $x = \sqrt{\dfrac{(a + b)}{d}}$	X = SQRT ((A + B)/D)
Describe computational procedure.	
Sum one hundred quantities	
$S = \sum\limits_{i=1}^{100} X_i$	DO 200 I = 1,100 S = S + X(I) 200 CONTINUE

The most common algebraic languages and their acronyms are:

Acronym	Meaning or Type of Orientation
FORTRAN	Formula Translator
BASIC	Beginners All-purpose Symbolic Instruction Code
PL/1	Programming Language, Version 1
ALGOL	Algorithmic Language
APL	A Programming Language

All the algebraic languages are very similar; having learned one of them, a user will find it quite easy to understand the others. A common characteristic of the algebraic languages is an emphasis on the users being able to write their own programs using the language rather than having to depend on a professional programmer.

FORTRAN is by far the most commonly used algebraic language. It is richer in features than the BASIC language which was developed as a language for time-sharing purposes. Widely used, BASIC is oriented toward simple problems and terminal operation. BASIC is easily learned and is well suited to the novice or occasional user. Both are surveyed in the chapter. PL/1, ALGOL, and APL are described and illustrated later in the chapter, but in less detail than FORTRAN and BASIC. PL/1 is a general-purpose language, but the programmer can treat it as an algebraic language, disregarding the other facilities.

Data Processing Languages

Often termed "business" or "commercial processing languages" to distinguish them from algebraic languages, the data processing languages emphasize the language capabilities for describing data processing procedures in information processing applications. These applications usually involve files, considerable manipulation of nonnumeric data, high volume of input and output, and arrangement of data on output documents. The processing procedures do not usually require extensive mathematical manipulation. Some common problems for which this type of language is suited are processing of payroll, inventory, and accounts receivable.

COBOL is the major language in this category. It is surveyed later in the chapter. PL/1 has facilities for commercial processing, and so it is an alternative to COBOL. Another alternative to COBOL is RPG, or Report Program Generator. It is an important language for small computers not having sufficient capabilities for COBOL and is therefore described in this chapter.

String and List Processing Languages

A string is a sequence of characters; for example, a sentence is a string. These languages are important in the handling of text material. A linguist desiring to search for word usage could make use of a string processing language, as could a writer using the computer to edit text. The major types of operations are searching for patterns, replacing one pattern by another, and inserting and deleting characters in the string. The languages might also be described as symbol manipulation languages. The following examples illustrate symbol manipulation problems:

A researcher wishes to count the number of times the term "sin," "saint," and "sinner" are used in a religious text.

A text of a technical report stored on computer magnetic tape is to be printed, but first the text is to be updated. All references to "United States of America Standards Institute" are to be replaced by "American National Standards Institute."

References are to be searched for titles with the words "computer" and "auditing."

The most important of the string manipulation languages is SNOBOL. It has gone through several versions, the most recent being SNOBOL4. "Text editors" are software packages which perform string processing functions.

A set of data items can be sequenced by putting them in physical order in storage. Another method is to attach a data item to each data element which specifies where the next item in the sequence is stored. This item, termed a "pointer," allows the data elements to be stored in any order; the pointers provide the means for processing in a given order. This arrangement is termed a "list." Examples of list processing languages designed for this purpose are IPL and LISP; they are quite specialized.

Multipurpose Languages

Why should a programmer need to learn a separate language for algebraic procedures, for data processing, and for string processing? Separate languages have some advantages, but since there is overlap among languages, a multipurpose language would appear to have advantages.

One of the earliest multipurpose languages was JOVIAL, developed as a language for military command and control applications. The most important of the multipurpose languages is PL/1. Another general-purpose language receiving academic use is PASCAL.

Simulation Languages

Simulations may be written in algebraic or multipurpose languages. However, a computer program to simulate operations involving queues can become quite complex and difficult for the programmer to handle. For example, a simulation of the operation of a job shop will involve many processing stations (machines) and many waiting lines of jobs waiting to be processed. Simulation languages have been developed to assist in describing simulation procedures (and especially queue discipline) for computer processing. The most common are GPSS (General-Purpose System Simulator), originally developed by IBM, and SIMSCRIPT, originally developed by Rand Corporation.

Specialized Application Languages

The list of languages could become quite long, but many of them are very specialized and not of general interest; others have received too little use to be of interest except to the specialist or perhaps the historian. Two examples will illustrate the very specialized languages:

Language	Purpose
APT (Automatically Programmed Tools)	To write programs to control machine tools.
COGO (COordinate GeOmetry)	To assist civil engineers in doing computations needed in surveying.

Survey of BASIC

BASIC (Beginners All-purpose Symbolic Instruction Code) is an algebraic programming language developed at Dartmouth College in the mid-1960s by John Kemeny and Thomas Kurtz. It was designed to make using the computer easier for students. It also has features which simplify the design of a compiler that translates a program in BASIC into machine code. There is a proposed American National Standard for a minimal BASIC language, but implementors have usually included additional features. These additional features are often termed "extended BASIC."

Overview of BASIC

The major application of BASIC is in time sharing in which the programmer-user has a typewriter input and output terminal. Some terminals use a visual display screen for output. Programs are typed and transmitted line by line to the computer. After the program is received, it is compiled and executed, and the results are typed on the typewriter or displayed on the screen. The terminal may also have a punched paper input and output. This allows a program to be prepared offline (without being connected to the computer) by being punched onto a paper tape. The punched paper tape is then transmitted to the computer, saving online connection time. BASIC is available on some computers for regular batch compilation (using punched card input), but this use of BASIC is much less common than its use as a time-sharing language.

Figure 6-1 shows the printout resulting from a programmer writing a simple program at a terminal connected to a time-sharing computer and having it executed. The programmer responses are underlined or otherwise noted. A glance at the program reveals that the language is very straightforward. There are statements to READ, PRINT, do computation, define input data, etc.

A BASIC program consists of a number of lines of coding, each of which must have a line number. The statements are numbered in increasing order from the first statement to the last. There may be missing numbers; in fact, it is a good idea to number so that statements may be inserted if necessary. The statements are rearranged in ascending order during compilation. This means that a statement to be inserted in the prior coding may be written anywhere in the program so long as it has a statement number which orders it correctly. Comments or remarks may be written in the program by a statement number and then the word REM (for remarks) followed by the comments. As an example, see lines 100 to 156 in Figure 6-1.

The last statement in a BASIC program has a statement number and the word END (line 270 in Figure 6-1). This signals the compiler that the program is complete and ready to be compiled. Execution of a BASIC program in time-sharing mode is signaled by the word RUN (with no statement number).

The most common types of BASIC instructions are replacement, input and output, control, and looping. Each of these will be explained and illustrated to provide insight into the language.

```
      76/10/13.  17.40.42.   TERMINAL:   157
   MECC/MERITSS.
   USER NUMBER: 3300919
   PASSWØRD
   ████████
   TERMINAL:     157,TTYD
   RECØVER /SYSTEM: BASIC
   ØLD, NEW, LIB, ØR GAME FILE: NEW
   FILE NAME: HØME
   READY.
   100   REM   PRØGRAM TØ CALCULATE AMØUNT ØF HØME
   110   REM   MØRTGAGE BASED ØN 25 YEARS ØF STATED
   120   REM   MØNTHLY PAYMENTS AND YEARLY INTEREST
   130   REM   RATES ØF 4,5,6, AND 7 PERCENT.
   140   REM   AUTHØR:  GØRDØN B DAVIS  9/7/76
   145   REM   LIST ØF VARIABLE NAMES
   150   REM       P = MØNTHLY PAYMENT
   152   REM       I = YEARLY INTEREST RATE
   154   REM       R = MØNTHLY INTEREST RATE
   156   REM       M = MØRTGAGE AMØUNT
   158
   160   PRINT "MØNTHLY PAYMENT ØF ";
   170   INPUT P
   180   PRINT "PERIØD ØF 25 YEARS"
   190   PRINT
   200   PRINT "INTEREST RATE","MØRTGAGE"
   210   FØR I = .04 TØ .07 STEP .01
   220       LET R = I/12
   230       REM   PERIØDS = 300 (25 YRS X 12 MØNTHS)
   240       LET M = P*((1.0-(1.0/(1.0+R)↑300))/R)
   250       PRINT I*100,M
   260   NEXT I
   270   END
   RUN

      76/10/13.  17.43.46.
      BASIC    PRØGRAM   HØME

   MØNTHLY PAYMENT ØF   ? 275
   PERIØD ØF 25 YEARS

   INTEREST RATE  MØRTGAGE
      4            52099.4
      5            47041.5
      6            42681.9
      7.           38908.9

   RUN CØMPLETE.
   GØØDBYE

   3300919   LØG ØFF    17.44.27.
   AFKI157   SRU      1.000 UNTS.
```

Procedures to get on the timesharing system from a terminal; note that this is to be a new program written in BASIC and called by the name HOME

Program to calculate amount of mortgage obtainable with a stated (input) monthly payment and various interest rates. The formula is:

$$m = p\left\{\frac{1 - [1/(1+r)^n]}{r}\right\}$$

where p = payment
n = months
r = monthly interest rate

User input

Output when program is run; user inputs monthly payment

Output based on monthly payment that was input

Sign-off procedures

FIGURE 6-1 Printout of steps in entering and executing a BASIC program using a time-sharing system. User inputs (other than program) are underscored.

Replacement Statements in BASIC

A replacement statement is used to define arithmetic operations to be performed and the memory location where results are to be moved and stored. As an example, the following statement says: Let the current value stored in a memory location called X be replaced by the result of the multiplication of 3.5 and the current value stored in a location called A.

The symbols used to indicate operations in BASIC are the following:

+	Addition
−	Subtraction
/	Division
*	Multiplication
↑ *or* ∧	Exponentiation

Parentheses are used to clarify the order of computation. Operations inside parentheses are performed first. See line 240 in Figure 6-1 for the use of these symbols in a formula.

There are mathematical functions which are frequently used in programming. The coding to perform these functions is contained in the compiler. To use these functions, the programmer merely codes the three-letter function name followed by the value or expression (in parentheses) to be used by the function. For example, the function to take the square root is SQR. The statement LET X = SQR(Y) will make X equal to the square root of the value of Y. If Y = 25, then X = 5.

Input and Output Statements in BASIC

Input and output in BASIC are very simple and fairly inflexible. There are provisions to call for data items which are included with the program, to call for data to be input from the terminal during execution, and to print the results in a standard manner with headings if desired. Editing and formatting of input and output are performed according to rules contained in the compiler. There are four input/output instructions:

READ list	Reads data from data block in the program.
DATA values	Defines data to be called for the READ statement.
PRINT list	Outputs data, headings, and labels.
INPUT list	Accepts data from the user terminal.

Where list is a sequence of variable names separated by commas or semicolons.

The INPUT statement is illustrated in line 170 and the PRINT statement in lines 160, 180, 190, 200, and 250 of Figure 6-1. Note that an arithmetic expression may be written in a PRINT statement (line 250). The result will be printed.

Control in BASIC

BASIC has statements for unconditional and conditional transfer of control:

1   Unconditional transfer of control   GO TO s   } s is a statement line number

2   Conditional transfer of control   IF condition THEN s

The unconditional transfer specifies the statement number to which control transfers (is executed next). The conditional statement specifies where control should go only if the condition is satisfied. If the condition is not satisfied, the program continues with the next statement in the sequence. The IF . . . THEN is used in coding a selection program structure.

Examples of the statements are:

10   IF H $>$ 40 THEN 80

10   GO TO 120

Looping in BASIC

In the looping or repetition structure, a set of instructions is executed a number of times. The BASIC instructions for looping consists of a FOR . . . TO . . . STEP instruction and a NEXT instruction. The FOR instruction is used at the beginning of a loop to establish the loop conditions; the NEXT instruction defines the end of the loop. As an example, in Figure 6-1 the FOR statement (number 210) defines the beginning of a loop in which the variable I will have an initial value of .04 and then be incremented by .01 until a value of .07 has been executed. The statements in the loop are 230 to 250. The statement to define the end of the loop is NEXT I in 260. The loops can operate on arrays of variables defined by a name and a subscript.

There are additional BASIC statements not mentioned (such as matrix instructions and statements to define functions and to use subprograms). BASIC has limited subprogram facilities for coding in a modular, structured format.

Survey of FORTRAN

FORTRAN (an acronym for FORmula TRANslator) is the most widely employed algebraic language and is available for use on almost all computers. Although not limited to mathematical problems, it is especially useful for problems which can be stated in terms of formulas or arithmetic procedures. This covers a wide range of problems. For example, FORTRAN is suitable for such diverse problems as analysis of sales statistics in a business and analysis of structural stress in designing a building.

Originally developed in 1957 by IBM in conjunction with some major computer users, FORTRAN has changed and evolved. In 1966, a voluntary American National Standard (ANS) FORTRAN was adopted with two levels of the language being defined—Basic FORTRAN and full FORTRAN. An international standard was also adopted. A revision of the FORTRAN standard was completed in 1977. The 1977 standard adds a few features to the older standard.

Overview of FORTRAN

The FORTRAN language consists of a vocabulary of symbols and words and a grammar of rules for writing instructions. The symbols, words, and rules utilize many common mathematical conventions. The instructions to the computer to carry out problem-solving procedures may be classified as follows:

Type of statement	Purpose
Input/output	To direct the computer to obtain data from a specified input device and to output data using a specified output device. To specify editing or formatting of data to be input or output.
Assignment	To perform arithmetic, logical, or character processing using data from the program or data read into memory by an input statement and to assign results to a variable name.
Control	To control the order in which the program is to be executed, to cause a set of one or more statements to be executed a specified number of times, or to call a subroutine.
Specification	To direct the compiler in the translation and program-building process.

The nature of a FORTRAN program can be illustrated by a short example. This sample program directs the computer to read three values called A, B, and C from a punched card, to sum the three quantities, to take the square root of the sum, to print the sum and the square root, and then to come to a halt.

FORTRAN statement	Type of statement
READ (1, 900) A, B, C	Input/output
900 FORMAT (3F10.2)	
X = A + B + C	Arithmetic assignment
Y = SQRT (X)	
WRITE (3, 900) X, Y	Input/output
STOP	Control
END	Specification (to compiler)

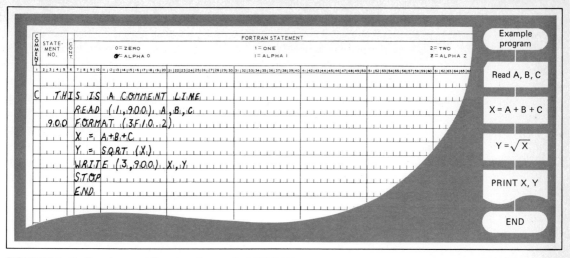

FIGURE 6-2   Coding sheet and flowchart for simple FORTRAN program to sum three numbers and take square root of the sum.

FORTRAN coding rules make it convenient to write the program on coding paper. Column 1 is used for specifying a comment line (by a C or an *). Columns 2–5 are used for a numeric statement label for any statement that must be referenced by the program. Column 6 specifies a continuation line. Columns 7–72 are for the statement. The example program on a coding form is shown in Figure 6-2.

Assignment Statements in FORTRAN

Since FORTRAN is a language for writing instructions to do the processing defined by mathematical formulas, it provides for the four specifications of a formula as part of an assignment statement.

Specification	How provided in FORTRAN
Quantities to be operated upon	Variable names and constants
Operations to be performed	Operation symbols and function names
Order of operation	Precedence rule and parentheses
Result designation	Variable names

Examples of variable names (up to six characters) are X, Y, ABLE, and Pl3. Constants can be 1.3, 7, or 4.15E10 (where E means to multiply the quantity by the power of 10 following the E). Variable names in FORTRAN can specify different types of data, the most common being real data which can have a fractional part and integer data which cannot have a fractional part. The operation symbols are +, −, /, * (for multiplication), and ** (for exponentiation). The equals sign means to assign (move) the results on the right of the equals sign to the storage identified with the variable name on the left. FORTRAN has a large number of functions which are used by coding the function name and the expression for which the result is to be evaluated or processed by the function inside parentheses. As an example, X = SQRT(Y) means to take the square root of Y and store the result in a storage location identified by the program as X. X = SQRT(Y + A) sums the value for Y and A and takes the square root of the sum. The order of operations in FORTRAN follows normal mathematical precedence—operations inside parentheses are performed first; and arithmetic operations are performed in order, with (1) exponentiation, (2) multiplication and division, and (3) addition and subtraction.

A few of the major, commonly used FORTRAN statements will be described in order to provide insight into the FORTRAN language. A program to compute the mean and standard deviation of a set of quantities and associated flowchart is illustrated in Figure 6-3. For clarity, the program is written as a set of blocks (very useful, but not required by the language). The first two blocks consist entirely of comments—the first set defining the program and the second describing each variable name in the program.

Input and Output in FORTRAN

The input/output statements use the word READ and WRITE (or PRINT). The form used in the two programs (Figures 6-2 and 6-3) specifies a unit number for the device to be used (in the examples, 1 is used for card reader and 3 for printer) and a FORMAT statement defining the FORMAT (i.e., editing) of the input or output. For example, FORMAT statement 900 in Figure 6-2 specifies that the results are to be read or printed in fields of 10 spaces with a decimal point (F specification), two digits being to the right of the decimal point. In Figure 6-3, FORMAT statement 940 in block 300 specifies an error message (used in case of an error in array size). The printed line consists of the 14 characters (defined by 14H) bARRAY SIZE OFb (b = blank) followed by a field of 10 positions for the integers in the array size printed without a decimal point (I specification) followed by the 28 characters bNEGATIVE,ZERO,OR TOO LARGE.

In the newer FORTRAN, the character output would also have defined by apostrophes, e.g., FORMAT ('bARRAY SIZE OF b' I10, 'bNEGATIVE,ZERO,OR TOO LARGE.') As illustrated by FORMAT 930 in Figure 6-3, a slash within a FORMAT means to terminate the current record (such as a card or a line) and go to the next record.

Control in FORTRAN

FORTRAN has a number of transfer of control statements; the most common are GO TO and IF. The GO TOs specify an unconditional transfer of control to statement number s. The IF statement specifies a condition such as a relation which is evaluated. If true, control goes to a specified statement number; otherwise, it continues with the next statement in the program. The condition is enclosed in parentheses:

IF (condition) s

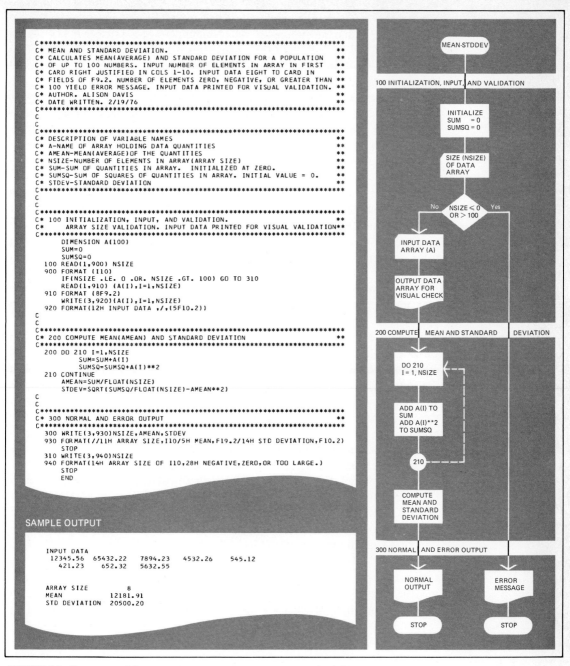

```
C*******************************************************************
C* MEAN AND STANDARD DEVIATION.                                   **
C* CALCULATES MEAN(AVERAGE) AND STANDARD DEVIATION FOR A POPULATION **
C* OF UP TO 100 NUMBERS. INPUT NUMBER OF ELEMENTS IN ARRAY IN FIRST **
C* CARD RIGHT JUSTIFIED IN COLS 1-10. INPUT DATA EIGHT TO CARD IN  **
C* FIELDS OF F9.2. NUMBER OF ELEMENTS ZERO, NEGATIVE, OR GREATER THAN **
C* 100 YIELD ERROR MESSAGE. INPUT DATA PRINTED FOR VISUAL VALIDATION. **
C* AUTHOR. ALISON DAVIS                                           **
C* DATE WRITTEN. 2/19/76                                          **
C*******************************************************************
C
C
C*******************************************************************
C* DESCRIPTION OF VARIABLE NAMES                                  **
C* A-NAME OF ARRAY HOLDING DATA QUANTITIES                        **
C* AMEAN-MEAN(AVERAGE)OF THE QUANTITIES                           **
C* NSIZE-NUMBER OF ELEMENTS IN ARRAY(ARRAY SIZE)                  **
C* SUM-SUM OF QUANTITIES IN ARRAY.  INITIALIZED AT ZERO.          **
C* SUMSQ-SUM OF SQUARES OF QUANTITIES IN ARRAY. INITIAL VALUE = 0. **
C* STDEV-STANDARD DEVIATION                                       **
C*******************************************************************
C
C
C*******************************************************************
C* 100 INITIALIZATION, INPUT, AND VALIDATION.                     **
C*      ARRAY SIZE VALIDATION. INPUT DATA PRINTED FOR VISUAL VALIDATION**
C*******************************************************************
      DIMENSION A(100)
      SUM=0
      SUMSQ=0
  100 READ(1,900) NSIZE
  900 FORMAT (I10)
      IF(NSIZE .LE. 0 .OR. NSIZE .GT. 100) GO TO 310
      READ(1,910) (A(I),I=1,NSIZE)
  910 FORMAT (8F9.2)
      WRITE(3,920)(A(I),I=1,NSIZE)
  920 FORMAT(12H INPUT DATA ,/,(5F10.2))
C
C
C*******************************************************************
C* 200 COMPUTE MEAN(AMEAN) AND STANDARD DEVIATION                 **
C*******************************************************************
  200 DO 210 I=1,NSIZE
      SUM=SUM+A(I)
      SUMSQ=SUMSQ+A(I)**2
  210 CONTINUE
      AMEAN=SUM/FLOAT(NSIZE)
      STDEV=SQRT(SUMSQ/FLOAT(NSIZE)-AMEAN**2)
C
C
C*******************************************************************
C* 300 NORMAL AND ERROR OUTPUT                                    **
C*******************************************************************
  300 WRITE(3,930)NSIZE,AMEAN,STDEV
  930 FORMAT(//11H ARRAY SIZE,I10/5H MEAN,F19.2/14H STD DEVIATION,F10.2)
      STOP
  310 WRITE(3,940)NSIZE
  940 FORMAT(14H ARRAY SIZE OF I10,28H NEGATIVE,ZERO,OR TOO LARGE.)
      STOP
      END
```

SAMPLE OUTPUT

```
 INPUT DATA
 12345.56  65432.22   7894.23   4532.26    545.12
   421.23    652.32   5632.55


 ARRAY SIZE          8
 MEAN         12181.91
 STD DEVIATION 20500.20
```

FIGURE 6-3 Program and flowchart for calculating mean and standard deviation.

Relational symbols used in conditions have a period before and after them. As an example, the IF statement in block 100 of Figure 6-3 tests whether NSIZE is less than or equal to (.LE.) zero or (.OR.) whether it is greater than (.GT.) 100. If true, control goes to statement 310 which prints an error message; otherwise the program proceeds with the READ following the IF.

Other control statements are STOP and END. The STOP statement terminates processing; the END statement (see both FORTRAN examples) specifies that there are no more statements in the program.

The FORTRAN DO Statement

A very important control statement used in a looping or repetition structure is the DO statement. The DO statement at the beginning of a loop specifies the statement number of the last statement in the loop (a CONTINUE statement in the example), the variable which will control the loop, the initial value, the terminating value, and the increment value for each repetition (if not 1). In the DO loop in block 200 of Figure 6-3, the DO statement (number 200) specifies number 210 as the end of the loop, the variable I as the loop control variable with an initial value of 1, a termination value of NSIZE (an input value), and an implied increment of 1.

The two statements following the DO illustrate subscripted variables. The variable called A(I) is part of an array A which was defined as having up to 100 elements by the DIMENSION statement in block 100. A(1) is the first variable in the array; A(2) is the second, etc. The program places the input values in array A; and subsequent statements write values from the array, sum the values in the array, etc. Since the loop causes the variable I to be 1, 2, 3, . . . , NSIZE, the first execution of the statement following the DO will be SUM = SUM + A(1), the second execution will be SUM = SUM + A(2), etc.

The READ and WRITE statements at the end of block 100 have implied DO loops within them. For example, READ(1, 910) (A(I), I = 1,NSIZE) means to read, using unit 1 (card reader) and FORMAT 910, the values of A(I) with the value of I varying from 1 by 1 until I = NSIZE (which was input earlier). If NSIZE is 3, the READ statement will read values for A(1), A(2), and A(3).

In the last two statements of block 200, the function FLOAT is used. As noted earlier, FORTRAN distinguishes between variables that can be only integer and real variables that can have fractional parts. Arithmetic expressions do not usually mix the types. NSIZE is an integer quantity, so the function FLOAT is used to convert it into an equivalent real quantity to avoid mixing the types.

Subprograms in FORTRAN

FORTRAN has limited facilities for a modular, structured program design. A FORTRAN program can be somewhat modular by the use of FORTRAN subprogram features. The major subprograms are function subprograms and subroutines. These are written as separate routines. The main program invokes their use and then control returns to the next statement following the invoking statement. For example, a main program and a subroutine might be linked as follows:

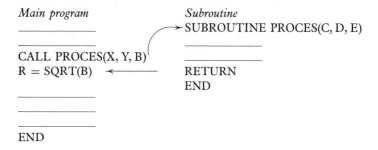

Main program

CALL PROCES(X, Y, B)
R = SQRT(B)

END

Subroutine

SUBROUTINE PROCES(C, D, E)

RETURN
END

One way data is passed from the calling program to the subroutine is through the parameter list in the CALL statement. These values replace the corresponding dummy parameters in the subroutine; for example, X, Y, B will be used by subroutine PROCES in place of C, D, E.

FORTRAN is a fairly rich language in terms of features. This brief survey has presented significant, commonly used statements. All the statements in Figure 6-3 have been explained. Read through the program, comparing it with the flowchart. The program computes the mean and standard deviation for an array of numbers. The *mean* is the average of a set of numbers. Finding the mean is quite simple—sum the quantities and divide by the number of quantities. The *standard deviation* is a measure of the distribution of the data around the mean. For computational ease, the following formula is used.

$$\text{Standard deviation} = \sqrt{\frac{\sum_{i=1}^{n} A_i^2}{n} - \text{mean}^2}$$

where A_i stands for each of the values in the array for which the standard deviation is to be computed, and n equals the number of quantities (called NSIZE in the program). $\sum_{i=1}^{n} A_i$ means to sum all the squares of A_i, with i going from 1 to n.

Survey of COBOL

COBOL (an acronym for COmmon Business-Oriented Language) is a high-level procedure-oriented language designed for coding business data processing problems.

A basic characteristic of business data processing is the existence of large files that are updated continuously or periodically. Business-type problems also tend to involve large volumes of input transactions and output of transaction documents and reports requiring editing and formatting of output data.

COBOL is not for the casual user, but because of its predominant role in data processing, the characteristics of COBOL should be understood by those who are involved in data processing, and COBOL should be a part of the programming language skills of every professional programmer.

Overview of COBOL

A COBOL program consists of four parts or divisions. These four divisions form a complete description of the program, including descriptions of the equipment required to run it, the form of the data files, and the processing steps to be performed.

Division	Purpose
IDENTIFICATION	Identification of the program
ENVIRONMENT	Description of the equipment to be used
DATA	Form and format of the data
PROCEDURE	Processing steps to be performed

Each division has a specific form. The general hierarchy of structure is for a division to be divided into sections. Each section contains paragraphs, and each paragraph consists of entries (in the IDENTIFICATION, ENVIRONMENT, and DATA DIVISION) or sentences (in the PROCEDURE DIVISION). Entries are composed of clauses terminated by a period. Sentences are formed from a sequence of statements and end with a period.

The PROCEDURE DIVISION contains the processing instructions (Figure 6-4). These instructions are interpreted in the context of the equipment described by the ENVIRONMENT DIVISION and the files and records described by the DATA DIVISION. The PROCEDURE DIVISION is machine-independent, which means that it can be compiled and executed on different computers without any coding changes. The DATA DIVISION describes the format of the data and is also machine-independent. The ENVIRONMENT DIVISION specifies the equipment to be used and assigns files to file storage equipment. It is a link between the machine-independent PROCEDURE DIVISION and the specific physical characteristics of the computer system being used. It must be rewritten if the problem is to be run on another computer. The IDENTIFICATION DIVISION is for documentation purposes and does not affect the machine-language program produced by the compiler. Each computer on which COBOL is implemented has a manual which describes the compiling procedures and details the way all computer-dependent features have been implemented for that computer. This manual is essential when using a computer to write, compile, and run a problem written in COBOL.

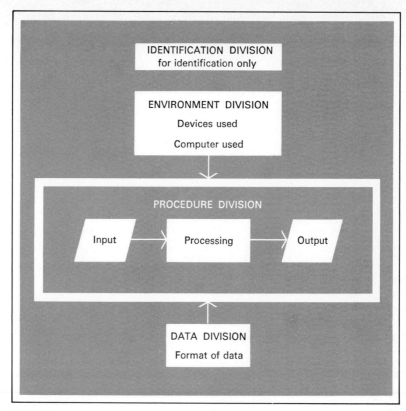

FIGURE 6-4 Purposes of COBOL program divisions.

The COBOL IDENTIFICATION and ENVIRONMENT DIVISIONs

A simple but complete COBOL program (Figure 6-5) will be used to explain the fundamental features in a COBOL program. The line numbers will be used to reference the COBOL statements.

The IDENTIFICATION DIVISION (lines 1 through 3) identifies the program as having an identifying name of PAYROLL. Line 3 identifies the author as Stanley Lau. Additional lines could be used to provide more identification. For example, comment lines (identified by an * in column 7) could contain text to explain the purpose of the program, etc.

The ENVIRONMENT DIVISION (lines 5 through 12) defines the program as having been compiled on a Control Data CYBER 74 (line 7) and to be run on the same model computer (line 8). Line 11 assigns the card reader (called INPUT by Control Data) as the device on which the PAYROLL-CARD-FILE will be read. Line 12 assigns the PAYROLL-LIST-FILE to the printer (called OUTPUT by Control Data).

The COBOL DATA DIVISION

The FILE SECTION of the DATA DIVISION provides a description of the files of records used by the program (lines 15 through 25). The PAYROLL-CARD-FILE is defined in line 17 as having no label record, a special record identifying the

```
00001          IDENTIFICATION DIVISION.
00002          PROGRAM-ID. PAYROLL.
00003          AUTHOR. STANLEY LAU.
00004          *
00005          ENVIRONMENT DIVISION.
00006          CONFIGURATION SECTION.
00007          SOURCE-COMPUTER. CYBER 74.
00008          OBJECT-COMPUTER. CYBER 74.
00009          INPUT-OUTPUT SECTION.
00010          FILE-CONTROL.
00011              SELECT PAYROLL-CARD-FILE ASSIGN TO INPUT.
00012              SELECT PAYROLL-LIST-FILE ASSIGN TO OUTPUT.
00013          *
00014          DATA DIVISION.
00015          FILE SECTION.
00016          FD  PAYROLL-CARD-FILE
00017              LABEL RECORD IS OMITTED.
00018          01  PAYROLL-CARD.
00019              02  PAYROLL-ID-NUMBER      PICTURE X(5).
00020              02  HOURS-WORKED           PICTURE 99.
00021              02  RATE-OF-PAY            PICTURE 9V999.
00022              02  FILLER                 PICTURE X(69).
00023          FD  PAYROLL-LIST-FILE
00024              LABEL RECORD IS OMITTED.
00025          01  REPORT-LINE                PICTURE X(132).
00026          WORKING-STORAGE SECTION.
00027          01  PAYROLL-LINE.
00028              02  FILLER                 PICTURE X(10) VALUE SPACES.
00029              02  PAYROLL-ID-NUMBER      PICTURE X(8).
00030              02  HOURS-WORKED           PICTURE Z(5)99.
00031              02  RATE-OF-PAY            PICTURE ZZ9.999.
00032              02  REGULAR-PAY            PICTURE $$$,$$9.99.
00033              02  OVERTIME-PAY           PICTURE $$$,$$9.99.
00034              02  GROSS-PAY              PICTURE $$$,$$9.99.
00035              02  FILLER                 PICTURE X(86) VALUE SPACES.
00036          01  REPORT-TITLE.
00037              02  FILLER                 PICTURE X(31) VALUE SPACES.
00038              02  FILLER                 PICTURE X(10) VALUE 'PAY REPORT'.
00039              02  FILLER                 PICTURE X(91) VALUE SPACES.
00040          01  TOTAL-LINE.
00041              02  FILLER                 PICTURE X(20) VALUE SPACES.
00042              02  FILLER                 PICTURE X(7)  VALUE 'TOTALS'.
00043              02  FILLER                 PICTURE X(5)  VALUE SPACES.
00044              02  TOTAL-REGULAR-PAY      PICTURE $$$,$$9.99.
00045              02  TOTAL-OVERTIME-PAY     PICTURE $$$,$$9.99.
00046              02  TOTAL-GROSS-PAY        PICTURE $$$,$$9.99.
00047              02  FILLER                 PICTURE X(60) VALUE SPACES.
00048          01  CALCULATIONS.
00049              02  REGULAR-PAY            PICTURE S999V99.
00050              02  OVERTIME-PAY           PICTURE S999V99.
00051              02  GROSS-PAY              PICTURE S999V99.
00052          01  PROGRAM-SWITCH.
00053              02  MORE-CARDS             PICTURE XXX.
00054          01  TOTAL-ACCUMULATORS.
00055              02  TOTAL-REGULAR-PAY      PICTURE S9(4)V99.
00056              02  TOTAL-OVERTIME-PAY     PICTURE S9(4)V99.
00057              02  TOTAL-GROSS-PAY        PICTURE S9(4)V99.
00058          *
```

FIGURE 6-5 Simple but complete COBOL program to prepare pay report (page 1 of 2)

```
00059              PROCEDURE DIVISION.
00060              MAINLINE-CONTROL-ROUTINE.
00061                  PERFORM INITIALIZATION.
00062                  PERFORM PROCESS-AND-READ UNTIL MORE-CARDS EQUAL 'NO'.
00063                  PERFORM PRINT-TOTALS-AND-CLOSE.
00064                  STOP RUN.
00065              INITIALIZATION.
00066                  OPEN INPUT PAYROLL-CARD-FILE.
00067                  OPEN OUTPUT PAYROLL-LIST-FILE.
00068                  MOVE ZEROES TO TOTAL-ACCUMULATORS.
00069                  MOVE 'YES' TO MORE-CARDS.
00070                  WRITE REPORT-LINE FROM REPORT-TITLE BEFORE ADVANCING 2 LINES.
00071                  READ PAYROLL-CARD-FILE
00072                      AT END MOVE 'NO' TO MORE-CARDS.
00073              PROCESS-AND-READ.
00074                  IF HOURS-WORKED OF PAYROLL-CARD GREATER THAN 40
00075                      PERFORM PAY-CALCULATION-WITH-OVERTIME
00076                  ELSE
00077                      PERFORM PAY-CALCULATION-NO-OVERTIME.
00078                  ADD REGULAR-PAY OF CALCULATIONS, OVERTIME-PAY OF CALCULATIONS
00079                      GIVING GROSS-PAY OF CALCULATIONS.
00080                  ADD REGULAR-PAY OF CALCULATIONS TO
00081                      TOTAL-REGULAR-PAY OF TOTAL-ACCUMULATORS.
00082                  ADD OVERTIME-PAY OF CALCULATIONS TO
00083                      TOTAL-OVERTIME-PAY OF TOTAL-ACCUMULATORS.
00084                  ADD GROSS-PAY OF CALCULATIONS TO
00085                      TOTAL-GROSS-PAY OF TOTAL-ACCUMULATORS.
00086                  PERFORM PRINT-PROCESSED-RECORD.
00087                  READ PAYROLL-CARD-FILE
00088                      AT END MOVE 'NO' TO MORE-CARDS.
00089              PAY-CALCULATION-WITH-OVERTIME.
00090                  MULTIPLY RATE-OF-PAY OF PAYROLL-CARD BY 40
00091                      GIVING REGULAR-PAY OF CALCULATIONS ROUNDED.
00092                  COMPUTE OVERTIME-PAY OF CALCULATIONS = (HOURS-WORKED OF
00093                      PAYROLL-CARD - 40) * 1.5 * RATE-OF-PAY OF PAYROLL-CARD.
00094              PAY-CALCULATION-NO-OVERTIME.
00095                  MULTIPLY RATE-OF-PAY OF PAYROLL-CARD
00096                      BY HOURS-WORKED OF PAYROLL-CARD
00097                      GIVING REGULAR-PAY OF CALCULATIONS ROUNDED.
00098                  MOVE ZEROES TO OVERTIME-PAY OF CALCULATIONS.
00099              PRINT-PROCESSED-RECORD.
00100                  MOVE SPACES TO PAYROLL-LINE.
00101                  MOVE CORRESPONDING PAYROLL-CARD TO PAYROLL-LINE.
00102                  MOVE CORRESPONDING CALCULATIONS TO PAYROLL-LINE.
00103                  WRITE REPORT-LINE FROM PAYROLL-LINE AFTER ADVANCING 1 LINES.
00104              PRINT-TOTALS-AND-CLOSE.
00105                  MOVE CORRESPONDING TOTAL-ACCUMULATORS TO TOTAL-LINE.
00106                  WRITE REPORT-LINE FROM TOTAL-LINE AFTER ADVANCING 2 LINES.
00107                  CLOSE PAYROLL-CARD-FILE, PAYROLL-LIST-FILE.
```

FIGURE 6-5   Simple but complete COBOL program to prepare pay report (page 2 of 2)

file which is not normally used with card files and files of print lines. There is one type of record in this file with the name PAYROLL-CARD (line 18). Lines 19 through 22 define the data items found on each PAYROLL-CARD. Each item has a name and a picture. The picture uses X's to describe that the data item is alphanumeric and 9's to specify numeric data to be used in computation. The character V specifies the implied decimal point in numeric data. PAYROLL-

ID-NUMBER consists of the first five characters (X(5)) on the card. The next two positions on the card are two numeric digits for HOURS-WORKED. RATE-OF-PAY (line 21) consists of four numeric digits with the decimal assumed after the first digit. In other words, if the data in card columns 8 through 11 is 3751, the program interprets it as 3.751. The last 69 columns of the card are not used, but COBOL requires that the entire card be defined. The term FILLER is used for that purpose (line 22).

The REPORT-LINE record (line 25) in the PAYROLL-LIST-FILE is defined only as consisting of 132 spaces, which is the number of spaces on a line of printing. There are three different kinds of output lines which are described in detail in WORKING-STORAGE (lines 27 through 47). Each type of line is moved in total to the REPORT-LINE for printing.

Output line data item pictures include editing characters to insert dollar signs, decimal points, commas, spaces, headings, etc. Insertion of characters in output editing is illustrated by line 32, which defines the field where REGULAR-PAY will be output as consisting of 10 characters. The string of dollar signs mean that a dollar sign will print next to the first nonnumeric digit except that the rightmost three digits with picture of 9.99 will print, even if zero. In other words, a value of zero for REGULAR-PAY will print as $0.00, a value of 495.37 will print as $495.37, etc. See Figure 6-6.

Lines 36 through 39 illustrate the coding of a heading line. The different parts of the line need no names because they will not be individually referenced in the programs, so the term FILLER is used. The entire output line is defined—either as spaces or as a heading 'PAY REPORT'.

Lines 48 through 57 are data definitions for data items computed by the program (instead of being input). For example, TOTAL-REGULAR-PAY (line 55) will be calculated by the program. The S in the picture specifies the arithmetic sign must be retained in processing.

```
                        PAY REPORT

    12355          45   5.200    $208.00    $39.00    $247.00
    12555          35   4.210    $147.35     $0.00    $147.35
    22345          25   3.210     $80.25     $0.00     $80.25
    32155          35   3.210    $112.35     $0.00    $112.35
    36542          42   5.210    $208.40    $15.63    $224.03
    45666          32   5.210    $166.72     $0.00    $166.72
    56213          45   3.210    $128.40    $24.07    $152.47
    75631          20   3.210     $64.20     $0.00     $64.20

             TOTALS         $1,115.67    $78.70 $1,194.37
```

FIGURE 6-6 Sample output from payroll program.

The COBOL PROCEDURE DIVISION

The program flowchart in Figure 6-7 describes the logic of the PROCEDURE DIVISION of the example program. Compare the flowchart with the program. The program is written in structured format—the MAINLINE-CONTROL-ROUTINE directs the performance of the three first-level modules: INITIALIZATION, PROCESS-AND-READ, and PRINT-TOTALS-AND-CLOSE. The module PROCESS-AND-READ directs the execution of lower-level modules PAY-CALCULATION-WITH-OVERTIME, PAY-CALCULATION-NO-OVERTIME, and PRINT-PROCESSED-RECORD. A program switch called 'MORE-CARDS' is used to decide when to end the program. MORE-CARDS is set to 'YES' in INITIALIZATION. When no more cards are available, MORE-CARDS is set to 'NO'. The module PROCESS-AND-READ is performed until MORE-CARDS is set to 'NO'. Control is then passed to the next statement, PERFORM PRINT-TOTALS-AND-CLOSE.

The PROCEDURE DIVISION is fairly understandable because of its English-like coding. Some comments to help in reading it are:

Line	Comment
66 and 67	OPEN means to prepare the file to be used.
68, 69, 98, 100–102, 105	MOVE causes data to be copied into the receiving data item.
101, 102	MOVE CORRESPONDING moves all data items with like names. Refer to lines 48 through 51 (CALCULATIONS) and 27 through 35 (PAYROLL-LINE) and note the like names.
107	CLOSE terminates the use of a file.

The program is simplified because there are no headings over the columns and there is no input data validation. However, the form of the program and the coding of the instructions are done in good COBOL programming style.

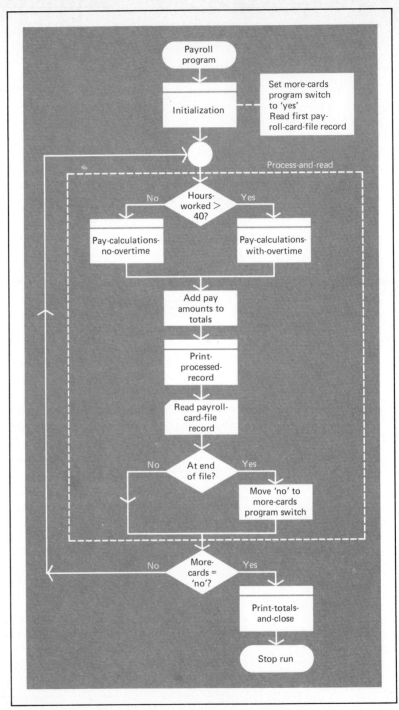

FIGURE 6-7 Program flowchart for payroll program with detail for PROCESS-AND-READ module.

A Short Introduction to Selected Languages

This section provides a short introduction to four important languages which each receive a significant amount of use.

The APL Language   Often termed Iverson's language after K. E. Iverson, APL (A Programming Language) is perhaps the most sophisticated of the modern programming languages. It is primarily a time-sharing language. The structure of the language and the available commands appear to be very effective in assisting users to develop and program problem-solving algorithms. The language is especially powerful in defining the processing of arrays of numbers and text-type data. Two features of APL that are different from other algebraic languages are an expanded character set for writing expressions and the fact that statements are executed from right to left without a precedence rule (although the factors inside parentheses are executed first). Some examples follow:

Symbol	Meaning	Example	Result
$\lceil$	Maximum	5⌈8	8
$\llcorner$	Minimum	5⌊8	5
÷	Divide	5÷2	2.5
*	Power	3*2	9
×	Times	4 × 5	20
≤	Not greater	4≤5	1 (1 for yes, 0 for no)
ρ	Size (number) of members of an array	ρA	10 (if array A has 10 members)

TABLE 6-1   SIMPLE APL PROGRAM TO COMPUTE MEAN OF AN ARRAY

APL program	Comments
▽ MEAN	Name by which this program is identified
[1] 'ENTER NUMBERS'	Print message to user
[2] X←□	Request input of set of data items called by an array or vector named X
[3] A←(+/X)÷ρX	Compute the mean (average) of all data items called X and assign to variable named A
[4] 'MEAN IS EQUAL TO'	Print heading
[5] A	Print mean
▽	End-of-program-symbol

In a terminal which does not have these symbols, alternative symbols are used.

A simple example of an APL program to compute the mean of an array will illustrate the language (Table 6-1). The key sentence to compute the mean [3] is a useful illustration. The elements of the sentence are:

ρX Number of quantities in array, i.e., the number of quantities that are being summed.

$+/X$ Sum all values in an array X.

$A \leftarrow$ Assign result to variable A.

Since $(+/X)$ is enclosed in parentheses, the summation is done first. Working then from right to left, the sum is divided by the number of quantities summed and the result is assigned to A. Even in this simple example, the power of a language with simple vector commands is apparent. Users of APL are very enthusiastic, and its applications are expected to grow.

The PL/1 Language

PL/1 (Programming Language, Version 1) is designed as a general-purpose language, combining the major features of both COBOL and FORTRAN and introducing features not found in either. It was introduced by IBM in 1960 in conjunction with the IBM System/360 series. The language has facilities for the realtime programmer and the systems programmer in addition to the traditional commercial and scientific programming features.

The PL/1 language is divided into modules or subsets for different applications and different levels of complexity. A programmer using one subset need not even know about the other modules. If the programmer does not state a choice among the various alternative specifications, the compiler automatically chooses a default interpretation. In each case, the default specification is the one most likely to be required by the programmer who is not using the advanced features.

Advocates point to advantages for PL/1 over FORTRAN and COBOL, but the economics of programming and program maintenance are such that many installations prefer to stay with existing languages rather than switch to a new language, even if it has new features. PL/1 has to date had only modest success against FORTRAN and COBOL, and apparently these two languages will expand to include the best of PL/1, rather than PL/1 becoming a dominant language.

PL/1 allows the programmer considerable freedom. For example, there are no special indentations or reserved columns on the coding sheet—a free format is used. This makes it easy to apply the concept of structured programming that indentation should show program structure. The language is very supportive of the block structure required for structured programming.

A PL/1 program is constructed from program elements. The basic program element is the statement. Statements are combined into large elements—the procedure or block. A statement in PL/1 is a string of characters terminated by a semicolon. A block begins with a procedure name and ends with the statement END procedure-name. Variable names may be up to 31 characters in length. A break character _ is used to provide a meaningful multiword name. In addition to the usual arithmetic operators of $+$, $-$, $*$, $/$ and $**$, there are the following:

Comparison operators		Bit-string (Boolean) operators
>	greater than	¬ NOT
>=	greater than or equal	& AND
<	less than	| OR
<=	less than or equal	
¬=	not equal to	

Some typical PL/1 statements are:

```
A = B**2;
X = Y/3 + 5;
IF HOURS > 40
    CALL OVERTIME;
ELSE
    GROSS_PAY = HOURS*RATE;
```

Data in PL/1 can be either numeric or string. String data consists of a group of characters or bits. Data can be grouped into arrays and in structures (hierarchies). A DECLARE statement is used to specify the array or structure attribute of the data. For example, a 2 × 3 matrix referred to as X is defined by the statement:

```
DECLARE X(2, 3);
```

A payroll record with the structure shown below

Payroll

Name			
Last	Middle	First	Hours

could be defined by the statement:

```
DECLARE 1 PAYROLL,
        2  NAME
              3 LAST CHARACTER(15),
              3 MIDDLE CHARACTER(15),
              3 FIRST CHARACTER(15),
        2  HOURS FIXED DECIMAL(2);
```

The numbers 1, 2, and 3 correspond to level numbers.

The programmer has considerable flexibility in input and output. Input/output is either record input/output, which consists of discrete records, or stream input/output, which is a continuous stream of characters. The input/output for records uses READ and WRITE statements, while stream input/output uses GET and PUT statements. The sample programs use the GET and PUT statements.

Three methods of designating the form of the data are data-directed, list-directed, and edit-directed. For example, assume data names of HOURS and RATE (hours worked and rate of pay) to be read from cards:

Method	Form of data on card	Explanation
Data-directed	HOURS = 42, RATE = 4.253;	Each data item is written with its data name.
List-directed	42,4.253;	The items are listed in order and separated by a space or commas.
Edit-directed	424253	The items are listed in order. The form of the data is defined by a format list.

Other important features of PL/1 are specifications by which the programmer can direct the computer to work on more than one procedure concurrently, as in multiprogramming. There is a sort verb by which the programmer can specify that a file is to be sorted. Storage allocation is also very flexible.

Two simple examples written in PL/1 do not illustrate the power of versatility of the language but do show its general form. Figure 6-8 shows a simple program to compute gross pay. Figure 6-9 is a sample program to prepare a mathematical table.

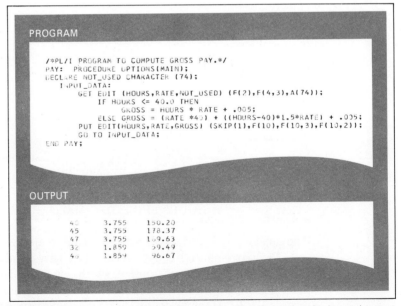

```
PROGRAM

    /*PL/I PROGRAM TO COMPUTE GROSS PAY.*/
    PAY:   PROCEDURE OPTIONS(MAIN);
    DECLARE NOT_USED CHARACTER (74);
       INPUT_DATA:
          GET EDIT (HOURS,RATE,NOT_USED) (F(2),F(4,3),A(74));
             IF HOURS <= 40.0 THEN
                GROSS = HOURS * RATE + .005;
             ELSE GROSS = (RATE *40) + ((HOURS-40)*1.5*RATE) + .005;
          PUT EDIT(HOURS,RATE,GROSS) (SKIP(1),F(10),F(10,3),F(10,2));
          GO TO INPUT_DATA;
    END PAY;


OUTPUT

          42    3.755    150.20
          45    3.755    178.37
          47    3.755    169.63
          32    1.859     59.49
          46    1.859     96.67
```

FIGURE 6-8 PL/1 program to compute gross pay and sample edit-directed output from program.

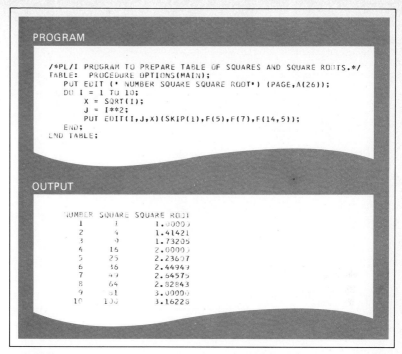

FIGURE 6-9 PL/1 program to prepare table of squares, square roots, and sample edit-directed output from program using exponent form.

The RPG Language

Report Program Generator (RPG) is a language in which the programmer writes the specifications for the problem and the compiler generates a program. RPG is offered by several manufacturers, but it is not standardized. This explanation is based on RPG for the IBM System/3 and System/370. RPG is well suited for the types of problems usually run on a small computer, so that it is an important programming aid for computers of this class. In fact, for small-business computers, it is the dominant language.

A problem is programmed in RPG by filling out specification forms. There are four basic ones and two additional forms for special situations. Not all are required, and a specification may consist of a single line.

Specification form	Major use
File description	Identifies the file as input, output, or combined. Associates file with an input/output device.
Input	Describes the records contained on the file and the location of the data fields.

Calculation	Specifies the operations to be performed and the data to be used.
Output	Specifies the arrangement of data on the output medium.
File extension	Provides additional information for chaining, using tables, and using direct access files.
Line counter	Specifies line control if report is to be written on tape or disk for subsequent printing.

The RPG specifications provide all information for the program. Each specification is punched into a card. The set of specification cards is read by the RPG compiler, and an object program is generated.

The sample program will use a simple gross pay computation (already presented in PL/1). Some headings will be used on the printed output. The input for the program is hours (columns 1–2) and rate (columns 3–6) on a punched card. The calculations are straight time for 40 or less hours and time-and-a-half for all hours over 40. The output is in the form shown in Figure 6-10.

The sample specification sheets are given in Figure 6-10. The file of cards containing the hours and rates is called the PDATA file. The input data fields are called HOURS and RATE. The output file is called REPORT. The result of the computations is GROSS for gross pay.

The file description form defines PDATA as an input file (I) to be read from the card reader. REPORT is defined as an output file (O) on the printer.

The input specification sheet for PDATA defines the data fields as columns 1 and 2 for HOURS, with no decimal position, and columns 3 to 6 for RATE, with the decimal position three places from the right.

The first action on the calculation sheet is the test to find out whether hours exceed 40. If they do, control proceeds to the line marked with 21; if hours do not exceed 40, control goes to N21 (NOT 21). 21 is an arbitrary designation. For over 40 hours, the computations prepare an amount TEMP2 which is a revised hour figure giving overtime credit. The H means to round the result.

The output specification of the report first defines the heading line and then the form and position of the variables on the detail line. The edit word ' ,$0. ' defines a dollar sign and decimal location in the output.

The ALGOL Language

ALGOL (ALGOrithmic Language) is an algebraic language similar to the algebraic features in PL/1. It is quite popular in Europe but has never achieved substantial use in the United States. ALGOL is well suited for structured programming because of its block structure. Each procedure is named, and the end of procedures are defined explicitly by the END command. Figure 6-11 illustrates a simple ALGOL program to compute a table (same problem as the PL/1 program in Figure 6-10).

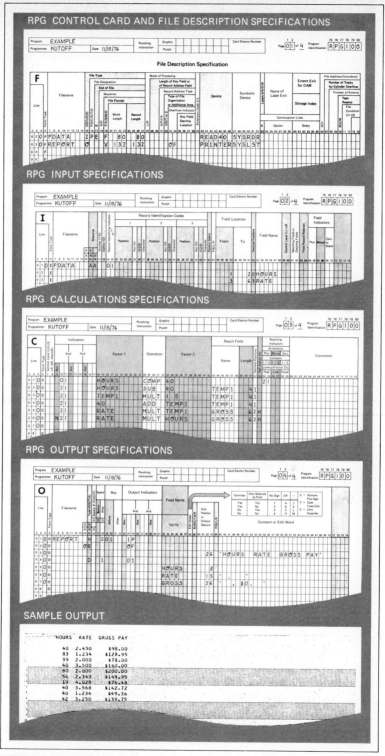

FIGURE 6-10 RPG specification sheets for program to compute gross pay and sample output from program.

```
'BEGIN'
   'REAL'B;
   'INTEGER' I,X;
   OUTPUT (61,'('↑'('NUMBER SQUARE SQUARE ROOT')',/')');
   'FOR' I:= 1 'STEP' 1 'UNTIL' 10 'DO'
      'BEGIN'
         X:= I↑2;
         B:= SQRT(I);
         OUTPUT (61,'('/4ZD,BBBBBBZZD,BBBBD.DDD')',I,X,B);
   'END';
'END'
```

FIGURE 6-11 Simple ALGOL program to compute table of squares and square roots.

Subroutine Packages

When developing and writing programs in languages such as FORTRAN or PL/1, the programmer should take advantage of statistical and mathematical routines which can be called by the user program. The programmer codes in FORTRAN or PL/1 and includes a CALL for the subroutine desired. Most large installations and university computer centers have extensive libraries of such routines. The two most common libraries are SSP and IMSL.

SSP (Scientific Subroutine Package) This set of over 200 mathematical and statistical routines is provided by IBM in FORTRAN or PL/1 and is available on most IBM equipment and some non-IBM equipment. A manual is available from the IBM Corporation.

IMSL FORTRAN Subroutines A set of about 200 FORTRAN callable subroutines has been developed and is maintained by International Mathematics and Statistical Libraries, Inc. A manual is available from IMSL. A computing center with this set of subroutines will have documentation available to users.

Some examples of the subroutines available in these packages illustrate their capabilities:

Major category	Example
Analysis of experimental data	Covariance analysis test
Basic statistics	Calculate means, standard deviation, and correlation coefficients
Eigen analysis	Eigenvalues and eigenvectors of a symmetric matrix
Random numbers	Generate normal deviates

Nonparametric statistics	Kendall's test for correlation
Sampling	Simple random sampling with continuous data
Vector-matrix arithmetic	Transpose product of a matrix

Other subroutine packages are also available. For example, IBM has a package of subroutines designed for forecasting called the Forecasting And Modeling System (FAMS).

Statistical Packages

It is rarely necessary for an investigator to code a computer program to do statistical analysis because prewritten computer programs are available for almost all statistical analysis. The statistical programs are self-contained sets of programs which perform statistical analysis based on user specifications. The user must define the form of the input data and specify the computational options desired. No knowledge of computer programming is required (although it may be helpful).

A few of the most common general-purpose packages and sets of routines are listed (in approximate order of use) to provide some idea of the options available. Manuals are listed, but later editions may be available. There are also a number of less used or specialized packages and routines that may be supported by a particular installation.

SPSS (*Statistical Package for the Social Sciences*)　A comprehensive program for processing common to the social sciences, it is maintained by the National Opinion Research Center, University of Chicago. A manual is available: Norman H. Nie, et al., *Statistical Package for the Social Sciences,* 2d ed., McGraw-Hill, New York, 1975, 675 pages.

BMDP and *BMD* (*Biomedical Computer Programs*)[1] Assembled and maintained by the Health Sciences Computer Facility at the University of California at Los Angeles, the newer BMDP contains 26 programs while BMD contains over 50 programs. These have wide use. Good user documentation is provided in the BMD and BMDP manuals: *BMD Biomedical Computer Programs,* University of California Press, 1973, 773 pages; *BMDP Biomedical Computer Programs,* University of California Press, 1975.

OMNITAB II　This is a large, unified set of computer routines developed by the National Bureau of Standards to do statistical and numerical analysis. It is available from the National Technical Information Service (NTIS), 5285 Port Royal Road, Springfield, Virginia 22161. A manual is available: *OMNITAB II Users Reference Manual,* U.S. Government Printing Office, Oct. 1971, 253 pages.

---

[1] For a comparison of BMD and BMDP programs, see James W. Frane, "The BMD and BMDP Series of Statistical Programs," *Communications of the ACM,* October 1976, pp. 570–576.

Figure 6-12 is a sample of specification input and resultant output for an SPSS program. The data consists of 70 pairs of data items for monthly gross income and amounts contributed to the Consolidated Fund drive. The specifications call for descriptive statistics and a scattergram (in which two extreme values were eliminated).

Because of the availability and power of these statistical packages and their ease of use, any student or researcher requiring statistical analysis should investigate them. The following list is suggestive of the range of processing performed by the statistical packages.

Data screening	Confidence intervals
Descriptive statistics	Nonlinear regression
Correlation and regression	Multivariate analysis
Analysis of variance	Factor analysis
Significance tests	

Other Packages for Programming

Some significant languages and packages which have not been discussed are file and data management systems and utility packages.

Software systems are available for managing files including extracting data and preparing reports. These systems range from those which manage single files to complex database management systems. Because of the language facilities available with such systems, they should be considered for use when available and when appropriate to the type of problem.

Utility software packages can perform a variety of tasks that otherwise would have to be programmed in a procedure-oriented language. Examples are utilities to copy files, print files, sort files, merge files, and perform text editing. The utilities are invoked through the use of job control cards.

SUMMARY Except for some special situations (and some minicomputers) machine-oriented programming has been superseded by the use of high-level languages and packages. The chapter reviews the range of languages and packages available for high-level programming.

It is useful to understand the general idea of translation from a high-level source language to machine-oriented instructions. This is done by a compiler. The task of a translator is to analyze each program statement and to produce a set of machine-level statements.

The type of languages that receive the most use are algebraic and data processing languages, but there are languages for string and list processing, simulation, and other purposes. There has been some attempt, as in PL/1, to provide a general-purpose language. The most used languages, BASIC, FORTRAN, and COBOL, are explained. Other significant languages (APL, ALGOL, PL/1, and RPG) are surveyed to provide a brief introduction to the variety available.

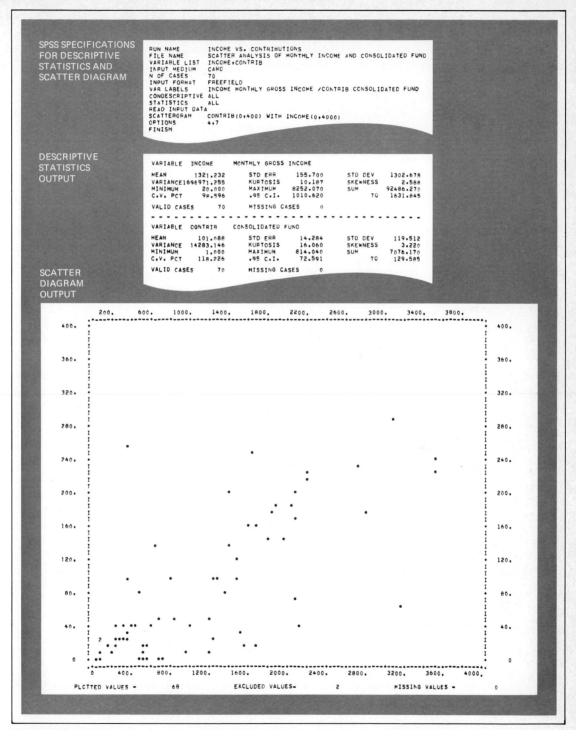

FIGURE 6-12 Example of specification input to SPSS statistical package and resulting outputs.

There are a number of statistical packages that provide compilation and execution based on specifications using a self-contained system. Another approach is to use subroutine packages which are obtained by call statements. These and utility packages can be very helpful in using the computer.

EXERCISES

1 Apply the considerations in selecting a language to each of the following situations.
   (*a*) A once-a-year analysis of distribution of salaries
   (*b*) A statistical processing performed now and then by market research
   (*c*) Payroll processing performed weekly
   (*d*) A mathematical formulation to be run only once
   (*e*) A simulation expected to take 600 hours of computer time

2 Describe the steps in using a high-level language for processing the solution of a problem.

3 How does a compiler translate a source program and produce an object program?

4 What is an algebraic language? How does it differ from a data processing language? Identify the orientation of the following languages: BASIC, FORTRAN, COBOL, PL/1, RPG, and GPSS.

5 Why should there be special languages for string processing and simulation? Be specific as to the exact type of processing that the language handles.

6 Define the orientation, the status of use, and the type of problem which is suited for APL, PL/1, ALGOL, and RPG.

7 Identify the following statements as APL, PL/1, or other language.
   (*a*) X = Y**2
   (*b*) X = Y**2;
   (*c*) COMPUTE X = Y**2.
   (*d*) A←(x/y)÷ρy
   (*e*) C = A + B
   (*f*) C = A + B;
   (*g*) IF GROSS-PAY>300 THEN GO TO ERROR_1;
   (*h*) ∇NEW

8 PL/1 is so large and complex that the occasional user cannot learn it all. Yet it is said to be a replacement for FORTRAN, which can certainly be used by the nonprofessional programmer. How is the solution to this problem approached in PL/1?

9 Describe the purpose of each of the specification sheets used in the RPG version illustrated in the text.

10 A student has a set of data to be analyzed. Describe the merits of writing a complete, new program, using a statistical package, or using a subroutine in a program.

11 A computer center has several statistical packages available including OUROWN and SPSS. Assuming OUROWN is more efficient in execution than SPSS, which should be used by:
   (*a*) A researcher who will share the results with colleagues?
   (*b*) A student running a short, one-time job?
   (*c*) The English department for evaluating each instructor each quarter?

12 How can one be sure that a subroutine or package is providing correct results?

13 Programmers argue about the merits of PL/1 versus FORTRAN. What are the considerations that have inhibited a change to PL/1?

3

COMPUTER
TECHNOLOGY

Part 3 emphasizes computer equipment and the way it operates to store data, perform computation, input or output data, and transmit data over communications facilities. Chapter 7 describes the way the computer represents data, surveys internal operations of the computer, and explains how data can be stored. Chapter 8 explains the equipment and methods by which data is prepared for computer processing, the equipment for input and output, and the facilities for transmitting data between different locations. The equipment for auxiliary storage of data and programs is described in Chapter 9, and an explanation is given of how data is organized for effective processing and retrieval.

Chapter

7

Internal Operations and Storage in a Computer

A programmer can write programs, an operator can perform his or her duties, and a manager can supervise computer operations—without understanding the internal workings of the computer. However, a general understanding of the internal operations of a computer is a useful background which may help in comprehending how most effectively to program and operate the equipment. This chapter presents a survey of the coding of data, circuitry, storage, and other internal operating features of computers.

The Coding of Data for Computer Processing and Storage

The computer operates with devices having only two states—electronic switches which are open or closed, electrical pulses high or not high, magnetized elements having one of two directions of polarities. The two states are represented by 0 and 1. They are called binary (meaning two) digits, a term abbreviated as *bits*. One can think of the computer as moving a string of 0s and 1s through its circuitry and storing strings of 0s and 1s in its memory:

But, the computer needs to be able to represent decimal numbers and alphabetic and special characters. In other words, the computer needs to be able to move and store strings of alphanumeric characters:

Since the computer needs to move and store at least 10 different numeric digits, 26 alphabetic characters, and more than 20 special characters (more than 56 in total) but can represent only 0 and 1, there must be a means for using the binary 0s and 1s to code the alphanumeric characters. There must also be a method for coding numeric data for computation. Although a programmer or operator will not normally be concerned with internal representations of data in binary, this data may at times be displayed or printed for his or her use. The use of strings of binary digits is not suitable for human operators, and therefore an operator notation is often used to represent the underlying binary coding.

The Binary Code for Alphanumerics

The way to represent many different characters using only 1s and 0s is to take sets of 1s and 0s and establish a code such that a certain pattern of 0s and 1s represents A, another pattern B, etc. How big will the set of 0s and 1s need to be to represent the alphanumeric characters? There will have to be enough different 1 and 0 combinations to allow a different combination for each of the alphanumeric characters and any other codes needed. For example, a 3-bit set will have eight combinations, as shown below.

Combinations of 0 and 1 with 3 bits

000	100
001	101
010	110
011	111

The number of bits to encode the alphanumerics is at least 6, but for reasons related to the need for more codes, most modern computers use a set of 8 bits. For example, the term 1 — A is coded as follows (an actual code being given only for illustrative purposes):

1	—	A
11110001	01100000	11000001

In other words, the computer moves and stores 1s and 0s (as represented by the two possible states), but sets of the 1s and 0s stand for (code) alphanumerics.

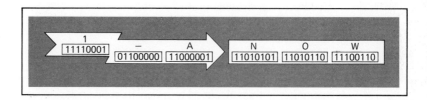

The computer can compare strings of these representations, move them about, rearrange them, and so on.

The Binary Code for Numerics

The coding of each character by a set of 8 bits works for numeric digits as well as for alphabetics. However, for arithmetic processing, 8 bits to represent a number is not efficient, and computers using 8 bits for encoding characters will split the 8 bits into two 4-bit sets for coding numerics. The coding concept is the same as with alphanumerics, with each 4-bit set representing a separate decimal digit. For example, the code for +103 is

1	0	3	+
0001	0000	0011	1100

The value assigned to each 4-bit set is determined by the rules for the binary number system. Note that there are bit combinations that are not used. Since only 10 of 16 combinations can be used to represent decimal digits, the remainder are available for other purposes, such as representing a positive or negative sign.

4-bit-set	Decimal value	4-bit set	Decimal value
0000	0	0101	5
0001	1	0110	6
0010	2	0111	7
0011	3	1000	8
0100	4	1001	9

The computer can perform arithmetic on these sets much like arithmetic on decimal numbers. Arithmetic operating on these sets is termed "binary-coded decimal" or "packed-decimal arithmetic."

The use of small sets to encode each digit is not the only method used by a computer to represent a decimal number for arithmetic processing. The second method is to encode numbers by using a long string of binary digits. The strings are actually a very large code. Depending on the computer, the string of bits can be 24, 32, 36, etc., bits in length. For example, the quantity 103 would be coded by a 32-bit binary string as:

00000000000000000000000001100111

Arithmetic performed on such strings is termed "binary arithmetic." In general, it is faster and less complicated for the computer hardware than binary-coded decimal arithmetic.

Operator Notation

The binary codes involving strings of 0s and 1s present no problem when in the computer in their electrical or magnetic representation, but frequently the operator (or programmer) wishes to write down a string of bits (say, for example, a string representing an error code). It is very error-prone and very inefficient to use the string of 1s and 0s. Ponder trying to write down a set of thirty-two 1s and 0s. It is common to write down the string using another related notation. The most common are hexadecimal, in which each set of 4 bits is written with an equivalent hexadecimal character (0 to 9 and A to F to represent the values from 0 to 15), or octal, in which each set of 3 bits is written with an equivalent octal character (values 1 to 7). As an example, it is easier and less error-prone to write the hexadecimal 6AF than the binary 011010101111.

Coding of Data on Input and Output

When it first enters the computer (say from punched cards or terminal input), the input data, whether alphabetic, numeric, or special characters, is encoded character by character into a binary character code, one bit set being used for each character.

The size of the bit set (usually termed a "byte") is 6 or 8 bits depending on the computer. The most common size is the 8-bit byte (used, for example, by the IBM System/370). The code structure of the byte is divided into two parts—a set of 4 (or 2 in a 6-bit byte) designated as a zone and 4 bits designated as a numeric portion. The zone bits perform the same function as the zone punches on a Hollerith punched card, indicating the group of characters to which the code applies. The specific character in the group is identified by the numeric coding. The set of bits may include error and control bits, but these will not be explained here.

As examples, the following are 8-bit byte codes for the IBM system/370.

Character	Zone	Numeric
A	1100	0001
B	1100	0010
M	1101	0010

Note that the zone bits for A and B are the same, but the numeric portion has a value of 1 for A and 2 for B. The zone code for M has a larger value than the zone code for B. The codes used thus define the collating sequence. When sorting data, an A is smaller than a B, and so on.

If the data is not to be manipulated arithmetically, it is stored in this character coding. However, if the number is to be used in arithmetic operations, it must be converted to a binary-coded decimal or binary form. Some computers perform arithmetic on the character-coded format, but the dominant design is for special numeric coding for arithmetic operations.

When data is to be output from the computer to a device such as a printer or a terminal, it must be encoded into a separate character code for each character to be output (including codes for the blank spaces in the output line). Data to be held in storage or written onto magnetic disk or tape may remain in either character code or computational code. The flow of data from input to output may vary depending on whether it is to be used in computations or to be manipulated as characters.

Number Systems for Computers The computer interprets coded data and performs arithmetic using the binary number system. The binary system is similar to the decimal system in the use of base, absolute value, and positional value. This is illustrated in Table 7-1 for the decimal system, which has a base of 10. Note that the positions are numbered to the left of the decimal point starting with 0 and to the right of the decimal starting with −1.

TABLE 7-1 SOME OF THE POSITIONAL VALUES IN THE DECIMAL SYSTEM

Position number	3	2	1	0	Decimal point	−1	−2
Position value (base of 10)	10^3	10^2	10^1	10^0		10^{-1}	10^{-2}
Quantity represented by position value	1000 Thousands	100 Hundreds	10 Tens	1 Units		$\frac{1}{10}$ Tenths	$\frac{1}{100}$ Hundredths

The decimal system has 10 absolute values represented by the digits 0 through 9. Each digit written in the decimal notation is interpreted as having a value equal to the absolute value of the digit (1, 2, 3, etc.) times the position value of the position it occupies.

The binary system uses the same concepts except that the binary system uses only two absolute values, 0 and 1, and the positional values are powers of 2 (Table 7-2).

TABLE 7-2 SOME OF THE POSITIONAL VALUES IN THE BINARY SYSTEM

Position	4	3	2	1	0	Binary point	−1	−2	−3	−4
Position value	2^4	2^3	2^2	2^1	2^0		2^{-1}	2^{-2}	2^{-3}	2^{-4}
Quantity represented by position value	16	8	4	2	1		$\frac{1}{2}$	$\frac{1}{4}$	$\frac{1}{8}$	$\frac{1}{16}$

The decimal equivalent of a number written in binary is found by adding the products of the absolute and positional values. For example, the binary 10101011.011 is interpreted as $171\frac{3}{8}$, as shown below.

The binary representation is used internally, and arithmetic operations are performed using rules for binary. However, when internal data is displayed or printed for programmer or operator use, it may use octal or hexadecimal notation (or decimal). The octal system has a base of 8 and absolute values from 0 to 7. The hexadecimal system uses a base of 16 and absolute values of 0 to 15 (with A to F representing 10 to 15). When binary data is displayed in octal, each group of three binary digits, starting at the binary point, is coded by an octal digit. For hexadecimal, each group of four binary digits is represented by a hexadecimal character. For example, 10110011 is 263 in octal and B3 in hexadecimal.

An Overview of the Internal Operation of a Computer

A computer must be able to perform certain fundamental operations internally:

Represent data and instructions
Hold (store) data and instructions
Move the data and instructions
Interpret and execute the commands of the instructions

These internal operations are carried out by the central processing unit (CPU) of the computer. The CPU contains three subunits—the control unit, the processing or arithmetic unit (pronounced a-rith-MET′-ic), and the storage unit. As explained in Chapter 1, these three units plus the input and output subsystems form the elements of a simple computer system (Figure 7-1).

There is no mechanical movement in the central processing unit such as one finds in an adding machine or mechanical calculator. It performs all operations electronically. The operations are directed by a program of instructions in the storage unit in which the data to be operated upon is also held. However, the storage unit is passive in that the data and instructions are merely held there. To be acted upon, the data and instructions must be moved into the control and processing units.

The information held in the storage unit is represented by the two states of the storage medium, for example, the open or closed states of integrated circuits or the

FIGURE 7-1 A computer system.

two magnetized states of ferrite (iron) cores. When data or instructions are moved from storage into the processing or control unit, the information being moved is represented by the two electrical states: pulse and no pulse. While being operated upon in the processing or control units, the data and instructions are held in registers.

The *registers* are devices designed to accept electrical pulse representations, temporarily hold the information by being in a given state, and then release the information in the form of electrical pulses when directed by control circuits. Computer operations, such as comparison and arithmetic, are performed by groups of logic (switching) circuits. This relationship is illustrated in Figure 7-2. It also suggests that much of the computer circuitry is for the purpose of controlling the movement of the electrical pulses. The circuits of the computer are designed to react to two electrical states of pulse and no pulse. Because they are using only two states, the switching logic can be described with Boolean algebra, the arithmetic of logic. The "truth" and "falsity" conditions of the Boolean analysis are identified with "closed" or "open" states in computer circuits which allow an electrical pulse to pass or not pass.

The computer is directed to perform actions by an instruction. The instruction is brought from main storage to the central processing unit and decoded. One part of the instruction specifies what the computer is to do. The other part specifies what the computer is to use in performing the operation (data from storage or a device).

Computer Circuits

The computer operates with electrical pulses. A binary 1 is represented by a sharp voltage pulse; a binary 0 by the lack of the voltage rise. A timing arrangement is used to distinguish the different binary digits being moved.

Pulse train						
Binary digit	1	0	1	1	0	0

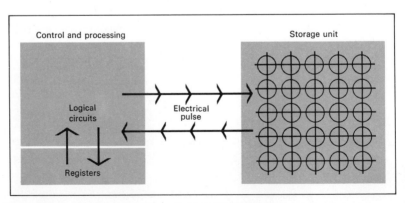

FIGURE 7-2 Relationship between storage and registers.

In order to form the pulses correctly, the computer will have amplifier circuits, which produce pulses of correct amplitude, and shaper circuits, which produce pulses of proper length. In general, the pulses will move through two basic kinds of circuits—switching or logic elements and bit storage elements or flip-flops (explained below). These basic circuits are the building blocks for the registers which hold information being processed and for the other functional units of the computer which encode, decode, accumulate, complement, and compare. The circuits are produced by the techniques of microelectronics.

Circuit Technology

The computer uses the same type of basic components as a television receiver or a radio. Transistors, resistors, diodes, and capacitors are assembled into circuits to control the flow of electric current. Early computers were large and produced substantial heat because they utilized vacuum tubes. The second-generation equipment changed to transistors. The trend in circuit technology has been toward small, fast, and very reliable circuits produced by microelectronic techniques. This same technology produces the circuits for pocket calculators.

Microelectronics is used to produce several entire logic circuits on a single chip. A typical chip might contain hundreds of components in order to form several interconnected circuits. The technology is also used to produce large numbers of memory circuits on a single chip. A typical memory chip might contain circuits to store 2048 bits. In other words, the density of memory circuits tends to be higher than for logic circuits. A chip is very small—say, $\frac{1}{16}$ in. square for a logic chip and $\frac{1}{8}$ in. square for a memory circuit chip (Figure 7-3). The chips are produced on a silicon wafer by a process of photomasking, etching, diffusions, and firings. Two major techniques are bipolar technology and metal-oxide semiconductor (MOS). Both produce miniturized circuitry. The trend in memory circuits is toward MOS.

Logical Circuits

The logical or switching circuits can be described using mathematical logic (also called Boolean algebra). The two states in logic, true and false, are represented by open and closed switches in the electronic equipment. To produce all possible logical functions, only three logical circuits need be used—AND, OR, and NOT (Figure 7-4). The basic circuits are combined in complex groupings to perform the switching for computer operation logic.

The AND gate (also called "AND block") can be thought of as an electronic element into which two (or more) wires enter and one wire exits. The logic statement A AND B is represented by the AND gate; i.e., for a pulse to come out on the exit wire, pulses must be sent into the element on *both* input wires. The truth table for A AND B presents the operating characteristics of the AND gate when 1 is used to represent a pulse and 0 a no-pulse.

The OR gate (also called "OR block" or "mixer") represents the logic statement A OR B. Like the AND gate, it has two (or more) input wires and one output wire. However, the OR gate will allow an output pulse if either or both of the input lines receive an electrical pulse. The truth table A OR B specifies the operating characteristics of the OR gate.

Microprocessor chip

Memory chip

FIGURE 7-3 Photomicrograph of integrated circuit chips used for processing circuitry (top) and for memory (bottom). Note the regularity of the memory circuit compared with the processor circuit. For actual size, see Fig. 1-6. (*Courtesy of Intel Corporation.*)

FIGURE 7-4 Logical circuits and corresponding truth tables.

The NOT circuit is very simple—the output is the opposite of the input. There are several common NOT notations; e.g., $\sim$A and $\overline{\text{A}}$ are two different ways of writing the opposite of A.

In the design of computers it is desirable to standardize as much as possible. Production is simplified by the use of combinations of standard logic modules. Two common modules are the NAND circuit (NOT AND) and the NOR circuit (NOT OR). The truth tables are not given since the inputs are the same as the AND and OR and the outputs are just the opposite.

Timing or Clock Circuits It takes time for electrical pulses to reach the proper level for representing a bit, and time for the pulse to travel through the computer. Also, operations in the computer must be performed in an orderly, timed sequence. The control of timing is performed by the use of control signals called "clock pulses" which are emitted from a central device called the "master clock." These timing signals are sent to all the logical components to keep them synchronized.

To illustrate the use of the clock pulse, assume a pulse A which must arrive at a point B at an exact time. By inserting an AND gate and a clock pulse, the pulse at A cannot pass until the clock pulse is also received.

Bit Storage Circuits

Circuits can be used as storage devices. Circuits, referred to as flip-flops, are used in the arithmetic, control, and storage units for remembering bit values during processing.

The term "flip-flop," as used here, refers to a device having two inputs (represented as 0 and 1, or "set" and "restore"), two outputs, and two stable states. When a pulse is applied to the set input, the flip-flop is set; when applied to the restore input, the flip-flop is cleared or restored. If the flip-flop is in one or the other of the two states, the corresponding output signal will be emitted, and the other output will be at the no-signal level. The output signal thus provides information on (stores) the most recent input of the flip-flop. The flip-flop maintains its state until altered by an input.

Other bit storage circuits used in developing the basic circuits of the computer are the trigger, or inverter, which is set by a pulse to the state opposite its state before the pulse, and the delay flop which has an output signal but only after a delay. The delay is used to slow down an electrical signal so that the bit represented by the signal appears one cycle later.

Functional Units

The circuits just described—gates, flip-flops, delays, etc.—are combined to form assemblies which perform specified functions necessary to computer operation. Examples of functional units are registers, accumulator, encoder, decoder, complementer, and comparator.

Registers   Registers are used to receive, hold, and transfer information used by the processing unit. A register is an assembly of bistable circuits (typically flip-flops). It acts as a temporary memory for the processing unit. There are usually several general registers which perform functions such as accumulate arithmetic results, hold the multiplier for multiplication, and hold the divisor for division. Other registers are an instruction register, which holds the instruction being executed, an address register, which holds the address of a storage location or device, and a storage register, which holds data taken from or being sent to storage. The important registers in the system are frequently connected to small lights on the computer console which display the contents of the registers.

Accumulator   An accumulator is an assembly used for addition. The design of the accumulator will depend on whether the computer uses a binary or a binary-coded decimal code and on whether the arithmetic is to be serial (one digit at a time) or parallel (all digits at once). The difference between a binary and a binary-coded decimal accumulator results from the difference in the rules for addition of these two systems. The major difference between serial and parallel arithmetic is in the number of adder units required. Serial addition uses only one 1-digit adder and adds successive pairs of digits one at a time. Parallel addition adds all pairs simultaneously, using a different adder for each pair of digits (Figure 7-5). The serial accumulator is slower than the parallel accumulator but requires less hardware.

The binary half-adder, composed of logic elements, is the basic addition circuit. There are several possible half-adder designs, all of which arrive at the result shown in Figure 7-6. In the half-adder, if there are pulse (1) inputs at A and B (but not both), the sum is 1 (a pulse). When both inputs are 1, the sum is 0, and there is a carry.

The half-adder is incomplete for addition purposes because it does not provide a carry to the next pair of digits to be added. The combination of circuits which correctly adds and carries is called a "full adder." It is essentially two half-adders

FIGURE 7-5 Comparison of serial and parallel addition.

FIGURE 7-6 Half-adder logic.

linked by a delay circuit. The delay flip-flop holds the carry bit and delays it one timing pulse so it can be added to the sum of the next pair of digits which have then entered the adder.

The net effect of the two half-adders and the delay is to produce a sum and carry (if any) from each pair of binary digits and the transmitting of any carry for combining with the next pair to be added. A simplified diagram of a full adder is shown in Figure 7-7.

Encoder, Decoder, Complementer, and Comparator

The encoder translates data from decimal form into binary-coded character form. The decoder, essentially the reverse of an encoder, translates the internal code back into decimal equivalents. In encoding, each input pulse (corresponding to an alphanumeric character) is converted into one or more binary digits.

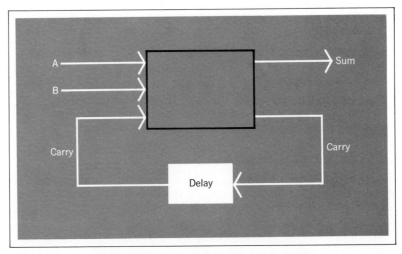

FIGURE 7-7 Simplified diagram of full adder.

Since computer subtraction consists of complementing the subtrahend and then adding, the subtraction operation requires special circuitry to perform complementing. Complementing is quite simple since the 1s complement of a binary number is each 1 replaced by a 0 and each 0 replaced by a 1. The inverter circuit performs in this exact manner.

Computer compare instructions form an important element in the modern digital computer. Several methods can be used in designing the comparison assembly. One common method compares pairs (or small groups of bits) until the larger of two quantities has been determined. For example, if 011011 and 010111 are to be compared, the comparison might proceed as shown:

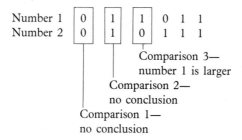

Computer Storage

The operation of the computer requires storage of instructions and data. There is storage in many different parts of the computer system (Figure 7-8). Storage may use different media but is all based on the use of two states to represent a binary digit. The most significant storages in the computer system are:

Storage	Explanation
Primary storage	The main memory which holds "active" programs and data. It uses, in almost all cases, semiconductor or magnetic core storage.
Secondary storage	Auxiliary storage to hold data files and programs not being executed. Lower cost. Generally uses magnetic disk or magnetic tape. Data and programs to be executed are read from secondary storage into primary storage for processing.
Buffer or cache storage	Small storage having very fast access for use in holding very active data. Used mainly with very high speed, large computers. The use is automatic, and the programmer is not usually concerned with it.

Control storage	Called "reloadable control storage" or (if read only) "read-only storage." Contains a computer program (called a "micro-program or microcode") for interpreting computer instructions and converting them to basic operations. Microcode in control storage is essentially a substitute for hardware. The programmer is not usually concerned with it.
Registers	Registers are essentially a form of storage used in processing.

This chapter emphasizes main memory; secondary storage is described in Chapter 9.

Two characteristics significant to primary computer storage are volatility and readout destructability. The major characteristic of secondary storage is access method (discussed in Chapter 9).

Characteristic	Description
Volatility	A storage medium is volatile if stored data is lost when power is removed. Semiconductor storage is volatile; core is not.
Readout destructability	Reading stored data may destroy the recorded data, so it must be restored by a separate operation. This is done automatically by the equipment, and the user is not aware of it. Magnetic core has a destructive readout; semiconductor storage does not.

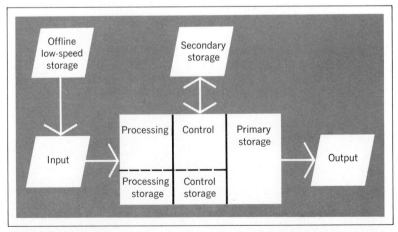

FIGURE 7-8 Elements of a computer system showing different types of storage.

The volatility of the semiconductor memory means that the computer system must make provisions to recover from a power outage by regularly storing important data on nonvolatile storage from which it may be read after the power is restored.

The two most common storage devices for main memory, semiconductors and magnetic core, are explained. Two less used methods of primary storage, thin film and plated wire, are described very briefly.

Semiconductor Storage

A major change in computer technology in the mid-1970s was the change from magnetic core as the dominant primary storage to semiconductors. The semiconductor memory consists of extremely small bit storage circuits (flip-flops) etched on a silicon chip. All the electronic elements to store a bit are placed in such a small area of the chip that a single chip can contain storage for thousands of bits (see Figure 7-3). The individual chips are arranged in groups to form a memory module complete with all interconnections to "plug in" to the computer.

The semiconductor storage operates on the principle of a flip-flop in which the switch is set to a 0 or 1 position by a write command which sets or restores the flip-flop. It remains in the same position until changed. Reading the bit storage consists of measuring the signals from the two possible outputs—one output indicates the switch has been set to 0, the other that it has been set to 1. As mentioned, power is required to maintain the 0 or 1 state. Therefore, stored data is lost whenever power is turned off or interrupted.

Magnetic Core Storage

Magnetic core storage is (and will continue to be) a significant medium for primary storage. A magnetic core is molded from a ferrite (iron) powder into a doughnut shape about the size of the head of a pin. The individual cores are strung on wires to form core planes. Several core planes stacked one on top of another form a core stack (Figure 7-9).

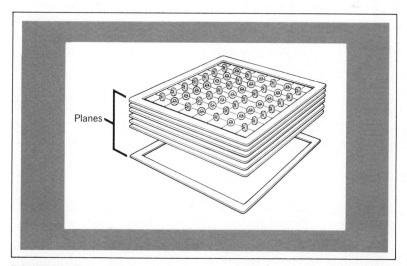

Planes

FIGURE 7-9 Core stack.

One of the experiments commonly carried out in an elementary physics course demonstrates that an iron bar can be magnetized in one of two directions: north-south or south-north. Similarly, a ferrite core can be polarized in two directions. These two directions of polarity form the two states of the core. A core can be placed in either state by the application of a magnetizing force. The direction of polarity will depend on the direction of magnetizing current. The computer designer selects one direction to represent a 0-bit and the other to represent a 1-bit. Once polarized in one direction, a core will retain that polarity until changed.

Figure 7-10 shows a single wire being used to apply current to the core. The typical arrangement uses two wires strung through the core. This arrangement is termed a "coincident-current core memory." One-half of the current required to switch the core from one polarity to another is applied to each of the wires when the core is to be "flipped." The cores are arranged in the planes with the intersection of two wires applying full current to only one core. This arrangement, shown in Figure 7-11, allows the computer to control the state of each individual core. These two wires will write on a selected core, but reading requires more wiring. Although there are several design possibilities, the most common organization of a core memory uses four wires through each core to accomplish reading and writing. In addition to the two wires for applying the magnetizing current, there is an inhibit wire and a sense wire (Figure 7-12).

A core is read by sending a current to polarize the core in a particular direction. If the core is already magnetized in that direction, nothing happens; if it is not, the core changes state. This changing or "flipping" induces a current. The sense wire picks up this current indicating that the core was in the opposite state prior to being changed. For example, if an electrical pulse is sent to write a 0 at a core position and the core is already in the 1 state, the writing of a 0 will flip the core. If a 0 is already there, no change will occur. The "flipping" induces a current which is picked up by the sense wire running through the plane. Only one sense wire is needed for an entire plane, since only one core is sensed at a time. In this case, if the core represented a 1, the sense wire will pick up a current; if a 0, there will be no current. Note, however, that reading by the writing of a 0 left the core position with a 0. In other words, a 1 would have been replaced by a 0 and a 0

FIGURE 7-10 Two-state representation with ferrite cores. (*a*) Current is applied in one direction to polarize a 1; (*b*) current is reversed and polarity flips to the opposite direction to represent a 0.

FIGURE 7-11 Selecting a core.

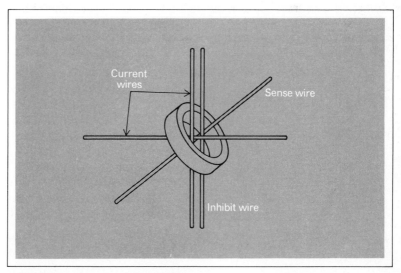

FIGURE 7-12 Closeup of a single core.

would have remained a 0. Reading a core in this way is destructive of the prior information, and to remedy this, the core must be restored to its former state. This is done by attempting to write a 1 at the position (the opposite current from that used to read the core). If no current was sensed during the read cycle, the restore cycle will simultaneously put an inhibit current in the inhibit wire. If the sense wire picked up a current during the read, no inhibit current will be used during the restore cycle. The result of this approach is to inhibit the writing of a 1 if the core was 0 and should therefore remain 0, and the writing of a 1 with no interference from an inhibit current if the core was flipped from 1 to 0 during the read cycle and is to be restored. The necessity to restore after reading is a technological disadvantage of core storage.

Thin-Film and Plated-Wire Storage

Although they have received much less use, thin film and plated wire represent storage technology that is found in existing computers. Thin-film memory is produced by depositing very thin spots of metallic alloy on a ceramic or metal plate. This spot performs in the same manner as the core, except that only two wires are required. A typical thin-film element consists of a rectangle about .025 by .050 in. with a thickness of about 1000 angstroms (.0000004 in.). This rectangle can be thought of as a bar magnet. Applying a current which causes the polarity to rotate but not to flip induces a current which indicates whether a 1 or 0 was stored (Figure 7-13). After the sense field is removed, the polarity is returned to its prior state by a digit pulse which "steers" the polarity back to a 1 or 0 state. An overlay of etched copper wires provides the circuitry necessary to connect the individual elements with the circuits which read and write.

Plated-wire memory or woven-wire memory uses a thin film which is desposited around a fine wire. This wire carries the write current during a write operation and is the sense line in a read operation. Insulated wires are woven across

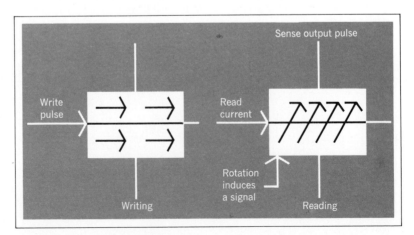

FIGURE 7-13 Thin-film memory.

the plated wire in a fashion similar to weaving cloth. The area where the insulated loop goes around the plated wire (Figure 7-14) forms a bit storage location. Reading is nondestructive.

Storage Addressing

Semiconductors, ferrite cores, and other storage devices are not usable unless data stored there can be retrieved when needed. In order to accomplish retrieval, each storage location has an address which identifies it just as a house address identifies a dwelling. Another comparison is a set of mailboxes in a post office. Each has a unique number which identifies the storage location (Figure 7-15). A person who wishes to store a letter in the box specifies the box number. Likewise, each set of semiconductors in a semiconductor storage or each set of cores in a core storage unit has an address. This address identifies the location so that data may be stored there, and data so stored may be retrieved. The address is a code which identifies the location for the computer circuitry. In other words, the computer circuitry

FIGURE 7-14 Plated-wire memory.

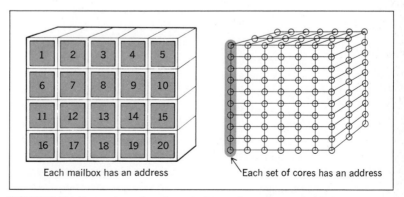

FIGURE 7-15 Comparison of mailbox number and core storage address.

associates a separate set of storage devices with each location designation. There is, for example, a set of semiconductors or ferrite cores which is identified by the location 347, another set associated with location 348. Each address refers to a set of storage devices, but how large the set is and what can be stored there depends on the word structure of the particular computer.

A computer word consists of the data which is stored or retrieved when storage to or retrieval from a memory location is specified. There are two basic approaches—fixed-length word and variable-length word. In addition, there is a byte-addressable word structure which combines many of the features of both.

Fixed-Word-Length Addressing

In a fixed-word-length computer, every storage location identified by an address consists of a fixed number of semiconductors, cores, or other storage representations. Some popular word sizes for fixed-word-length machines are 24, 30, 32, 36, 48, and 60 bits. The computer designer makes a choice of word size, and all addresses then reference that number of bits. If the computer is designed with a 48-bit word, each reference to a memory location will access 48 bits. The computer may be able to manipulate parts of words such as small groups of bits which encode characters, but the basic operations always move a fixed word.

Variable-Word-Length Addressing

The variable-word-length or character computer has an address for each set of bits which can encode one character. If it requires 6 bits to encode a character, each 6-bit set (not counting control bits) will have an address assigned to it. Thus, if the number 39 is in storage, the 3 will occupy one storage location having an address, and the 9 will be in another contiguous storage location with a separate address.

If each character is stored in a separate storage location having a separate address, how is a number such as 945823, which takes up six separate storage locations, accessible? If it were necessary to specify each of these six locations in order to access the number stored there, the procedure would become quite cumbersome. This is, however, not necessary. A group of storage locations can be accessed by specifying only a single storage location which defines the starting location for the group of characters that make up the word. Since the number of characters in the group can vary, the number of memory locations accessed is variable. Because the computer begins at the starting location given and picks up all succeeding bit sets until the end of the word is indicated, there must be a method of specifying the end of the word. Two methods are in use, an older method being the use of a special control bit called a "word mark" set to 1 in the code of the character at one end of the word, the other end of the word being addressed. The other, most common, method of variable word addressing (used in the System/370) is explicit specification of length in the instruction. In this approach, any instruction which specifies a variable-length word gives the leftmost starting address plus the number of locations to be included in the word.

Byte-addressable Combination

Most modern medium- and large-scale computer systems are designed so that fixed and variable words can be used in the same computer. This is done by having a byte-addressable organization. A byte is a group of bits which form a subunit of a computer word. In IBM's System/370, which are byte-addressable computers, each 8-bit byte has an address. Four such bytes make up a 32-bit fixed binary word, the address of which is the address of the first byte. When an instruction references a fixed binary word, the computer automatically stores or retrieves 4 bytes. The computer also has instructions which specify a fixed length of 2 bytes (half-word) and 8 bytes (double word). In addition to these fixed-word-length instructions, there are variable-word-length instructions which specify the first byte of the word and the number of bytes to be included.

Virtual Memory

The virtual storage technique was implemented as early as 1959 (in the Atlas computer at Manchester University, England) and in several computers thereafter, but widespread use across the entire range of computer sizes began in the 1970s. Virtual storage is a method for hardware and software management of application programs (stored in primary and secondary storage), so that an application program need not be restricted in size to the storage space in main memory. In other words, the programmer can write programs as if the computer had practically unlimited main storage (for example, up to 16 million bytes in one computer), even though the main computer storage is only a fraction of that size. Since only a part of the program is active and need be in main storage at any one time, the program is divided into small sections called "pages" (say, 2000 to 4000 bytes in size). A group of pages is sometimes referred to as a "segment." The pages that are active are placed in main memory; the remainder are stored on a direct-access file such as a disk or drum from which they may be loaded as needed.

It is useful to distinguish between the physical (real) storage addresses in main memory and program-generated (virtual) storage addresses. Each instruction and each data item in main storage during program execution is located in a physical storage location, with a real address. In the real storage approach, each program is assigned physical addresses for all instructions and data. In the virtual storage approach, the program has addresses for instructions and data, but these addresses are understood to be relative addresses which will allow the physical locations to be identified at execution time. With virtual storage management, at any given time during execution some pages of a program may be in main storage, possibly in noncontiguous page frames (sets of real storage locations each of which holds a page). Other pages will be in external page storage. When an instruction being executed calls for the data in location 3764, the hardware and software which manage the storage access must determine where the page is located which has the virtual address 3764. If the page is currently in main memory, the virtual address of 3764 must be translated into the real address. If the page is in the external page storage (say, on disk), the page must be transferred to main storage (called "demand paging"), and the address of 3764 translated to the real address in the page. The movement of pages of instructions into main memory, the identification of page location, and the translation of a virtual address to a physical address are performed by hardware and software. Tables which contain the location of pages and main memory addresses for main memory pages are maintained by the operating system. A hardware mechanism (IBM calls it DAT for dynamic address translation) automatically translates each virtual address into a physical address by means of a table look-up procedure.

The operating system monitors page usage; pages not in use are written back to external page storage and pages needed are brought in. Several programs may be in process concurrently so that the paging process may place a significant demand on the central processor and the input/output resources. Under certain conditions, the paging activity becomes so high that little productive work is done. This is termed "thrashing." The software which manages virtual storage monitors page usage and automatically makes changes to eliminate thrashing.

The use of virtual storage has the advantage of eliminating program storage constraints and thereby increasing flexibility of storage use. Virtual storage techniques may improve storage utilization. The disadvantages are the computer resources required to manage the virtual storage. For example, the operating system is larger (requires more storage), the direct-access storage devices must be faster, and additional computer power must be provided to compensate for virtual storage resource use. On balance, virtual storage is a significant development and will tend to be utilized in most medium- and large-scale systems.

Effect of Word Structure on Computer Design

In terms of understanding the difference between computers, the word organization is an important distinction. The differences between fixed-word-length, variable-word-length, and byte-addressable computers are, for the most part, a natural consequence of the different word organizations. In the fixed-word-length computer, every instruction or data word has exactly the same number of bits. All the circuitry is designed to accept this basic block. The variable-word-length computer word can range from one character up to many characters. Computer circuitry cannot therefore be designed to handle a fixed group of bits other than the small number associated with a single character. These two approaches lead to the hardware characteristics (Table 7-1) usually found in computers using these word

TABLE 7-1 HARDWARE CHARACTERISTICS FOR DIFFERENT WORD-LENGTH DESIGNS

Characteristics	Fixed word length	Variable word length	Mixed byte-addressable
Length of word	Specified	Variable	Both
Registers	Addressable	Storage-to-storage	Both
Arithmetic	Usually binary	Binary-coded decimal	Both
Transfer for data	Parallel	Serial	Both

organizations. One of the important distinctions is the use of addressable registers versus the use of a storage-to-storage approach. This leads to other important differences.

The Use of Addressable Registers

As explained, a register is a set of storage devices where data or instructions are moved in order to be operated upon. The main storage is passive, merely holding the data and instructions; the register is active storage. A register may be addressable, so that the programmer can write an instruction to load it with the contents of a storage location or to copy its contents into a regular storage location. Or a register may not be addressable, being called into use automatically by the circuitry of the computer.

The use of addressable registers requires a fixed-length word because the register is designed to accept and hold a specified number of bits. When addressable registers are used, data is moved into a register, operated upon, and then moved back to a storage location. The trend in the design of fixed word-length computers is for several addressable registers. For example, IBM's System/370 computers have 16 general-purpose registers for fixed word-length instructions.

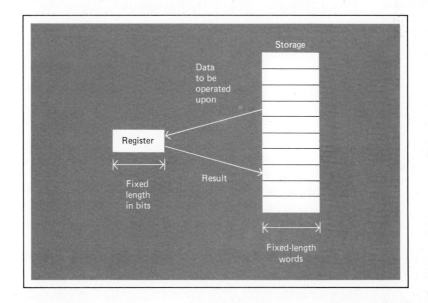

The advantage of a register approach is the speed which can be attained. Data can be transferred from storage to register in parallel, i.e., all bits simultaneously. This is possible because all words contain the same number of bits no matter how small or large the value. If a 32-bit memory location, for example, is storing the number 1, it will have 31 leading 0-bits and one 1-bit. This can be transferred in parallel from storage to a register in exactly the same time as a large number. Once in a register, the arithmetic operations can also be performed in parallel.

Storage-to-Storage Approach

When the word length is variable, transferring the entire word into a register is precluded because the register size cannot be exactly specified. Instead of using an addressable register, the variable-length instructions are executed in a storage-to-storage approach in which a single character or byte is read from storage into a nonaddressable register, operated upon, and the result stored back in a character or byte location. For example, if a 6-digit and a 4-digit number are to be added in a character machine, the addition will be performed serially, a pair of digits at a time. The result will be stored a digit at a time in memory, replacing one of the operands.

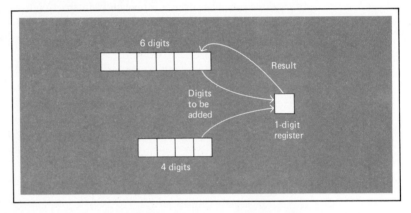

This approach removes the limitation imposed by a fixed-length word. Operands may be as small or as large as necessary. However, this flexibility is achieved at a loss in speed because the storage-to-storage approach must operate in serial fashion.

The Problem of Precision

"Precision" refers to the number of significant digits which are used to express a quantity. The precision for a fixed word-length computer is the size of the word. If, for example, a 32-bit binary word is used, the largest quantity which can be represented is 2,147,483,647. If a larger number is to be stored, two words can be used as if they were a single location. This is known as "double precision." Double-precision hardware is available on many large-scale computers; for small computers, the use of two words for one quantity is handled by program instructions. Another approach to representing very large or very small numbers is floating point in which a number is represented by two parts of a quantity and an exponent which specifies the scaling of the quantity.

Comparing Memory Sizes

In references to a computer, the primary storage is designated in terms of the number of addressable storage locations. Yet an addressable location may range from a large fixed word to a group of bits encoding a single decimal digit. Because of design considerations, memory sizes will usually come in rather odd numbers—multiples of 4096. The term K is used to refer to thousands of addressable locations rounded to the thousands. Thus, 4096 storage locations are termed "4K memory." A 32K memory may actually be 32,768 locations.

Since the storage is described in terms of addressable storage locations and these locations vary widely in their capacity and versatility, the comparison of memory sizes requires some analysis. An initial analysis can be made in terms of the capacity of the storage with respect to alphanumeric characters, decimal digits, and instructions.

Comparing Storage of Alphanumeric Characters

The storage capacity for alphanumeric characters will depend on the number of bytes of storage, each of which encodes one alphanumeric character. This is influenced by the word orientation of the computer.

Word orientation of computer	Method of representing alphanumerics
Binary	Bytes of 6 to 8 bits within a binary word
Binary-coded character	One character per bit set (of, say, 6 bits)
Byte-addressable	One character per byte (8 bits)

As examples, a Control Data Cyber 170 60-bit fixed word-length computer stores 10 alphanumeric characters in each word using 6-bit bytes, the Honeywell 2000 character code uses one location to encode each character, and the byte-oriented UNIVAC 90 series stores one character in each 8-bit byte.

Comparing Storage of Numeric Data

There are two problems in comparing storage of numeric data. The first arises from the difference between encoding numeric data in binary-coded decimal versus binary and the second because of the unused bits in a fixed-word format. In binary-coded decimal encoding of data, each digit is encoded by one bit set, the size of the bit set being 4, 6, 8, or 9 bits, depending on the computer architecture. In packed decimal, an 8-bit byte is divided into two 4-bit sets each of which encodes a digit. However, the sign also requires a separate 4-bit set. In packed decimal, a 9-digit number takes 10-bit sets (5 bytes) in storage. Coding numeric data in binary-coded decimal uses only the storage needed to encode the data words.

Encoding in binary uses a string of binary digits. A binary representation will take roughly 3.36 bits to encode each numeric digit. The maximum size in number of decimal digits which can be represented by a 32-bit computer word, for example, is computed as 31 ÷ 3.36 (31 because 1 bit is reserved for the arithmetic sign), or 9.2. A 32-bit word (31 bits plus sign) can, therefore, encode any number up to and including 2,147,483,647. Coding in binary in a fixed-word computer uses an entire word even if only a single digit is to be stored. There can, therefore, be wasted storage space. However, many binary computer designs allow small binary words (say 8 or 16 bits) for encoding small numbers.

Comparing Storage Space for Instructions

In the simplest case, all instructions are the same size in terms of storage, and one instruction, in a fixed-word-length computer, will occupy one memory location. Although some computers follow this simple approach, most computers have instructions of different length. The IBM System/370, which has a 32-bit word, uses instructions which are 16, 32, and 48 bits (2, 4, or 6 bytes) in length. Another factor complicating comparison of instruction storage is the type of instructions available. The instruction repertoires of different computers vary in power, so that a single instruction in one computer may suffice for what takes several instructions to do in another computer.

The comparison of memory sizes is not a simple matter when all factors are considered properly. In order to make a meaningful comparison, one must know something about the data to be stored, the program to be run, etc. Such an evaluation is beyond the scope of this text, but with the background obtained in these chapters a rough evaluation can be made, and this is usually satisfactory considering the fact that there are many uncertainties in any computer comparison. To illustrate the effect of the three elements to consider in looking at memory size, Table 7-2 gives these measures for three computers having different storage addressing.

Most computer systems can be obtained with a main storage capacity chosen from a large range of possible memory sizes. In the usual case, the storage can be increased by later addition of storage modules. In choosing the size of memory to be installed, one must consider not only the probable necessity for data and

TABLE 7-2 EXAMPLE OF COMPARING MEMORY SIZES

| Computer | Orientation | Code | Memory size being compared | MAXIMUM STORAGE IF ALL DEVOTED TO | | Addressable locations to encode one instruction |
				Alphabetics	Numerics	
IBM System/370	Model 115 small general purpose	Byte-binary	65K	65,536	131,072	2, 4, or 6
Honeywell 2000	Small commercial	BCD	65K	65,536	65,536	1 to 12
UNIVAC 1100/40	Large general purpose	36-bit binary	65K	393,216	393,216	1

program storage but also the storage requirements of the various programming and operating aids described in Chapter 3. Typical primary storage size in computer configurations is increasing in size because of changes in storage technology, reductions in cost, and increased need for storage by system and application software. In the small IBM 1401 computer, 16K was a popular storage size; a comparable storage size for a mid-1975 to 1980 small computer is likely to be 65 to 131K. Many medium-large to large systems have megabyte memories (millions of bytes). The range of storage sizes is indicated by the following primary storage sizes typically available for computers introduced after 1975. In all cases, the storage uses metal oxide semiconductors.

Size of computer	Range of primary storage size
Small	65 to 262K
Medium	131K to 2 megabytes
Large	524K to 6 megabytes
Very large	1 to 12 megabytes

A Computer Operating Cycle

Most computers are designed so that a fixed interval of time is allowed for each operation. A computer which uses fixed time intervals to determine when to initiate the next operation is known as "synchronous." A less common design, the asynchronous computer, initiates the next operation when a signal from the current operation indicates a completion. In both cases, exact timing is necessary to proper operation. The basic timing interval is a pulse emitted by the electronic clock circuits. Since each operation takes a specified number of pulse times, the control circuitry will initiate the proper commands at the correct intervals. The clock time may range from a few microseconds (millionths of seconds) to a few nanoseconds (billionths of seconds).

A frequently mentioned figure in computer timings is storage cycle time. This is the time required to obtain a word from storage. Storage cycle times are in the microsecond or nanosecond range. A typical time to read from a fast semiconductor storage is in the range from 200 to 800 nanoseconds. By way of contrast, the time required to obtain data from secondary storage is measured in thousandths of seconds (milliseconds).

A Basic Cycle A basic computer cycle can be divided into two parts—the instruction cycle and the execution cycle.

Instruction Cycle **1** An instruction is obtained from a main storage location and transferred to the central processor. The instruction is composed of an operation code specifying what is to be done and the address of the data or device to be operated upon (operand).

2 The operation code is transferred to an instruction register and decoded.

3 The address of the operand is transferred to an address register.

4 The address of the next instruction is determined.

Execution Cycle **5** If the operand address refers to information stored in memory, the information is obtained from storage and placed in the storage register.

6 The operation specified by the operation code is performed, using appropriate registers.

The address of the program instruction is found in an instruction counter. This counter is set to the address of the first instruction when the program of instructions is begun. When an instruction is brought from storage, the counter automatically advances to the address of the next instruction. If an instruction occupies one storage location, the counter will advance by 1; if two locations, by 2; etc. This procedure assumes that instructions are stored in sequence in main memory. For many of the instructions, this sequence assumption is correct. The program itself may specify a break in the sequence. In this case, the instruction counter is reset to the instruction address specified.

Speeding Up the The speed of the basic computer cycle may be improved not only by faster
Operating Cycle circuitry but also by hardware features which allow faster storage access, concurrent operations, and look-ahead. Faster primary storage access is obtained by the use of a very high speed buffer (cache) storage. This storage may be quite small, but the trend is toward a size in the range from 8 to 32K. Data items that are in active use by the program are placed in the buffer storage, thereby reducing the data access time. When the program first accesses a data item, it is also loaded into the buffer memory (perhaps along with adjacent data). In most cases, this approach will mean that the very active data will be quickly available in buffer memory. A hardware feature automatically accesses buffer memory instead of regular primary storage for blocks of data items that have been moved there. In other words, the computer software and hardware automatically load and use the buffer storage, so the programmer can ignore it.

The basic cycle of the computer is sequential with one operation following another. It is possible to provide additional hardware, so that certain operations can overlap. For example, many of the operations in the instruction and execution cycle can overlap. Storage of data (from the last operation) and accessing of the storage for the next instruction can be overlapped. In addition to overlapping basic operations, the computer can be designed with several independent processors to handle groups of operations concurrently. This is the concept of distributed processing. As implemented in the central processor, distributed processing is the use of separate processors to handle input and output, instruction processing, and service operations (involving the operator console, system diagnostics, and error-recovery operations). The concurrent use of these three independent processors speeds the overall rate of computer processing. The concept can be extended to more processors.

Look-ahead is a method of reducing instruction and data access time. A set of registers (called a "stack") is loaded with a set of instructions. When the first instruction in the stack is executed, it is dropped from the stack, and the next instruction (following the last one in the stack) is added to the bottom of the stack. This means that the computer can look ahead to the instructions in the stack and put data called for by the instructions in the buffer storage. It can execute small loops (a common operation) very rapidly because the instructions are all contained in the stack.

The Microprogram in the Operating Cycle

The computer has some very fundamental operations which direct the flow of pulses in the circuitry. These basic operations are combined into higher-level operations such as add, move, and compare. This combining of fundamental operations into a higher-level operation can be done by computer circuitry, or it can be programmed into a central processor control program. Because the control program is dealing with low-level operations, it is termed a "microprogram." A combination of wired circuitry and microprogram is also possible. The microprogram is essentially a substitute for additional circuitry. It adds flexibility to a computer because a computer can, by the use of different microprograms, change the instruction available to the programmer.

In the operating cycle, the instruction to be executed is decoded by the microprogram which executes a set of microoperations to execute the instruction. This sequence is slower than wired circuitry, but adds to the number of instructions that a computer can efficiently execute. The microcode can be used to provide programmers with high-level instructions which cannot be cost-justified in the hardware.

The microprogram is contained in a special control storage. This storage was, in some earlier computers, a read-only storage that was loaded at the factory. Current computers use the concept extensively with a reloadable control storage. The smaller computers are likely to have larger control storage because the smaller computers put functions in the microprogram that are wired in the larger computer.

Microprograms are written by specialized programmers and are usually furnished to the installation by the hardware vendor. For example, IBM System/370 microprograms are furnished on diskette (a small floppy disk—described in the next chapter). The microprogram is read by a special disk drive incorporated in the central processing unit.

Alternatives in Computer Design

From this survey of the internal operations and storage of computers, it can be seen that there are several major design alternatives that are of general interest. There are summarized briefly below, with additional comment where there has been no previous discussion.

Characteristic	Discussion
Timing of operations	Computers operate with either synchronous or asynchronous timing. Synchronous timing assigns fixed times to operations; the end of the fixed time for the current operation is the basis for initiating the next operation. Asynchronous timing initiates the next operation after a signal is received that the previous operation is completed. Most computers are synchronous.
Microprogram	Microprograms (also called "stored logic") are used in place of wired circuits to increase the number and variety of instructions that a computer will accept. They are placed in a special control storage.
Transfer of information	Transfer of information is either serial (digit by digit) or parallel (a block or a word at a time). Parallel transfer is faster and is used in most very high speed computers.
Arithmetic circuitry	The basic operation of addition can be performed serially (digit by digit) or in parallel (all digits at once). The parallel mode requires more circuitry than the serial mode but is faster.
Type of numeric representation for arithmetic	Numeric data to be used in arithmetic can be represented internally in binary or binary-coded decimal (packed decimal) form. Both forms may be found in the same computer.
Type of arithmetic processing	Arithmetic may be binary (on pairs of binary strings) or binary-coded decimal (on pairs of bit sets each encoding a digit).
Storage-addressable unit	The addressable unit may be a fixed-length word or a variable-length word. The same computer may be designed to address either fixed- or variable-length words by using a byte-addressable format.
Program addressing	Program addressing may be to real addresses or to virtual addresses (in virtual storage).
Buffer storage	A buffer or cache memory is used to speed instruction and active data access by having the very active elements in a special high-speed storage.
Look-ahead	An instruction stack holds a block of instructions, allowing the computer to look ahead and perform instructions more quickly.
Distributed processors	Independent processing units may be assigned to specific tasks such as operator communication and input/output management.

SUMMARY   The internal operation of the computer is binary, i.e., based on two values or conditions. Examples of the two-valued orientation are:

1   Data is represented in binary or a variation based on binary.

2   Storage in the processing and control units makes use of a bistable (two stable states) device, the flip-flop.

3   Information being moved is encoded by having an electrical pulse represent a binary 1 and a no-pulse a binary 0.

4   The switching circuits are two-valued and can be described using the two-valued arithmetic of Boolean algebra.

The chapter has surveyed the circuits and functional assemblies from which a computer is built, providing a background for understanding how to program and operate a computer.

The characteristics of storage were surveyed, and storage for main memory was described. The dominant form for primary storage is semiconductors, with magnetic core having substantial use. The methods of reading and writing on a core were explained. Thin-film and plated-wire were also reviewed.

The concept of address is a means for identifying storage locations to be used. These addresses can be real or virtual. Storage addresses must be understood in the context of the word structure for the computer being used. The fixed- and variable-word-length organizations are basic alternatives, while a byte-addressable structure is being used to provide both methods in a single computer.

Several important design alternatives have now been presented. These are synchronous versus asynchronous timing, microprogrammed stored logic versus hardware circuitry, parallel versus serial data transfer, parallel versus serial arithmetic, binary versus binary-coded decimal representation and arithmetic, fixed versus variable word length, real versus virtual program addresses, buffer storage, look-ahead instruction stacks, and distributed processors. These alternatives are not independent; once a decision is made as to word, character, or byte addressing, other characteristics are also decided. For example, variable-word-length operations are performed serially, and the arithmetic is binary-coded decimal.

EXERCISES   **1**   Considered individually, which of the following design alternatives provides for faster operation?
(*a*) Synchronous versus asynchronous timing
(*b*) Parallel versus serial data transfer
(*c*) Parallel versus serial arithmetic
(*d*) Hardware arithmetic versus microprogrammed arithmetic
(*e*) Fixed versus variable word length
(*f*) Binary versus binary-coded decimal arithmetic
(*g*) Real versus virtual program addressing

2   In the processing unit, data is either being moved or being held in temporary operating storage. How are binary digits represented in these two cases?

3 Give the truth table for:
   (*a*) A NOR circuit   (*b*) A NAND circuit
4 Define the following terms:
   (*a*) Flip-flop   (*g*) Address
   (*b*) Register   (*h*) Double precision
   (*c*) Encoder   (*i*) Word (in computer)
   (*d*) Byte   (*j*) K (in reference to storage)
   (*e*) Half-adder   (*k*) Microprogram
   (*f*) Clock circuit   (*l*) Buffer memory
5 Explain the difference between:
   (*a*) Synchronous and asynchronous timing
   (*b*) Parallel and serial addition
   (*c*) Binary and BCD arithmetic
   (*d*) Real and virtual storage
6 Explain the characteristics (in terms of design alternatives presented in the chapter) that are associated with both variable and fixed word designs. How can both designs be implemented in the same computer?
7 What terms are used to refer to thousandths, millionths, and billionths of a second?
8 Computer memory sizes are usually defined in terms of the number of addressable storage positions. Compare the amount of storage in the following computer memories. Make a general evaluation of the effective memory.
   (*a*) 40K variable word-length computer
   (*b*) Fixed word-length (36 binary bits) 32K computer
   (*c*) Byte-addressable 32K computer
9 How does virtual storage work? Define page, segment, demand paging, page frame, external page storage, and thrashing.
10 Explain how each of the following can store a binary digit. In each case, how is it read?
   (*a*) Semiconductor   (*b*) Core   (*c*) Thin-film
11 Explain the most common method for specifying word length in variable word addressing.
12 What is the difference between using addressable registers and storage-to-storage operations?
13 What is the difference in precision obtainable in a fixed- versus a variable-word structure?
14 How is a buffer storage used?
15 Explain a distributed processing hardware design.
16 Using a rough figure of 3.3:1 as the ratio of binary digits needed to encode a digit of a decimal number when using straight binary, approximately how large a number (expressed in decimal digits) can be encoded by (*a*) 24 bits, (*b*) 32 bits, (*c*) 48 bits, and (*d*) 60 bits?
17 What takes place during the instruction cycle?
18 How is the instruction counter used in obtaining the address of the instruction to be used?
19 A computer instruction may specify "Branch to storage location 1029." What happens to the instruction counter?
20 How is a central processor kept in synchronization?
21 For the computer available to you, determine the following:
   (*a*) Synchronous or asynchronous
   (*b*) Storage cycle time

(*c*) Number of accumulator registers

(*d*) Serial or parallel addition

(*e*) Complete add time (for two 5-digit operands if addition is performed serially)

(*f*) Fixed versus variable-length structure or both (based on byte addressing)

(*g*) Binary or BCD addition (or both)

(*h*) Hardware or programmed floating point operations

22 Using the storage address and coding structure for the computer available to you, determine the following for main memory:

(*a*) Size in addressable units

(*b*) Number of alphanumeric characters that can be stored if all storage is used for them

(*c*) Number of instructions that main storage will hold

(*d*) Number of numeric characters storage can hold

Chapter

8

Data Preparation, Input, Output, and Data Communications

Data to be used in computer processing must be made available in machine-readable form. This may involve data preparation to record and enter data into processing, or an application may make use of secondary storage which holds data that has already been prepared or which holds the results of prior processing that is needed in the current processing. The computer application inputs (reads or accepts) data from devices such as card readers, magnetic tape units, magnetic disk units, or terminals. The results of computer processing are either written onto secondary storage for subsequent use by a computer application or written or displayed in a form that is readable by persons receiving the data. The trend in information processing is to have some applications online, receiving data from remote terminals via data communications facilities and transmitting results back to the remote site to be printed or displayed.

This chapter explains the process and the devices for data preparation, original input, and human-use output. It includes an explanation of data communication operations and facilities. Secondary storage devices are described in the next chapter.

Data Preparation Activities

Data preparation is used to refer to the activities which bring data to the point of input to processing by a computer application. A major part of data preparation is data entry, and that term is often used to refer to the data preparation activities. Five major data preparation activities are:

1   Recording the transaction
2   Transcribing to machine-readable form
3   Validating the data
4   Converting data to input medium
5   Batching for input

There are a number of alternatives in the design of data entry for computer applications. These alternatives affect the manner in which data preparation activities are performed, and some application design alternatives eliminate some data preparation activities.

Recording the Transaction   A transaction is broadly defined as the occurrence of an activity or event (such as a sale, a purchase, enrolling a student, or performing a measurement). Data about the transaction must be recorded in order to provide input to computer processing (for purposes such as sales accounting, purchases recordkeeping, student records, and statistical analysis).

The recording of data during the execution of a transaction can make use of a variety of recording technology. Five major approaches are listed below together with examples of the technology employed. The data entry devices are described later in the chapter.

Approach to transaction recording	Data entry technology
1 Recording on a document for subsequent conversion to machine-readable form	Paper document for conversion by keypunching, keyboard to disk, terminal, etc.
2 Recording on a document in a machine-readable form	Typing document with optically readable typing font or printing characters for reading by optical character reader.
3 Recording with a turnaround document from a previous, related transaction	Document may be in a machine-readable form (punched card or optically readable printing), or it may not be machine-readable and need conversion.
4 Recording which produces both a document and a machine-readable input	Point-of-sale device which produces document (such as cash register tape) and also records transaction on a machine-readable medium (such as magnetic tape, magnetic disk, or paper tape).
5 Recording via a terminal	A visual display terminal or a typewriter terminal.

The first two methods utilize a document to record the data. Careful document design (beyond the scope of this text) is important in reducing the time required for recording data and in reducing recording errors. In the following examples, the use of the boxes for social security numbers reduces the chance that a number with too few or too many digits will be recorded. Asking for a person's name without specifying the order is error-prone. For names such as DAVIS BITTON and HART WILL, which is the last name and which is the first? (One is a historian and the other an accounting professor—the order of both names is first/last.)

Error-prone

Social Security No. _____

Name _____

Better

Social Security Number ☐☐☐-☐☐-☐☐☐☐

Name (please print) ☐☐☐☐☐☐☐☐☐☐

Last

☐☐☐☐☐☐☐☐☐☐

Given Name and Initial

Documents which will be converted by subsequent manual data entry should be designed to aid efficient and error-free entry. For example, data items that are to be entered by keying should be clearly identified (with boxes or small numbers, etc.) and should be on the document in the order in which they are to be entered. Documents to be read by optical scanning should be designed to meet the requirements of the equipment. Background boxes and lines, optical-scanning guide characters, etc., may be necessary.

The use of turnaround documents is a variation on the first two methods. A turnaround document is included with a transaction as a document to be returned as part of the completion of the transaction. It may be machine-readable or may require conversion as does any nonreadable document. For example, a gasoline credit card billing will usually contain an optically readable statement or a punched card portion to be returned with the payment (Figure 8-1). This turnaround document, which represents a record of the payment, is an input to the processing of receipts. No further data input is required to record the payment unless there is a partial payment. The use of turnaround documents is very important in business data processing because much of the data from the transaction is needed for subsequent, related transactions.

In many applications a receipt or other document is prepared by a machine

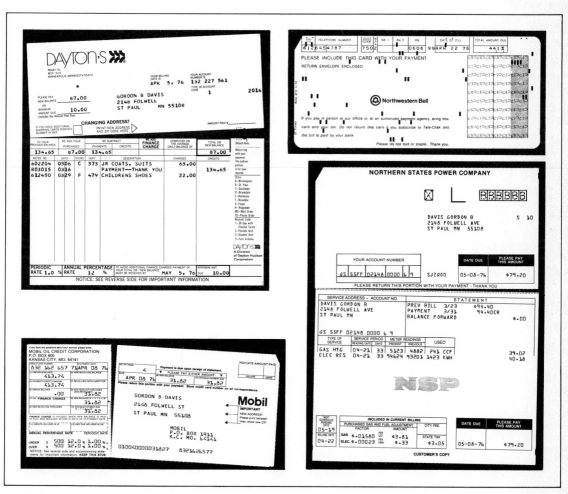

FIGURE 8-1 Examples of turnaround documents used in customer billing.

which can also produce a machine-readable record of the transaction for subsequent processing by the computer. For example, the checkout counter at a discount department store may produce a register tape for the customer and a machine record for sales analysis and inventory accounting.

Computer terminals are being used extensively both to capture data for subsequent processing and to enter data for immediate processing. Terminals can be used for direct entry to the computer or can be used offline with data being accumulated for subsequent input to the computer. The major advantage of terminals is the logic capabilities that are available for assisting the person performing data entry and for validating data while it is being entered.

Transcribing to Machine-readable Form

Transcribing to machine-readable form is required for original documents and turnaround documents that are not machine-readable. The methods of transcribing (using devices to be explained later in the chapter) are:

1 Keypunching into cards

2 Keyboard to disk, diskette, or tape

3 Key entry at a terminal

4 Recoding in a machine-readable form (such as typing in a machine-readable type)

Transcribing data in machine-readable form usually requires some verification to ensure the correctness of the conversion. There are a variety of techniques, a common method being a duplicate keying of critical data fields for comparison with the original keying. Differences indicate an error (in original keying or rekeying) to be corrected.

Data Validation

In addition to checking the correctness of transcribing, data needs to be validated for correctness. As noted in Chapter 3, this vital function can be performed during data preparation, prior to input, or during input. In some applications, validation can be a visual review of the input data; in all cases, logic validation tests should be performed on the data before it enters the processing run. Such logic validation requires the logical capabilities of a computer program. For data entry methods using devices with stored logic capabilities (keyboard to disk and terminals), the data validation may be performed during original recording or during conversion activities, depending on how the application is designed. An early detection of errors by data validation during data preparation not only provides cleaner data, but also improves the effectiveness of error correction processes (Figure 8-2).

Conversion to Input Medium

In some cases of data preparation, the existence of data in a machine-readable form does not mean that it is ready for input to processing runs. The data is often converted to another computer storage medium. In many cases, documents en-

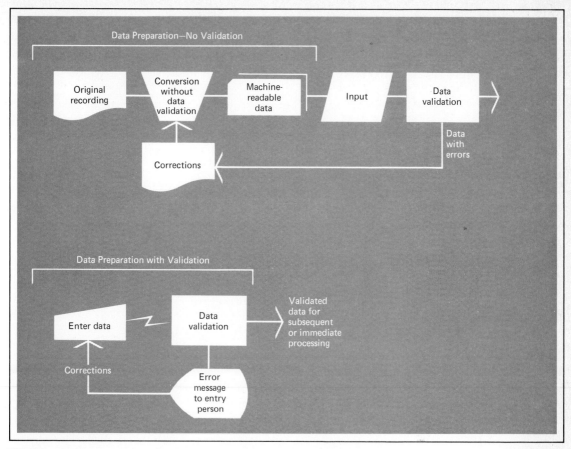

FIGURE 8-2 Examples of data validation during and subsequent to data entry.

coded for optical reading and documents encoded with magnetic ink characters are not input directly into the computer but are read by a special reader which may write the data onto magnetic tape or magnetic disk for subsequent input rather than input directly to processing. Paper tape, small magnetic tape cartridges, and diskettes are sometimes used as input from terminals, but in the typical data processing situation, data on these media requires conversion to a higher-speed input medium such as regular magnetic tape or magnetic disk storage.

Batching for Input For considerations relating to processing efficiency and control over completeness and correctness of processing, it is frequently desirable to assemble batches of transactions. As explained in Chapter 3, one major approach to processing, periodic processing of batches of data, is referred to as "batch processing." The batching of data, if batch processing is to be performed, occurs during the data preparation phase. It can be performed at two points, depending on the data entry technology being used (Figure 8-3):

1 After recording on documents but prior to conversion activities.

2 After terminal entry. (Terminal entry, if connected directly to the computer, allows immediate processing, but transactions can also be entered and batched for subsequent processing.)

Alternatives in Data Preparation Design The discussion of data preparation activities has described several alternatives in data preparation. Two major sets of alternatives are dependent on the type of processing:

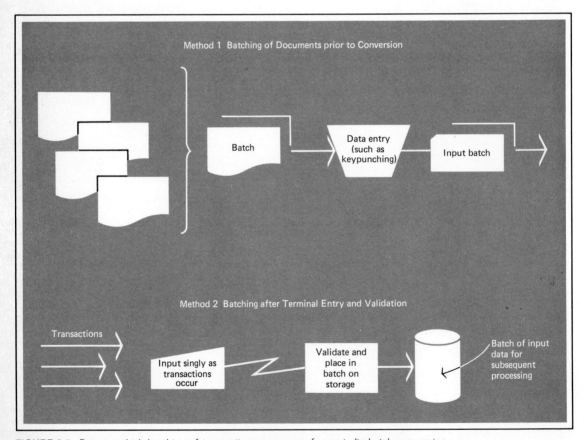

FIGURE 8-3 Point at which batching of transactions may occur for periodic batch processing.

Type of processing	Data entry
1 Immediate online processing	Entry of transactions as they occur via a terminal with validation. No batching, no conversion to machine-readable form, and no conversion to input medium activities.
2 Periodic processing	Alternatives: (a) Input via a terminal with validation and batching for subsequent processing. (b) Document record with batching before conversion to machine-readable form. Validation dependent on conversion device. Machine-readable records produced by entry or recording device. (c) Document in machine-readable form. Conversion to input medium. Validation dependent on conversion device.

The data entry devices to implement these alternatives can be classified into offline devices for converting data originally recorded in a form that was not machine-readable, offline devices for original data recording in machine-readable form, and terminal data entry devices.

Offline Data Transcription Devices

The three devices described in this section are used to transcribe data originally recorded in batches of documents that are not machine-readable to equivalent data in machine-readable form. In addition to the card punch, keyboard to disk, etc., and magnetic ink devices described here, the optical typing method described in the next section can be used in a data transcribing mode.

Card Punches and Verifiers   Although it is being replaced in many new systems, the most commonly used data entry device is still the keydriven card punch. It is estimated that there are about one-half million of these units in service. The majority produce traditional 80-column Hollerith cards, but there are a significant number of keypunches for 96-column cards.

In data entry using keypunches, the keypunch operator is given a batch of documents from which one or more items per document are keypunched into cards. The punching is based on instructions as to how the data is to be entered. After the batch of documents has been keyed, the punched cards and documents are given to a second operator who rekeys the entire set of data for each card or may rekey only important data items. The verifier (or card punch in verifier mode) detects differences between the two punchings. The data for each card for which there is an error is rekeyed and reverified.

There are three generations of keypunches in terms of the technology used in the devices:

1   The pre-1960 keypunches with a restricted keyboard. The IBM 026 is the major punch of this era.

2   The 1960s keypunch with an expanded keyboard and improved technology. The IBM 029 is the major example.

3   The 1970s keypunch with buffered input before punching. The UNIVAC 1700 and 1800 series and the IBM 129 are examples (Figure 8-4).

The buffered keypunch has a small memory called a "buffer" into which the data is keyed. After all the contents of the card have been entered, the card is punched with data from the buffer. By using two such buffers, the current card contents may be keyed in while the preceding card is being punched. Also, since there is no punching until the entire card contents have been keyed, errors may be corrected in the data still in the buffer. The most recent models of keypunches have added limited processing capabilities for data validation.

An evaluation of the unbuffered and buffered keypunch characteristics suggests that for infrequent use of the keypunch or use of the keypunch by untrained, occasional users, an unbuffered keypunch is satisfactory. But when a modest volume of records is to be transcribed to machine-readable form, a buffered unit should be selected because of the increased speed (say, 50 percent greater).

Keyboard to Disk, Diskette, or Tape   The basic idea of the keyboard to disk, diskette, or magnetic tape devices is to record data on a magnetic medium rather than on punched cards. These devices are generally an alternative or a replacement to card punch and verifier (Figure 8-4). In all cases, these devices offer less noise and greater key entry speeds than is possible in keypunching of cards.

The keyboard to magnetic tape (or keytape) was first introduced in 1964. Although there are existing installations, few new keytape units are being installed because of the superiority of keydisk systems. In keytape units, data is keyed by an operator and recorded on magnetic tape. The magnetic tape allows backspacing, correction, etc. Depending on the model, the magnetic tape can be a regular tape or a cassette. The regular tape can be used directly as input; it is necessary to pool the cassettes and create an input tape.

The key to diskette unit (first introduced by IBM in 1973 as the IBM 3740 data entry system) uses an 8-in.-round floppy or flexible disk to record keyed data (Figure 8-4). The diskette holds a maximum of 1898 records containing up to

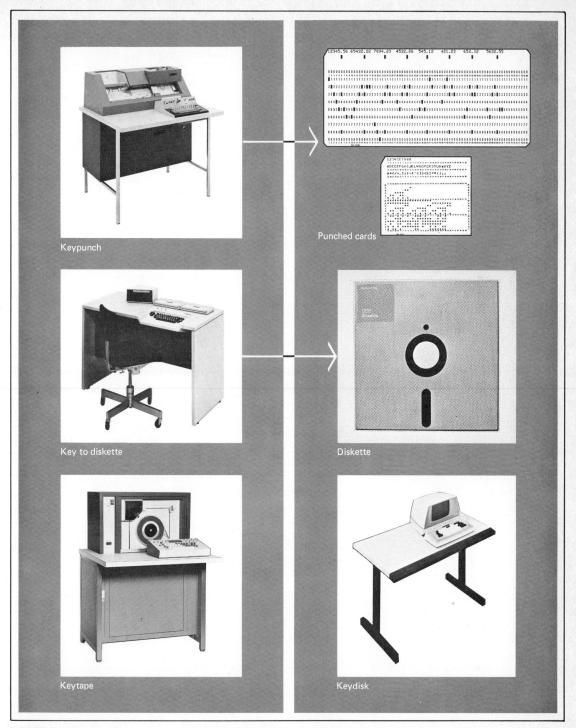

FIGURE 8-4 Keyboard data entry equipment for conversion of recorded data to machine-readable form.

243,000 characters of data. This is the equivalent of 1900 or more punched cards. It is permanently housed in a plastic envelope, is quite rugged, and can be mailed since it weighs only 8 oz. The cost of a diskette (about $8) is greater than the cards (say, $3) it replaces, but the diskette is reusable. Also, the data can be corrected on the diskette during verification. The data entry system using the diskette has a small six-line CRT display to show status information and to display the data being entered. Simple data editing and data validation functions can be performed while data is input. The diskettes must be transferred by a separate device to a regular magnetic tape for input to processing.

The keydisk system is currently the most popular keypunch replacement device. In a keydisk system, a minicomputer processor manages input from several key stations. Data from each station is recorded on a magnetic disk shared by several key stations. The operators at the different stations may work on different jobs at the same time; the different input formats are controlled by the shared processor. Each operator has a visual display unit for display of messages, formats, input data, etc. The minicomputer can be used for rather extensive data editing and data validation techniques. When the batch of data is complete on the disk, it can be validated by rekeying data and comparing the second keying with the data fields on the disk. The batch is transferred from the disk by the minicomputer to a magnetic tape for use in input.

In comparison with keypunching, if there is a substantial volume of data entry and a variety of input formats, and if validation procedures can be applied, a shared processor keydisk system is probably most effective. Data entry rates are generally 50 percent greater than standard keypunches and slightly higher than buffered keypunches.

Magnetic Ink Character Recognition (MICR) Encoders The encoding of documents with magnetic ink characters is limited almost exclusively to banking and especially to turnaround documents such as checks. The magnetic ink characters use a standard type form accepted by the banking community. The standard characters, consisting of numbers plus some special characters, are visually readable by banking personnel. The magnetic ink characters identifying account number, bank number, and check number are precoded; the amount is encoded on each check in a batch using a magnetic disk ink encoder, a manually operated keyboard device (Figure 8-5). Batches of checks are sorted by a special sorter and read and transferred to magnetic tape (or disk) by a special reader. The reader senses the magnetic pattern formed by the characters. A character can be read even if crossed over, creased, or otherwise made illegible for visual reading.

Offline Recording of Data in Machine-readable Form

Many applications require a document that is readable by both humans and machines. Two major methods will produce such a document with a single recording of the data: (1) optical character and optical mark encoding and (2)

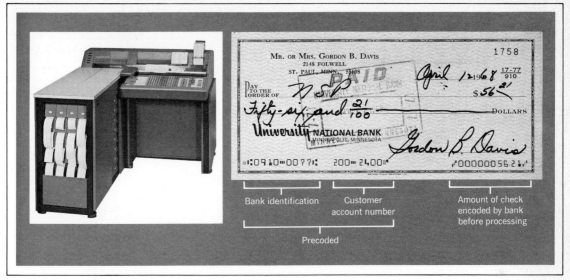

FIGURE 8-5 Magnetic ink character recognition equipment.

devices which produce computer-readable data as a by-product of the recording of the transaction and making the necessary transaction document (point-of-sale devices are an example).

Optical Character and Optical Mark Encoding

Encoding for optical character recognition (OCR) at data entry may involve one of three major methods (Figure 8-6):

1 Typing data in a machine-readable type font
2 Handprinting characters
3 Making marks in designated areas on a document

The data encoded in optical characters is read by equipment which either writes the data on magnetic tape for input to processing or inputs directly to a computer.

The typing of data in a machine-readable form may make use of a regular typewriter font, but typically a special optical font is used. The data to be converted to machine-readable form is typed, usually on special input forms which simplify the reading of the data. In fact, forms design is a critical factor in most OCR applications. Readers may be designed to read a single font or multiple fonts.

Handprinting of characters is a limited method of data entry. It requires discipline in handprinting legible characters and is therefore most useful in terms of small amounts of input. For example, a turnaround document may be complete except for partial payments, and these may be handprinted before the document is read (see NSP bill in Figure 8-6). The handprinting must be done in premarked areas, one space being marked for each character.

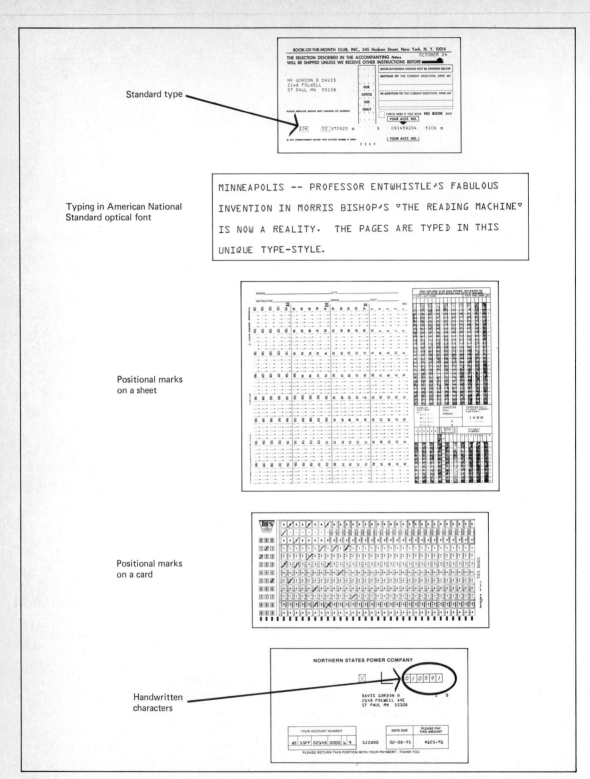

Standard type

Typing in American National Standard optical font

MINNEAPOLIS -- PROFESSOR ENTWHISTLE'S FABULOUS INVENTION IN MORRIS BISHOP'S ᵛTHE READING MACHINEᵛ IS NOW A REALITY. THE PAGES ARE TYPED IN THIS UNIQUE TYPE-STYLE.

Positional marks on a sheet

Positional marks on a card

Handwritten characters

FIGURE 8-6 Documents which can be read using optical scanning.

Optical mark encoding makes use of predefined areas (say, small squares) which are marked with a slash or other sign to indicate the value selected. These require a relatively simple technology to read compared with optical type font or handwritten characters. The optical mark technique is most appropriate for simple inputs such as answers to multiple-choice examinations or meter readings.

There are multimedia systems available which have optical scanning plus key entry equipment with a visual display unit. Documents are read optically and displayed, and the keyboard is used to add more data or to enter data not readable by the optical scanning. This combination is a significant technological development.

In all optical reading machines, the characters to be read are scanned by some kind of photoelectric device. The photoelectric cells convert the symbols on the document into an analog or digital representation that is analyzed by a recognition unit. The recognition unit matches patterns from the scanner against internally stored reference patterns. Patterns which cannot be identified cause the document to be rejected. There are a number of different methods for recognition. Some of the more common are:

1 *Matrix matching* This method of total character recognition compares individual elements of the scanned character with the elements of all characters which can be identified by the reader. A character is recognized when it matches exactly or quite closely one of the reference patterns. Any type font may be programmed.

2 *Feature or stroke analysis* A character is recognized on the basis of the stroke or line formation of each character. The technique requires a special printing font.

3 *Curve tracing* In this method, especially suited for recognizing handwritten characters which vary in size and shape, a spiraling spot of light follows the outline of a character. Characters are identified by observations as to vertical lines, horizontal lines, etc.

Reading speeds range from, say, 70 to 2400 characters per second. Reader reliability is important. Two measures of reliability are the reject and error rates. The reject rate is the percentage of documents (currently running from 2 to 10 percent) which the reader cannot read. The reject rate can vary considerably depending on the quality control exercised over the form, the recording of the data, etc. The error rate (currently less than 1 percent) is the percentage of documents on which a character has been incorrectly identified. Reentry of characters or data rejected is generally done offline but may use the multimedia keyboard system mentioned earlier.

Optical character recognition equipment is sufficiently expensive that an installation must have a volume range of over, say, 7000 input documents per day which could be read optically (roughly equivalent to the work of six to eight keypunch operators) before such equipment is likely to be economical. Optical mark equipment is fairly low in cost but is generally applicable for simple recording of quantities or questionnaire results. If there is a large volume and the source documents can be made suitable for optical scanning, OCR should be considered. If even parts of each document can be read optically, a multimedia optical reader/keyentry system should be evaluated.

Point-of-Sale Devices

Point-of-sale (POS) devices are used primarily by department stores and supermarkets for data collection while the sale is being entered. The devices have memory and logic processing capabilities. In the case of a department store, the POS device accepts entry of customer account number, product code, etc. The devices accumulate product sales data, customer billing data, etc., and may communicate with a central computer for credit checking. Other data is generally recorded on tape for later input to processing. The supermarket POS systems read product data by scanning a product code printed on every item. The register is connected to a minicomputer which contains prices for all items. The price plus product data is used to produce a register tape for each customer. Sales and inventory data are accumulated by the computer (Figure 8-7).

Point of sale is very useful but adds cost to the recording equipment. The advantages of input validation, automated pricing, credit verification, inventory control, etc., may be sufficient to justify the added cost. The trend is clearly toward use of this type of equipment at point of sale in large supermarkets and large department stores.

Keyboard to Paper Tape Devices

Paper tape is a very limited purpose input/output medium. It is produced as a by-product of input in a variety of business devices such as cash registers, accounting machines, and adding machines. Teletype machines can prepare paper

Supermarket system

Department store terminal

FIGURE 8-7 Data entry using point-of-sale devices. (*Courtesy of International Business Machines Corporation.*)

tape while they are in offline mode. The paper tape is then used as a higher than manual speed input for online transmission of data. This medium consists of a paper tape punched with 10 characters per inch (Figure 8-8). Speeds for reading range from 350 to 2000 characters per second (with lower speeds from typewriter attachments). Both eight-channel and five-channel codes are in use. In concept, paper tape can be thought of as being a continuous punched card. This presents advantages such as the fact that no individual record can be lost or put out of sequence because all are on the continuous tape. However, paper tape is more difficult to correct and is less flexible for sorting, etc.

Terminals

Data may be entered into computer processing through terminals. The devices used for terminal data entry can be classified in several ways:

1 Nonintelligent terminals
2 Intelligent (programmable) terminals
3 Remote batch terminal

The terminals can be connected to a computer either directly by cables, if near the computer, or by data communications; or the terminals may be used to accumulate data for subsequent input. The latter option of accumulating data is especially feasible if the terminal has programmable logic and a magnetic recording medium such as diskette or tape cassette. There is a trend toward the use of microprocessors in the terminals (as an alternative to hard-wiring) to implement terminal control for data communications.

Reel of paper tape

FIGURE 8-8 Punched paper tape using American National Standard code for information interchange (ASCII).

Terminals are rapidly growing as significant elements in data processing configurations. Costs have continued to decrease (cost is about $1000 to $4000 per terminal). It is estimated that there are over 2 million terminals of all types in operation. Terminals are used in connection with data communications to put the input next to the point of origin and to put the output next to the user. This has advantages because data can be validated at entry rather than later and corrections made by the originator. Output can be received directly by the user, reducing the output distribution delay. Terminals allow the computer files to be interrogated at locations remote from the computer. Terminals must be used in immediate processing but can also be used for periodic processing.

Intelligent and Nonintelligent Terminals

The intelligent terminal is also known as a "programmable terminal" or a "logic terminal." The intelligent terminal essentially contains a small computer processor and a fairly small memory. This means that a program can be stored in it to direct the operation of the terminal, validate input, direct communications with a larger computer, etc. Because the intelligent terminal contains a program and can perform many data input validation tasks, it is possible to enter data via an intelligent terminal, validate it for correctness, and then to either transmit the data for immediate processing or record it for subsequent processing. The trend is toward at least some logic in terminals.

A nonintelligent or nonprogrammable terminal must be connected to a computer which accepts data, sends back messages, etc. Input is either processed immediately or stored by the computer for subsequent processing. Teletypes and typewriters used as time-sharing terminals are nonintelligent terminals.

Visual Display Units and Teleprinters

Terminals generally have a keyboard by which to enter data. The terminals may have a magnetic tape cassette (or perhaps a diskette) for recording input or output. The output technology may be a visual display, a teleprinter, or both (Figure 8-9).

Visual display units may be designed for alphanumeric display only, or they may be designed for graphic output as well (to be described later in this chapter). Most terminals are limited to alphanumeric display because of the extra cost of graphic capabilities (several times more expensive). Visual display units are frequently referred to as CRTs because all but a few visual display units utilize the dominant cathode-ray tube technology. Alternative display technologies are light-emitting diodes (LEDs) such as those used in calculators, plasma, and liquid crystal. The most common technique for forming the characters on the CRT screen is the dot matrix. A typical dot matrix consists of 35 dots (seven dots high by five dots wide). The dots required to form a character are displayed. An alternative technique uses a stroke method in which short, straight lines are drawn.

Some capabilities which may be found in the commonly used alphanumeric display terminal are:

1 Control of a cursor which defines where data is to be entered.

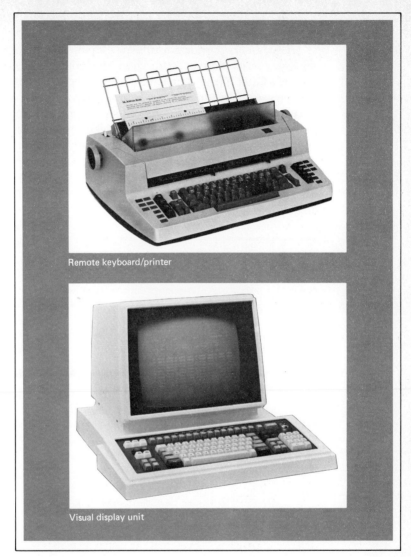

Remote keyboard/printer

Visual display unit

FIGURE 8-9 Alphanumeric terminals.

2 Editing to insert a character in a line, delete a character in a line, and insert or delete a line.

3 Character or field blinking to draw the operator's attention to vital data.

4 Brightness control to highlight some data.

It is common practice to have a format displayed on the screen to guide input (much like a paper form). This requires the format to be protected so that it is not altered by the keyed-in data. Only the filled-in data is transmitted, not the formats.

The formats may be received from the computer or from attached cassettes or diskettes.

Teleprinters provide a hard copy output. The printing mechanism generally employs a serial printing approach in which one character is printed at a time. A few use a faster line-at-a-time technology. The printing technique may be impact or nonimpact. The printing may be full-character or a character image formed by a matrix of dots. Full-character serial impact printing can generally achieve speeds of 10 to 30 characters per second; for higher speeds, it is necessary to use alternative impact technologies such as the matrix printer or alternative nonimpact methods in which the image is produced by an electrothermal (heat) technique on special paper.

The display terminal and teleprinter terminal each have advantages and disadvantages, as noted below:

Basis for comparison	Comparative advantage of visual display unit versus teleprinter
Cost	Teleprinters can be obtained at lower cost, but average cost of display units is dropping.
Output speed	Displays are much faster. Typical visual display output is 300 to 1200 characters per second compared with 10 to 30 characters a second for teleprinters.
Editing, data entry, and formatting	Displays frequently provide extensive capabilities; teleprinters do not.
Reliability	Both are reliable, but visual displays are totally electronic and therefore inherently more reliable.
Output medium	The teleprinter provides a permanent, hard copy; visual displays do not.

These comparisons suggest that the visual display is superior for input or retrieval where speed of output editing and formatting are important, but the teleprinter is superior for applications requiring hard-copy output.

Remote Job Entry Terminals

A remote job entry (RJE) terminal uses a remote batch terminal that groups data into blocks for transmission to a computer. A remote job entry terminal is a remote batch terminal that can initiate (from a remote site) the execution of an application by a computer at another location, transmit the data for the program, and probably receive back and print the results of the application program. The RJE terminal therefore typically consists of a remote console, input device, and output device (Figure 8-10). It has program storage capability to control input communications,

FIGURE 8-10 Remote job entry terminal. (*Courtesy of Data 100 Corporation.*)

output, etc. It may, in fact, be a small computer that can be used as either a job entry terminal or a standalone computer.

Transfer of Data between Input/Output Devices and the Computer

Two major types of input and output can be identified—the input and output from devices directly connected to the computer (often called "peripherals") and input/output from remote devices over data communications facilities. This section describes input and output from peripherals. The peripheral devices are described later in the chapter except for secondary storage peripherals, which are explained in the next chapter.

Input/Output Cycle An input operation for a peripheral device begins with a program instruction from the central processor which sends a command to the input device to read a record. Reading takes place (frequently by having an input medium such as punched card or magnetic tape move through the input device). Information is read and converted to the code used by the computer system. The coded information is transmitted to the internal storage and stored in memory locations assigned to hold the input record. The data is then available for use by the processing instructions.

An output operation is essentially the reverse of the input procedure. The data to be written is arranged by program instructions in a set of storage locations assigned for this purpose. An instruction to perform output causes the data from the output storage locations to be copied and transmitted to the input/output device which writes it on an output medium.

An input or output device is directed by a control unit. The control unit decodes the input/output command from the central processor and effects operation of the device or devices. Other functions are coding, decoding, and checking of data transmitted between the CPU and the device. The connection between the central processor and the control unit is generally via a channel which is essentially equipment for managing data transfer between the central processor and one or more input/output device control units.

The cycle of activity for an input thus has a sequence approximately as follows (the output cycle is similar):

1 The computer decodes program instructions to read the contents of one block (also called a "physical record"), using a specified input device.

2 A signal is set to the control unit for the device which starts the device in operation. If the device is busy or inoperable, an interrupt or conditional transfer of control is executed, depending on the way the program is written.

3 The device reads the contents of the physical record and encodes it into electrical signals.

4 The control unit codes the data signals and checks them.

5 The data is transmitted to the specified storage locations in main memory via a channel.

6 A signal is transmitted to the central processor that the input operation is completed.

Major input and output design considerations are a result of the difference between input/output speeds and internal processing speeds. To provide a rough understanding of the speed of input/output devices relative to internal speed, a high-speed card reader reads at, say, 1200 cards per minute or 20 cards per second. This is one card every 50,000 microseconds. An average medium-size computer is able to execute from 5000 to 15,000 instructions in the same period of time. The efficiency of the system is therefore increased if the input and output operations can be overlapped or performed simultaneously with computation.

Data Channels Data channels are the method by which the slow input/output operations can be kept from delaying the internal processing. A typical data processing procedure consists of three phases—input, processing, and output. Data is read from one or more devices, the data is processed, and the results are written using one or more output devices. In the absence of any provisions for simultaneous operation of CPU and input/output units, the CPU would be idle a good part of the time (Figure 8-11). By the use of data channels, simultaneous operations by input/output devices and the central processor are allowed (Figure 8-12).

A data channel consists of hardware circuitry which controls the movement of data between the primary storage and the input or output devices. It can be thought

FIGURE 8-11 Processing cycle with no simultaneous operations.

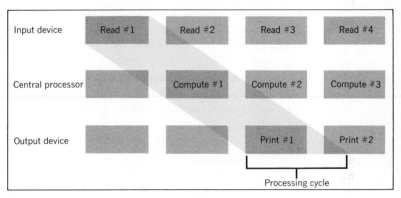

FIGURE 8-12 Processing cycle with simultaneous operations.

of as a separate, small processing unit used only for managing the transfer of data. Each channel has facilities for accepting input/output instructions, addressing input/output devices, obtaining its control information from storage, directing and buffering information transfer, and performing similar functions necessary for an orderly transfer of data. Normally the channel is connected not to an input/output device itself but to the control unit which matches the channel interface (connection) to the internal requirements of the device (Figure 8-13).

The channel is activated by a program instruction which identifies the channel, device, and other data to control the operation. After the CPU has activated the channel and identified the command word, it is free to continue other processing. Once started, the channel will control the quantity and destination of the data transmitted between main storage and the input/output devices without further

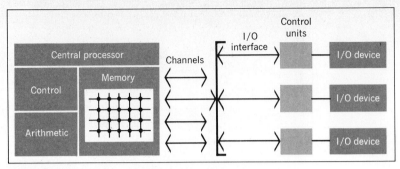

FIGURE 8-13 Use of channels for input and output.

supervision by the central processing unit. Several channels may be operating simultaneously because each is an independent unit.

Channels use an interrupt procedure. When the data transfer is complete, the channel interrupts the central processor to indicate completion of the transfer. The channel will also interrupt processing if an error condition is detected in the input/output device or channel. When the interrupt occurs, the central processor halts processing, examines the channel status, takes appropriate action (such as an error-handling routine) if there is an error, or provides a new channel command word if the interrupt signals the completion of the previous command and there is more input/output to be performed. The simultaneous operation of several channels means the possibility of a number of interrupts occurring simultaneously and other conflicts among the channels. These conflicts are handled by a pre-established priority procedure and the setting up of a waiting line of requests to be serviced.

Although some channels, referred to as "selector channels," can service only one device, it is not always necessary to have a separate data channel for each separate device to be operated simultaneously. A high-speed device will monopolize a channel (sometimes termed a "burst" mode), but slower devices like a card reader or printer can share a channel. The shared channel, frequently called a "multiplexor channel," has a number of subchannels, each of which can sustain an input/output operation. In this mode, sets of data from several devices are interleaved together in the channel. The channel keeps track of these different segments and sends each to its proper destination (Figure 8-14).

The number and capacity of channels supplied with a computer are important elements affecting the capabilities of the computer system. The number of channels is important because this determines the number of devices which can be operated simultaneously. The capacity of a channel is significant because some devices provide a very high rate of data transfer and therefore need a high-capacity channel.

Punched Card Input and Output

Although there is increased use of input, through alternatives such as terminals and keydisk systems, the most common input medium for introducing source data into computer processing is the punched card. Cards are read by a card reader and

FIGURE 8-14 Modes for channel operation.

punched by a card punch. These two units may be housed in the same cabinet or separately.

The reading of cards requires the following steps:

1 The cards with data punched in them are placed in the read hopper of the card reader.

2 On a command from the computer, a punched card is moved past two separate sensing stations (although some readers use only one).

3 The configurations of punches and no-punches are read by the two stations and are compared to detect read errors.

4 The configuration of punches and no-punches is converted to internal computer code and transmitted to the computer for storage.

5 The card is deposited in an output stacker.

Card readers may use two different methods of sensing the existence of punches—photoelectric cells or wire brushes. In the photoelectric-type reader, punches are detected by photoelectric cells activated by light passing through the punch holes. In the brush-type reader, the card is passed between a wire brush and a metal roller. If there is a punch, the brush makes electrical contact with the roller, thereby sensing a punch. The input/output control systems will normally handle tests for off-normal conditions in the equipment or error conditions and provide operator messages. Examples of these conditions are read error, input hopper out of cards, full output stacker, and card jam.

The punching of cards under computer control requires an online punch.

Most punches punch a row or column at a time as the card moves under a set of punch dies. Once punched, the card is moved into an output stacker. Card punching is normally much slower than card reading because of the additional mechanical action required.

Output Devices

The peripheral devices for output discussed in this section provide final output for human use rather than being secondary storage for subsequent processing. Output devices already described in the chapter and therefore not described here are visual display terminals, teleprinter terminals, and punched card output.

Line Printer   There are two types of high-speed printers—impact printers, which print by means of a type bar or wheel pressed against a paper and ribbon, and nonimpact printers, which form an image by chemical, photographic, or electrostatic means. Most printers in use employ the impact approach, but newer nonimpact printers using electrostatic methods offer an attractive alternative.

Several different impact printing methods are in use; the most common are the chain printer and the printer drum. In the chain printer (Figure 8-15), the print characters are mounted on a chain which moves horizontally in front of the paper. The chain may contain several sets of the print characters. As the character to be

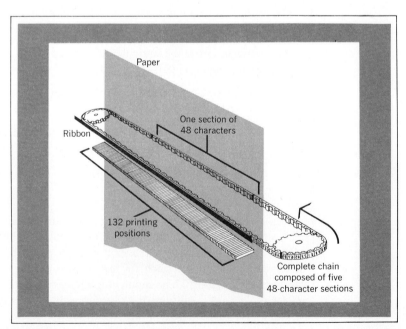

FIGURE 8-15 Print chain.

printed passes in front of each position on the paper where it is to be printed, a magnetically controlled hammer behind the paper presses the paper against the typeface to print the character. Moving one character set of the chain past the paper is thus sufficient to print a line. The entire process for printing a line takes from one-fifth to one-fiftieth of a second, depending on the speed of the printer. The chain is removable, so that more than one type face and set of special characters may be used.

The print drum method uses a metal drum with rows of characters engraved on it. During printing, the drum revolves, moving each row of characters (for example, the row containing A's) past the print hammers. The print hammer for a position is activated when a row of characters to be printed passes, and the hammer presses the paper against the drum to print the character. A somewhat uneven line is sometimes produced by this method.

The vertical spacing of the paper is frequently controlled by a plastic or paper loop on the printer (Figure 8-16), although some printers are controlled completely by program instructions. The loop contains several rows or channels. Punches in these columns designate the positioning of the paper. The tape loop control is activated by a character placed in the first position of the print line. This character is sensed, but not printed, by the printer, and it activates vertical spacing. The

FIGURE 8-16 Tape loop for vertical spacing control. (*Courtesy of International Business Machines Corporation.*)

punched tape loop will position the paper at the top of a page and at different vertical positions on the page (required, for example, by a preprinted form). The tape loop for vertical movement of printer paper is similar in concept to the tab stops for horizontal movement of the carriage on a typewriter.

The very high speed nonimpact printers use electrostatic methods (similar to a Xerox copier) on plain or specially treated paper. The image to be transmitted is prepared in different ways depending on the make—one uses a laser beam, another a set of styli, and a third a character drum and light beam. Some of the printers are for offline only, others for online use. The speeds range from 4000 to 18,000 lines per minute. The process allows forms to be added as a background to the printed output.

Graphic Display Terminal

In contrast to the alphanumeric display terminals, a graphic display terminal provides drawings as output on a screen. Almost anything that a graphic artist can draw with lines (straight or curved) can be displayed (Figure 8-17). They are used in interactive design, in presentation of data for business or engineering use, and for pictorial representations. The relatively high cost and specialized nature of the graphic terminals tend to limit their use.

FIGURE 8-17 Graphic display terminal output. (*Courtesy of Tektronix Corporation.*)

Graph Plotter   A graph plotter is a device for drawing graphs. Both plots and smooth graphs are possible. A swimsuit manufacturer, for example, uses the graph plotter to draw different size patterns based on the standard pattern of the swimsuit designer. A variety of plotting techniques are used. Figure 8-18 shows the use of the graph plotter for plotting data.

Audio Response   A stockbroker, wanting the latest quotation for a security listed by the New York Stock Exchange, dials a special code number. The response is immediate as a voice speaks the quotation over the telephone. The entire transaction is handled by a computer using a voice response unit. The computer interprets the input code number, obtains the data from storage, and transmits the answer to the audio response unit. This unit selects, from a magnetic drum, words and phrases of prerecorded vocabulary which then form a spoken reply. The reply is limited to a relatively small number of words and phrases, but the inquiries and responses can make use of an ordinary telephone. The response unit is suited for applications such as credit inquiry and inventory status where the reply vocabulary can be standardized.

Computer Output Microfilm   Computer output microfilm (COM) prepares data on microfilm, either as a roll or as a microfiche. In a common technology the COM device displays data on a CRT screen, and this screen is exposed to microfilm (Figure 8-19). Other methods of exposing the film are also used. At speeds up to 30,000 lines per minute, the rate of recording is faster than printing—about 25 to 50 times faster. The microfilm is small and easily stored. About 2000 frames are stored on a roll. It is read with a microfilm reader. A computer-generated index is used to locate the proper roll or microfiche and to find the right frame. The cost of the microfilm for a page of output is only one-half to one-eighth the cost of a sheet of printer paper. A forms overlay may be used to print headings, lines, etc., to make the output more readable. Additional microfilm copies may be made at very low cost.

The COM equipment is fairly expensive, and so small users who wish to use it take data files to a service center offering COM processing. Costs and processing difficulties are being reduced, so this output method is likely to receive much use by medium and large data processing centers which have applications with extensive printouts needed largely for reference purposes. Such printouts are bulky, take large storage space, and are difficult to access. Archival storage of data files required to meet legal or government regulations is another use.

Data Communications

Data communication is employed to reduce the time required to move data from a point of origin to the computer and from the computer to a point of use. It reduces the time requirements from the hours or days involved in mail or messenger

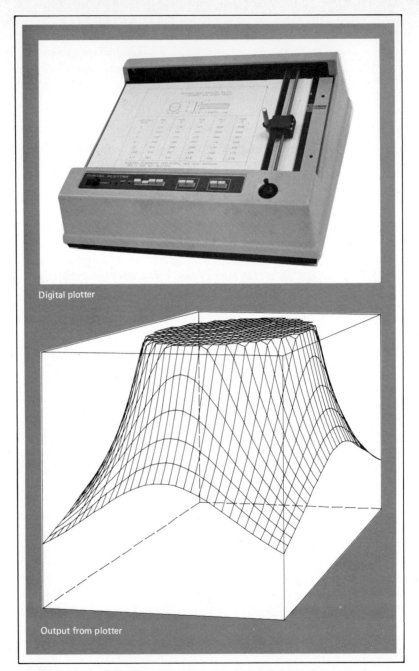

Digital plotter

Output from plotter

FIGURE 8-18 Graph plotter and its output. (*Courtesy of Tektronix Corporation.*)

transportation to the few seconds or minutes for electrical transmission. Data communication should be considered whenever the benefit from this immediate movement of data is expected to exceed the extra cost of the communication.

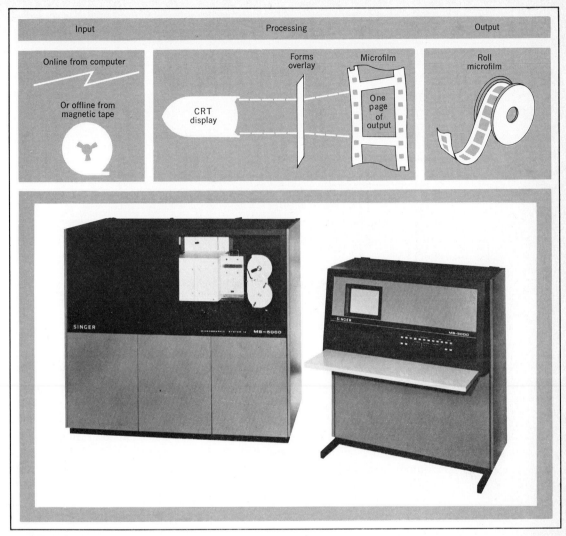

FIGURE 8-19 Computer output microfilm. (*Courtesy of Singer Company.*)

Data Transmission   Data is transmitted by an electrical signal or wave form which is defined by the strength of the signal (*amplitude*) and its duration in time (*phase*). The *frequency* of a wave form is the number of times the form is repeated during a specified interval. These three characteristics are diagrammed in Figure 8-20. The signal is an analog or electrical equivalent of the communication input. If the basic shape of a wave form is known, a few measurements at selected time intervals (in other words, a sampling) provide the receiving instrument with enough data to identify the signals. In order to sample during the interval when a bit is transmitted, the receiving terminal must be synchronized with the sending terminal. The standard unit of signaling speed is a "baud," which is one pulse or code element per second.

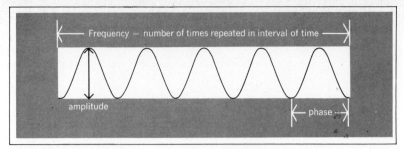

FIGURE 8-20 Diagram of waveform.

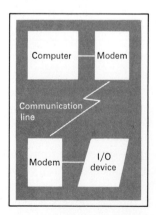

FIGURE 8-21 ASCII code.

The most important code used in data communications is the American Standard Code for Information Interchange (ASCII) (Figure 8-21).

A transmission medium is usually separated into many independent bands or data paths, each consisting of a range of frequencies assigned to it. Band width is an important consideration in data communications. This term refers to the range of frequencies accommodated within a band on a transmission medium. There is a device to convert the constant-level direct-current pulses of the computer equipment into signals suitable for transmission and to perform the reverse process for the receiving terminal. The conversion is called "modulation" and "demodulation." The device is referred to as a "modem" or "data set."

An electrical signal must be repeated or regenerated at intervals along the transmission medium to replenish its strength. The typical analog signal is amplified in whatever shape it is received. In other words, distortions are carried along the line. The newest technology is for a method of regeneration using digital logic which analyzes the signal received and creates a new, clean signal to send along the line. The communications network using this method is called a "digital transmission network." Because of the techniques used, transmission speed and quality are improved. Also, a modem is not required.

Communications Facilities

Some of the types of communications facilities are telephone and telegraph cables, radio, microwave, and satellite. Although under certain circumstances an organization may install its own communications facilities, most communication utilizes the facilities of the public telephone and telegraph companies, the largest of these in the United States being the American Telephone and Telegraph Company (Bell System) and Western Union. There are specialized common carriers which, in certain locations, offer only data communications facilities.

There are three modes of operation for communication facilities—simplex, half duplex, and full duplex.

Mode	Description
Simplex	Communication in only one direction. Used, for example, for a remote device which receives but does not send.
Half duplex	Communications in both directions, but in only one direction at a time.
Full duplex	Communications in both directions at the same time.

Service can be divided into three classes on the basis of band width. Band width determines the maximum transmission speed because the width of a band affects the frequency range that can be accommodated, and a high-frequency state provides for faster communication. The three classes of band width therefore represent three classes of capacity.

Class	Description
Narrow band (low speed)	Communication facilities capable of transmitting data in the range up to 300 bits per second. Typical speeds are 45, 57, 75, and 150 bits per second depending on service used. The Western Union TWX/Telex falls into this class.
Voice grade (medium	Channels used for human voice communications. Speeds range from 600 to 4800 bits

speed)	per second, although some higher speeds can be obtained.
Broad band (high speed)	Communication facilities having a higher band width than voice band width and therefore used for communication involving high data-transfer rates, say, 20,000 to 500,000 bits per second.

The services available to a user from the communications companies include leased lines or public switched lines (the term "lines" commonly refers to all types of communications facilities, even though they may use nonwire methods such as microwave). Leased lines provide users with a specific communications path dedicated to their use only. The switched line (also termed "dial-up"), on the other hand, provides access to the communications network. For the switched line, the path of connections and routing of a message may vary from use to use because the automatic switching equipment in the network selects a path from the many available connections and lines when the connection is dialed. The leased line is more expensive, but its quality is known, and it is available for use at any time. The switched line is less expensive, but it must be connected for each use (through dialing), and the quality of the connection may vary considerably from time to time.

The volume of data transmitted by a single terminal is never high enough to utilize the capacity of a voice-grade line. If several terminals are in use, they can share a single line through the use of a multiplexor. There are various approaches to multiplexing, but essentially the multiplexor divides the line into small segments and arranges the simultaneous transmission of data from a number of devices. A multiplexor at the receiving end reverses the process.

A relatively new concept in data communications services is a value-added network (VAN), also called "packet switching." Users of the service transmit data to a collection point where a minicomputer assembles the data into one or more segments (packets). An address for the destination is attached to each packet. Packets from many users going to diverse locations are transmitted through a high-quality leased line to another minicomputer which transmits each packet to its destination, after stripping off the address, etc., used in the switching. In other words, many users share a high-quality line. The concept can be extended to a network of lines.

Processing Data Communications

The communications carrier provides the transmission facilities. When multiplexors are used, they may be provided either by the carrier or by the user. When the transmitted signal reaches the user, there must be facilities to process it such as line protocol, communications processor, telecommunications access software, and a communications monitor.

The line protocol is associated with line control. If several lines come into a single computer, there are several methods of accepting messages. One method is for the terminal to send when ready and to interrupt the central processor in order for the message to be accepted; the other approach is for the computer to poll the devices (frequently but in turn) to see if there is a message to be accepted. A message generally consists of a heading and a text. The heading defines the terminal, the transaction code, priority, identification of sender, etc. The message has information separators for start of heading, start of the text to be transmitted, end of the text, and end of the transmission. The format of messages, the characters to use as separators, the control character sequence, etc., are the line protocol. There is no single standard line protocol. IBM has proposed a single protocol to be used in all its equipment. The overall communications network design is termed SNA (system network architecture) by IBM; the protocol is called SDLC (synchronous data link control).

Communications processors are small computers which are dedicated to the handling of data communications. They are also termed "front-end processors" because they handle all data communications functions, relieving the central processor of message control activities such as polling, character and message assembly, data code conversion, message editing, error control, message buffering and queuing, and message switching. Such activities can overload the central processor but can be handled by a small, but fast, minicomputer designed for the function. Most systems with significant data communications use a front-end processor.

Software packages, called "telecommunications access methods," are available for sending and receiving messages from terminals, addressing and polling terminals, queuing messages, message logging, system recovery, etc. Acronyms for the IBM packages are BTAM, QTAM, TCAM, and VTAM, with AM standing for access method and T for telecommunications. Other vendors offer similar software.

The management of data communications can become quite complex as the variety of requirements and equipment expands. A specialized software system may be required to handle the data communications and to manage the interface with other software. The data communications software, called a "data communications monitor," is a comprehensive package to manage a wide range of data communications functions.

Applications of Data Communications

Five examples will illustrate the use of data communications in computer processing.

Application	Comments
Data entry	Data is entered for processing via terminals at remote locations. The input data is transmitted (immediately or in a batch during off hours) to the computer over the communications network.
Inquiry processing	Each remote location has an inquiry device connected to the central computer. An example is an online reservation system in which any agent can use a remote device to interrogate the reservation file.

Time sharing	Shared use of a computer by each user having an input/output device connected via communications lines to the central computer, discussed further in Chapter 10.
Data collection	In data collection applications, data from a remote station is transmitted to a central processing facility. An example of data collection with data communications is a system which employs recording devices on the factory floor. When beginning a job, the worker inserts a plastic identification badge and a punched job card into a data collection device in the factory. The data collection device transmits this data to a central computer facility. When the job is completed, the worker repeats the process and keys in the actual number of units produced. By this means, data on the location of each job, job time, and amount produced in the shop is made known immediately to the central computer.
Message switching	An organization which has a number of widely separated locations will normally have a communications network to handle the transmission of messages from one location to one or more other locations. An efficient method of handling this message traffic is to have two-way communication between each remote location and a central message switching center with computer switching. The switching center receives messages, stores them, and transmits them to the designated receiving terminals.

SUMMARY

Data preparation activities (also termed "data entry") record transactions. These activities largely determine the quality of the data that is input to processing.

Data recording can be in a form not readable by machine, in which case the data must be transcribed. The major devices for offline transcription are card punches, keyboard to disk, diskette, or tape, and magnetic ink character encoders. The data may be initially recorded in machine-readable form. Examples are optical character or optical mark encoding, point-of-sales devices, and keyboard to paper tape devices. Data may also be entered via terminals. The data may enter processing immediately or be batched by the terminal or by the computer for subsequent processing. The terminals may be intelligent, performing validation and other functions, or nonintelligent, in which case the computer to which they are attached performs all processing during entry. Terminals are generally of three types: visual display units, teleprinters, and remote batch terminals.

In all but the simplest data processing system, the method for buffering between the input/output unit and the central processor is the data channel which, operating independently of the central processor, manages the transfer of data between the main storage and the input/output device. The data channel is started by an instruction from the central processor, which then proceeds to other processing steps. When the channel detects an error or when it is through with the transfer, it interrupts the central processor.

The chapter discussed two devices in some detail—card reader and line printer. Other input/output devices were discussed in less detail (card punch, graphic terminal, graph plotter, audio response, and computer output microfilm). Input/output devices which are secondary storage, such as magnetic tape and magnetic disk, are discussed in the next chapter.

Data communications are an important element in systems which provide input and output from remote locations. The chapter surveyed data transmission, communication facilities, processing of data communications, and applications of data communications in computer processing.

EXERCISES

1 Define the flow of data preparation activities for the following data entry technology:
   (*a*) Data is recorded on documents and keypunched. Processing is batch (periodic).
   (*b*) Data is typed onto machine-readable forms. Processing is batch (periodic).
   (*c*) Data is recorded on paper documents. Transcription is by online terminals. Processing is batch (periodic).
   (*d*) Data is entered into an intelligent terminal which transmits data each evening to a central computer where the batch is processed.
   (*e*) Data is entered via a terminal and processed immediately.
   (*f*) Data is handwritten on documents and then retyped in optical characters.

2 How are turnaround documents used? Trace the preparation, sending, turnaround, receipt, and processing of a turnaround document in customer billing.

3 Compare keypunches with keydisk devices. Under what conditions would each be suitable?

4 Explain the advantages or disadvantages of paper tape relative to punched cards as input/output media.

5 Define the conditions which suggest the use of:
   (*a*) MICR encoding   (*b*) Optical mark encoding   (*c*) Paper tape

6 A friend borrows one of your checks with MICR coding of account numbers, crosses out your account number, and writes his own. Assuming no further action to make changes, which of the following will happen? Explain.
   (*a*) Your account will be charged.
   (*b*) His account will be charged.
   (*c*) The MICR reader will reject the check.

7 What do the following letters, abbreviations, or acronyms stand for?
   (*a*) OCR   (*c*) I/O   (*e*) CRT   (*g*) RJE
   (*b*) MICR   (*d*) ASCII   (*f*) COM

8 Describe or explain the following with respect to terminals:
   (*a*) Difference between intelligent and nonintelligent terminals
   (*b*) The characteristics for deciding whether to use a visual display or a teleprinter
   (*c*) Remote batch terminal

9 Compare nonintelligent terminals and keydisk units for entering data for subsequent batch processing.

10 How can an audio response unit deliver a different message to each inquiry (say, inquiries are for current stock quotations)?

11 How does a remote batch terminal fit into the concept of distributed processing?

12 Define the role of each of the following in the input/output cycle:
   (*a*) Interrupt   (*b*) Data channel   (*c*) Device controller

13 Fill in the following table with alternative methods or processes (not all will have three alternatives).

Item	1	2	3

(*a*) Vertical spacing of paper on printer

(*b*) Methods of accepting data communications message
(*c*) Printer mechanism for impact printing
(*d*) Sensing of punches on card reader
(*e*) Band widths in data communication
(*f*) Modes of operation for communications facilities
(*g*) Methods of optical character recognition
(*h*) Types of data communications lines

14 What difference does band width make for data communications?
15 With respect to data communications, define or explain:

(*a*) Protocol	(*e*) Packet switching
(*b*) Access method	(*f*) Band
(*c*) Communications monitor	(*g*) Interface
(*d*) Multiplexor	(*h*) Front-end computer

16 Diagram and explain the hardware and software for data communications involving:
(*a*) One terminal over a voice-grade line
(*b*) A variety of terminals at different locations
17 Under what conditions is a front-end computer desirable?
18 Describe uses for minicomputers in data preparation, input, output, and data communications.
19 An organization has large volumes of output. Describe how visual display terminals, computer output microfilm, and nonimpact printing may be used in system design to do the output.
20 Describe how a university can use optical and optical mark encoding to process grades.

Chapter

9

Secondary Storage and Computer Data Structures, Files, and Databases

Data Concepts and Data Organization
Data Items
Records
Blocks
Files
Information Structures
File Management

Secondary Storage Media and Devices
Magnetic Tape
Magnetic Disk
Other Media and Devices

File Organization for Data Processing
Sequential File Organization
Random File Organization
Indexed Random File Organization
Indexed Sequential File Organization
Selecting a File Organization

List Organizations for Information Retrieval
Simple-List Organization
Inverted-List Organization
Ring Organization

Database Concepts and Management
Schema
Database Administrator
Users and Suppliers of the Database
Data Management Systems

Sorting for File Processing

Summary

Exercises

Data must be organized in some manner in order for processing to be feasible and efficient. Data items are organized into records. A collection of related records is termed a "file." Files are created when the need for a particular collection of records is recognized. This may necessitate obtaining new data from source documents, or it may involve a selection of records from existing files. A set of logically related data files is called a "database." The creation and maintenance of files and databases is the major factor in the workload of a computer information processing system. These files and databases are stored on secondary storage devices. In this chapter, secondary storage devices, data structures, file organization, file management, databases, and related topics are discussed.

Data Concepts and Data Organization

Data must be organized in order for processing to be feasible and efficient. There are four major levels of data organization: item, record, file, and database. This section describes item, record, and file; the database concept is explained later in the chapter.

Data Items A *data item* describes some attribute of an object of data processing. For example, if the object of data processing is an employee, a data item may describe the attribute "name." Another data item may describe the attribute "age," a third may describe the attribute "social security number." Data items may form a hierarchical relation among themselves. For example, the attribute "date" is composed of three subitems: year, month, and day. These are termed "elementary items" because they have no subitems into which they can be divided.

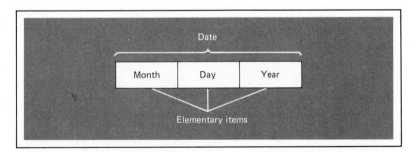

An item is sometimes termed a "field," but a field is the storage space on the physical data processing file medium, whereas the data item is what is stored there. This is most easily seen on a punched card. Sets of columns are defined as fields in which specified data items are punched.

Data items are of either fixed or variable length. For example, names and addresses vary considerably in the number of characters required, but two numeric digits will handle the age of any employee.

Records Data items which relate to an object of data processing are combined into a record for that object. If the object of processing is a customer, items such as customer number, name, address, balance due, and credit rating form the record for the customer. Other examples are an employee record for payroll processing, a sales order record for sales order processing, and a parts record for parts inventory processing. Each record in the file is identified by a record identifier or record key. An employee account number, employee identification number, and a part number are examples of identifiers that could be record keys.

Each data item for a record occupies a field on the storage medium. The sum of the storage required by the various record fields is the storage required by the record. Records of a given type may be all the same length (fixed length) or may differ in length (variable length). There are two reasons that records differ in length (Figure 9-1).

1 The size of the fields required differs because the length of the data items varies among records. For example, names differ in length.

2 Some fields will not be present on all records, thereby reducing the size of the record.

In general, it is simpler to program for and to process fixed-length records, but the potential savings in storage space may offset the difficulties of variable-length records.

Where variable-length records are employed, a method is required to specify the length of variable-length fields (if used) and the variable length of the record. Two methods are encountered:

1 A length field is used. For example, a length field may be set as the first item on the variable-length record to specify the length (say, in characters) of the record.

2 A special symbol may be inserted as the last character in a data field or the last character in the record. The computer program reads the field or record until the termination character is sensed, thereby defining the end of the field.

Some records may be divided into two parts—a master portion containing relatively permanent data and detail or trailer portions. For example, an accounts

Two Reasons for Variable-Length Record

| Name | Age | Dept. | Rate | Soc. Sec. |

| Name | Age | Dept. | Rate | Soc. Sec. |

Variable length because of variations in item length

| A | B | C | D | E |

| A | C | E |

Variable length because of variation in items included

Two Methods for Specifying Variable Length

Item

| Item length | Name | Item length | Address | |

Record

| Record length | |

Use of length field

Item

| Name | * | | ← Marks end of field or record

Record

| | * |

Use of termination character

FIGURE 9-1 Variable-length records.

receivable system which keeps track of individual invoices might have a master record portion containing fairly permanent customer data, such as name, address, and credit rating, plus several trailer records or repeating records, each containing data on an unpaid invoice.

Blocks　A *block* is the group of characters that are read or written with each read or write operation on the storage medium. For example, a single punched card is read or written with each operation, so the punched card is a block. A record is a concept related to items which logically belong together; a block relates the physical storage of data. Blocks are, in other words, the smallest unit of data moved from or to a physical file device. A block may contain part of a record, one record, or several records. Although blocks may be of variable length, it is usually convenient to have them of fixed length because the main memory area into which a block is read has to allow for the largest-size block that is going to be read by the application.

Files　A collection of related records is called a *file* (also called a *data set*). Examples are a payroll file containing all employee records related to payroll and an accounts receivable file containing all customer records related to accounts receivable processing. Files are created when the need for a particular collection of records is recognized. This may necessitate obtaining new data from source documents, or it may involve a selection of records from existing files and restructuring them into a new file. The creation and maintenance of files is a major factor in the workload of a computer information processing system. Files are kept for a variety of purposes. Four main types are usually identified.

File Type	Purpose	Examples
Master file	Relatively permanent records containing statistical, identificational, and historical information. Used as a source of reference and for retrieval.	Accounts receivable file, personnel file, inventory file
Transaction file (also called "detail file")	Collection of records describing transactions by the organization. Developed as a result of processing the transactions and preparing transaction documents. Used to update a master file.	Sales invoice file, purchase order file, pay rate change file
Report file	Records extracted from data in master files in order to prepare a report.	Report file for taxes withheld, report file for delinquent customer accounts, report file for analysis of employee skills
Sort file	A working file of records to be sequenced. This may be the original or a copy of the transaction file, master file, or report file.	

　The record key is used as the basis for sequencing and searching of files. The record key for this purpose can be numeric such as a social security number or alphabetic such as a name. More than one identification field can be used as a key, and therefore the same record may be sequenced on one key for one file and on another key in a second file. For example, a customer file for a department store might be sequenced on account number for processing of sales and customer payments, but by customer name in the file used by accounting personnel responding to customer inquiries.

Information Structures

An information structure defines the relation that data has for the user. For example, the user defines a person's last and first names as having an important relation to each other and the person's address as being related to his or her name. Information structures can be classified as hierarchic or associative (Figure 9-2). The *hierarchic structure* is one in which there is an inferior-superior relation. For example, the invoices in an accounts receivable file belong to a customer (the customer is the owner of the invoices), so the invoice records bear an inferior relation to the record of the customer who is to pay them. Each invoice may have line items which reflect merchandise the customer ordered and received. These line items are in an inferior (belong to) relation to the invoice. This hierarchic relation exists in many parts of the file. On the other hand, the term *associative structure* defines records as related if they have the same value for a data item. Examples are records for employees in the same department which have an associative relation because they all have the same department number, or records for employees which are related because the employees are all women.

In contrast to information structures, the file organization or file structure is the logical formatting of the file for storage purposes. It may be sequential, random, indexed, indexed sequential, etc. The major file organizations are described later in the chapter.

The distinction between physical storage relation and the logical relation among data records is important. The physical storage depends upon the storage medium that is used and the physical relationships that will make processing most efficient. The logical relations exist in the minds of the users and are not necessarily the same as the physical storage. For example, a file of customers for a department store may be physically stored in sequential order by customer account number. But a large number of logical relations can exist among the records in the file. The credit manager may think of the file as consisting of two associative groups: nondelinquent and delinquent customers. A marketing manager may visualize the data in terms of zip code areas where people live (especially if the store uses direct mail or other promotion that can be identified with zip code areas). The task of file organization is to create a file such that any logical relation can be converted into a physical relation for processing.

File Management

File management refers to all activities relating to the creation, updating, and use of files. These activities can be classed as:

1   File creation
2   File processing and maintenance
3   Selection (retrieval)
4   Extraction

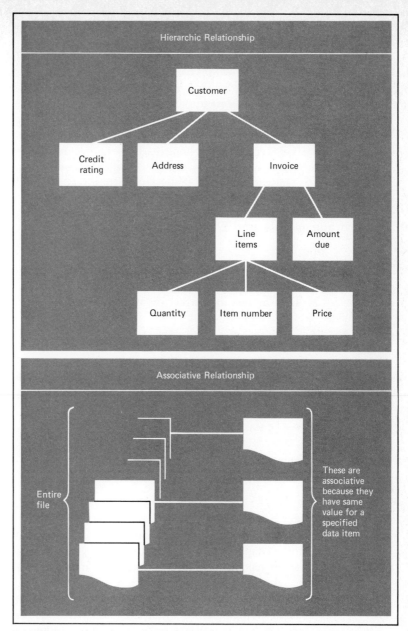

FIGURE 9-2 Information structures.

File creation can refer to the establishing of an entirely new file or the conversion of an existing file in noncomputer form to a computer file medium. The conversion of existing files is one of the difficult problems of converting to a computer system or from one computer system to another.

File maintenance is the updating of a file to reflect the effects of nonperiodic changes by adding, altering, or deleting data. To maintain a master file, new records are added and obsolete or erroneous records are removed. File processing, on the other hand, is the periodic updating of a master file to reflect the effects of current data, often transaction data in a detail file. File maintenance may be performed either in a separate run or in conjunction with file processing runs.

Selection refers to the retrieval of a record from the file. This search process can be very straightforward or quite complex, depending on the file organization.

Extraction is the copying of selected records from a file to form a new file for analysis, report preparation, etc. For example, from the file of all employees, the records of employees with over 20 years of service may be extracted in order to perform an analysis of the characteristics of these employees.

Secondary Storage Media and Devices

The major purpose of secondary storage is to store:

1   Programs or parts of programs not being executed
2   Data needed for current or subsequent processing

The emphasis in this chapter is on the storage of data which is grouped into records, files, and databases.

The two major secondary storage media are magnetic tape and magnetic disk. These are described in some detail. Other media such as magnetic drum, cartridge, extended core, and laser are described briefly. A significant distinction in secondary storage is access. A magnetic tape has serial access so that the nth record on the tape cannot be accessed until the first n-1 items have been read. For example, the first four records must be read one after another (serially) in order to access the fifth. Magnetic disks offer direct access because any storage location can be accessed directly without reading other locations.

Magnetic Tape   Magnetic tape consists of a plastic base coated with an iron oxide coating. Tape measuring $\frac{1}{2}$ in. wide is most common, but some high-capacity tapes are 1 in. wide. A reel of tape is normally 2400 ft in length, but smaller sizes are also used. Magnetic tape provides very effective and inexpensive storage. A single tape can store several million characters at a price of about $15 per tape.

The recording of data on magnetic tape is similar in concept to a home tape recorder. Writing (recording) on the tape destroys the previous contents; reading (playback) may be repeated, since it does not alter the contents. For data recording purposes, the tape is divided into channels which run parallel to the edge of the tape. A single character (or part of a word) is encoded on a vertical frame or column. A typical nine-channel tape will contain four numeric bit positions, four zone positions, and the parity position (Figure 9-3). The older, less common seven-channel tape contains two zone positions instead of four. There is a read-write head for each channel.

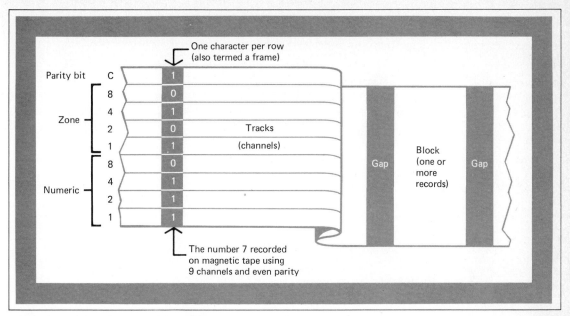

FIGURE 9-3 Recording of data on magnetic tape.

The *tape density* is the number of frames per inch of tape. The common nine-track densities are 800, 1600, and 6250 bits per inch. The older seven-track tapes use 200, 556, or 800 bits per inch. The effective transfer rate is the tape speed in inches per second (75, 125, and 200 are typical) times the density per inch. This is illustrated by a fairly slow, medium, and high speed tape unit:

Ranking	Tape speed, inches per second	Density	Transfer rate, thousands of bits per second
Slow	75	800	60
Medium	125	1600	200
High	200	6250	1250

Increasing the speed and density reduces the time that a frame will be under the read-write head and increases the need for precise positioning and timing. Rewind time is also a factor in tape processing. Tapes written on one model of a tape unit may not be able to be read on another model tape unit because of difference in channels, density, speed, recording method, etc. Where necessary, special tape-to-tape converters are available to handle this task.

Several methods, all quite similar, are used to drive the tape past the read-write heads and to permit starting and stopping the tape quickly. A vacuum-operated tape unit is illustrated in Figure 9-4. Figure 9-5 shows a tape read-write head.

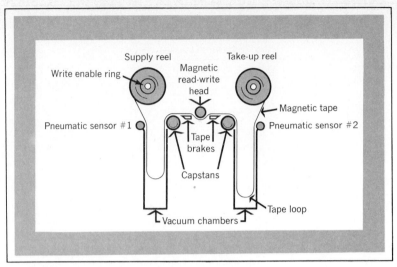

FIGURE 9-4 Vacuum-operated tape unit.

FIGURE 9-5 Two-gap read-write head.

Data records are written on a magnetic tape in a sequence determined by the record key. There is no tape address. When a record is to be found, the tape records are read serially, and the key for the record to be located is compared with the key of each record until there is a match.

Data is physically stored on the tape in blocks. The blocks are separated by an interblock gap. The most common gap length is .6 in. for 800 and 1600 bpi densities and .3 in. for 6250. The tape drive reads a block when a tape read instruction is given. The interblock gap allows the tape drive to detect the end of the block and also to accelerate to the speed required for reading and to decelerate after reading. Some magnetic tape units will read while the tape moves in the reverse direction as well as the forward direction.

The start and stop time associated with the end of a block means that reading time for a file is shortened if the blocks can be made as long as possible. One limit on size is the amount of memory space available for the block when it is read into the main storage. Several records may be put in the same tape block for tape read purposes (Figure 9-6). The capacity of a reel of magnetic tape is increased through blocking because long blocks with many records reduce interblock gaps compared with many short blocks (Figure 9-7).

The first record on a file of magnetic tape records is frequently a header label containing identification information about the file. The OPEN instructions for input files on magnetic tape will cause this header label to be read and perform

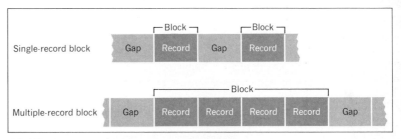

FIGURE 9-6 Blocking of records on magnetic tape.

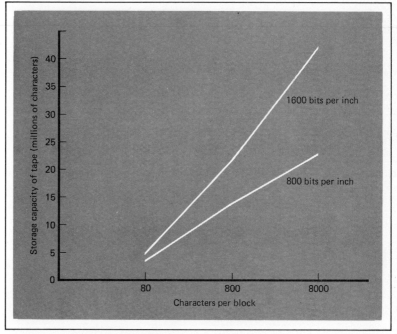

FIGURE 9-7 Storage capacity of magnetic tape as function of density and block size (2400-ft reel and interblock gap of 0.6 in.).

checking to make sure the file is the one called for by the program. When the OPEN instruction is used to open an output file on magnetic tape, it will write a standard header label record. The last record of the file may be a trailer label containing control information such as record count or control totals (Figure 9-8).

In comparison of the performance of tape units, the effective speed and capacity of the units depend on a combination of the following operating characters:

1 Tape density (characters per inch) ⎱
2 Tape speed (inches per second) ⎰ Define transfer rate
3 Size of interblock gap
4 Start-stop time
5 Rewind speed
6 Ability to read or write in both directions

The advantages of magnetic tape over punched cards, evidenced by its extensive use in data processing, are as follows:

Speed	The transfer of data from magnetic tape to internal memory or from memory to tape is performed at a much higher speed than with punched cards.
Convenience	Tape is more compact than cards and easier to handle.
Capacity	A single tape can hold several million characters. The equivalent of tens of thousands of punched cards may be stored on a reel of tape.
Low cost	A reel of magnetic tape (at about $15) costs less than the punched cards it can replace, and it is reusable.

Magnetic Disk A magnetic disk unit consists of rotating metal disks on which data may be stored. The disk unit is frequently referred to as "random access" or "direct access" storage because any storage position can be read or written directly without having to serially read other records. This direct access, although not strictly random in

FIGURE 9-8 Use of header and trailer labels.

access time, allows processing to be handled on unsequenced input data and without having to process any records not related to the transactions.

A magnetic disk file consists of a stack of disks rotating on a common shaft. There are from 5 to 100 disks measuring $1\frac{1}{2}$ to 3 ft in diameter. In appearance, the disk file suggests a stack of phonograph records (Figure 9-9). The disk units may be classed according to the number of read-write heads (or arms) and the removability of the stack of disks as follows:

1 Heads
    (*a*) Moving head (single head serves more than one track)
    (*b*) Fixed (head per track)
2 Stack
    (*a*) Fixed
    (*b*) Removable (disk pack)

The most common method in terms of numbers of units installed is the moving head with one arm per disk and a removable disk pack.

The access arm for a disk contains two read-write heads—one for the top and one for the underside of the disk. To read or write a record, an access arm must be positioned on the disk over the location to be used. The arm (if a moving head) moves in and out to locate itself in the correct spot. The heads float on a cushion of air 35 μ in. (microinches) from the surface (about one-fifth the height of a smoke particle or one-tenth that of a fingerprint). This closeness requires close alignment to avoid head crashes against the surface.

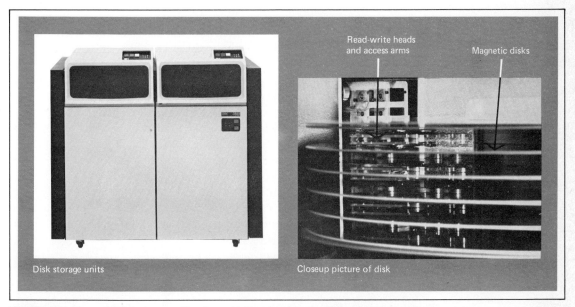

Disk storage units

Read-write heads and access arms

Magnetic disks

Closeup picture of disk

FIGURE 9-9 Magnetic disk storage. (*Courtesy of International Business Machines Corporation.*)

Same track on each disk to form a cylinder

FIGURE 9-10 Accessing of a cylinder using a read-write arm for each disk.

All the arms in a moving-head disk move in and out together. When one arm is positioned over a track on one disk, the other arms are automatically positioned on the same track on all disks. These tracks are termed a "cylinder" (Figure 9-10). Some disk units are available with a read-write head for each recording track, an arrangement that eliminates arm movement altogether. Disk units can have fixed disks or portable, replaceable disk packs. Some system programs and some frequently used files are required to be available virtually all the time. For this reason, an installation may need to have some fixed disk storage and some removable packs. The storage capacity of units varies, but a fixed disk unit may store several hundred million characters, while each replaceable disk pack will store in the 2- to 200-million character range.

A single disk pack does not have sufficient capacity for large online file processing. The trend is toward the use of multiple-pack storage subsystems such as the one illustrated in Figure 9-9 storing between 800 million and 1.6 billion bytes.

Disk technology is also being applied in other ways. Small "floppy" disks about the size of a 45 RPM record are being used for microprograms and other functions. Small single disks are being used to provide low-cost and low-capacity online storage for small computer systems.

When comparing the performance of disk units, the following operating characteristics are important. There are considerable differences in performance, but some figures for commonly used medium- and large-capacity disk systems provide some idea of disk performance.

| | PERFORMANCE | |
Performance characteristic	Medium capacity	Large capacity
1 Access time, milliseconds	60	30

2	Storage tracks on each disk (also defines number of cylinders	200	400
3	Data transfer rate, bytes per second	312,000	806,000
4	Storage capacity per pack, millions of bytes	29–58	100–200
5	Maximum online storage in a subsystem, millions of bytes	233–466	800–1600

Storage with a capacity of a hundred million characters is capable of holding the written portion of 40 to 50 average textbooks, but due to the storage structures and technical requirements, not all available storage is actually used. The effective capacity is less than the theoretical capacity.

Data is stored in and retrieved from identifiable locations on a disk file. The locations are uniquely identified by an address consisting of disk face, track on the disk face, and perhaps sectors of the track (Figure 9-11). The block for disk reading

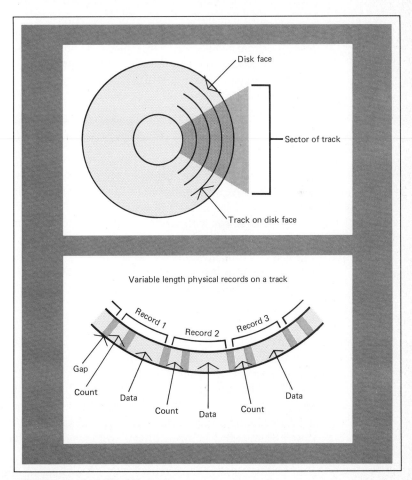

FIGURE 9-11 Disk file addressing.

and writing is typically either a sector, an entire track, or a portion of the track defined by a variable-length record.

The time to access a record in disk storage consists of the seek time and the rotational time.

1 *Seek time* This is the time required to position a movable read-write head over the recording track to be used. If the read-write head is fixed, this time will be zero.

2 *Rotational time* This is the rotational delay to move the storage location underneath the read-write head.

The seek time is much more significant than rotational time. Data on disk files is frequently organized to reduce the seek time.

A major system design and programming consideration with disk storage is the identification of the disk location of a record to be used in processing. In order to obtain a given record without searching a large number of records, some method of determining where a record is stored is needed. If, for example, the inventory records are maintained on a disk file, a withdrawal transaction will be used to update the balance on hand for the item. To process this transaction, the storage location on the disk on the master inventory record must be identified. The identification and location methods are explained later in the chapter in connection with file organization.

An evaluation of storage characteristics suggests that disk files have an advantage over magnetic tape in cases where direct access capabilities are needed or desirable. A disk file can be used exactly like a magnetic tape with records stored and processed in sequence. However, the advantage of having files on magnetic disk is that alternative processing modes may also be used which take advantage of the direct access characteristics of the disk.

By comparison with magnetic tape, disk storage transfer is faster and access is direct. The major disadvantage of magnetic disk storage is that disk files are more expensive than magnetic tape (about 20 times more for removable disk packs having a storage capacity anywhere from one-fourth as great up to about the same as a reel of tape).

Other Media and Devices Secondary storage devices of less importance are magnetic drums, magnetic cartridges, mass core, and laser storage.

The magnetic drum is similar in concept to a fixed-stack magnetic disk. Read-write heads read or write as the drum revolves at high speed. The advantage of a drum over a disk is generally in access time. This means that drums will tend to be used for high-speed direct access secondary storage. However, there are large, slower drums which compete directly with magnetic disk units and head-per-track disks which compete with drums.

The cartridge (Figure 9-12) is a very high capacity storage concept pioneered

IBM 3850 mass storage system

Mass storage cartridges

Honeycomb and access mechanism

FIGURE 9-12 A cartridge mass storage system. (*Courtesy of International Business Machines Corporation.*)

by IBM (called by IBM the Mass Storage System). Data is stored on small individual rolls of wide magnetic tape housed in small cartridges. The cartridges are stored in cells in a honeycomb-like structure. Any cartridge can be retrieved and ready for use in a few seconds (say, 4 to 8 seconds). Up to 472 billion bytes can be placed online. This is equivalent to 4700 high-capacity disk packs or storage sufficient for more than 200,000 books of average length.

Core storage has many advantages for direct access because there is no movement of the storage medium, thereby eliminating a major source of operating delay and difficulty. However, core is more expensive than other media. Recent developments in fabrication of core storage have resulted in a large-capacity core storage unit for use as secondary storage. At present, use of core storage is limited to large-scale systems having a need for very high speed secondary storage.

Laser storage uses a coated strip as storage medium. A bit may be recorded by having a laser beam burn a tiny hole in the coating or by changing a magnetic field with the laser. For the laser hole technology there can be a hole for representing each bit location. Recording is permanent as with a punched card. To read the card, a lower-powered beam scans it to detect the presence or absence of a bit. Because laser beams can be positioned very accurately and can make and detect extremely small holes, a coated strip can store millions of bits.

File Organization for Data Processing

The objectives of a file organization are:

1 To provide a means for locating records for processing, selection, or extraction
2 To facilitate file creation and maintenance

In attempting to achieve its objectives, the file organization should be designed to take advantage of the characteristics of the equipment and the data processing system. Some key considerations in file design are the following:

Considerations	Comments
File storage access method	Serial access or direct access
File size	Affected by number of records, record size, block size, and the method of storing the data on the file medium
Item design	Fixed or variable
Cost of file media	Cost highest for direct fast access devices such as drum and disk, lowest for serial slow access storage medium such as magnetic tape
File maintenance processing and inquiry requirements	Frequent online updating and retrieval versus periodic processing
Need for a database	Database expands record sizes and increases complexity of file management
File privacy	Security provisions to restrict access and to restrict the making of changes to the file

The file organizations are divided, for the sake of explanation, into organizations used primarily in data processing applications and the list organizations especially applicable for information retrieval. The data processing organizations are sequential, random, indexed random, and indexed sequential.

Sequential File Organization   In sequential file organization the records are stored physically in order by the record key. If, for example, the records are for employees and the key is employee payroll number, employee 475 will precede employee 476 on the physical file storage. Sequential file organization is very common because it makes effective use of the least expensive file medium—magnetic tape—and because sequential processing at periodic intervals using a batch of transactions is very efficient. For small data processing systems using punched cards, sequential organization is always used because of the difficulty of alternatives. A disk storage device can be used much like a magnetic tape. The data records are stored sequentially starting at some location so that the first storage location has the first record, the second storage location has the second, etc. If the first location is known, all subsequent locations are filled with data records very much like a magnetic tape. Sequential organization on a disk is often termed SAM for "sequential access method."

When a file is organized sequentially by record key and is accessed serially, there is no need to know specifically where any record is stored, only that it is in order by the sequencing key. Locating any particular record is performed merely by starting at the beginning of the file, reading each record, and comparing its key with the record which is being sought. Efficiency of processing thus requires that all transactions to be processed against a file should be organized in the same order as the file so that the first record on the file to be sought will be found first and the transaction which needs that record will be processed first, the second transaction will find its corresponding record next, etc. In this type of sequential processing using a serial access file, the entire master file is passed through the computer for any type of processing run involving transactions to be processed against the file (Figure 9-13). This is one reason it is desirable to hold transactions until a

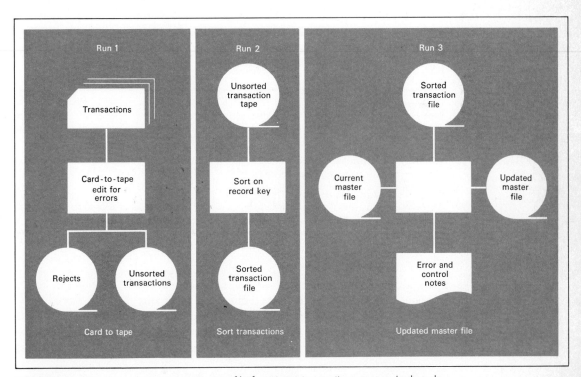

FIGURE 9-13 Runs to update a magnetic tape file from input transactions on punched cards.

reasonable sized batch can be processed. Sequential processing organization is therefore oriented toward periodic batch processing.

The efficiency of sequential organization in locating data required by inquiries depends on the type of inquiry. If the inquiry is for a specific record identified by its key, a serial file such as magnetic tape is searched from the beginning until the record is found. A disk file using sequential organization may search for a specific record by a binary search procedure. This is performed by going to the middle record in the file and comparing the key of that record with the key of the desired record. If the desired record is on the second half of the file, the search continues using only that half. The middle record of the half is examined, and the search then continues with the upper or lower half of that segment. This halving and comparison processing continues until the desired record is located. The binary search is quite efficient. For example, to locate a record with a given key out of 2000 records requires that only 11 records be accessed and compared. All requests involving selection criteria (such as customers living in Falcon Heights having incomes between $10,000 and $15,000) are processed by reading the entire file and checking each record to see if it matches the criteria. Because of the need to pass the entire sequential file to obtain a subset for processing, secondary files are sometimes maintained. The difficulty in using secondary files is in the extra work in updating them.

In evaluation of the sequential file organization, both the updating process and the inquiry from the file need to be considered. If there is sufficient level of activity and transactions can be batched, the sequential design is excellent for master file updating. The advantages and disadvantages of sequential organization when updating master files are the following:

Advantages	Disadvantages
File design is simple—locating a record requires only a sequence key.	Entire file must be processed no matter how low the activity rate.
If activity rate is high, the simplicity of the key as the method for accessing makes for efficient processing.	Transactions must be sorted in the same order as the file.
Low-cost file media (magnetic tape) can be used.	File is always out of date to the extent that a batch has not been processed.

Random File Organization

The advantage of a direct access storage device is that any location can be read without reading the locations preceding it. This means that data stored on the direct access file can be obtained directly if the address of the record is known. The problem of file organization for data processing using direct access storage is therefore how to store the data records so that, given a record key, its storage location can be found.

It would be ideal for direct random access if the record keys could be the same as the identification number for the disk storage locations, but this is almost never the case, and therefore other means must usually be found. Stated another way, the task is to take a set of record keys and map them into a set of disk storage location identifiers. If the record keys ran sequentially with no gaps, this might be a fairly simple matter, but such a condition almost never exists. In addition to gaps, many identification codes are not sequential because they are designed to be significant, such as showing territory or product line.

Because of the infeasibility of making a simple transformation, other methods must be used. The most common arithmetic procedure to transform the record key into a storage address is termed "randomizing" because transformation of the nonsequential numbers to a range of storage addresses is based on the uniform distribution of random digits. If, for example, 100,000 storage locations are to be assigned and the occurrences of the digits 0 to 9 in each position of the storage addresses are tallied, there will be 10,000 1s, 10,000 2s, etc. Therefore, a procedure which takes part of or all the record identification number or record key and produces a random number will generate storage addresses falling somewhat uniformly in the range of the assigned storage identifiers. This procedure is also called "hashing."

The best-known and most frequently used technique for producing addresses by randomizing is division of the key by a positive integer, usually a prime number. The remainder obtained from the division becomes the address locator. The prime-number divisor is usually chosen to be approximately equal to the number of available addresses. There are additional methods, but all attempt to do the same thing—to generate a set of addresses which will map the keys into the storage area as uniformly as possible.

A major difficulty with the randomizing procedure is that some addresses will never be generated, whereas two or more record keys may produce identical disk addresses (synonyms). This is also called a "collision." In that event, one of the records is stored at the generated location with the synonym being stored in an overflow location. The overflow can be handled in one of several ways.

1   The overflow record can be stored in the first available location following the location where it should be found. On any retrieval for which the desired record is not in the location specified, the procedure is to search succeeding locations until it is found.

2   A special data item field in each record points to (identifies) the address of the first overflow record for which the same address was generated. If a third synonym was produced, the overflow address linkage for it is put in the second record, etc. When retrieving a record, the program examines the program at the key-generated address. If it does not have the same key, the program looks at the pointer field and goes to the overflow location for the record.

3   Special overflow areas are used. If the record is not found at the generated address, the program goes to the overflow area which is searched sequentially until the record is found.

Overflow becomes a severe problem if most of the storage locations are used. If, say, 50 percent of the locations are used, overflow is generally not a problem; if 80 percent of the locations are used, overflow will usually become quite large, and this can increase substantially the average number of accesses to locate a record. In this and other disk-addressing methods, it is frequently desirable to have the basic method of obtaining an address refer to a bucket instead of a single record location. A group of records is stored in the bucket, which is then searched sequentially to find the appropriate record. The use of buckets increases storage utilization, and the sequential search of a block or bucket is not typically a substantial hinderance to processing efficiency when compared with the increased use of storage and the reduction in overflow records.

The advantages of the random storage approach arise primarily in situations where the records need to be located randomly and quickly as in online inquiry and online updating. If a random organization file is to be processed sequentially, it would generally need to be copied onto another file and sorted into sequential order. The random approach is often termed "direct access method" or "basic direct access method" (BDAM).

Indexed Random File Organization

Instead of attempting to locate addresses by randomizing, separate indexes may be maintained in which the address of the record being sought is found. Indexes are frequently in order by record key, thereby allowing the index to be searched either sequentially or by a binary search process to locate the address of a record. In some cases, a sequential index is not desirable, and an indexed organization may be created using a tree index.

A tree index consists of the key of a record, a left branch address, and a right branch address. When the file is created, the first record is placed in the first position in each index. The key of the second record to be stored is compared with the first record key. If its key is greater, the right branch of the first record points to the second index address. If it is less, the left branch index address of the first record is set to point to the second address. When the third record is added, it is referenced as being one part of the tree (see Figure 9-14). The result looks much like a tree and is therefore called a "tree structure."

When searching for a record with the tree index, the search starts at the beginning of the file index and by means of a comparison branches through the tree until the desired index is located. The resulting tree search can be reasonably efficient. The storage is efficient since there is a high packing density.

Indexed Sequential File Organization

Indexed sequential file organization is essentially a compromise between sequential access and random access methods. It is often referred to as ISAM for "indexed sequential access method." The records are stored on the disk sequentially by record key so that sequential processing may be performed, but indexes are also maintained to allow direct retrieval based on a key value.

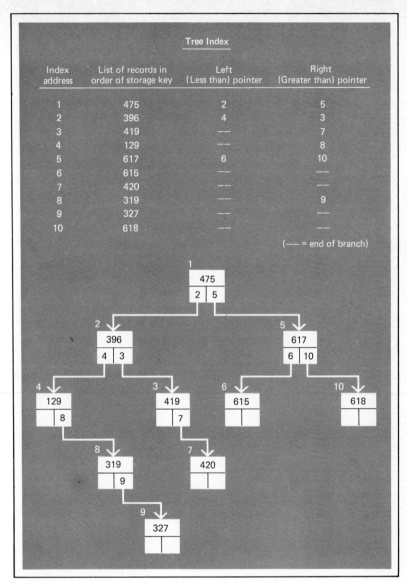

FIGURE 9-14 Tree indexing of randomly organized records.

In order to directly access a particular record with ISAM, the index is searched and the key is located which then provides the address for access. Note that even though the file is sequential, it can be updated with transactions in random order because the index may be used for directly locating a record for updating. If the file is to be processed sequentially, the index need not be used. In updating the file, the records to be updated are read, updated, and written back in the same location. If a new record is to be inserted in the sequence, completely reordering the file is inconvenient. The record to be inserted is placed in a special overflow area, and a special indicator is placed in the record occupying the location immediately preceding the location where the record will be inserted to indicate the address of the missing record in the sequence. A record that is deleted leaves an empty space. Periodically the file is reorganized to eliminate the overflow addressing and the empty locations.

The indexed sequential organization may be modified slightly to assist in sequential ordering, yet to allow for easy insertions into the file without frequent reorganization. A common method is to arrange records in blocks or buckets with the index referencing the block number. This reduces the size of the index but means that once the block is located the block must be searched sequentially. Since the block is usually small, such a search is not a serious processing impediment. Blocks are organized with extra locations so that the records may be added or deleted from the block without reorganizing the rest of the file (Figure 9-15). It is

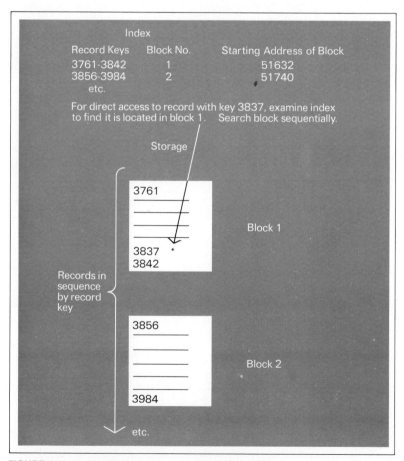

FIGURE 9-15 Indexed sequential organization using blocks.

generally desirable to use special index sequential software to build the file and indexes and to update and reorganize. Such software is available from both the hardware manufacturers and independent software vendors.

Indexed sequential organization is very popular for direct access storage files because it combines the best features of sequential organization with features of direct access by means of the index. Disadvantages are the extra storage requirements caused by the need to allow for insertions to the file, the extra storage for the indexes, the extra processing required in using indexes, and the need to periodically reorder the file.

Selecting a File Organization

In summary, the use of a serial access medium such as magnetic tape for file storage requires sequential organization for efficient processing; direct access media allow sequential, random, indexed random, and indexed sequential organization. The file medium can therefore be a constraint in the organization chosen. The serial access approach to sequential batch processing requires the entire file to be passed, so that by comparison with direct access, it is inefficient to process in the batch-oriented sequential manner if there are few transactions. However, rarely will all records in the file be active. In most files of any size, a 10-percent activity rate (transactions affecting 1 of 10 master records) represents a substantial level of activity. Two major factors in deciding on a file organization are therefore whether processing is to be periodic on batches of data or immediate on single transactions and, if performed on batches of data, the activity rate of updating.

Other considerations in selecting a sequential or nonsequential organization are concurrent processing of files, sorting requirements, and file integrity. One of the processing economies achieved in direct access processing is the concurrent processing of several files. When a sale is recorded, the account receivable can be posted, the inventory withdrawal written, etc., at the same time. In sequential processing using, for example, magnetic tape, this would require several different runs. Nonsequential or random organizations of the file allow processing to be performed on data which is not sequenced. Transactions which update the file or inquiry transactions requiring file access can be handled in random order as the transactions are received.

In processing a transaction against a random organization using a direct access file, the record to be altered is copied from direct access storage, updated, and then written back in the same location (Figure 9-16). This replaces the prior contents of the location. If the updating was in error, the record prior to updating is no longer available. This is in contrast to the approach of creating a whole new file when using serial access and rewriting. Especially in online processing, the direct access file is exposed to the risk of incorrect updating. Special backup and reconstruction must therefore be provided.

Random organization allows for rapid access to a record. However, it requires extra processing time to obtain the address (if address is derived or obtained from an index). Unlike a sequential organization which can fill all locations, the random organizations tend to not use all locations. Randomizing techniques cannot com-

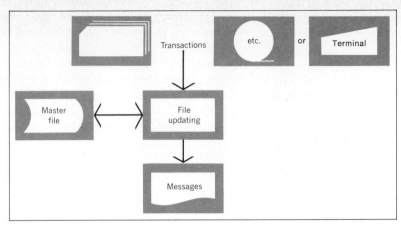

FIGURE 9-16 Direct access processing.

pletely pack the file, and the use of overflow locations increases the average access time. The file must be reorganized periodically to reduce overflow and to eliminate records to be dropped from the file.

The major criteria for selecting among the nonsequential access methods are speed of access (random is usually best), packing of storage (random is worst), ease of meeting processing needs (indexed sequential supports sequential output better than other methods), and level of difficulty and frequency in building and re-organizing the file, given the applications using the files.

List Organizations for Information Retrieval

The problems of access are most severe in information retrieval applications, and an alternative to sequential or random organization is to use some form of list organization. In a list organization, relations among records are established by pointers so that there need be no special physical organization of the file. The use of pointers allows different logic organizations to be established without regard to the actual physical arrangement. A pointer in a record consists of a data item (occupying a field) which gives the address of another record. If the file is on a disk, the pointer to a record is the disk address of that record. There may be many pointers in a record because many different relations may need to be established. List organizations are methods for building structures with the pointers. The most common are simple lists, inverted lists, and ring organizations.

Simple-List Organization In a simple list an entry in an index points to the first record. The first record in the list points to the second logical record, the second logical record points to the third, etc. The last record in the logical sequence contains a special symbol in the pointer field (Figure 9-17). This is also termed a "threaded list." The sequence of

FIGURE 9-17   Simple list.

the physical records is not important because the pointers are specifying the logical relation. For example, in order to establish a logical file involving all employees by department, an index is established with the different department numbers and a corresponding entry into the first employee in the file belonging to that department. If the employees in department 417 are to be read, the search begins with entry for 417 in the department index which has a pointer to the first employee in the department. The first record for department 417 will point to the next record which contains an employee working in department 417, etc. A record can be a part of several logical files because there can be many pointers in the same record.

The updating of a list by inserting a record requires that the pointer of the preceding logical record be changed. If a record has multiple pointers, deletion of the record requires that all pointers be revised. If there are only single, forward pointers, there is no method for going backward in the list to revise the prior pointers. Merely by inserting backward pointers which point to the preceding record, it is possible to insert or delete records easily. This also allows the list to be searched in either direction.

Inverted-List Organization   The list concept of the simple list may be extended. For example, a fairly comprehensive list of characteristics may be established as an index with a pointer to the first record in the file which has that characteristic and with pointers from each such record to the next record having the characteristic. Whereas a sequential file can be thought of as being accessed only through the record key, a full set of characteristics would allow the file to be accessed through any characteristic. The file is then said to be "inverted." In other words, all indexing is by content rather than by record key (Figure 9-18).

FIGURE 9-18 Inverted file.

The index in an inverted list may be expanded to include a list of all records having a specified characteristic. The pointers are then dropped from the records because the index has the complete list (Figure 9-19). In other words, in a file of personnel at a university all the people born in 1930 will be listed by record identifier following the characteristic "born 1930." This allows searching of the index for the content which is to be found in the file, rather than having to search the file itself. Since the fully inverted file makes every data value available as a basis for search and retrieval, it is excellent for information retrieval applications, especially where the retrieval requirements cannot be specified in advance. The disadvantage is that the index for a fully inverted file will be quite large, and a somewhat modified form is usually the most practical approach for day-to-day use.

A problem in an inverted list is how to efficiently store the list or directory of records containing each characteristic. There is generally no way to determine the length of the list prior to its creation, and the length of the list can change as the data changes. For example, if an attribute in the index is sex—say, male—a company with all male employees would list every single employee record as belonging to this list.

Ring Organization A ring organization is a list which has pointers going both forward and backward. The first record is an index record which specifies the nature of the ring, and the

File sequenced by name

Disk address	Name	Age	Code for occupation	Code for salary range
224	ANDERSON L.	32	1	2
225	FLINT C.	23	7	4
226	THOMAS H.	42	3	3
227	PORTER N.	39	7	4

Content indexing for inverted file

Age index	
Content	Disk address
23	225
32	224
39	227
42	226

Occupation index	
Content	Disk address
1	224
3	226
7	225,227

Salary index	
Content	Disk address
2	224
3	226
4	225,227

FIGURE 9-19 Use of content indexes for inverted files.

last record in the list points to the first. This allows retrieval to proceed from any record, either backward or forward, until the entire list has been examined.

This is a very useful organization because it provides a facility to retrieve and process all the records in any one ring while branching off at any or each of the records to retrieve and process other records which are logically related. For example, a retrieval request may involve injured employees. When one is found, the next question is, "Who does he or she work with?" This question is answered by taking the pointer for department number and following the list through all employees who are part of that same list until the ring brings the list back to the originating record (Figure 9-20).

Database Concepts and Management

A database is a set of logically related files organized in such a way that access to the data is improved and redundancy is minimized. There can be several databases to reflect several logical groupings of files. The database concept is made operational by a database management system, a software system which performs the functions of creating and updating files, retrieving data, and generating reports. All

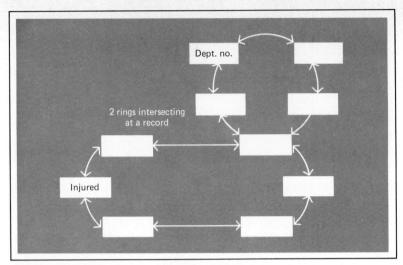

FIGURE 9-20 Ring organization.

data in the set of files can be accessed by any program having the right to use the database. In general a database needs to be on direct access storage in order to implement the concept. Because many different user programs may access the database, it is controlled by a separate authority established for this purpose. The database concept can result in efficiency of storage and efficiency in processing. The efficiency of storage stems from the elimination of redundant files. If each application has its own file, there will be many applications that will be essentially duplicating files. The efficiency of processing arises not only because of the reduction in file storage but also because logically related data items which might otherwise be maintained in separate files are now found in a single file and the processing can take advantage of this fact. A single updating will update an item for all processing applications which use that item, thus reducing the inconsistencies and errors which often occur among separate files. The database reduces the necessity for sorting, comparison, and merging which are often required if separate files are maintained and then merged for interrelated processing. It improves efficiency for retrieval of information because all the files are found logically related in a single place. Two major concepts connected with database are the schema and the database administrator.

Schema The *schema* is a definition of stored data, i.e., it describes the database. Essentially one can think of the schema as a dictionary which describes all the data items in terms of entry type, length, name, etc. The schema is written in a data definition language which describes the data and logical relations between data entities. The schema is thus a comprehensive directory of all data items in the file. It is convenient to have two types of schemas—the conceptual schema which describes the logical structure of the database and an internal schema which defines the physical structure of the database.

In a large database the schema can include a substantial number of items. Any application program will, however, use only a small subset of the items on the database. The subset is described by a user schema or subschema (also termed an "external schema"). The subschema is essentially a description of the items that are to be used in an application program. A programmer writing an application program therefore describes the data which he or she needs by a subschema. The subschema must be compatible with the schema, but it need not be concerned with the physical storage. For example, a schema may have a large record with many fields for each employee. A program requiring only two of the items, say, pay rate and age, defines a subschema for only these two items. The binding of the subschema to the schema is done by the software system and need not concern the application programmer.

The *data manipulation language* (DML) is a language (also called a "database command language") which the programmer uses to transfer data between the program and the database. A DML statement will be a mixture of a host language such as COBOL and special database instructions.

The consequence of the concept of database management and schema/subschema is to remove the database from the control of the individual programmer. All uses of the database must be handled through the database management software. This allows the integrity and security of the database to be under better control than if all programs were allowed to operate directly. Also the individual programmer no longer need be concerned with the physical records. The programmer works with only logical records defined by the user schema.

Database Administrator

The concept of the database which is independent from the application programs and is not available to the application programmers except on a controlled basis means that someone must exercise control. This person is known as a "database administrator." In other words, a function is required to manage and control the database in order to preserve its integrity, maintain its definition, and prevent unauthorized usage or change.

One of the major problems of a database is security. When, for example, there were separate files for different programs, security could be maintained merely by physical security over the files. A program not needing a file would not call for it. In the database approach, a substantial amount of data is collected for use by a variety of programs, some of which are not authorized to access all the data.

The database administrator has responsibility for the database. This means that he or she has responsibility for the schema and exercises validity and access authority for subschemas. The administrator's activities include defining and organizing the database, providing for protection of it, and preparing documentation of it.

Users and Suppliers of the Database

The persons who are affected by the database are its users and suppliers. The users are those who program applications utilizing the database for persons in the organization who desire information. The suppliers are those who must provide input for storage into the database.

The supplier of the data for the database will find that there is greater emphasis upon integrity of the input data than when only individual applications were involved. The effects of an error can now affect much of the organization, whereas formerly individual files could often be in error without affecting the rest of the organization. For example, the personnel file could be in error without affecting the payroll processing. The measures for data integrity will therefore be measurably strengthened when a database is used and a database administrator enforces the data quality standards.

When individual parts of the organization maintain data files, the amount of quality control over the data is connected with the use to which it is put by that part of the organization. However, with the database and database administrator the level of data integrity must suit organization-wide objectives rather than the needs of an individual organizational unit. In other words, the database is viewed as an organization-wide resource. The centralization of data requires a well-conceived plan governing the development of the database and access to the data. Some users may notice the need for formal security codes and formal procedures for establishing the right to access data.

The users of data will find that the directory issued by the database administrator provides substantially enhanced knowledge of the data resources in the organization. The ability to perform analysis will be considerably improved both by a greater knowledge of data availability and by the retrieval capabilities and report generation capabilities of the database software. These capabilities are generally available to both programmers and nonprogrammers.

The programmer, in using the database, will find that many of the tasks formerly done need not be performed. The data administrator will arrange for such matters as security, backup, and data integrity. All the physical problems of the storage will be separated from the programmer. At the same time, the programmer is restricted in what can be done to the data. The programmer can extract any data for which his or her program has valid security access but cannot alter fields in the data without permission from the data administrator.

Data Management Systems

A data management system enables a user to create and update files; to select, retrieve, and sort data; and to generate reports. Data management systems are an extension of prior concepts in software. In first-generation computers, the programmer was required to write in machine-oriented code, and all functions had to be written for each program. It was soon found that many functions could be generalized and used by all programmers. This was especially true of input/output functions, and so macro instructions were added to assembly languages so that the individual programmer did not have to write the input/output code. Other functions soon became generalized, such as sorting and report generation, and this software is found as part of the generalized software support for a data processing installation. The data management system is an extension of these ideas to the management of the files of an organization. There are two types of data management systems—file management systems and database management systems. The difference between the two is in their scope. The file management system handles individual files, whereas the database management system has the capability for managing an entire database as well as an individual data file.

Two different approaches are used in database management systems. One is the self-contained system which has its own language with which to write programs to retrieve data, etc.; the other is the host language system in which the database management system provides an interface to programs written in a high-level language such as COBOL. Early systems were usually of the self-contained variety, while later systems favor the host language design. Both approaches provide a convenient user inquiry and report preparation capability.

A number of data management systems are available. Each computer manufacturer offers one (generally as extra-cost software); in addition, a number of data management systems are provided by software vendors. Some examples of data management systems in use are:

FILE (DATA) MANAGEMENT		DATABASE MANAGEMENT	
Name	Vendor	Name	Vendor
MARK IV	Informatics MARK IV Systems Co.	TOTAL	Cincom Systems, Inc.
EASYTRIEVE	Pansophic Systems, Inc.	IMS	IBM
DYL-260	Dylakor Software Systems	DL/I	IBM
CULPRIT	Cullinane Corporation	ADABAS	Software AG
SCORE	Programming Methods	System 2000	MRI Systems, Inc.
		IDMS	Cullinane Corporation

Substantial reductions in the time required to program file maintenance and report functions have been reported by installations using data management systems. The newer data management systems continue to improve in generality, flexibility, and quality. These systems are an important element in the trend in processing systems design to greater data independence, more powerful but simpler-to-use languages for data access, and improved operating performance.

Sorting for File Processing

Sorting is an important data processing activity requiring a significant part of the data processing time. Transactions are sorted for three reasons, all related to efficiency:

1 Efficiency in processing
2 Efficiency in distribution of output
3 Efficiency in subsequent retrieval

Transactions may need to be sorted for ease of processing if the processing involves reference to files or involves file updating. Although never required in the absolute sense, sorting of transactions into the same order as the reference or master file is for all practical purposes required for files accessed serially (such as files on magnetic tape). Sorting into the file sequence is sometimes required and often done for improved processing efficiency when the reference or master files are on direct access devices.

Sorting of output for distribution is important both for efficiency and control in distribution. Some examples illustrate this need:

Paychecks are processed in order by employee number but are distributed to each department for issuance. Before the checks are printed, the transaction file is sorted so that the checks are printed in order by department. Control totals and employee counts for control over payroll check distribution are based on departmental employee counts, etc.

Customer statements of amounts due are prepared from a file organized by customer account number. The mailing of the bills requires that they be sorted into zip codes. Before the customer statements are printed, the output file must be sorted by zip codes.

Copies of customer statements are filed for reference purposes on computer output microfilm. Depending on the requirements, this reference output may need to be in customer number order or alphabetical order.

Sort routines are provided as part of the software furnished by the manufacturer, so that individual installations need not write the sort programs. The sort routine is used by specifying the key on which the file is to be sorted, the record length, and similar characteristics. There are a number of different algorithms for sorting. The discussion on sorting will use magnetic tape and simple merge sorting as the example.

There are two steps in merge sorting a tape file. The first is establishing the initial sorting strings, and the second is the merging of these strings into a single, sequenced string. A *string* is a group of records which has been sequenced. The merging process will be explained first.

Two strings sequenced on a key can be merged into a single, sequenced string by looking at the keys of only two records at a time. In other words, no matter how long the two strings, only the next record from each string needs to be in main memory for the sort comparison. This merging of strings is illustrated in Figure 9-21 for two strings of four records.

The two merging strings come from two different input magnetic tape units, and the merged string that results is written on one of two output tapes, alternating

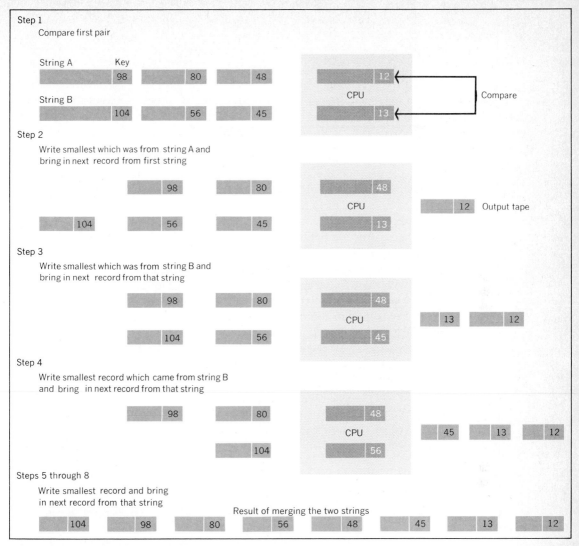

FIGURE 9-21 Merging of two strings.

between the output tapes. When the input tapes have been read, the output tapes become input for the next merge. Suppose there are 15,360 records to be sorted and there are 512 initial strings each 15 records in length; the number of passes, string length, and number of strings are shown below.

Pass number	String length at end of pass	Number of strings on each output tape
1	30	256
2	60	128

3	120	64
4	240	32
5	480	16
6	960	8
7	1920	4
8	3840	2
9	7680	1
10	15,360	1 on final tape

The initial strings are usually established by reading in a group of records and sorting them inside the computer. By doing this, the number of sorts can be substantially reduced. For example, in the case of the 15,000-record file, initial strings of 60 instead of 15 reduce the number of passes by 2, a 20 percent reduction in sorting time. The size of the initial sort is limited by the size of the memory since the records are held there during the sorting. The internal sort can take several forms. The methods are illustrated by exchange sorting (Figure 9-22). Starting with the first record in a list, the key of that record is compared, one at a time, with those following. If any key for a record lower in the list has a higher key (for an ascending sort), the records exchange places in the list, and the new record key is used to continue comparing to the end of the list. The first item is now the largest in the list. The second item is then compared with the third, etc., until the largest key (with its record) is in the second position. The process continues as shown for a list of four keys in Figure 9-22. Depending on the expected order of the data prior to sorting, alternative sorting algorithms may be more efficient than exchange sorting. Note that in tape sorting the key length does not, for practical purposes, affect the length of time for the sort. The final sequence is checked by the final merge.

SUMMARY   An understanding of data is fundamental to understanding of computer processing. The chapter defines the basic data concepts of item, record, block, and file. Information structures and file management activities were also explained.

Secondary storage media and devices are used for storage of data files. The characteristics of the two major media, magnetic tape and magnetic disk, were

STEP	1	2	3	4	5	6	FINAL
RECORD	82 ⎞ Exchange	98 ⎞	98 ⎞	98	98	98	98
KEYS	98 ⎠	82 ⎠ No	82 ⎠ No	82 ⎞ No	82 ⎞ Exchange	87	87
	49	49 ⎠ exchange	49 ⎠ exchange	49 ⎠ exchange	49 ⎠	49 ⎞ Exchange	82
	87	87	87	87	87	82 ⎠	49

FIGURE 9-22   Exchange sorting.

described in some detail; other devices and media were surveyed. The distinguishing difference between magnetic tape and magnetic disk is record access. Access to records on magnetic tape is serial; for magnetic disk, it is direct. Most of the advantages and disadvantages stem from this difference.

The organization of files affects both storage requirements and speed of processing. It is convenient to separate the file organizations used primarily in processing applications from the list organizations required for efficient information retrieval. Four data processing organizations were explained—sequential, random, indexed random, and indexed sequential. Three list organizations were described—simple list, inverted list, and ring structure.

A database is a set of logically related files organized to improve access and minimize redundancy. The database is maintained independently of the applications programs. The database is described by various schemas—an overall schema and various user schemas (or subschemas) to define the data for individual applications. A database administrator controls the database and the procedures for access.

Data management software aids in file management and in retrieving data from files. A database management system manages a database. It provides capabilities for creating and updating the database, selecting data, generating reports, etc. It is required for effective implementation of the database concept.

Sorting is a fundamental operation for data processing. In this chapter, a basic approach to sorting was explained using magnetic tape as an example.

EXERCISES

1 Define the following terms:
   (*a*) Data item   (*f*) Information structure
   (*b*) Record   (*g*) Master file
   (*c*) File   (*h*) Transaction file
   (*d*) Block   (*i*) Sort file
   (*e*) Database   (*j*) Pointer

2 Explain and contrast the following pairs of terms:
   (*a*) Item and field
   (*b*) Logical files and physical files
   (*c*) Record and block
   (*d*) Serial access and direct access
   (*e*) Fixed length and variable length
   (*f*) Hierarchic and associative data relationships

3 Explain how a variable item design affects storage and processing requirements.

4 Take the first name on each page of the telephone book for the first hundred pages and calculate the relative advantage of a variable-length name field over a fixed-length name field. Assume a field size item to indicate length for the variable approach.

5 A processing job involving 2000 records of a maximum length of 300 characters is to be processed once a month. The fields vary in length. Should the item size be fixed or variable? Explain. Would your answer change if there were 20,000 records of 1000 characters maximum and 100 characters minimum?

6 Define each of the following with respect to magnetic tape processing:

(a) Interrecord or interblock gap   (e) Density
(b) Blocking   (f) Transfer rate
(c) Header label   (g) Address
(d) Trailer label   (h) Record key

7 Define each of the following with respect to disk processing:
(a) Track   (e) Stack
(b) Sector   (f) Index
(c) Face   (g) Address
(d) Cylinder

8 What types of storage devices are likely to be used under the following circumstances:
(a) A small retailer using punched card billing forms
(b) A manufacturer interested in up-to-the-minute inventory status information
(c) A large credit-granting agency with need for rapid access for active accounts and slower-speed access to other accounts
(d) A large retailer sending out monthly bills

9 Explain the way a record is located on:
(a) Magnetic tape file   (b) Disk file

10 Compute the number of 80-column punched card records that can be stored on a magnetic tape that is 2400 ft long and uses gaps between blocks as follows:
(a) One record per block:
(1) 800 bytes-per-inch density (.6-in. gap)
(2) 1600 bytes-per-inch density (.6-in. gap)
(b) Ten records per block for both 800 and 1600 bytes per inch.

11 Figure 9-7 is based on nine-channel third-generation equipment. Prepare data on older equipment with a .75-in. gap and densities as follows:

Density	BLOCK SIZE		
	80	800	8000
200			
556			

12 Complete the table of effective transfer rates in characters (bytes per second) for the following (assuming tape speed of 125 inches per second):

Block size in characters (bytes)	DENSITY (BYTES PER INCH) AND INTERBLOCK GAP (INCHES)		
	800/.6	1600/.6	6250/.3
80			
800			
8000			

The basic formula is:

$$\left.\begin{array}{l}\text{Transfer rate} \\ \text{(in bytes per} \\ \text{second)}\end{array}\right\} = \text{bytes per inch} \times \text{tape speed (in inches per second)}$$

But the effective transfer rate must take into account the gap which requires time to read but has no data. Calculate an effective total of bytes per inch to use in the above formula as follows:

$$\text{Effective bytes per inch} = \frac{\text{block size in bytes}}{(\text{block size/bytes per inch}) + \text{gap (inches)}}$$

13 A company has 190,000 records on magnetic tape, one record per block. Each record is 60 characters. The tape is 2400 ft, the density is 800 bpi, and the interrecord gap is .6 in. By packing 10 records in a block, the number of tapes will be reduced from _____ to _____ (show your computations).

14 Assuming a cost of cards at $1.50 per 1000, a cost of tape at $15, 80-character records, .6-in. interblock gap, and 800-bpi density, calculate the cost of tape storage relative to card storage (assuming full utilization of both and ignoring reusability factors).

15 If a number is multiplied or divided by a prime number such as 17, the resulting digits (especially the middle digits) are relatively random. That is, the occurrence of 0s, 1s, 2s, etc., will be approximately the same in each digit position. How might this fact be used to generate disk addresses from identification numbers?

16 Define the following acronyms:
(a) DASD   (c) BDAM   (e) IMS
(b) ISAM   (d) SAM

17 Explain the logic of a sequential file update run. Why must a sort run have preceded it?

18 Explain the organization of a sequential file. Explain how it is used in:
(a) Updating run
(b) Retrieval request
(c) Preparing report arranged in different sequence

19 Assume the same file is organized sequentially on magnetic tape and also on a disk. How would the search process differ for the two files for obtaining the record of student Jennifer Davis? The file is organized in name sequence.

20 Explain the random file organization.
(a) How is a record located?
(b) How is overflow handled?

21 Explain a tree index. What are the advantages and disadvantages?

22 Prepare a tree index like the one in Figure 9-14 for the following record keys received in the order given:
976   811   894   419   444   519   821   318
709   845   518   240   917   320   200

23 Explain indexed sequential organization. How are blocks used to reduce index size and reorganization needs?

24 Explain what a pointer is and how it is stored in a record.

25 Explain a simple list. Why might it be called a "threaded list" or "knotted list"? Why are forward and backward pointers sometimes used?

26 Explain an inverted file. Why might it be called a "content-indexed file"? Why are pointers not used in the records?

27 A bit index is a string of bit positions, each of which identifies the existence (1-bit) or nonexistence (0-bit) of a value for an attribute. It can be very efficient as an index for a partially inverted file. Construct a bit index for the values for the following three attributes in a partially inverted file of three records.

Record key	Salary class	Sex	Education code
180	1	Male	4
190	2	Male	7
200	1	Female	6

28 Explain a ring organization. How is it used in information retrieval?

29 In a ring structure, an individual Gordon Clark has been found to be part of the ring which identifies sophomores. We wish to find some other characteristics (the record contains several pointers). How is this accomplished?

30 Explain how the files would be processed for the following:
 (a) An inquiry to select all male students majoring in mathematics who are 19 years old.
  (1) Using a file organized sequentially
  (2) Using a file organized randomly
  (3) Using an indexed sequential file
  (4) Using a fully inverted file
 (b) Select the records for Flint Stanford and Marie Alison, two students on the file. ID numbers are known.
  (1) Using a sequential file
  (2) Using a random file
  (3) Using an indexed sequential file
  (4) Using a fully inverted file

31 What are the characteristics of a database?

32 Explain the difference between the schema and subschema.

33 What are the duties of a database administrator?

34 Explain and contrast file management systems and database management systems.

35 Explain the difference between a host language system and a self-contained data management system.

36 Perform an exchange sort for groups of four of the following numbers and then do a merge sort. Show your strings at each stage.

256	072	296	416
024	288	592	664
096	576	736	656
384	152	888	312
768	134	944	248
536	432	104	984

4

EFFECTIVE OPERATION AND USE OF THE COMPUTER

The first three chapters in Part 4 relate primarily to operations and management of the computer resources of an organization; the last one, Chapter 13, is a summary of current and prospective developments in the entire field of computers. Chapter 10 provides the student with insight into how a computer center operates and describes the alternatives of using an outside computer service center and a time-sharing service. The important areas relating to methods for ensuring accuracy of computer processing and for security of computer resources are described in Chapter 11. A significant management issue is the selection and procurement of new or replacement hardware or software. A commonly used approach is explained in Chapter 12.

Chapter

10

Operating an Inhouse Computer and Using Outside Computer Services

An organization may have an inhouse computer, it may use an outside data processing service organization, or it may use a combination. The decisions and the management of the resulting operations are significant not only because of the expense of the operation or service but also because of the computer operations' role as a service department which accepts input data, performs processing and storage, and provides information. If the function is not well managed, the activities of the entire organization can be impaired.

This chapter discusses both managerial and operating considerations for a computer installation. Students frequently find it difficult to visualize what is happening as the computer operator puts a job into the computer. The section on operating the computer describes how a program is loaded, etc. Another section describes the operating system which manages much of the computer operations. Alternatives to an inhouse computer are explained, both service centers and time sharing.

Structure and Management of Computer Processing in Organizations

The data processing function should be structured and managed according to the same principles used in the rest of the organization. This includes a plan of organization and standards for procedures and performance. The activities in managing the development and running of an application illustrate both the overall flow of work and the management requirements.

Organization Computer processing departments usually follow one of two forms of organization with respect to systems analysis and programmers—the functional or the project organization. These two alternatives are illustrated in Figure 10-1.

The organization charts do not show the location of the computer department in the overall structure. In the most common plan the data processing department reports to the chief financial officer or chief accounting officer, such as financial vice-president, treasurer, or controller. There is, however, a growing tendency to move the data processing executive to a higher position in the organization with a title such as vice-president of management information systems.

As information systems have grown in size and complexity, basic functions of analyst, programmer, operator, and data preparation have been subdivided into further specialties. Some of the major functions which now exist or are beginning to emerge in some organizations are the following:

Position	Description
Information analyst	Works with users to define information requirements. Develops user procedures and instructions. Understands the organization, management, and decision-making functions. Has an ability to work with people.

System designer	Designs computer-based processing system to provide the information specified by the information analyst. This function requires higher technical capability than does that of information analyst. May specialize in area such as data communications.
Systems programmer	Writes specialized software such as operating systems and data management systems. Has technical proficiency in hardware and software.
Application programmer	Designs, codes, tests, and debugs computer programs for applications. Some installations separate programming into commercial or business applications and scientific applications with separate programming groups for the two types.
Maintenance programmer	Works on the maintenance (changes and corrections) of existing programs.
Database administrator	Administers and controls the organization database.
Computer operator	Operates the computer equipment.
Librarian	Stores and issues the computer files on tapes and disks. Files documentation. Maintains record of usage.
Control clerk (also called input/output control clerk)	Records control information and reviews performance of control procedures.
Information systems planner	Plans the future of the information system.

A Master Development Plan

An organization should not develop computer processing applications without an overall plan. As explained in Chapter 3, such a plan is often termed a "master development plan." It describes what the information system will consist of and how it is to be developed. The master development plan provides a framework for all detailed planning of applications, equipment selection, staffing, etc. In general, it contains four major sections (refer back to Figure 3-1).

1 Organizational goals and objectives
2 Inventory of current capabilities
3 Forecast of developments affecting the plan
4 The specific plan

Procedural and Performance Standards

Procedural standards are established by defining clearly and exactly how each job is to be done. This provides each person with a clear description of what is expected and the methods and techniques to be used. The standard methods provide a discipline to the data processing operations, which reduces training difficulties, increases the effectiveness of review and supervision, minimizes the effect of personnel turnover, and provides a basis for performance evaluation. A standard operating procedure manual specifies for all personnel the standard methods to be

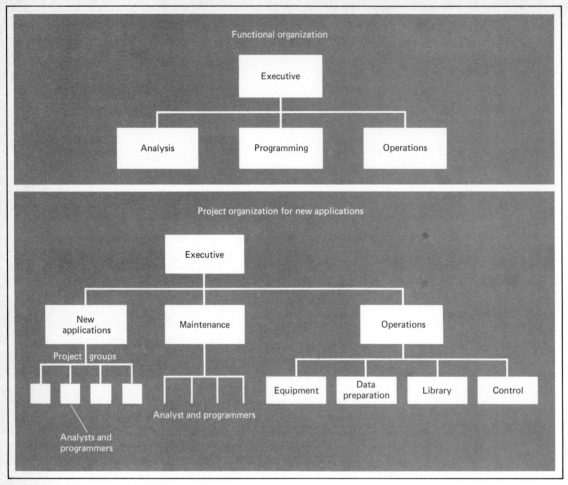

FIGURE 10-1 The basic organizational patterns.

used in that installation. This includes standard procedures for systems analysis, programming, and operating. The manual may also include organization charts and job descriptions.

Performance standards aid in planning, in controlling costs, and in evaluating performance for both equipment and personnel. Equipment standards for each separately operated unit specify the amount of time the equipment should be devoted to setup, production, scheduled maintenance, and unscheduled maintenance. The performance standards for a unit of equipment provide a basis for scheduling work, evaluating operator performance, spotting units to be replaced or repaired, etc.

Performance standards for systems and programming personnel are more difficult to establish than equipment standards because of the problems in estimating a task that has a substantial element of creativity. However, performance estimates can usually be made sufficiently close for management purposes. In one approach to estimation, each assignment is divided into tasks. For example, a programming job may be divided into tasks, and the assignment evaluated in terms of its size and complexity. Preestablished times for size and complexity categories are then applied to arrive at time estimates for performing each individual task using the standard methods for the installation (Figure 10-2). Once a performance standard has been estimated, it provides a basis for scheduling work and evaluating individual progress and performance. This approach is useful for both systems analysis and programming. Equipment operator jobs are machine-paced, and therefore operator scheduling is based on machine standards.

Facilities Management Many companies have had difficulty in managing their data processing installations. An alternative is the use of facilities management. A firm offering facilities management will take over a company's data processing operation and run it for a fee. By applying standardized management techniques, the facilities management firms appear to achieve substantial savings. The major problem is that of disengagement should the user of facilities management services decide to terminate the arrangement.

Management Activities in Development and Running of an Application In order to visualize the management of a computer installation, the management activities connected with the development life cycle presented in Chapter 3 will be surveyed.

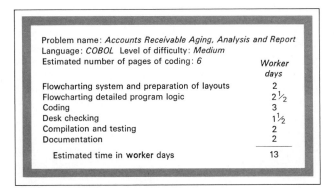

FIGURE 10-2 Estimating programming time.

Steps in life cycle	Management activities
Problem recognition and definition (feasibility assessment)	When the need for a computer application is recognized, a systems analyst is assigned to work on the project. A project name and/or number is assigned for keeping track of time devoted to the project. After a preliminary investigation, the project will be given a time budget for completion of the feasibility phase. The result of this phase will be a feasibility report with cost estimates. If the decision is favorable, the project is placed into the work schedule.

Information analysis and system analysis and design	As work proceeds, the information and systems analysts report the time spent on each element of the job on a time sheet and make an estimate of time to completion. For example, time may be reported by the basic tasks such as the following (or even in more detail):
	    Information requirements
	    Application specifications
	    Layout of inputs, reports, and files
	    System flowcharts
	    Development procedures
	The supervisor reviews progress based on time reports and time estimates and approves the work when it is completed.

Procedure and program development and conversion	The job is then assigned to a programmer who is given the system analysis specifications, a job number, and a time budget. The job is scheduled as with the systems analysis. The programmers record time by each phase of the job, such as:
	    Program planning
	    Coding
	    Desk checking
	    Assembly or compilation
	    Testing
	    Documentation
	    Conversion
	The hours are summarized by the clerical staff and compared with the time budget. The job, when completed, is analyzed by the supervisor for programming evaluation purposes. The supervisor reviews the program (for clarity and maintainability of coding, adequacy of testing, documentation, etc.) while it is being written and also before it is released for production use. Based on either delays or early completion, the programmer schedule is revised. The data processing executive is furnished with a periodic summary of program status for managerial review.

Operation and maintenance: Running of program	The operations supervisor prepares a production schedule showing the jobs to be run, the expected running time, and the time each job is to be completed. A new job is inserted in this schedule. When the time arrives for the job to be run, the operator obtains the program and any data files

from the program and file library. Using the operator instructions for the run as a guide, special forms (if any) are obtained, and the program, forms, and data files are loaded into the equipment. The program is then run. The running time is recorded either automatically by the computer or by the operator. The times are summarized by job and by major operating category and reviewed by the data processing management. A record of delays, errors, and other conditions which required corrective action is made and summarized for management review purposes.

Control and distribution of output

The control clerk logs in any control figures prepared when the data was recorded or converted. The control clerk records the computer control totals and checks for any discrepancy. The clerk examines the output for obvious errors and then distributes it according to the instructions in the run manual documentation. Any errors reported by the users are logged in, investigated, and corrected. A report of such errors is made periodically to the data processing management.

Correction and maintenance

Users may decide that there should be a change in the output. Errors may appear that were not detected in the testing. A maintenance programmer is assigned to make the change. The change is planned and approved. After the program changes are made, the programs are retested. The change documentation is added to the application documentation.

Operating the Computer

There are differences in procedures for operating different computers, but there is usually an operator console, instructions must be loaded into memory, there must be a method for starting the program, and there are provisions for specifying successful or unsuccessful terminations.

The Computer Console

The computer console (Figure 10-3) contains a control panel by which the operator monitors the action of the computer. The console may be mounted on the cabinet housing the central processor, or it may be a separate unit. Usually associated with the console is a low-volume input/output device, such as a typewriter or visual display unit. The control panel lights, switches, dials, and the console typewriter or visual display unit are used to:

1 Manually instruct the computer

2 Display the condition and status of the computer equipment and the input/ output devices

FIGURE 10-3 Computer console for IBM System 370/145. (*Courtesy of International Business Machines Corporation.*)

3 Display the contents of registers

4 Alter the operation of the equipment

5 Alter the contents of registers or other storage locations

6 Diagnose equipment malfunctions (by maintenance personnel)

The small incandescent lights on the panels of many computer consoles usually display the contents of the various registers. During the running of the program, the lights change too rapidly for the contents to be read. During debugging or when the computer halts, the register contents may be an aid in determining what has happened.

Various lights indicate the operation or condition of important assemblies in the central processor and in peripheral equipment. For example, there may be an overflow light, parity-error indicator, temperature warning light, indicators to display the results of program comparison tests, and lights to indicate off-normal conditions for peripheral equipment. Each item of equipment will have on it a small number of buttons and lights. The buttons are to start, stop, reset, etc., while the lights indicate off-normal conditions. For example, a light on a printer may indicate it is out of paper.

The console typewriter or visual display unit is used by programs or operating systems to send messages to the operator and by the operator to respond. Manual intervention to change the running of a program is frequently handled through the console keyboard.

Loading the Program into Memory

When the source program is assembled or compiled, the result is a machine-language program on some machine-readable medium, such as magnetic tape or magnetic disk. The program is generally stored in a program library. The library may be managed by a software package designed for that purpose. These program library packages are often termed "librarian software."

Each instruction must be stored in memory, so it must be assigned to a separate memory location. This assignment may be absolute, in which case the same instruction will always be put in the same location, or it may be relative, and the specific address is assigned by the load program which is part of the operating system. In relative addressing the assembled or compiled program contains addresses starting at location zero, and the loader adds a constant to arrive at the actual addresses to use.

Instructions will not automatically place themselves in the designated locations. There must be a procedure to take each instruction and place it in the location specified for it. This is accomplished by a load routine in the operating system. The load routine is put into memory in order to read and store the program to be loaded. A load routine may also be part of each program to be loaded. How does the load program get into memory (or the program to load the loader)? One general approach is a "bootstrap" technique. The first instruction entered into memory loads the next one, which loads a third, and so on until a small number of instructions are loaded. These few instructions then load the remaining instructions. A special load button on the console is sometimes available to read the first record into memory to start the bootstrap operation.

Starting the Program

The load program, as its last step, will usually transfer control back to the operating system or perhaps directly to the operating program just loaded and start execution. A message is typed or displayed to the operator to specify that the program has been loaded.

The computer console provides some means for specifying a starting address and transferring control to it. This is necessary in order to allow the operator to start or restart a program at a point other than the beginning. The branching may be done through console switches, dials, or console keyboard.

Successful and Unsuccessful Terminations

Once started, a program may be terminated for one of several reasons.

1 Successful completion
2 Programmed error termination
3 Continuous loop
4 Invalid operation

Successful completion of a program is indicated explicitly by a console message from the program, from the operating system, or from both. Programmed error halts are each associated with a specified console message. By reference to the instructions, the operator can determine the exact reason for the error halt. A program may occasionally get into a continuous loop (executes a sequence of steps over and over again) from which there is no exit. If allowed to continue, the computer would never stop performing the same loops. The reason for this is an error in programming. A loop of this sort may sometimes be spotted by a recurrent pattern on the console lights, but in most cases it is detected because of excessive running time. The expected maximum running time for a program is part of the operator instructions. If the program exceeds this limit, a loop is assumed and the run is aborted. Many computer centers automatically apply limits to small problems written in FORTRAN or similar languages; unless the writer of the program specifies a longer running time, the automatic limit is used. Most recent computers have a clock which can be interrogated by the program for this purpose. A program may also hang up because of an invalid operation or location (usually because of improper instruction modification). For example, a program instruction may send control to a location which contains data. The computer will attempt to use the data as an instruction and, if this is impossible, will halt.

Operating Systems

An *operating system,* also called "OS," "supervisor," "monitor," or "executive," is a set of routines to manage the running of the computer. Operating systems range in complexity from simple systems which manage only basic functions to very complex ones. In general, the more sophisticated the computer system, the more complex the operating system required to manage its use. The philosophy underlying the operating system is that the computer should perform those operator tasks which it can do faster and more accurately and that the computer should be kept operating as continuously and as effectively as possible. For simple, second-generation systems, the operating system was a convenience; for third-generation systems, it is essential to efficient operation.

Managing of Assembly and Compilation

Consider the steps, as shown in the table on page 299, required to compile and run a program written in a high-level language such as FORTRAN, both with and without an operating system.

Operator only	Operator and operating system
1 Operator examines program and determines that it is a FORTRAN program.	Operator: Puts program into card reader along with other jobs. Job and control cards are included with each program deck. (Typical job control cards are shown in Figure 10-4.)
2 Operator records start time, operator, and program name on a log.	
3 Operator locates copy of FORTRAN compiler.	
4 Operator loads FORTRAN compiler into storage (manual start).	Operating system automatically:
5 Operator starts FORTRAN compilation (manual start).	1 Determines that program is FORTRAN program to be compiled.
6 At completion, operator examines program printout to see if successful compilation.	2 Loads compiler and starts compilation.
7 If yes, operator loads FORTRAN program into storage (manual start).	3 Checks for successful compilation.

8 Operator determines if all input/output units are properly loaded with input data, cards, paper, tapes, etc.

9 Operator starts execution of program (manual start).

10 At completion, operator decides if it is a successful termination. If so, unloads all input/output media associated with program.

11 Operator writes time of completion on computer log and notes errors or other conditions.

12 Operator examines programs to be run and chooses next one to work on.

4 Loads object program and starts execution.

5 Provides messages to operator regarding any duties he or she may have.

6 Prepares a record of the time taken by the program, records error conditions, and updates operating statistics.

7 At successful completion goes on to next program.

Some of the tasks typically performed by an operating system are given in the following list:

Program loading
Interrupt handling
Scheduling of input/output operations
Operator communications
Job-to-job communications
Job accounting
Job scheduling and management

The scheduling of input/output may include the use of an input/output control system which will perform label verification, assignment of buffer areas in memory

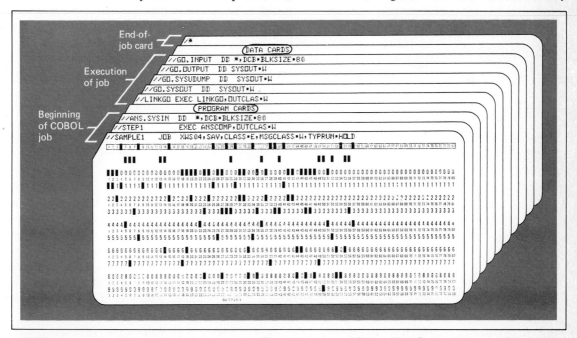

FIGURE 10-4 Job cards for a simple job using Job Control Language (JCL) on IBM System/370 under full operating system (OS) to (1) read a COBOL source program, (2) compile it, (3) execute it using data from the card reader, and (4) print the resulting compilation listing and output on the printer.

for use in input and output, error checking and recovery during input/output operations, etc.

Managing of Scheduling and Multiprogramming The job scheduling and management activity of the operating system can become quite complex. Their purpose is to provide a steady flow of work to the computer. Scheduling can be divided into two types—sequence scheduling and concurrent scheduling. A sequence-scheduling supervisory program selects the next program to be run on the basis of such factors as time of day, priority rankings of the programs in the job stack, and availability of input data. Only one program is scheduled into memory at a time.

The concurrent-scheduling program not only schedules the sequencing of programs but also directs the concurrent processing of two or more programs. This technique for having the computer handle several programs concurrently is known as "multiprogramming" or "parallel processing." The programs are placed in different sections (partitions) of memory, and the operating system switches control from one to the other. For example, a program to read cards and print their contents may be run concurrently with a program to update a file. The control routine in the operating system first gives control to the read/print program. This initiates a read-a-card instruction. Control is then shifted to the file update program. When the card for the first program has been read, the second program is interrupted and control is passed back to the first program, and so on. Since the read/print routine can proceed no faster than the reader and printer can operate, the central processing unit would be idle much of the time if multiprogramming were not used. The partitions can be fixed in size (sometimes termed MFT) or variable in size (MVT). Many computers operate with virtual storage, i.e., programs are written as if there were unlimited main memory. The operating system segments programs into pages and brings in pages as required during execution. The virtual storage version of an operating system (IBM calls it OS-VS) is therefore more complex than an operating system using only real storage.

Computer Performance Measurement and Improvement

In early-generation computers, measurement of computer utilization was simply elapsed time. This is no longer satisfactory for any but the simplest systems. The central processor and channels operate independently. The CPU can process while the channel is managing the reading or writing of data. Two or more channels can be active concurrently. Several jobs may be in execution in multiprogramming mode. Program pages may be in and out because of the use of virtual storage. But no computer system is completely utilized during the time it is operating. The CPU may have to wait because it cannot continue until it receives data from the channel. The channel may not operate because there are no requests. Jobs may be waiting on storage or input/output resources or be waiting for pages from virtual storage. Computer performance measurement (or computer performance evaluation) determines how well the operating system and application programs are utilizing the hardware for a given job mix, so that corrective action may be taken. Data collection for performance evaluation may be from:

1 Job accounting statistics that are prepared by the operating system [called "system measurement facility" (SMF) by IBM], or a manual job log if there is no automated job accounting

2 Hardware monitor

3 Software monitor

The hardware monitor is a data collection device attached by probes to the circuitry of the computer. It records the occurrence of specified signals by the CPU, memory, and channels. The data is recorded on tape for batch processing. It imposes no load on the computer system and does not interfere with the program. The hardware monitor is best suited for determining hardware component utilization and identifying resource conflicts. Examples of utilization measurements are CPU active (not idle), channel active, program partition active, and operating system active. The cost is fairly high because of special equipment and training in its use.

The software monitor is a high-priority application program or routine inserted into the operating system which collects detailed data on the behavior of the software and operating system during operations by sampling. At established intervals, the monitor routinely interrupts processing and gathers data from internal tables and status registers maintained by the CPU and by the operating system. The data is recorded, say, on magnetic tape, and analyzed. The program requires internal memory space, file space, and some operating time. The measurements have sampling errors. The software monitor is less expensive than hardware. It is suited for determining which jobs are unnecessarily holding onto resources and which jobs must wait for resources.

Experience suggests that the use of monitors can be very productive in improving performance where used properly. But "to put on a monitor to see what we find out" has generally been unsuccessful. The most successful approach is hypothesis-testing where the system is studied and operations analyzed to formulate performance improvement hypotheses. Measurement tools are then used to collect data for testing these improvement ideas.

Another method of performance improvement is optimization of program coding for more efficient execution. The use of certain coding features can vary in execution time, and when programs are executed in a virtual storage environment, coding that requires frequent jumping from page to page can be very inefficient. Yet to go over every program and recode it for efficiency would be very time-consuming and costly. It is not necessary to do so because a small percentage of the coding will be used over and over again, and this small percentage (say, 10 percent) can be examined closely for optimization purposes. In order to collect data on which parts of the code are being used, some compilers provide special measurement instructions; or the user can write some instructions to do this. Users who have analyzed their programs for improvement have been able to achieve substantial savings in running time.

As a rather dramatic example of the impact of performance measurement, a brokerage firm reported a 90 percent reduction in CPU use and a 75 percent reduction in elapsed time after changes following performance evaluation.[1] The firm had an online system for displaying current account information on visual displays. Nightly updating of the database took so long the system was not ready by morning. A software monitor was employed to collect data on program execution and use of resources. A heavy user of CPU time was a library routine for computing the size of data. The use of this routine was eliminated by some relatively minor program coding changes. This reduced the time by half. Other measurements showed waiting time for tape reel mounts. Changes were then made to eliminate this delay.

Using a Service Center for Computer Processing

A data processing service center or service bureau is an organization which provides data processing service to outside clients on a fee basis. There is considerable diversity in the data processing service center industry, but established firms tend to be able to provide a complete data processing service rather than merely renting equipment time. A typical well-established data processing service organization has qualified personnel to analyze customer requirements, write programs, etc., as well as having control over appropriate equipment. Most service centers have standard prewritten software to meet common processing requirements.

A data processing service can be used either in place of manual processing or to supplement an existing internal machine data processing installation. An application which can profitably be turned over to a service center will usually have one or more of the following characteristics:

1 Significant volume of records.

2 Considerable computation.

3 The data must be rearranged in several ways to obtain different tabulations or to perform different computations.

4 The time available for processing is too short for the regular inhouse processing staff, or there are insufficient personnel.

5 The application requires specialized knowledge or special equipment not available inhouse but found in the data processing center.

The service center is an obvious option for a small business or for a business which does not wish to have an inhouse installation. However, even if an organization has

---

[1] "Monitor Cuts CPU Time 90% on Broker's Daily Run," *Computerworld*, May 10, 1976, p. 15.

its own data processing equipment, it may still use a service center for reasons such as the following:

1 Special or periodic overloads

2 Projects requiring specialized handling, specialized knowledge, or special equipment (such as computer output microfilm)

3 Need for experience and assistance in connection with a conversion to new equipment

Types of Service Centers The diversity of service center organizations makes them somewhat difficult to categorize. The following different classifications are useful:

TABLE 10-1 CLASSIFICATION OF DATA PROCESSING SERVICE CENTERS

Ownership	Control of equipment	Frequency of processing	Type of equipment	Processing orientation
Manufacturer	Owner or prime lessee	Batch	Computer	Commercial
Independent	Block time lessee	Remote batch	Time-sharing computer	Scientific
Organization-affiliated		Time sharing	Specialized	Industry specialist
University				Full line

Most of these classifications are easily understood. The control of equipment classification is based on the fact that some service organizations are owners or lessees of their equipment, whereas others use block time (i.e., blocks of computer time) on installations which have excess time.

Periodic batch processing according to a schedule is offered by almost all service centers. Some offer time-shared processing on demand. Remote batch is a compromise between the two. A job is transmitted from a remote device and enters the job stream. It is executed in batch mode without interaction such as frequently occurs in time sharing. The results can be transmitted back to the input/output device at the user installation. Some processing centers are specialists in the type of work they do. For example, a center may specialize in data processing for automobile dealers or in scientific processing for architects. Specialized equipment is required for processing for banks, for processing optically marked tests, etc.

Method of Operation Although the organizational structure for a data processing service center may vary, there tend to be three major functions: sales, consulting/programming, and production.

The sales function is carried on by sales representatives who call upon customers to explain the services offered by the organization. They analyze customer requirements and present proposals for performing services.

The purpose of the consulting and programming function is to perform system analysis and prepare specialized system designs for each customer's unique requirements. If the system is accepted by the client, the service organization also prepares programs.

The production department performs the data processing activity for the firm. This is typically divided into three separate areas: data preparation, quality control, and data processing. The quality-control activity is concerned with controlling customer records and ensuring that the work is done correctly and on time. An account representative or account supervisor in the quality control group is assigned the responsibility for customer contact regarding the data processing.

Another way of describing how a service center operates is to trace the handling of a continuing commercial data processing contract, such as preparation of a payroll or preparation of accounts receivable. The representative who first calls on the customer may work out the solution and make an estimate, especially if the system is relatively uncomplicated and fits standard procedures already developed by the center. If the system is complicated or unique, systems analysts will prepare layouts, system flowcharts, programs, etc. Once the system is agreed upon and programs have been prepared, the client's files are converted to machine-readable form in order to get the system started. These files are then typically (but not always) stored at the service center. Thereafter, documents received from the client are logged in by the data processing center, checked for appropriateness by the control unit, then transcribed to machine-readable form (and verified). The data processing group obtains the master file from the quality-control group, runs the program, and turns the results back to quality control. The account representative examines the master records and the processed reports for completeness and accuracy and returns the master file to the storage area. The completed reports are either picked up by the client or transmitted by messenger service or mail. An error listing accompanies the reports. The client is advised through the error listing or through a call from the account representative as to the procedures to be followed to take care of the errors in the next data processing cycle.

Method of Charging for Service

There are three basic approaches to charging for data processing center services:

1 Fixed price
2 Time and materials at standard rate
3 Cost plus fixed fee or percentage

The fixed fee is preferred in most cases, with the understanding that changes not agreed on in advance can cost extra. It is well suited for standard program packages or for those cases where specifications for the customer's system are firm and few changes are to be anticipated. The fixed-price contract may take the form of a fixed fee, plus a charge for each item processed. There is usually a minimum charge for each processing period for recurring jobs. The minimum reflects the fact that there is an administrative cost associated with each client no matter how small the job.

Charging on the basis of time and materials at a standard rate is suitable where the problem and procedures are well defined but the running time, number of runs, or number of transactions are not known. It is also a useful method of charging in cases where the client's own program is being used. The basis of cost plus fixed fee or percentage is applicable where the problem or procedures are not well defined.

As a general principle, reruns due to erroneous input data or errors caused by the customer are charged to him. Reruns caused by the program being unable to handle conditions which were not excluded when the contract was taken are presumably the responsibility of the service center. In all cases, however, these should be discussed beforehand rather than after the fact.

Using a Time-sharing Service

Time sharing is the concurrent use of a single computer system by many independent users, each user having his or her own programs, each expecting fast response, and each operating independently without an awareness of the use of the facility by others. Time sharing is popular for universities and for certain types of scientific and engineering computation.

Basic Characteristics Time sharing may be viewed as an extension of multiprogramming in which the computer works on several programs concurrently, going from one to another for the purpose of maximizing the use of the system hardware. Time sharing adds the notion of servicing all programs frequently enough that a user does not become discouraged with the waiting time. The direct access to the computer by many users is the reason that a time-sharing system is also referred to as a multiple-access system.

Time sharing may be used internally within an organization or by a data processing service center. A university, for example, may have a central computer facility with remote terminals at various points on the campus from which many faculty members and students simultaneously make use of the computer. A data processing service center which offers time sharing provides continuous access to the computer.

A time-sharing computer arrangement will typically have the following characteristics:

1 Each user has one or more input/output devices connected to the central computer by communication lines (Figure 10-5). The most common input/output terminal devices are the typewriter and visual display device. The most common communication connection is over the facilities of a telephone company.

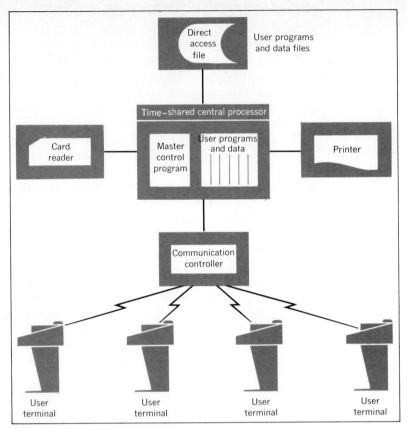

FIGURE 10-5 A time-sharing computer system.

2 Each user acts independently of the others who are connected to the system. Each user sends data and instructions from the terminal, acting as if he or she were the sole user.

3 The central computer accepts the data and instructions arriving simultaneously from many users and, by giving each user a small but frequently repeated segment of computer time, services all users concurrently. For most problems, the computer can send the requested output back almost immediately.

4 The user's data files are maintained at the central computer center. The user instructions to the computer identify the files to be used. The system is designed to prevent one user from making unauthorized access to the files of another user.

5 Each user has a private set of programs, plus access to a set of public programs.

6 The data files, program files, and input/output devices are all directly connected to the computer, so that processing can be performed at random as transactions occur or requests are made.

Time sharing may make use of a computer which does only time sharing, or time sharing may be provided by a part of the computer resources dedicated to that activity, the remainder being available for regular processing. The latter arrangement is sometimes called a time-sharing option (TSO). In either case, the operating system must have special routines for managing the sharing of the computer memory and processing time.

Methods for Sharing a Computer

In time sharing, the computations associated with a problem typically are not run continuously until the answer is obtained, because this might mean that a program requiring a long running time would cause an excessive delay for other users. Instead, each user is given a small amount of computer time with such frequency that the access appears to be continuous.

In implementing this sharing arrangement, there are two problems: sharing the main memory and sharing the central processor. Sharing the main memory is a problem since there is a limit on the size of storage, such that all the program sharing the processor cannot be in memory at once. Sharing the central processor presents difficulties because the computer must switch between programs, giving each a share of the time so that no program is noticeably delayed.

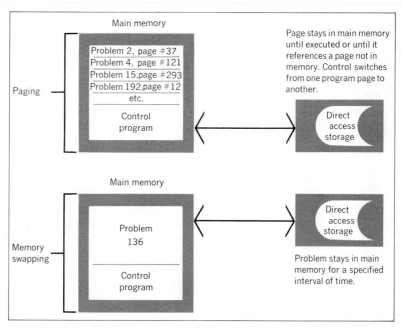

FIGURE 10-6 Methods for sharing main memory in time sharing.

There are many schemes for sharing the main memory (Figure 10-6). These may be classified as (1) paging and (2) memory swapping. In paging, each program is broken into small sets of instructions. These pages may range from a fairly small number of instructions to quite a large segment of a program. For example, one large scientific system uses pages of 1000 computer words, while another business-oriented service uses pages of only 64 words. When a program is to be run, a single page (or a small number of pages) is brought into memory and executed. Any reference by this page to another page in the program will necessitate bringing that page into memory. The previous page is no longer needed, and its memory space can be released. Pages from many programs may be in memory simultaneously, thereby allowing the computer to switch between programs.

In the memory-swapping approach, the entire program is moved in or out of main memory. Only one program is in memory at a time, and it is allowed only a very short residence before it is rolled out in favor of the next program. Both alternatives require a sophisticated program to supervise the operation and high-speed transfer rate from secondary storage.

If pages from many programs are in memory at the same time, the computer shares the processing time among them. Two methods may be used for deciding when to switch between them. One method is to switch at the end of a very short time slice. Each program gets its slice of time if it can use it. This is very useful in scientific processing where the time for any one problem is not known. The other method is to switch each time the program being executed has to wait for a direct access file reference or for an input/output operation. A program may thus execute and wait many times before its execution is complete. If memory swapping is used, each program gets a small amount of processing time before being moved from memory to be replaced by the next one. The program then waits its turn, repeating the cycle until it is finished.

An Evaluation of Time Sharing

The sharing by remote users has benefits from interaction and immediate processing. It introduces new cost elements because of the need for terminal devices and communications lines. It also results in added operating time at the computer center because of the time required to switch programs in and out of main memory and to switch from processing one program at a time to processing many programs, each for a short but frequently repeated interval of processing time.

If a time-sharing arrangement is deemed advisable, some of the selection considerations are response time, terminal devices used, programming language, amount of systems assistance provided, control features, and stability. Time sharing dominates in the field of "short" problems—student, research, and engineering-type computations where immediate response speeds the other work of the user. A limited amount of time sharing is being used for commercial processing (such as order processing).

SUMMARY   The management of the data processing organization can make effective use of traditional management methods. These include job descriptions, organization charts, a master development plan, standard procedures, and performance standards. Where a company does not wish to be involved in day-to-day management, operations may be turned over to a facilities management firm.

The operation of the computer is under the direction of the operating system. The operator makes use of the computer console and the console typewriter or visual display unit to communicate with the computer. The operator does not have to load the individual programs into the computer; this is usually done by the operating system on the basis of job instructions and job control cards.

The complexity of operations when a computer is doing multiprogramming, using virtual storage, etc., makes it difficult to evaluate operating performance and to know how to make changes for improved efficiency. Performance measurement improvement methods include the use of job statistics, hardware monitors, and software monitors to collect data by which performance improvement hypotheses may be tested.

An inhouse computer is not the only alternative. A user may consider a data processing service organization. Almost all such organizations offer batch processing service; a smaller number offer time-shared use of a computer. Because of the unique characteristics of time sharing, an organization with an inhouse computer may still make use of outside time-shared computing.

EXERCISES   1   Define the following terms:
    (a) Facilities management   (e) Multiprogramming
    (b) Loader   (f) Paging
    (c) Bootstrap technique   (g) Memory swapping
    (d) Operating system

2   Explain the difference between the duties of a systems programmer, an applications programmer, and a maintenance programmer.

3   Explain the difference between an information analyst and a system designer.

4   Define the general content of a master development plan.

5   What can the operator learn from the console lights?

6   What are the advantages and disadvantages in using facilities management firms?

7   How is a program loaded? How does it get started? What causes it to stop?

8   What are the advantages of the use of performance standards?

9   Why should an installation adopt standard procedures?

10   What is the purpose of job control cards?

11   Why would an operating system with variable partitions for multiprogramming be more complex than one with fixed partitions? Why would virtual storage make the operating system more complex?

12   Explain the difference between hardware and software monitors.

13   The data processing manager feels that monitors should be used to "see if anything pops out." Contrast this with the hypothesis approach and explain why the proposal

by the DP manager is not likely to be effective.

14 Why might a company with an inhouse computer use a service center?

15 A service center went into bankruptcy. What happens to the client files at the service center?

16 A data processing service center offers a payroll service—preparation of checks, tax reports, analyses, etc. What method are they likely to use in charging for the service?

17 List advantages and disadvantages of time sharing for
(*a*) Scientific processing   (*b*) Commercial data processing

18 What event might make a time-sharing user aware of other users?

19 What is the difference between paging and swapping for time sharing?

20 What must the operating system do to operate in time-sharing mode?

21 One company reported dramatic savings from transferring some jobs from time sharing to batch. Why were these savings possible?

Chapter

11

Quality Control and Security in Computer Processing

Computer data processing removes many traditional procedures for the detection and control of errors. A clerk doing data processing by hand or using a calculating device which produces a visible record will scan the results of his or her work and will question answers which appear to be unreasonable or not "right." In the computer installation, computations are performed at electronic speed, and intermediate results are stored in the computer in a form which cannot be scanned visually. Metal disks, metal drums, and plastic tape hold the files in which records are stored. Since the data stored on the magnetic surfaces cannot be read without a machine conversion, questions arise about the state of various records and the accuracy of computations made by the machine. How does a person know, for example, that the results of a statistical computation are correct or that the accounts-receivable file contains the data it should? A related question which applies to files where there are no visible records is the extent to which the concern should protect itself against the destruction of the records either through an accident or through malfunctioning equipment. There is also the problem of internal control. In data processing by hand or by mechanical equipment, there is typically a sufficiently large staff involved in processing any given set of figures so that the division of work and the various cross-checking procedures provide considerable control against inaccuracy and fraud. The computer staff, on the other hand, is small and has under its control the computations and records which previously were divided among large staffs of clerical personnel.

Too often, computer centers operate with a higher error rate than is necessary because management does not insist upon a lower error frequency. Error control is not without cost, and a manager needs to understand the method for error control and the attendant problems in order to evaluate the value of tighter control against its cost.

This chapter describes the methods for quality control over computer data processing. The emphasis of the chapter is upon controls in a data processing environment rather than controls for one-time scientific or engineering problems. However, one section of the chapter discusses quality control for one-time computational problems.

An Overview of Quality Control in Data Processing

The control over the quality of computer data processing should be established not just by having a correct program but by a series of controls which are applied at each stage of processing. The flow of processing is shown in Figure 11-1. Error detection and control procedures can be applied at each of the activities in the flow:

Data recording
Data transmittal to data processing
Data preparation for processing
Input to processing
Processing

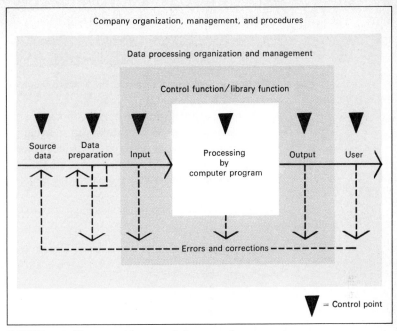

FIGURE 11-1   The control framework for computer processing.

Files and programs
Output
Distribution of output
Output use

Control procedures for these different control points are described in the chapter. Not all will be applicable to each application. The designer of an application must choose the appropriate methods from the available techniques. These techniques are applied in an organizational framework—both the overall organizational controls and the specific organization of the data processing equipment.

Organization for Data Processing Control The data processing organization exists within a larger organizational framework. As such, data processing should be subject to standard organizational controls. Significant control is exercised by top management, data processing management, and the control function and library function within data processing.

Top management has the overall responsibility for data processing. This consists of:

1 Authorization of major changes or additions to hardware and acquisition of purchased software

2 Authorization of major applications to be put on the computer system

3   Postinstallation review of actual cost and the effectiveness of hardware, software, and applications

4   Review of organization and control practices of the data processing function

5   Evaluation of performance based on a performance plan or standard of performance. This will include
    (*a*) Cost of data processing activities compared with planned cost
    (*b*) Frequency and duration of delays in meeting processing schedules
    (*c*) Error rates for errors detected at various control points

The data processing management is responsible for:

Recruiting, training, and supervising performance of data processing personnel

Supervising completion of projects to design and implement applications

Supervising day-to-day operations

Preparing plans, budgets, project justification, etc.

Errors in operation will be reduced if the installation has standard procedures which are followed by all personnel. This will include standard programming practices, standard operating procedures, and standard control procedures.

The control function in a data processing installation consists of activities which monitor the processing and ensure that no data is lost or mishandled during processing. In small installations, the control activities may be performed by the data processing manager and a clerk; in large installations, there will be a separate staff. The duties of the control function will include:

1   Logging in batches of input data and recording control information

2   Recording progress of work through the department

3   Reconciling control totals produced at various stages of processing

4   Scrutinizing console log and/or preparation and analysis of control reports from system performance data

5   Supervising distribution of output

6   Liaison with users regarding errors, logging correction requests, and recording corrections made

7   Maintaining error log and preparing error report

A librarian function in the operations part of the organization maintains control over data files and programs. The librarian is responsible for storing magnetic tapes, disk packs, card decks, etc., on which the data files and programs are stored. The librarian may also be in charge of the documentation records. Data files and programs are issued to computer operators on the basis of the schedule of jobs to be run. They are returned to the librarian after the job has been completed. One of the duties of the librarian is to record the condition of magnetic tape with respect to read-write errors encountered, unusable portion of tape, etc. The librarian may also be responsible for offsite storage of backup files and backup copies of programs.

Building Error Control into Applications

Error control in a computer application begins with the application design and is aided by quality control procedures during the development process. The design should provide for adequate input validation, for control comparisons and control outputs during processing, for data in the outputs that will aid users in detecting errors, and for an audit trail to trace the processing performed. The development process should produce error-free, maintainable programs. Suggested approaches which aid in this objective are top-down modular design, chief programmer team, structured programming, structured walkthroughs, and a comprehensive test plan for checking the application. Special care should be taken to prepare instructions and procedures for handling and correcting errors detected during processing.

Conceptual Basis for Control Techniques

Redundancy is the basis for control techniques. *Redundancy* has a precise definition in communication theory, but for the purposes of this discussion can be defined more broadly as an extra element in a code, an operation, etc., which would not be necessary except for the need for error control. In general, as redundancy is increased, error detection is improved. However, there is a cost associated with redundancy, and too much redundancy can reduce system effectiveness. For example, one check bit in a code is quite good at detecting most transmission errors. Two redundant code elements improve the error-detection rate and allow some automatic correction of errors. But the extra error detection and error correction are obtained at the price of increased transmission time, extra circuitry, etc. The check bits themselves introduce possible errors in transmitting them, performing the checks, etc. The extra check bits are redundant in that they would not be necessary if transmission were 100 percent correct.

The concept of redundancy in error control will be observed in most of the controls described in the chapter. Redundancy does not, however, provide automatic error control; error-control procedures must be designed to use the redundant elements to detect errors. For example, a check bit does not detect an error in transmitting a code. This is done by circuitry which uses the check bit. Examples of redundant elements which are explained in the chapter are:

Parity or check bit
Read after write check
Check digit
Hole count
Two read stations

Control total
Hash total
Key verification
Echo check

**Evaluating
Error Controls**

The major error-control procedures to be presented in this chapter provide for protection against almost any type of error. Despite the availability of these methods, one still hears about payroll checks being written for $1 million instead of $100. In these cases, elementary control features have not been used. On the other hand, error controls, like all other controls, require an expenditure of resources. Programmed controls require programming effort; they also take up valuable storage. In other words, controls need to be part of the data processing system, but they can be expensive; therefore, before implementing a control, the designer should evaluate its merits by asking such questions as

1 How frequently might this error occur?
2 What are the monetary consequences of the error?
3 What are the nonmonetary consequences of the error?
4 What is the cost of detecting these errors?
5 If the error is missed at this point, will it be detected later?
6 What are the consequences of late rather than early detection?

Control over Data Preparation and Input

The flow of control in data processing starts with data preparation and moves to input procedures, processing, output, and distribution of output to users. Data preparation and input are the weakest links in the chain of data processing. The input data for processing may be in error for one of four general reasons: (1) It may be incorrectly recorded at the point of inception; (2) it may be incorrectly converted to machine-readable form; (3) it may be incorrectly read or otherwise entered into the computer; or (4) it may be lost in handling. Controls should therefore be established at the point of data creation and conversion to machine-readable form, at the point the data enters the computer, and at points when the data is handled, moved, or transmitted in the organization. Table 11-1 presents an inventory of methods which the system designed can use in order to achieve the level of error control required for an application.

**Procedural Controls
and Data Review**

Standard clerical practices and well-designed data forms impose procedural controls on the creation of data. For example, if a part number is to be written on a document, boxes may be printed which contain the exact number of spaces required for the part number. Any clerk writing a part number containing less or more digits than the quantity required will notice the error. For example, bad and

TABLE 11-1 METHODS FOR INPUT DATA ERROR CONTROL

At point data is created and converted to machine-readable form	At point data is first put into the computer	At points data is handled, moved, or transmitted
Procedural controls	File label	Transmittal controls
Data review	(internal)	Route slip
Verification	Tests for validity:	Control total
Check digit	Code	External file labels
Input echo	Character	
Terminal validity checks	Field	
	Transaction	
	Combination of fields	
	Missing data	
	Check digit	
	Sequence	
	Limit or reasonableness test	
	Control total	

good document designs (from an error-control standpoint) for collecting a social security number are shown below:

Bad	Social security number _____
Good	Social security number ☐☐☐-☐☐-☐☐☐☐

Where direct input terminals are used, templates over the keys, identification cards, and other procedural aids help to reduce input errors. Turnaround documents (described in Chapter 9) reduce data entry errors because the data to be entered is prepared by a prior computer operation.

Some installations make a review examination of data (especially codes which identify part number, product, etc.) before it is converted to machine-readable form. This checking may be performed in connection with the addition of information, or it may be an entirely separate step.

Verification of Conversion to Machine-readable Form

When data is punched into cards or keyed onto tape or disk, the accuracy of the data conversion can be tested by mechanically verifying the keypunching operation. For keypunching of cards, this may require two separate keydriven machines (a card punch and a verifier) or a single machine which can operate in both punch and verify modes. The data is first punched by a keypunch operator. The punched cards and original data are then given to a verifier operator who inserts the punched card in the verifier and rekeys the punches using the original source documents. The verifier does not punch, but instead compares the data keyed into the verifier with the punches already in the card. If they are the same, the punched card is presumed to be correct. A common indication that this check has been performed is for the verifier to place a notch at the end of the card or over the column containing the difference. Similar verification is used with a keydisk or keytape device where data is keyed and recorded directly on a magnetic disk or tape. The same device is used (at separate times) both to record data and to verify it. The verification process includes the correction of errors.

Verification is a duplicate operation and therefore doubles the cost of data conversion. Various methods are used to reduce the amount of verifying. One method is to verify only part of the data. Some data fields are not critical, and an error will not affect further processing. Examples are descriptive fields containing vendor name, part description, etc. which, under most circumstances, are not critical. The use of prepunched cards, prepunched stubs, and duplication of constant data during keypunching may allow verification to be restricted to the variable information added by the card punch. A second approach used with statistical data is to verify only if the keying error rate is above an acceptable level. Each operator's work is checked on a sample basis. If the error rate is acceptable, no verification is made; if not, there is complete verification. Other control procedures to be explained may be substituted for verification, e.g., a check digit on an account number or a batch control total.

Check Digit In most applications involving an identification number, it may be verified for accuracy by a check digit. A check digit is determined by performing some arithmetic operation on the number. The arithmetic operation is performed in such a way that the typical errors encountered in transcribing a number will be detected. There are many possible procedures. For example, a simple check digit procedure might be as follows:

1 Start with a number without the check digit.

2 Multiply each digit by the weight assigned to the digit position. Examples are $1 - 2 - 1 - 2, \ldots$, and $1 - 3 - 5 - 7 \ldots$.

3 Sum the individual digits in the resulting products plus the digits not multiplied.

4 Divide the sum-of-digits by the modulus and save the remainder.

5 Subtract the remainder from the modulus to give the check digit.

6 Add check digit to number (at end or elsewhere).

The most common modulus is 10; the next most common is 11. As an example, assume the number 47648, modulus 10, and weights of 1 – 3 – 5 – 7 – 9:

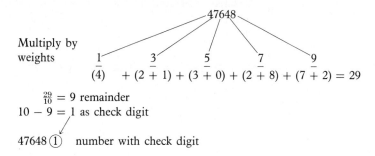

$\frac{29}{10} = 9$ remainder

$10 - 9 = 1$ as check digit

47648 ①   number with check digit

Note that check digit procedures are not completely error proof. For example, if weights of 1 – 2 – 1 – 2 were used, 47846 and 47678 would yield the same check digit. It is, however, unlikely that transpositions of this form will occur. The check digit does not guard against assignment of an incorrect but valid code, for example, the assignment of the wrong but valid identification code to a customer.

The checking of the code number for the check digit may be performed by either a data preparation or data entry device such as a keypunch, keydisk, or intelligent terminal, or it may be programmed into the computer. The use of the check digit as part of the preparation device or terminal has the advantage that an incorrect code is detected before it enters the computer process. A data item checked by a check digit does not normally need to be verified. Examples of uses are charge account numbers, employee pay numbers, and bank account numbers.

Input Echo and Terminal Validity Checks

When data is input via a terminal (either offline or online), the data being input can be displayed in a manner that will facilitate visual review and verification of input. For example, the input data can be formatted to aid in the review (with labels, separation into data items, lining up decimal positions, etc.). Also, codes and abbreviations can be expanded to identify the meaning of the code. If input is code 47 for $\frac{1}{2}$-in. strapping tape, the terminal might display CODE 47 1/2 INCH STRAPPING TAPE.

As previously mentioned, intelligent terminals can be programmed to perform validity checks on input data. Nonintelligent terminals can transmit to a computer which may perform validity tests as part of the process of data acceptance from the terminal. The types of validity tests that can be made are described later in the chapter. In either case, when errors are detected, an error message may be displayed and an immediate correction made.

Input Validation

Before data is used in updating computer files or other computer processing, it is usually tested for errors to the extent possible or appropriate in the light of the consequences of input errors. A separate input validation run or input editing run may be used, or the checking may be performed at the time of processing. Input validation is usually performed even if the data was validated at an input terminal. If errors are detected, the erroneous transaction or the record found to contain an error is shunted aside, rather than having the computer stop in order to make corrections. There will be some control output at the time of the input validation (Figure 11-2). A complete analysis of the rejected transactions may be prepared immediately or subsequently. The erroneous records will usually be written on an error file. Items which are rejected are corrected and reentered at a later run.

One approach to error handling is a circulating error file or error log. All rejected transactions are added to the error file. Those responsible for corrections are given an error report. When corrections are made, the error transaction is removed from the error file. As a result, there is a file of uncorrected transactions which is subject to review. If an error is not corrected, managerial action may be taken. An error log in which rejected transactions are recorded and then checked off when corrections are made is also used to prevent duplicate corrections.

Error controls at the point data is entered into the computer are file labels and tests for validity. Control totals are used at this point, but these totals are such a basic procedure and useful in movement controls as well that they are described separately.

A file label is a record at the beginning and also possibly the end of the file which contains identification and control information. These records are used to ensure that the proper transaction file or master file is used and that the entire file

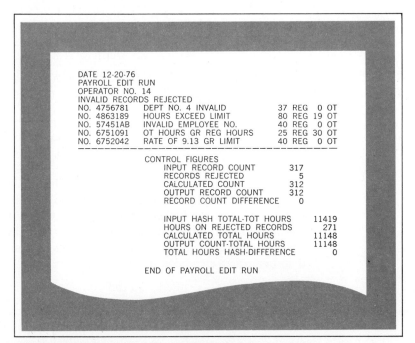

```
DATE 12-20-76
PAYROLL EDIT RUN
OPERATOR NO. 14
INVALID RECORDS REJECTED
NO. 4756781    DEPT NO. 4 INVALID          37 REG  0 OT
NO. 4863189    HOURS EXCEED LIMIT          80 REG 19 OT
NO. 57451AB    INVALID EMPLOYEE NO.        40 REG  0 OT
NO. 6751091    OT HOURS GR REG HOURS       25 REG 30 OT
NO. 6752042    RATE OF 9.13 GR LIMIT       40 REG  0 OT
─────────────────────────────────────────────────────────
                 CONTROL FIGURES
                     INPUT RECORD COUNT        317
                     RECORDS REJECTED            5
                     CALCULATED COUNT          312
                     OUTPUT RECORD COUNT       312
                     RECORD COUNT DIFFERENCE     0

                     INPUT HASH TOTAL-TOT HOURS      11419
                     HOURS ON REJECTED RECORDS         271
                     CALCULATED TOTAL HOURS          11148
                     OUTPUT COUNT-TOTAL HOURS        11148
                     TOTAL HOURS HASH-DIFFERENCE         0

                 END OF PAYROLL EDIT RUN
```

FIGURE 11-2 Sample output from input validation run.

has been processed. The label at the beginning is the header label which identifies the file. It is considered good practice to label all files with header labels. Typical contents are

Name of file
Creation date
Purge data
Identification number
Reel number (for magnetic tape)

The trailer label is the last record and summarizes the file. When used, the trailer label contents normally include

Record count
Control totals for one or more fields
End-of-file or end-of-reel code

The data can be subjected to programmed tests by the computer in the input validation run or by a programmable terminal at data entry to establish that it is within the limits established for valid data. Some examples of validation which can be done are:

1 *Valid code* If there are only a limited number of valid codes, say, for coding expenses, the code being read may be checked to see if it is one of the valid codes.

2 *Valid character* If only certain characters are allowed in a data field, the computer can test the field to determine that no invalid characters are used.

3 *Valid field size, sign, and composition* If a code number should be a specified number of digits in length, the computer may be programmed to test that the field size is as specified. If the sign of the field must always be positive or must always be negative, then a test may be made to ensure that there is not an incorrect sign. If the field should contain only numerics or only alphabetics, then a test may be made to determine that the field does indeed contain a proper composition of characters.

4 *Valid transaction* There is typically a relatively small number of valid transactions which are processed with a particular file. There is a limited number, for example, of transaction codes which can apply to accounts receivable file updating. As part of input error control, the transaction code can be tested for validity.

5 *Valid combinations of fields* In addition to each of the individual fields being tested, combinations may be tested for validity. For example, if a sales representative code may be associated with only a few territory codes, this can be checked.

6 *Missing data* The program may check the data fields to make sure that all data fields necessary to code a transaction have data in them.

7 *Check digit* The check digit is verified on identification fields having this control feature.

8 *Sequence* In batch sequential processing the data to be processed must be arranged in a sequence which is the same as the sequence of the file. Both the master file and the transaction file may be tested to ensure that they are in proper sequence, ascending or descending as the case may be. The sequence check can also be used to account for all documents, if these are numbered sequentially.

9 *Limit or reasonableness* This is a basic test for data processing accuracy. Input data should usually fall within certain limits. For example, hours worked should not be less than zero and should not be more than, say, 50 hours. The upper limit may be established from the experience of the particular firm. Input data may be compared against this limit to ensure that no input error has occurred or at least no input error exceeding certain preestablished limits. Examples are:
   (*a*) The total amount of a customer order may be compared with the customer average order amount. If this order exceeds, say, three times the amount of the average order, then an exception notice may be printed.
   (*b*) A material receipt which exceeds two times the economic order quantity established for the particular item might be subject to question.
   (*c*) A receiving report amount may be compared with the amount requested on the purchase order. If there is more than a small percentage variance, then there is an assumption of an error in the input data.
   (*d*) In a utility billing, consumption is checked against prior periods to detect possible errors or trouble in the customer's installation.

Control Totals Control totals are a basic method of error control to determine whether all items in a batch have been received and processed. The control total procedure requires that a control figure be developed by some previous processing and that the current data processing recompute this amount, comparing the resultant total with the previous total. Control totals are normally obtained for batches of data. The batches are kept to a reasonable size, so that errors can be easily isolated. For example, the sales slips to be processed by computer are first added on an adding machine to arrive at a control total for the sales in the batch. A control total for payroll might be the number of employees for which checks should be prepared. Control figures may be financial totals, hash totals, or document or record counts.

Financial totals These are totals such as sales, payroll amounts, and inventory dollar amounts which are normally added together in order to provide financial summaries.

Hash totals These are totals of data fields which are typically not added. The total has meaning only as a control and is not used in any other way in data processing. To determine that all inventory items are processed, a control total might be developed of the inventory item numbers, and this control would be compared with the sum of the item numbers obtained during the processing run.

Document or record count In many cases, rather than obtaining a financial total or hash total, it may be sufficient merely to obtain a count to ensure that all documents or records have been received and processed.

Control totals prepared prior to computer processing are furnished to computer processing as an input data item. The computer is then programmed to accumulate control totals internally and make a comparison. A message confirming the comparison should be printed out even if the comparison did not disclose an error. These messages are then subject to review by the control clerk (Figure 11-3).

When processing is performed online as transactions occur, there is no batch control because the transactions are not batched. However, it is possible to apply the batch concept. Transactions are accumulated during a period such as a day. Batch totals are also accumulated for various groupings of transactions (logical batches). At the end of the period, logical batch totals are available for checking against other counts or physical data collected by operations. The transactions may be sorted and printed as a logical batch listing. For example, there may be a listing of transactions by terminal or by salesperson (Figure 11-4).

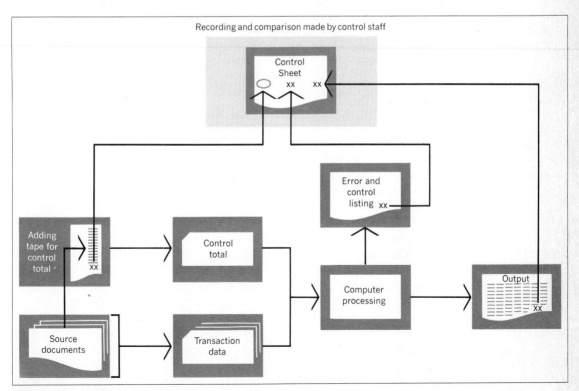

FIGURE 11-3 Use of control totals.

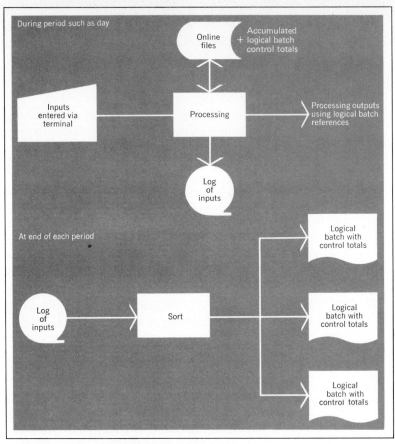

FIGURE 11-4 Use of logical batches in online processing.

Movement and Handling Controls

Transmittal controls, route slips, control totals, and external file labels are examples of controls over the internal handling and movement of input data. The objective of these controls is to prevent (or detect) the loss or nonprocessing of data. Control totals have already been explained, and external file labels are described in connection with file safeguards. Only the transmittal controls and route slips are discussed in this section.

When data is moved about through an organization, there is always a possibility that it may be lost or otherwise diverted from the proper processing channels. To ensure proper identification of data as it moves through the company, and more especially as it moves through the data processing steps, it is customary to use some form of status identification. As batches of data enter the data processing center, they may be logged on a listing showing the data received. As each batch passes a data processing station, it is registered, recording the fact that the batch has been processed. The batch itself usually carries a route slip which indicates the path of processing which it should follow and provides spaces to keep a record of processing performed. After data documents have been processed, they are canceled by marking or perforating to prevent accidental or deliberate reprocessing.

Control over Processing

Control over processing makes use of programmed controls. The processing should provide a processing trail which is suitable both for internal needs and as an audit trail for audits of the organization.

Programmed Control over Processing

The types of program controls which test the computer processing are the limit or reasonableness test, the crossfooting or crosstesting check, and control figures.

As with input data, a control over processing can be exercised by program steps which test the results of processing by comparing them with predetermined limits or by comparison with flexible limits which test the reasonableness of the results. In a payroll application, the net pay can be checked against an upper limit, an amount such that any paycheck exceeding the limit is probably in error. In a billing operation for a relatively homogeneous product, such as steel bars and plates, the weight of the shipment may be divided into the billing in order to develop a price per pound. If the price per pound exceeds the average by more than a predetermined percentage, a message will be written for subsequent follow-up to determine if the billing is in error.

It is frequently possible to check computer data processing in a manner similar to the manual method of crossfooting. Individual items are totaled independently, and then a crossfooting total developed from the totals. For example, in a payroll application, the totals are developed for gross pay, for each of the deduction items, and for the net pay. The total for net pay is then obtained independently by taking the total for gross pay and deducting the totals for each of the deduction items. If this crossfooting does not yield identical figures, then there has been some error in the program of processing.

Control figures developed in a manner similar to the input control totals can be used for testing the data processing within the machine. For example, the number of items to be invoiced in a billing run may be used as a control total and compared with the number of items billed on invoices.

The Processing Trail

The processing trail (or audit trail) consists of references, intermediate printouts, listings, etc., which document the flow of processing such that

1   Any transaction can be traced to the accounts in which it is aggregated and the report totals of which it is a part.

2   Any total in a report or in an account can be explored and traced back to the detailed transactions from which it was aggregated.

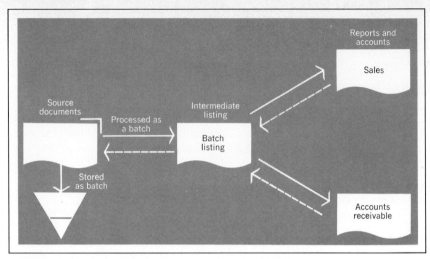

FIGURE 11-5 Processing trails.

Two examples will illustrate the concept of the processing trail.

Assume a credit sale which is to be traced to the accounts receivable record and to its inclusion in the sales figure. The sales invoices are probably batched and given a batch number. As part of the processing, the sales for the batch would be added to the sales total, and each individual sale would be added to the appropriate customer accounts receivable account. The batch itself might be listed. Any source sales transaction can be traced first to a transaction listing with a batch number and then to the recording of sales totals. The sales can also be traced via the batch reference to each sales entry in the accounts receivable detail file. The reverse procedure in this case is quite simple. The accounts receivable and sales entries have batch references which point to a transaction listing and to the batch of transaction documents (Figure 11-5).

The provisions for a processing trail may take several forms, but in all cases, there must be a means for tracing from the source document forward to the final aggregation and back from the aggregation to the source document. For batch processing, this is done by such references as batch number, document number, date of processing batch, etc. When processing is performed online on individual transactions rather than on batches of data, each transaction is identified by a unique identifier which is input or is assigned by the computer. Logical batches (stored for access or printed) form another basis for an online audit trail (refer back to Figure 11-4). References in records which point to the updating transaction use the unique identifier for the transaction and/or the reference to the logical batch.

Control over Output and Distribution

Before being distributed, the output from computer processing should be checked in two ways:

1 Comparing of control totals on output with previously prepared control total (balancing to input controls)

2 Screening to spot obvious errors

The distribution of output should be controlled to ensure that only those authorized receive it. Part of the control documentation for an application is the distribution list.

Persons receiving the output are an important error-detection control point, and provisions should be made in the system design for error feedback from recipients of output.

Hardware Features for Control over Equipment Malfunctions

Computer hardware consists of both mechanical parts (such as card reader transport) and electronic elements. The electronic portion is very reliable; the mechanical portion is somewhat less error-free. Both need periodic maintenance. The

TABLE 11-2 METHODS FOR ERROR DETECTION IN COMPUTER HARDWARE

Method of error detection	Description	Example
Redundant code character	Extra bit in coding of data. The number of 1-bits is summed. The parity bit is the 1-bit or 0-bit which makes the sum of 1-bits equal to an odd number (if odd parity).	Parity check bit C 1 ← Check bit B 0 6-bit A 0 code 8 0 with 4 0 parity 2 1 bit 1 1 Number 3
Duplicate process	Same operation is performed twice and the results compared.	Two read stations for card reader
Echo check	Signal sent to device to perform an operation; device returns a signal verifying that equipment was activated.	Printer echo check (Are print wheels in proper position?)
Validity check	Only certain results are correct.	Validity check on codes received from card reader
Equipment check	Test that equipment is operable.	Testing of photoelectric cells on card reader using them

error-control methods used with hardware are summarized together with one or more examples in Table 11-2.

Computer Installation Security

A data processing installation should establish and follow procedures which safeguard the hardware, programs, and data files from loss or destruction. If loss or destruction does occur, advance provisions should have been made for reconstruction and recovery. Security involves physical safeguards, procedural controls, a retention and reconstruction plan, and insurance.

Physical Safeguards The physical safeguards may be classified as fire protection, access security, protection, and off-premises storage. The National Fire Protection Association calls for housing the computer in a noncombustible environment, storage of vital records in storage cabinets having a class C rating (1 hour at 1700°F), separate air-conditioning and power controls readily available in an emergency, and a fire extinguishing system. A sprinkler system can damage the equipment, so a Halon gas extinguishing system is preferred.

The computer room houses both expensive equipment and vital records. Some records may be confidential, and so access to the computer center should be restricted to those having a legitimate need to be there. The access security may be a key, a badge-activated lock, a guard, etc. Such access security provisions should be supported by personnel practices to screen applicants to avoid security risks, to recover keys and badges upon termination of employment, etc.

In the case of terminals which provide access to computing resources and/or to the organization database, there must be special safeguards. Unauthorized use of the computer is a misuse of organizational assets. In most organizations, there is confidential information in the files which should be restricted—salary data, for example. Security should be especially strong for changes by a terminal user of data in the master files. There is no method of completely restricting access, because any safeguards which are programmed can be changed through programming. The terminal use restrictions can be quite effective, however, by setting up provisions such as the following:

1 A "lockword" or "password" which the user must provide in order for file access to be accomplished. The passwords may provide varying degrees of access. For example, a password may identify a user as time sharing only, access only, or access and update.

2 A catalog of eligible users which is checked before access.

3 Scrambled data fields for confidential information. The data field is unscrambled for users who establish a need to know through a password. Other

users who may accidentally obtain access get only meaningless data. This cryptography approach to coding of confidential data may also be used to prevent data being sent over communication lines from being "tapped" by an unauthorized person.

Off-premises storage is used to provide a further safeguard for essential data processing records. Space can be rented in a secure, fireproof location, or another storage location in the same company can be used.

Procedural Controls   Procedural controls can be used in the management of a computer center in order to minimize the possibility that an operator error will result in the destruction of a data or program file. Some common methods are external labels, magnetic tape file protection rings, and library procedures.

Files should be clearly labeled so that the operator will know the file contents. Punched card files are usually labeled on the top of the deck by the use of a felt marking pen. File name, identification, and date are commonly written. The first and last cards are also labeled. Magnetic tape reels and disk packs are labeled with a paper label attached to the tape reel or disk pack.

A physical safeguard used to prevent writing on a magnetic tape and destroying information prior to the release date for the tape is a removable plastic or metal ring, the absence of which will prevent writing on the tape.

Library procedures provide for recordkeeping to maintain a log of the use to which tape reels and disks have been put and for a systematic method to store tapes and packs that allows them to be easily located or replaced in the storage racks.

Programs should be protected against loss by documentation which is updated when changes are made. A copy of the documentation and all updating changes should be stored off-premises along with data files and copies of the programs. Programs should be protected against undocumented changes by a change approval and documentation procedure. After a program has been approved and put in use, there will be a need for program changes. These should be approved by the program manager or data processing manager. A record of the change should be prepared and filed with the run manual for the program (Figure 11-6). The changes should be carefully tested.

The program change record is useful in keeping documentation current. It is very time-consuming to correct all documentation each time a program change is made. Instead, a change record is included with the documentation. The original

DATA PROCESSING PROGRAM CHANGE RECORD

Program name or description

Change number _____

Date
change effective _____

Program number

Change initiated by _____ Date _____
Change request approved by _____ Date _____

Description of purpose or reason for change

Description of changes made (and effect on this and other programs)

Change made by _____ Date _____
Change tested by _____ Date _____
Change posted to run manual _____ Date _____
Change posted to operator instructions _____ Date _____
Review of changes _____ Date _____

FIGURE 11-6 Program change notice.

documentation, plus the change records, form the current documentation.

The source program in machine-readable form used in making changes should be safeguarded by the librarian and issued only upon authorization. Some organizations use program library management software which performs program updating and automatically provides a record of all changes and data needed for reconstruction if the change is to be removed.

Retention and Reconstruction Plan

The retention plan of a data processing department provides a means for record or file reconstruction. Source documents are retained at least until the computer file has been proved and balanced with its controls. However, other considerations may require a longer storage period for these documents. Important master files should be reproduced and a copy maintained in secure storage, preferably off premises.

A retention plan for magnetic tape is generally accomplished by the use of the son-father-grandfather concept. The files retained under this concept on, for example, a Wednesday (assuming daily processing) would be

Wednesday's file	(Son)
Tuesday's file	(Father)
Monday's file	(Grandfather)

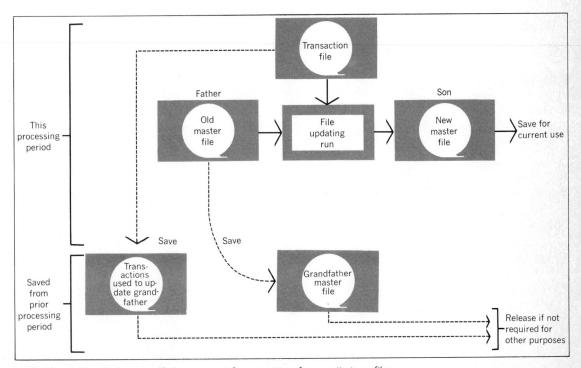

FIGURE 11-7 Son-father-grandfather concept for retention of magnetic tape files.

If, during processing on Thursday, the Wednesday tape were destroyed, Tuesday's tape would be processed again with Wednesday's transactions to recreate Wednesday's master tape. If no other processing or retention considerations require keeping the tape longer, the old grandfather can be released when a new one is produced (Figure 11-7).

Disk file processing, unlike magnetic tape, does not automatically produce a duplicate, updated copy of the file. To provide for reconstruction, the disk must be duplicated before processing to provide a reference point and all transactions saved until the next reference file copy is made. The reference copy can be put onto another disk or a magnetic tape.

Computer security requires not only a retention plan but also a contingency plan. This will cover disruptions such as fire, bomb threats, etc., and will define the procedures for reconstruction in the event of loss of a file or destruction of equipment. The plan will include backup physical facilities through either the manufacturer, a service center, or another user. It may include special programs to facilitate reconstructing of files. As an example of the problem, a recent news item reported a wildcat strike by bus drivers who had not been paid at the appointed hour. The reason for the delay was the bankruptcy of the service bureau which processed the payroll. The files and programs were not transferrable to another service bureau, and the payroll had to be prepared by hand. The manual processing was too slow to meet the deadline.

Insurance   Insurance should be part of the protection plan of a data processing installation. The major risk is fire unless work is performed for others, in which case there should be liability insurance for errors or omissions in doing the work. The ordinary fire insurance policy is limited in its coverage of risks associated with losses connected with data processing. Therefore, many organizations take special data processing insurance coverage.

Although the number of losses arising from dishonesty of data processing employees is apparently quite small, the risks associated with the concentration of the data processing function in a relatively small number of people suggest that bonding (fidelity insurance) of data processing employees is a desirable practice.

Auditing of Computer Processing

Because of the possible damage from undetected and uncorrected errors, it is desirable to have some computer processing audit procedures. These audit procedures may be performed by the control section and by an internal audit group. Investigations should be made on a regular basis of conditions which suggest possible errors. Examples of such investigations are:

1 Investigation of all limit violations, such as payroll checks which exceed the maximum allowable.

2 Investigation of discrepancy between computer records and physical count, such as the difference between the physical inventory counts and the perpetual record maintained through the computer.

3 Investigation of items which change radically for no apparent reason, such as an expense which has been fairly constant and then changes without apparent cause.

4 Investigation of items where statistical analysis indicates a change from normal relationships. For example, the gross profit percentage in a business will tend to be constant and can therefore be used as a standard for comparison with data produced by the computer.

As a part of the regular auditing by the internal and external auditors, there should be a review of the processing control organization and practices and tests to determine compliance. Independent tests should also be made on data files to check the quality of records.

The concentration of processing in a small number of files and few personnel increases the possible damage from malicious destruction and also increases the possibility of certain types of computer-based fraud. The dangers from fraud are probably overemphasized, but they do exist. The protection against such fraud rests primarily on proper control practices, but auditing can assist in identifying risk and detecting possible fraud. The audit can also review and test security provisions and practices.

Quality Control for Computational Programs

The emphasis so far in the chapter has been on quality control over business data processing. The one-time nature of scientific or statistical processing does not require the full range of controls. However, it introduces new problems of quality assurance for the computational programs—in the statistical software used and in the individual programs.

In the case of statistical software furnished by the manufacturer or by software houses for general use, the packages tend to be good. However, there may be errors in them. For example, a statistical package used for several years at a university was found to have an error in one of its routines. This was detected when the same problem was run using this routine and a similar routine on another computer. A routine may work well in most cases but not handle conditions such as negative numbers, etc. The problem of arithmetic precision may cause different statistical packages to yield slightly different results. The user of a statistical package may find it so convenient to obtain output that the necessary thought of its applicability may be overpowered by the availability. On balance, a user of statistical packages should exercise care in selecting the package to use (and understanding what it does) and should perform reasonableness tests on the results.

Quality control over user-written computational programs can be improved if steps such as the following are taken:

1 Test all conditions in the program with special attention to negative and zero data if these are not expected. Test the program with data values at each breakpoint and at the breakpoints plus one and minus one. If, for example, processing is different for data having a value less than 100 (i.e., 100 is the breakpoint), tests should be made on data values 99, 100, and 101.

2 Print out all input data as part of the output of the program.

3 Print out intermediate results if this can be meaningful in evaluating the resulting computations. For example, an iterative procedure which is converging to an answer may tally the number of iterations and print every nth result.

SUMMARY   A major problem with computer data processing systems is control over the quality of the processing. The responsibility for quality extends from top management down to the control function in the data processing department. Top management should require adequate justification before approving projects and should follow with reviews of performance. The data processing department should be organized to provide for division of responsibility and a clear assignment of duties, including the control function and library function. Documentation and other desirable management practices should be included.

The control over data entry and input is very important because most errors occur at this point in the processing. The equipment, on the other hand, is very reliable and, in general, has adequate controls. Programmed controls over processing can detect some program errors. The programs themselves should be controlled to prevent unauthorized changes. Also, a protection plan for computer files, programs, and program documentation should be part of the operations of a computer installation.

This chapter has surveyed the major techniques and major considerations associated with the different control points. Adequate controls have a cost associated with them. Therefore, data processing management should understand control practices and evaluate their use on the basis of the cost of the control versus the consequences of an error being undetected at that point in the data processing cycle.

EXERCISES

1 Explain the concept of redundancy and how it applies to error detection.

2 A systems analyst made the discovery that double-entry accounting has a large amount of redundancy. He stated that his "system" would eliminate this and use only single entry. Evaluate this from the point of view of error control.

3 In a well-known fraud, a computer programmer working for a service bureau wrote a program for a bank which listed all overdrawn checking accounts. This same programmer was sometimes assigned as a night operator to run the job. One evening, he inserted a patch to have the computer ignore his account number if it were overdrawn. He then proceeded to overdraw his account. What control features would have prevented or detected the fraud?

4 Examine the following two check-digit procedures to determine the relative merits of each. Apply the procedures to the number 37657123 and evaluate the probability of simple transpositions giving the same check digit.
Method 1: See textbook
Method 2: Same as method 1, except that the weights are 1 – 2 – 1 – 2 . . . .

5 Write down any 10 six-digit numbers. Test each of them to determine if you have a valid account number, assuming the last digit is a check digit and the method is the one presented in the text.

6 Both inside and outside recipients of output are important elements in the control framework. Evaluate the effectiveness of customers as control elements in detecting *and* reporting errors. What other nonprocessing considerations are relevant in deciding to depend on customers to detect and report errors?

7 What is the purpose of the control function? What are the duties which might be assigned?

8 How might an error in keypunching of input data get past the verification process?

9 What is the purpose of input data validation?

10 What validation might be used to detect the following input data errors:
(a) Transcription error creating wrong customer account number
(b) Pricing error—wrong price used
(c) Quantity written as number of pounds but issued in tons, not pounds
(d) Wrong plant coded in shipment instructions—plant does not stock item
(e) Seven-digit salesperson code used instead of eight-digit product code
(f) No price entered

11 A computer at the University of Waterloo was held "hostage" by a group of campus dissidents occupying a campus building. When the police finally began to clear the building, the dissidents "killed" the hostage. At Fresno State College, a student threw an incendiary device through the glass window and into the computer room. The computer was completely destroyed. Assume that you are the director of computer services for a university and outline steps you should take to safeguard your computer facilities. Assume that the computer is used for both academic purposes and university data processing.

12 The internal auditor for a large mutual fund made a check of computer room security during the evening and found that there was a period of one-half hour when no employee was present. The room was wide open. Other than malicious destruction, what was at risk?

13 A large credit-card company has the following procedure for handling customer complaints about billings. An indicator is set in the customer record, and the customer receives a notice with the next billing stating that "Your communication has been received. Please pay undisputed amount." The complaint is turned over to an

investigator who may or may not get to it. However, the computer is programmed to start dunning the customer starting 1 month from the first notice. Describe how this procedure might be improved.

14 Evaluate, using the criteria given in the chapter, the merits of controls to:
   (*a*) Prevent item quantities on purchase orders prepared by the computer from exceeding certain limits
   (*b*) Prevent shipping-order errors
   (*c*) Prevent billing errors
   (*d*) Prevent sales-analysis errors
   (*e*) Prevent overpayment of wages to an employee

15 The master payroll file on magnetic tape was inadvertently written over by another processing run.
   (*a*) What elementary operating control procedure was not used?
   (*b*) How can the installation recreate the master file?

16 Why is a hash total used?

17 What errors will a parity bit procedure detect? Which will it not detect?

18 An agent specializing in industrial espionage offers the sales data from any sales office of a competitor. The competition transmits the data over communications lines. You inform the competitor and suggest protective measures. What might these measures be?

19 How is an input echo used in detecting and correcting errors?

20 Define possible duties of internal auditing with respect to computer processing.

Chapter

12

Acquisition of Computer Hardware and Software

Acquisition of computer hardware and software is an important topic not only because large expenditures may be involved but also because the computer can alter the operation and management of an organization. Computer hardware and software that do not meet the needs of the organization represent a loss of the expenditures made and, usually more important, may result in significant loss due to the disruption of the organization. No major acquisition of hardware or software should be undertaken without adequate investigation and careful planning of the implementation.

Evaluating hardware or software systems is a complex task and one which cannot adequately be described in a single short chapter. On the other hand, the overview of this chapter should assist the student in understanding the factors involved in evaluating the desirability of computer hardware or software acquisitions, in selecting a specific system, and in the installation of the selected system.

Criteria for Evaluation

The fundamental criterion in a business organization for deciding whether to install a new computer system, replace an existing computer, obtain a software package, or implement a new application is whether the system will help to produce greater profits. For a nonprofit or government organization, the criterion is whether the computer will result in either reduced operating costs or significantly improved ability to provide service to customers, clients, or the public.

The benefits can be classified into three categories:

1 *Cost displacement* This would include all decreased operating costs through reductions in personnel, reductions in space utilization, etc.

2 *Operation efficiencies* This would include the benefits arising from better information. Examples are reduced inventory (reduced costs for carrying inventory), improved scheduling of production (less idle time), and reduction in billing time (faster collections).

3 *New methods* The computer produces benefits from new methods of operation and management. For example, an immediate response system allows new methods of order entry, production scheduling, management analysis, etc.

4 *Intangible benefits* This includes items for which the benefits are difficult to quantify, such as improved service (improved responsiveness to inquiries and improved delivery time), more timely analyses for planning and control, and improved analysis for decision making.

In the early days of computer usage, most computers were justified on the basis of direct clerical cost displacement. It should be noted that, in a large percentage of cases, these cost reductions were not achieved. Today, the emphasis is on increasing profits through the use of the computer. The latter criterion is more nebulous than direct cost reductions but should not be ignored. There are also other considerations, such as the fact that some businesses could not return to manual processing even if they wished; the large clerical staffs which the computers replaced may no longer be available. The processing of checks, for example, is now so completely computerized that it would be virtually impossible for a bank in a large city to process checks manually.

Studies have shown that companies with aggressive and alert managements tend to be extensive users of computers. However, these facts are not sufficient to justify a computer or a move to acquire a more sophisticated model.

Cost Characteristics of Computer Installations

It is difficult to make general statements about cost characteristics because the costs may vary considerably from installation to installation. Nevertheless, it is useful to describe general tendencies in terms of percentages of total costs. The first breakdown is in terms of percentage of total expenditures devoted to the major objects of expenditure (objects for which expenditures are made, such as personnel or hardware).

Object of expenditure	Percent of total cost*
Personnel	60
Equipment and equipment maintenance	25
Supplies	5
Building and overhead	10

*Author's estimates.

Note that supplies and equipment and equipment maintenance are only 30 percent of total expenditures, whereas personnel are double the equipment and supplies cost. The trend has been for the equipment costs to decrease as a percentage of total expenditures and for the personnel costs to increase. This trend is likely to continue. The supplies figure is surprisingly high because, although paper, cards, etc., are inexpensive, the computer system makes use of massive quantities.

The object of expenditure indicates what the expenditures purchase. Another very meaningful breakdown of the same costs is to show the functions or purposes for which they are spent. For this division, four major functions are identified: development of new applications, maintenance on old applications, operations (running current applications), and administration. In other words, these are the reasons why personnel were hired, equipment installed, etc. In the beginning of a new installation, the percentages would be much higher for new applications. These figures show the breakdown for a continuing installation in operation for some time.

Expenditure by function	Percent of total cost*
New applications (investigating, designing, planning, and implementing)	20
Maintenance to correct and update existing applications	10
Operations (data preparation, data entry, and execution of existing applications)	65
Administration	5

*Author's estimates.

Two-thirds of an installation's expenditures go for current operations to run existing applications. About one-third goes for developing new applications and maintaining old ones. The relationship between new applications and maintenance of old ones is important because it emphasizes the fact that to keep a computer application in use requires a continuing expenditure. Changes will be made, it will need to be updated to become consistent with some other system, some latent errors will need to be corrected. This maintenance expenditure is significant, representing half as much as is spent on developing new applications.

There is a substantial start-up cost to get a completely new system (as opposed to a replacement system) selected, installed, tested, and ready to run. Making a general statement is difficult, but start-up costs may equal one-half to one whole year's expected operating costs after installation.

Guidelines for Success in Using a Computer

Some computer installations have been very successful; others have been plagued by trouble. What is the difference? Equipment problems are rarely to blame for the troubles of a computer installation. Failure of the manufacturer to deliver software on schedule or failure of the software to meet specifications may be quite disruptive, but the major elements of success are within the company. These are:

1   Top management participation and support

2   Adequate planning and control

3   Adequate consideration of human problems caused by the introduction of the computer and a program of action to handle the problems

Top management participation and support are necessary conditions for success. Since the installation of a computer can be disruptive to the organization, the entire organization must understand that top management is solidly behind the new system. Lower levels of management will tend to support what is clearly being supported by top management. The top management also needs to be involved in deciding on the broad outlines of the new system. The design, as far as top management is concerned, must be "our design" and "our system," not "your design" and "your system."

The installation of a new or replacement computer system extends over a long period of time. If it is not properly planned and controlled, the different activities will not be achieved on time, and the parts of the system will not mesh correctly. The planning and control of the steps in installing a computer system should utilize standard management techniques. This means that responsibility should be defined, criteria and objectives should be specified, schedules and deadlines should be established, work assignments should be made, and procedures should be established for spotting deviations from this plan.

Installing a new computer data processing system in a proper manner requires many months of preparation prior to the moving in of the equipment. As a rough guide, installing a batch-oriented medium-scale data processing system in an organization which has not had a computer before requires from 12 to 24 months from the point that the decision is made to investigate the feasibility of the computer system until the system is running satisfactorily with the first applications. Figure 12-1 gives a reasonable approximation of minimum times. However,

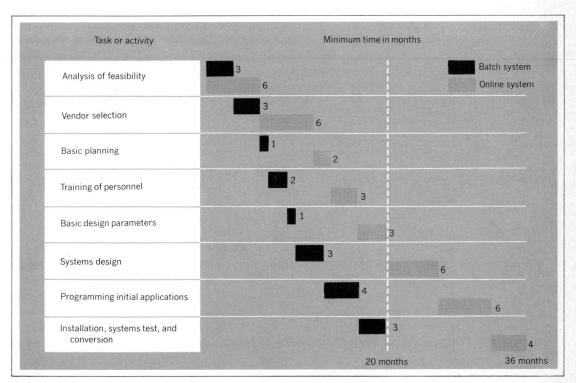

FIGURE 12-1 Minimum times for implementing a new medium-scale computer data processing system.

the total elapsed time may, in some cases, be reduced by performing some tasks simultaneously, rather than one after another. Assuming that the decision has been made to install a computer, the total elapsed time until the system is operating is not likely to be less than 9 months for a batch system and 18 months for a complex online system. Where replacement computers are to be selected and installed, the time required is dependent on such variables as the transferrability of the old applications to the new system. A reasonable estimate for the time between the decision to replace and its implementation might be two-thirds of the original time estimates between decision and implementation.

Small business-oriented computer systems can frequently be installed in a much shorter period of time than the more complex systems because the vendors provide prewritten applications which are modified only slightly for each user. The use of the "canned" application packages allows installation of a small business computer and operation of its basic applications in, say, 3 months after vendor selection.

In the matter of human problems caused by the introduction of computers, some form of resistance to the change by both clerical and supervisory personnel is the rule rather than the exception. A computer system (or a substantial change to a more sophisticated system) will cause changes in the organization. Jobs will be eliminated, there will be a change (reduction or increase) in the status and prestige of some employees, and there will be a change in the work environment. Reducing the impact of change can be accomplished by a policy of education about the change, the reasons for it, and the nature of the change, plus a policy of participation in considering the change. It is generally agreed that resistance to change will be decreased to the extent that persons influenced by the change are able to have some "say" in the planning and implementation of the change. There is some inclination on the part of systems designers for computer-based systems to disregard the opinions and suggestions of experienced employees because of their own zeal in the use of the computer. The management needs to be perceptive to this type of problem and recognize that experienced employees can usually make even a mediocre computer system work and can cause a well-designed system to fail. Their cooperation is therefore vital to success.

An Approach to Selection of a New or Replacement Computer System

The process of selecting computer hardware and software is similar to the process of selecting production machinery. Although there are some similarities in selection methods, it will be useful to discuss new or replacement computer system selection separately from specific software package selection. A general approach to the analysis of the desirability of a computer system consists of the following steps which are carried out or supervised by a study group:

Feasibility study
Preparation of manual of specifications

Obtaining of equipment proposals
Selection

The first three steps are described in this section of the chapter; selection of the computer equipment is the subject of the next section.

The Study Group A recommended approach to computers is to form a committee or task group to direct the evaluation study. For most organizations, the committee should consist of middle-management personnel who represent the principal functions of the business, plus an executive from the systems function. One of the major problems in systems design is understanding the requirements of the different portions of the organization. The use of middle-management personnel who are reasonably high in the organization and can speak authoritatively about the requirements of their functions gives authority and scope to the work of the group. They can also be freed from part of their responsibilities in order to allow adequate time for this assignment. Although the members of the study group do not have to be technically proficient, they should have a reasonable overall understanding of data processing. A short training course for the committee may therefore be desirable. The task group must be provided with technical staff support. For an organization with a computer installation that is studying the value of a new or expanded system, the staff support can come from the data processing systems staff. For an organization without prior experience, the use of outside consultants is frequently advisable. If used, consultants should work with, guide, assist, and otherwise aid the study group by providing the experience and technical expertise which the committee may not have. It is not usually advisable to turn the entire evaluation process over to outside consultants without having them work with an internal group.

**The Feasibility
Study** The purpose of the feasibility study is to investigate the present system, evaluate the possible application of new or revised computer-based methods (and also noncomputer methods), select a tentative system, evaluate the cost and effectiveness of the proposed system, evaluate the impact of the proposed system on existing personnel, and ascertain the need for new personnel.

To define an improved information system, the study group must understand the information requirements of the organization. This understanding may be obtained by the dual process of examining the existing data processing system to determine what is currently being done and of investigating through interviews and analysis what information needs to be provided that is not being furnished by the existing system. Data on the cost of operating the current system needs to be collected in order to make a cost-benefit analysis for a new system.

The data collection procedure consists of interviews with personnel who prepare and who use information. This leads to analyses of system objectives, of decision processes, and of necessary information for processing and decision purposes. The information analysis will include preparation, movement, use, and storage of documents, reports, files, records, and data items. The result of the data collection will be:

1 Description of events which lead to data processing and the response time and accuracy needed by the system user.

2 Samples of all input, output, and file documents.

3 Description of use of information and the processing performed by each person receiving or issuing documents.

4 Information and document flow within the organization.

5 Description of all files. The description includes the use, rate of growth, inquiry rate (why and by whom), and frequency of updating (if a master file).

From this documentation of events, documents, information flow, and files, a description of the existing system can be organized and new systems laid out. Techniques for the system design are system flowcharting, grid charts, networks, specification sheets, layouts, etc.

When conducting interviews, the staff of the study group should seek to discover the information and data processing requirements not satisfied by the current system and to find out what information is needed. In this phase, it should be recognized that many persons do not know what they need or can use. Some analysis is then required to help the user perceive what information would be useful.

From the information obtained in the feasibility study, the study group formulates one or more tentative systems, then makes rough estimates of their cost and their ability to meet system objectives. From these tentative systems, one of which should usually be a modified version of the present system, a system is selected as the best solution and is then analyzed further in terms of personnel impact, cost benefit, and suitability in terms of the needs to be met. Care should be taken to design the system to take advantage of the special capabilities of the new or replacement computer rather than merely computerizing or speeding up an existing system.

The personnel impact portion of the feasibility study assembles data on the impact on company personnel of the proposed system. Rough plans are formulated for orienting, training, counseling, and adjusting the work force to the computer system. Estimates are made of the cost of the adjustment.

The cost-benefit study summarizes the benefits to be expected from the computer, the expected cost, and expected savings. A useful approach is to separate the tangible, measurable benefits from the intangible. The tangible benefits are used to estimate an expected savings and rate of return. The intangible benefits may also have benefits assigned to them; they are used in a judgmental decision process after the tangible benefits have been evaluated. Table 12-1 shows a summarized analysis. This would be supported by an analysis showing more detail. The figures are rough because specific equipment has not yet been selected. For the purposes of an

TABLE 12-1 PRELIMINARY COST-BENEFIT ANALYSIS FOR COMPUTER SYSTEM

Estimated initial cost of a new computer system		
Cost of site preparation	$xx	
Analysis and programming of basic applications	xx	
Cost of training, file conversion, parallel operations, etc.	xx	
Total one-time costs		$xx
Estimated annual operating costs		
Computer and related equipment rental or amortization and maintenance	$xx	
Software rental	xx	
Program maintenance	xx	
Operating personnel	xx	
Space charges, supplies, power, etc.	xx	
Total operating costs		$xx
Annual savings from displaced costs plus value of operation efficiencies and new methods less annual operating costs		$xx
Rate of return (rate at which present value of savings equals present value of one-time costs)		xx%
Intangible benefits (list)		

investment analysis, the life of a system is probably about five to eight years. Six years is probably a satisfactory compromise unless added facts are available which dictate otherwise.

The results of the feasibility study together with the recommendations of the study groups are summarized and presented for top management approval. If the project is approved, the next step is to prepare a manual of specifications for use in procurement.

Manual of Specifications

The *manual of specifications* is a statement of requirements which defines specifically what is to be accomplished by the proposed computer. It is a fairly detailed document. Most of the data needed for it is collected in the feasibility study. The document serves both as a summary of the proposed system for internal purposes and as a statement for use in inviting equipment proposals from vendors of data processing equipment. The system specifications will usually include the elements listed in Table 12-2.

The underlying concept for the manual of specifications is that the company should define its requirements and that the vendor proposals will be measured against these specifications. However, the rather complete specifications of the system requirements should not be used to discourage innovative suggestions by the vendors. The manufacturer preparing a proposal should be allowed to suggest alternative or improved methods for achieving stated objectives.

TABLE 12-2 ELEMENTS IN A MANUAL OF
SPECIFICATIONS FOR SYSTEM PROCUREMENT

1 Introduction
  (*a*) Description of organization
  (*b*) Summary of requirements
  (*c*) Current equipment
  (*d*) Selection process (criteria to be used, form of responses, etc.)
  (*e*) Acceptance tests

2 System requirements
  (*a*) Hardware features required
  (*b*) Software required
    (1) Compilers (FORTRAN, COBOL, RPG, etc.)
    (2) Utility packages (e.g., sort routine)
    (3) Application packages (e.g., linear programming, payroll
        processing)
    (4) Operating system
  (*c*) Support required
    (1) System designers provided by vendor
    (2) Backup facilities
    (3) Test time and facilities
  (*d*) Constraints
    (1) Planned delivery date for equipment and software
    (2) Time constraints on processing
  (*e*) Desirable features not required to meet specifications
  (*f*) Capability for future growth

3 Major applications (for each, the following)
  (*a*) System description
  (*b*) File description including current size and growth rate
  (*c*) Input data specifications and volume of input
  (*d*) System flowcharts for each run and run descriptions giving
    (1) Frequency of processing
    (2) Volume of transactions
    (3) Suggested method of processing

Obtaining On the basis of a preliminary screening, four or five vendors may be invited to
Equipment submit proposals. Each vendor is provided with a copy of the manual of specifica-
Proposals tions and the rules for submitting proposals. There may be follow-up interviews
with vendors to clarify any misunderstandings or uncertainties in the specifications.

   When the proposals are ready, the manufacturer's representative is usually
provided with an opportunity for a presentation to the study group. At this
meeting, he or she will summarize the proposal and answer questions. The
manufacturer's proposal should normally contain the points listed in Table 12-3.

Deciding on the Computer System

The manual of specifications plus the manufacturer's proposals provide input for
the decision process on equipment selection. The need for a systematic alternative
has prompted the use of ranking methods. There are a number of methods for

TABLE 12-3 OUTLINE OF INFORMATION NORMALLY FOUND
IN A MANUFACTURER'S PROPOSAL

1 Proposed equipment configuration
    (*a*) Equipment units
    (*b*) Equipment operating characteristics and specifications
    (*c*) Options or alternative configurations
    (*d*) Ability of the system to expand (modularity)
    (*e*) Special requirements as to site and other installation costs

2 Cost of proposed configuration
    (*a*) Rental and purchase price by unit
    (*b*) Extra shift rental
    (*c*) Maintenance contract if a unit is purchased
    (*d*) Software rental

3 Availability of specified software and special software packages

4 Systems support
    (*a*) Systems analysis included; cost for added services
    (*b*) Programming services included; cost for added services
    (*c*) Customer maintenance engineer availability
    (*d*) Customer education support and schedule of rates

5 Terms
    (*a*) Acceptance of specified delivery date or proposed alternative delivery date
    (*b*) Payment terms
    (*c*) Lease-purchase and other options
    (*d*) Amount of test time to be provided

6 System performance for specified applications
    (*a*) Changes in design if different from that specified in requirements
    (*b*) Timings (how long each application takes)
    (*c*) Changes in timings using optional equipment

7 Other information

evaluating throughput for evaluation purposes; the major methods are discussed below.

When a vendor is selected, an order is placed. The contract with the manufacturer is usually based on a standard contract form. However, there are still many points for negotiation. For example, the assistance to be provided by the manufacturer—number of systems analysts who will assist in implementing the system or number of hours of free test time—may vary from installation to installation depending on the negotiations. Now that equipment costs are firm, a final cost analysis can be prepared.

**Ranking of
Equipment
Proposals**
The evaluation may be simple if only one manufacturer can satisfy specifications; but in general, several manufacturers will respond with proposals worthy of consideration. Since there are a number of considerations, both quantitative and subjective, one method is to rank each manufacturer by a point system. For each criterion for evaluation, a possible number of points are assigned, and then each manufacturer is rated by assigning part of or all the possible points. A summary for

such an analysis is given in Table 12-4. There is a supporting analysis for each of the summary criteria. For example, software evaluation might include such sub-criteria as

Operating system evaluation
COBOL evaluation
FORTRAN evaluation
Report generator evaluation
Data management system evaluation
Storage requirements
Other software evaluation

Evaluation criteria will receive various weights from different users. The major questions are whether the proposed equipment will perform the job in the time allowed, its relative cost, and whether it has sufficient flexibility to expand as more applications are added. A system should allow for growth—in file size, in number and scope of applications, and in volume of transactions. Most systems can provide for growth by the addition of equipment options. For example, a stripped-down, minimum-memory-size computer may have its power increased by adding faster input/output units, more storage, or special instruction packages. A compatible family of computers allows the user to move from one computer in the

TABLE 12-4 SUMMARY SHEET FOR POINT-RANKING METHOD OF COMPUTER EVALUATION

		PROPOSALS		
Criteria for evaluation	Possible points	A	B	C
1 System performance (42 percent)				
(a) Hardware performance	60	60	41	42
(b) Software performance	60	39	43	31
(c) Expansion capabilities	55	41	48	30
2 Vendor capabilities (25 percent)				
(a) Vendor performance	40	25	32	21
(b) Maintenance and backup	20	14	18	13
(c) Installation support	20	12	18	12
(d) Staff preference	25	15	20	5
3 Cost (33 percent)				
(a) Rental price	50	35	23	40
(b) Terms for extended use	20	17	5	18
(c) Ongoing educational cost	25	21	9	17
(d) Maintenance and backup cost	20	15	10	14
(e) One-time system and education cost	20	18	11	14
Total points	415	312	278	257

family to a larger size without reprogramming. It is necessary to evaluate not only the existing software but also the probability of promised software being available when expected.

In evaluating hardware and software, it is frequently desirable to program and run a test problem to try out the effectiveness of the software and to evaluate the operating problems. The manufacturer will usually provide time for testing. Frequently, an order must be placed before any test machine is available. But the practice in the industry is to use the initial sales order as a basis for scheduling machine delivery. When the delivery time is close (say, 6 months), the order is firmed. Thus, there is usually sufficient time to evaluate by test runs the equipment which may not have been available when the initial order was placed.

In evaluation of equipment, the alternative of a mixed system should be considered. Several firms offer plug-in compatible peripherals (say, a tape unit or a disk unit) which have higher performance at a lower cost than the manufacturer's units. The main disadvantage of these independent peripherals is in the added management problems of dealing with more than one vendor and related questions of responsibility for equipment-caused failures.

Comparing Throughput Performance

The study group should make an analysis of the applications timings furnished by the manufacturer and conduct an independent analysis of the computer capabilities. There is no foolproof method for selecting the best computer system; there are too many uncertainties. However, a combination of the stated system times for the applications contained in the specifications and independent evaluation of throughput provide a reasonably good basis for decision.

If the programs have not yet been written, how can a valid time estimate be made? For some computer runs using utility packages such as the sort routine, the times can be estimated with a high degree of precision. Some jobs are input/output bound, so that as long as the computational steps stay within the bounds of the input/output times, these times can be used. Other routines can be evaluated by estimating number of instructions required and multiplying by an average time per instruction. The proposal should be checked to ensure that all estimating procedures are specified. The time estimates should include handling and setup time where required and should show the timing for each unit of the configuration for each run; these times should be summarized by day. Such a summary shows the peak requirements, since some runs are daily, others weekly or monthly, and provides an estimate of the peak load of the system.

There should also be some independent evaluation of the manufacturer's times. This can be performed using data from computer information services and by specially constructed kernel or benchmark problems. The information and analysis services available for this purpose range from a computerized analysis (which makes independent timings for a specified list of computers and compares them for decision-making purposes) to comparisons based on instruction times or standard benchmark problems.

In using evaluation techniques, it should be kept in mind that the real criterion for measuring system performance is throughput. The comparisons that are made are in lieu of the complete throughput analysis, which cannot be made in advance because all programs would have to be written and running. The following frequently used methods of comparison are listed together with comments on their effectiveness:

Comparison techniques	Comments
Memory cycle time	Extremely gross measure. Unreliable because systems differ in hardware organization, overlapping of operations, etc.
Add time	Extremely gross measure. Perhaps useful when comparing computers with same hardware organization.
Instruction times	Very gross measure since the frequency of instruction use must be considered.
Instruction mix times (average for a mix of instructions)	An average instruction time based on the expected frequency with which each instruction is used for different types of applications. Gross measure, but better than unweighted instruction time. At best, it is a measure of raw internal computing power.
Kernel problem	Sample problems are coded with the system's own instructions and time. Especially useful for standardized mathematical applications. Gives a measure of internal performance. Does not reflect the input/output, multiprogramming, operating system, etc.
Standard benchmark problems	Standard problems of a type normally performed. The problem is coded, and time to perform the standard task is estimated or measured by running it. Standard benchmark problems usually reflect the type of jobs done but are not a sample of the complete processing system as it will operate.
Simulation	The characteristics of the proposed system are compared with the characteristics of available computers, and the performance of the different systems are simulated by a computer program.

Converting to a Computer System

Rarely is a computer delivered shortly after the order is signed. Usually there is a lapse of several months. Within the limits of possible delivery dates, the installation date should be planned at the customer's convenience rather than at the manufacturer's. The conversion to a new or replacement computer is a major project and should therefore be carefully scheduled and coordinated. The conversion must be supervised, preferably by the new data processing manager (if a new system) or by the current manager (if a replacement computer). The installations may be assisted by the study group. Some of the preparatory activities are site preparation, training, preparation of initial applications, file conversion, and cutover to the new system.

Site Preparation and Training

A medium- or large-scale computer will usually require some special site preparation. The manufacturer will provide complete specifications for the electrical, space, air-conditioning, and other needs of the equipment, and a site-planning engineer from the vendor will usually be available for assisting in site planning. This planning may include physical security and provisions for an uninterrupted power supply.

Initial training of staff in programming and using the equipment will typically be available from the manufacturer. The amount, type, and cost of training should be agreed upon when the contract is negotiated. Manuals and other instructional materials are normally available from the vendor.

Preparation of Initial Applications and Cutover

The initial applications to be run on the computer should be written and debugged prior to delivery of the equipment. In other words, when the computer is working and turned over to the organization, the first applications should be programmed, debugged, and ready to run. As part of the agreement to rent or purchase the equipment, the user should have negotiated with the computer manufacturer for a certain number of hours of time on that model computer at the manufacturer's test facilities. Additional time may of course be purchased. This provides the customer with computer time to assemble or compile, debug, and test programs prior to the installation data. The customer's personnel can also gain experience in operating the equipment. Testing is also required with application packages or systems (such as standard accounts receivable application) obtained from the vendor, but the preparation and testing time may be substantially reduced.

Prior to the beginning of processing, all master files must be prepared. For a completely new installation, this will normally involve extensive conversion of data to punched cards or keydisk and then to the computer file storage medium. This must be done with care and with a substantial amount of control and checking, so that the initial file is correct. If the conversion is from one model computer to another, the old files possibly may be run on the new equipment without change. If not, a conversion program may be necessary, or special equipment such as a tape-to-tape converter may be used.

When converting from one computer system to another, various methods or combinations are used to ease the problem of rewriting programs.

Method	Explanation
Emulation	An extra-cost feature, it is usually implemented by a microprogram (in a special storage) which executes the instructions of the old computer on

	the new one by interpreting each old instruction into its equivalent in the new instructions. Programs do not run as fast under emulation as when they are rewritten in the language of the new computer.
Simulation	Does the same function as the emulator except that it is a regular program which interprets each instruction and executes the equivalent instructions in the new machine. Generally slower than emulation.
Conversion routines	Routines which produce source programs for the new computer from the source program for the old system. Used both for symbolic languages and for making required changes for various high-level languages, such as FORTRAN or COBOL.

During the start-up for a new system, unforeseen difficulties may arise in the processing programs. Also it is often difficult to obtain a proper cutoff. For these reasons, it is usually a good idea to run both old and new systems in parallel until the new system is found to be operating satisfactorily (say, 2 to 4 weeks). A cutoff point is then established, the files are updated to the cutoff point, and all transactions initiated after that point are recorded using only the new system.

The specifications used to solicit vendor proposals should have included equipment acceptance criteria. The sales or rental contract with the vendor should also state explicitly the conditions for acceptance of the equipment. Several criteria may be used such as percentage of downtime for repairs, performance of hardware and operating system on benchmark problems, software performance in compilation, etc. These acceptance tests should be run successfully before the equipment is accepted.

Computer user organizations may be a useful source of information for the user. These organizations are operated by the participating users of the same equipment but are supported by manufacturers. The groups share information, pressure the manufacturer, establish standards, etc.

Postinstallation Review

In preparing for a computer system, cost and benefit estimates are made. But it often happens that the cost savings are not realized and the benefits are not as great as projected. A computer system disturbs existing jobs and procedures, and, frequently, the personnel will duplicate the work of the computer because they do not trust the new system or do not understand the new procedures.

A postinstallation review is a desirable procedure to detect unrealized benefits, cost reductions not made, and lack of adherence to the new system. Measures may then be taken to improve performance. If there are substantial deviations in cost or performance by the computer processing group, they should be reviewed in order to appraise the cause and to assess possible courses of action. Plans for a postinstallation review probably improve the planning and estimating performed in deciding on the computer. If it is known that there will be a follow-up, estimates and plans are likely to be made more carefully than if such an appraisal is not anticipated.

Financing Use of Computer Equipment

There are three major approaches to financing the use of computer equipment— rent or lease from a manufacturer, purchase or lease from an independent leasing firm. The terms which can be negotiated under each of these methods will depend on the manufacturer, the leasing agent, and the negotiating strength of the user.

Rental or Term-Lease from the Manufacturer

Rental or fixed-term lease is the most common financing method. There is a rental or lease price which includes maintenance for using each piece of equipment and, depending on the manufacturer, a rental price for each software system. Manufacturers differ in the rental agreements they offer, but a common approach calls for a base rental for 176 hours of actual use per month. This represents one 8-hour shift per day for the average month of 22 working days. Hours above 176 are charged at a lower rate (a common percentage is 10 percent of the implied hourly rate for the first 176 hours). The trend in computer rentals is to reduce the second- and third-shift rental charges. The use of computers on a rental agreement can usually be canceled by the user on fairly short notice, say, 1 to 3 months. Most manufacturers offer a reduced rental rate for users who sign a long-term lease (2 to 5 years) for the equipment. For example, the basic rate may be reduced and extra use charges may be eliminated. Users can also rent with options to purchase.

The major advantages of renting or leasing are the absence of a large capital outlay, the assumption by the manufacturer of all maintenance, and the removal of the risk of obsolescence for the user. The latter risk is not entirely removed, since a user has large amounts invested in special site preparation, training, programming, and other costs which are lost if the computer must be replaced by one of another manufacturer. The major disadvantages of rental or fixed-term lease is the higher total cost. The manufacturers have tended to base rentals on 5-year life, but computers being installed are likely to be used longer than this—probably closer to 8 or 9 years.

Purchase of Equipment

The major incentive for purchase is the savings to be had over the life of the equipment. There is also a tax advantage because of the investment credit provisions of income tax law. The purchaser assumes a risk with respect to the reliability of the equipment, amount of maintenance, and obsolescence.

If the equipment is purchased, separate arrangements must be made for maintenance. Several possible arrangements are:

1   Maintain equipment using own personnel

2   Purchase a complete parts and labor maintenance agreement from the manufacturer

3   Pay for maintenance personnel on an hourly rate when needed, and pay for parts as used

The maintenance risk varies for different units in the computer configuration. For example, central processors are very reliable, while disk files or magnetic tape units, because of the precision required in their moving parts, are more likely to require frequent maintenance. Therefore, some installations will purchase part of their equipment and rent the rest.

One consideration in a maintenance program is the need for a continuing relationship with the manufacturer. As weak points are discovered or improvements are found desirable, the manufacturer usually makes field changes in the equipment. Since these occur throughout the life of the equipment, a purchaser will want to be aware of them so that a decision can be made as to whether they should be made.

An impediment to purchase is the risk of obsolescence. The possibility of outgrowing a system can be guarded against by acquiring a system with growth possibilities, both in the basic system and in available options for adding equipment.

When the risk of obsolescence has been considered, the decision of purchase or rental becomes a standard problem in capital expenditure analysis. A rough rule of thumb frequently cited is that a computer installation with a useful life of more than 5 years should be purchased rather than rented. However, a specific analysis should be made.

Third-Party Leasing of Computers

A company which has examined the obsolescence and reliability problems and has concluded that purchase is the best alternative may not have funds available, or may find that using the funds for purchasing computers will restrict future sources of funds. Under these circumstances, the possibility of leasing from an independent leasing company should be examined.

A third-party lease typically provides for the purchase by a leasing company of the specific equipment configuration desired by the user. The leasing company then leases it to the user. Lease agreements vary, but usually they have provisions such as the following:

1   User agrees to lease for a minimum period, say, 5 years, with purchase and trade-in options.

2   The lease payment includes a maintenance contract and other charges.

3   There is no additional charge for second- or third-shift operations (except perhaps some additional maintenance charges).

4 After the minimum period, the lease charges drop to a lower rate.

5 If the lease is terminated before the minimum period is up, there is a termination charge.

Acquisition of Software Packages

As explained in earlier chapters, there are two general types of software: system software and application software. System software consists of programs or sets of programs to support the efficient use of the computer. Examples are operating systems, database management systems, job accounting systems, and compilers. Application software refers to programs or sets of programs that perform a specific processing application. Examples are accounts receivable, inventory control, and statistical analysis.

Traditionally, system software was provided by the hardware vendor and application software was prepared by the user. Software was, during the early years of computing, included as part of the hardware, without extra cost. Most (but not all) manufacturers now price it separately. There is therefore an incentive for the user to evaluate alternative software packages.

The acquisition of independent (proprietary) system software instead of system software from the hardware vendor is generally based on improved efficiency, enhanced capabilities, or lower cost of the proprietary software. About half of all proprietary software in use is system software.

The acquisition of proprietary applications packages is an alternative to user development of the application programs. The application can be implemented more quickly and frequently at a lower cost. However, the package may not exactly meet the needs of the user. A small computer user may not be able to justify application development costs to make the application exactly what is needed; a larger user is more likely to do so. Because of the lower cost, reduced risk (because the package exists for testing), and reduced implementation time, software packages should always be considered as an alternative to inhouse development.

Sources of Software Packages The main sources of proprietary software packages, both system software and application software, are the following:

Source	Comments
Hardware vendor	Traditional source of system software. Many have variety of application packages.
Software house	Companies which specialize in development of software.
Software brokers	Companies which market software devel-

oped by others. Software package quality tends to vary considerably from this source because the software has such a variety of development environments.

User groups	User groups have traditionally exchanged software. However, there is no support for the packages which are exchanged and documentation is generally inadequate.

A user in search of potential packages for evaluation should inquire of the hardware vendor. In addition, a search may be made using reference sources for software. The most comprehensive source is the *ICP Software Directory,* a listing of proprietary software packages. Other useful sources are analytical services such as *Datapro* and *Auerbach Software Reports* and the computer magazines which carry news and advertising about software packages.

Evaluating a Software Package

A necessary precondition to software package evaluation is a determination of requirements. The problem to be solved should be defined, the basic processing functions specified (inputs, processing, and outputs), and requirements for interface with the operating system and other applications identified. The requirements can be used in requesting vendors to present their packages for consideration. On the basis of the requirements, many of the potential packages can be eliminated, leaving only a small number for detailed evaluation.

In the evaluation, a formal point method may be used similar to the one proposed for hardware. Or a less formal method may use a series of analyses which will clarify the differences among the packages. The following are useful steps. The sources of data are the package vendor, package documentation, current users of the package, and rating services.

1 Compare functional capabilities of package with the requirements that have been developed.

2 Evaluate any hardware constraints in using the package on the computer system. Storage requirements and equipment usage are examples.

3 Evaluate software problems in using the package. Will the operating system, compilers, etc., interface properly with the package?

4 Evaluate computer operating characteristics such as throughput timing, ease of installation, ease of operating. How good are the operating instructions?

5 Evaluate use characteristics such as input requirements, report formats, controls, audit trails, error detection and error handling, and special forms. How good are the user instructions?

6 Evaluate the maintainability of the package. How well is it documented for

maintenance? Is it written in a disciplined form that is easily maintained? Is it coded in a standard language? Who will maintain the package?

7 Evaluate the flexibility of the package in meeting changing needs and growth.

Users of packages report considerable differences in quality, especially as reflected in documentation for users, operators, and maintenance programmers. The investigation of package characteristics is therefore essential to successful acquisition and use.

Packages which still appear viable after the preceding investigation should be demonstrated in some manner. Perhaps the best approach is to use benchmark tests at one's own installation. Some packages are not large enough to justify the expense of benchmarking and may be demonstrated at another installation, or a trial use period for the most likely package may be used as a method of final evaluation.

Contract negotiations for software packages are important. They should cover points such as guarantee period, return privileges if the package is not satisfactory, penalties for late delivery, support by vendor in installation and maintenance, agreed upon modifications, list of deliverables, and performance standards the package must meet.

SUMMARY In evaluating the acquisition of new or replacement computer systems, there are some cases in which industry practices or competitive pressures require computerization. In most cases, the decision is based on cost and benefit. The costs can be determined with reasonable accuracy; benefits require considerable estimation.

A major change in the cost characteristics of computer installations has been a reduction in the relative importance of equipment costs as a percentage of total cost. This is now on the order of 25 percent and continuing to decrease.

Success in computer selection and installation seems to depend on the participation and support of top management, adequate planning and control, and adequate steps to alleviate the human problems caused by the dislocation resulting from the computer system.

An approach to investigation of new or replacement systems described in the chapter includes a study group which conducts a feasibility study and, if the decision is to proceed, prepares a manual of specifications for the system. This is used for obtaining and evaluating equipment proposals. The decision on the computer equipment can be systematized by the ranking method of assigning weights to various evaluation criteria and assigning points to each manufacturer for each criteria. The evaluation of throughput is the most complex evaluation, and various methods may be used. These range from very simple comparisons to complex simulations.

Converting to a new computer system also requires careful planning and scheduling. A period of parallel operation is needed to make sure the system is debugged. At the end of an initial period of operation, a postinstallation review is essential to assess performance compared with plans.

The methods of financing the use of computers were also discussed in the chapter. These are rental, purchase, or lease from an outside vendor. There are advantages and disadvantages to each. The majority of users still rent or lease from the manufacturer, but there is a perceptible trend toward purchase.

The acquisition of software packages, either system software or application software, is of increasing importance because there is a trend toward increased use of packaged software. The general approach to software acquisition is to develop a statement of requirements, conduct a search for suitable candidates, and then evaluate the packages using data from the vendor, current users, evaluative services which report on packages, and results of demonstrations. Packages differ considerably in quality, and therefore a careful evaluation is necessary.

EXERCISES

1 An executive in a company with a successful computer installation was called by a friend, an executive in another organization, who asked if he might come and have a chat. He stated, "We are getting our computer in a couple of months and are looking for ideas on how to use it." Evaluate the position of the company making the inquiry.

2 What criteria can be used to evaluate the following proposals:
   (*a*) Proposal to obtain a computer primarily for payroll processing now being done by a large number of clerks.
   (*b*) Proposal to obtain a computer primarily for production scheduling and inventory control. It would replace clerks using manual methods and would also allow the use of advanced techniques.
   (*c*) Proposal to obtain a small scientific computer for linear programming applications.
   (*d*) Proposal to put remote inquiry stations at all sales offices. Sales representatives would be able to make direct inquiries about status of inventory, items scheduled into production shipments, etc.

3 What is the advantage of a middle-management study group committee?

4 Under what circumstances is it appropriate to rely on manufacturers' representatives?

5 What is the manual of specifications?

6 What should be included in a run description?

7 Why is a new system run parallel with the old one? What problems does this create?

8 Assume you are asked to advise the financial vice-president of a distributing company in the following situation. The company built a new warehouse with automated handling equipment. The system relies on a computer to process data in a way not previously done. The company was told that this processing was feasible. It is now 2 months until the new warehouse will be ready. No programs have been written, and the manufacturer says that a larger machine will be required. What should he do?

9 Why would a company buy peripherals from another vendor?

10 In 1969, IBM unbundled—i.e., it started charging extra for most software, systems engineers, and customer education, which had formerly been provided without charge. Rentals were reduced slightly. Evaluate the effect of this decision on:
   (*a*) An existing installation that was renting
   (*b*) An existing installation that had a purchased machine
   (*c*) An independent software company
   (*d*) A competing manufacturer which did not unbundle

11 A new computer system has been installed. A program written in the predecessor

machine language is to be run once a month. Evaluate the relative merits of emulation, simulation, and conversion routines.

12 How can a vendor estimate times for runs which are not yet written?

13 Suggest the applicability of the various methods of comparing computer performance for the following situations:

(*a*) Comparing two models in the same family of computers

(*b*) Comparing two computers with similar word organization

(*c*) Comparing several computers for use on a wide range of scientific problems

(*d*) Comparing several computers for rather standard data processing tasks—mostly sorting, file updates, and reports

(*e*) Comparing several computers for all-round use

14 What major methods of ownership and financing use of a computer are employed? Under what conditions is each method appropriate?

15 In the postinstallation review it is found that the monthly cost displacement savings that were predicted did not materialize to the extent planned and these savings will never offset the conversion costs. What action should be taken? Explain.

16 What should the company do to be ready to use the computer when it arrives?

17 How can resistance to the introduction of a computer be reduced?

18 Compare the typical reasons for lease or purchase of proprietary system software and the reasons for lease or purchase of proprietary application software.

19 What are the sources of package software? Evaluate the general quality of products attainable from each source.

20 Explain an approach to evaluation of software packages.

Chapter

13

Current and Prospective Developments in Computer Hardware, Software, and Applications

The field of computers is changing so rapidly that it is difficult to speak authoritatively of future developments because these are being so quickly translated into current use. Therefore, the distinction will not always be clear as to what is currently being done and what is going to be done soon. This chapter provides a point at which these developments can be discussed. Some of these developments are already being implemented, while others are unknown to actual installations. Some developments will be only mentioned to make the reader aware of them; others will be discussed in more detail.

Articles describing future developments in computer systems frequently refer to the "fourth generation," but the term is generally undefined. There has been general agreement on first-, second-, and third-generation equipment, the distinction being based primarily on circuitry. The first generation was marked by tubes, the second by transistors, and the third by microcircuitry. It is not yet clear what the distinguishing characteristics of a fourth generation might be. IBM's System/370 was introduced 5 years after the first installation of the System/360. However, it is an improved and enhanced system rather than one that is radically different. The use of semiconductor memories is a new development, but it does not seem to be a change of the magnitude that occurred between the first- and second- or second- and third-generation equipment. Micrologic is an important element in the new computers, but the idea has been implemented for several years. Large-scale integration provides faster, denser circuitry, but is an extension of third-generation microcircuitry. In essence, there is no agreement on what a fourth generation means, or whether it has yet arrived. This chapter, therefore, avoids that terminology.

Developments in Computer Hardware

There has been a clear and continuous trend in hardware toward reduced size, reduced cost, increased speed, and an improved cost/performance ratio. This trend is likely to continue. At the same time, users are finding it valuable to have greatly improved capabilities to support more complex processing requirements. The result is that users have more hardware in more complex configurations.

Circuitry The past size reduction in circuitry has been dramatic. An integrated circuit the size of the letter "O" contains elements that required several cubic feet of space in first-generation tube circuits and several cubic inches of circuit boards in second-generation equipment. Current large-scale integration (LSI) technology provides 1000 to 2000 circuits on a chip, and further increases in density are forecast.

Circuit speed has increased many times, and cost has been reduced to a fraction of that in early computers. This trend to faster, lower-cost circuitry will continue. For example, IBM reports devices performing binary switching in less than 10 picoseconds ($1/10^{12}$). This is more than a thousand times faster than currently available circuits. The device, called a Josephson junction, uses only 1/10,000 as much electric power as a transistor.

Very low cost microcomputers or computers on a chip have made it feasible to place computer logic in peripheral devices, terminals, etc. This trend is expected to continue.

Processor Design

The design of the central processor is being influenced by the availability of low-cost circuits, by the need for flexible design, and by the need for improved performance for certain activities. The low cost of circuitry means that many functions performed by software may be included in the hardware. The need for flexible design is accomplished by stored logic in a control storage. A computer with stored logic capabilities may be microprogrammed to accept instructions for any other computer. New functions can be added to the equipment by means of changes in the microprogram (also called "firmware"), whereas adding new hardware functions might be impossible, and attempting to execute them using software might be too slow and cumbersome.

Several small processors can be included in the processor design to handle separate functions. There can be a small processor for input/output channel control, a processor for data communications control, a database processor, etc. The concept of multiple processors can be extended to multiple arithmetic processors to achieve an array or pipeline processor which can simultaneously process entire arrays of data, an ability valuable in high-volume computation applications such as weather forecasting.

Data Capture, Data Preparation, and Data Input Devices

Data capture, preparation, and input are still major problems in computer processing. The trend is clearly toward the replacement of keypunches with keydisk systems and for various methods of direct entry. The trend in terminals for data capture and data preparation is the inclusion of some logical capabilities (intelligence) so that data may be validated while it is being recorded at the terminal. The terminals frequently include devices to read coded documents, such as various optical codes.

An interesting development to watch is voice recognition equipment. It has had limited use but appears to have high potential in certain applications, especially where the person doing the input has both hands busy and is required to provide only simple input. Current equipment can recognize a small number of words (say, 20 to 40 words). Since there are individual differences in speech, the equipment is "trained" to recognize a set of spoken words as pronounced by each individual using the system.

Output Devices

In general, there is a trend toward a greater variety of output devices. Audio output and computer graphics are receiving increased use. The increased volume of data to be output is being handled by the use of visual display devices (instead of typewriters) at terminals, nonimpact printers, and computer output microfilm. The nonimpact printers provide very high speed output. Various technologies are employed; a significant one is the use of a laser beam to write the characters on a rotating drum that is electrostatically charged. The drum prints on paper in much the manner as an electrostatic (say, Xerox brand) copier. Examples of maximum printing speeds are 13,000 lines per minute offered by one manufacturer and 21,000 by another. This contrasts with 1000 to 2000 lines per minute for high-speed impact printers. Computer output microfilm (COM) also achieves high-speed output that takes much less storage volume than paper output. The major constraint to the general use of laser printers and COM is the high cost of the devices, and so they are justified only for large-volume users.

Storage Devices Semiconductor memory has replaced core memory as the major storage technology for main memory. There has been substantial improvement in magnetic storage density, and so magnetic tape and magnetic disk still dominate secondary storage. These magnetic storage devices are expected to be improved further with increased densities and lower cost. However, current and prospective developments suggest that alternative higher-density, lower-cost storage may become available. Two alternatives that appear promising are holographic storage and magnetic bubble memory.

There are two forms of holographic storage—mechanically driven and optical. In the mechanically driven type, data bits are stored by a laser beam (a very tiny, concentrated beam of light) which records a 1-bit by burning the coating on a tape or film. The recording is permanent in the same way as a punched card. The spot is read by a laser beam of lesser power which detects the existence or absence of a hole. Each hole is very small so that, in one existing device, 13 million bits can be recorded per square inch. This method is in use, but major problems are the mechanical movements to position the beam and the nonerasable character. The optical holographic methods are in a more experimental state. A laser beam is passed through an array of light valves to produce a binary pattern of darkness and light. The pattern can theoretically be very large, say, 100,000 bits. This pattern is stored on a light-sensitive material such as thermoplastics, or on ferroelectric crystals. The stored data is read by directing a laser beam to the desired hologram, and an image of the page of light patterns is sensed and analyzed into 0 and 1 bits. If practical optical memories become available, they would provide high-density storage of very large capacity at low cost.

A newer approach to computer storage technology is a magnetic bubble memory. The technology is based on tiny magnetic domains or "bubbles" that appear in certain kinds of crystalline materials under the control of magnetic and electrical fields. The presence of a bubble signifies a 1-bit, the absence a 0-bit. A train of bubbles can be shifted from cell to cell in a shift register to read the storage. Storage density is very high, about 1 million to 100 million bits per square inch.

Data Communications Facilities Virtually all computer systems have the capability for remote input and output via data communications facilities. The demand for data communications has grown very rapidly, and future growth in demand is expected to be high. Trends in data communications are higher speed, greater reliability, and lower cost. These results can be achieved by special digital networks based on electronic switching. Such networks are in operation and can be expected to increase in scope and use.

System Configuration

Trends in system configurations reflect a shift toward the computer as a utility which is designed to service remote users with both interactive computing and terminal-directed batch processing. Two trends to support the computer utility are multiprocessor configurations at central sites servicing a large number of users and dispersed or distributed systems.

Large, centralized systems providing interactive processing are tending toward the use of more than one processor, with the processors dividing the tasks. There are efficiency considerations supporting such configurations, but perhaps more important is the need for the reliability which can be obtained in a multiprocessor system.

An alternative trend in large systems is to disperse the processing capability. Remote sites are provided with minicomputers to perform much of the processing and to maintain local data files. Only selected tasks are transmitted to a larger, central computer which also maintains the organization-wide database.

The concept of the computer network can be extended to networks in which the computer system for one organization is interconnected with the computer system of another organization. An example is the computer for an airline reservation system being able to make reservations on an interconnecting line by directly communicating with the computer for that airline.

Developments in Computer Software

Hardware improvements have been spectacular and rapid; software improvement has been much slower and generally delivered less than promised. Current and prospective developments are for simplified operation and improved performance for system software and for greater use of leased or purchased application software.

The trend in computer systems is to a network of CPUs, input/output processors, and communication processors with the scheduling and allocation of resources under the control of the operating system. The operating system provides automatic management of files, data communication, and input/output. The trend is for the operating system to be internally more complex, but less complex for the user. The trend is also to design hardware facilities that will make the operating system more efficient.

Improved performance of software is being achieved not only in increased throughput but also in reduction of errors. The emphasis on programming discipline (as described in the text) is resulting in a marked reduction in errors in software.

The use of purchased (or leased) application software is expected to continue. The supply of well-written, well-documented, and flexible application packages has substantially increased the attractiveness of using such packages. The trend in small computers is for the vendor to provide a large selection of such packages as part of the support for the system.

Developments in Information Systems

The use of computers is extending into a wide variety of applications ranging from space flight to computer-assisted surgery. A major area of development is in the use of computers by organizations to support management and decision making. Such information systems are so large that researchers have proposed automation of many of the system-building functions.

Management Information Systems

An organization has transactions that it must process in order to carry out its day-to-day activities. The payroll must be prepared, sales and payments on account must be posted: these and others are data processing activities and might be termed clerical in nature; they follow rather standard procedures. The computer is useful for these clerical data processing tasks, but a management information system performs other tasks as well and is more than a data processing system. It is an information processing system applying the power of the computer to provide information for management and decision making.

A management information system (or MIS), as the term is generally understood, is an integrated, man/machine system for providing information to support the operations, management, and decision-making functions in an organization. The system utilizes computer hardware and software, manual procedures, management and decision models, and a database.[1] Chapter 2 describes the pyramid nature of an MIS and the way an MIS affects different users.

When an MIS system is in use, there is a systematic collection and storage of data not previously obtained. More online entry and retrieval devices may be utilized. There is an increased availability of current, accurate information for all levels of personnel. Reports, responses to information requests, analysis, planning, and decision making receive improved processing and information support. The implementation of such systems is one of the most challenging areas in the application of computers. It is anticipated that the development and refinement of systems based on the MIS concept will continue to be a major objective of organizations using computers.

Automation of Information System Design

Programming has received most of the attention in terms of improving system-building performance by automating various programming tasks, use of facilitating software in programming, modularization, etc. The analysis and design of infor-

---

[1] For a comprehensive discussion, see Gordon B. Davis, *Management Information Systems: Conceptual Foundations, Structure, and Development,* New York: McGraw-Hill, 1974.

mation systems are more difficult and more crucial tasks. Some work has been performed to systematize and automate this process; considerably more needs to be done.

Methods have been proposed for quantitatively describing system require-ments, so that algorithms can be applied to the design process. The next step is to automate the system-building task. Major elements in the approach being followed by a major research project[1] are indicative of the kind of research activity to be expected:

1 Development of a problem statement to describe requirements of an informa-tion processing system completely and unambiguously.

2 Development of computer programs to analyze information system problem statements for errors and to produce output analyzed in a form useful for physical design of information processing system.

3 Development of algorithms to design optimal information processing system and for reorganizing of data.

Impact of Computers on Organizations and Individuals

Computers are already present at all levels of organizations. An individual in an organization making extensive use of computers cannot remain unaffected by changes in information processing systems. A significant change expected in such organizations is in organizational structure. The effect on the individual is in such areas as job content, reduction in allowable individual behavior, and privacy. The structure of the computer industry raises societal, economic power issues.

Impact on Structure of Organizations   In the speculation as to the impact of computers on the organizational power and status structure, most attention has been concentrated on the middle-management level. The reasoning is that computers provide top management with a greater span of control and that many of the judgmental decisions usually handled by middle management will be programmed into the computer. Therefore, less middle management will be required, and its power and status will decline.

However, one might argue that most of the time of middle-management personnel is spent on tasks which are motivational or which require unstructured decision making or judgmental reasoning. Therefore, although some decisions may be taken from them and central planning may further restrict their range of decision making, all other middle-management functions will remain. The prob-lems of managing people are still critical and are not computerized. Furthermore, the frequency of change may make it more difficult than was thought to routinize many middle-management decisions.

[1] ISDOS project at the University of Michigan. See Daniel Teichroew and Hasan Sayani, "Automation of Systems Building," *Datamation*, August 15, 1971, p. 25-30.

The question of whether complex computer systems will cause organizations to centralize operations that have been decentralized is not yet answered. In a decentralized organization, planning and decision making at the individual plant or other facility are delegated to the local manager. In a centralized organization, all important decisions are made by a central staff at the headquarters. It is clear that some individual decisions are being centralized—an example is centralized inventory control, in which a computer system keeping track of all inventory at all locations is usually able to make better decisions than the individual managers. On the other hand, the economic and managerial considerations which have prompted some organizations to decentralize are still strong. Examples are the need for local response to changing conditions and enhanced motivation.

On balance, however, it seems quite clear that the computer has already had some impact on organization and management and will have greater impact as more complex computer-based information and control systems are implemented. It is likely that the most successful systems will be ones that divide tasks between the worker and the computer (a man-machine system) rather than fully automated systems. In a task-division system, the decisions by computer are structured, routine decisions, the decisions made by the worker are the unstructured, difficult ones. And even computer decisions will need to be monitored. It would take an executive with an excess of faith in computer programs (written by mere mortal programmers) to let important decisions be handled automatically by a computer without human review.

Quality of Individual Life

Computers have created interesting and challenging new jobs and have eliminated many fairly routine clerical tasks. On the other hand, some computer-based jobs are quite routine, such as keypunching or key-entry of data. Automated systems provide users with increased processing and data retrieval capabilities, yet the systems tend to require that users be regimented to a fairly rigid discipline with regard to input, etc.

The use of computers in systems with which individuals must deal, e.g., billing and payroll, often results in a sense of frustration and alienation. It took the author 1 year to get a simple billing error straightened out with a credit card organization. Repeated notes requesting adjustment were ignored. Computerized notices were automatically generated which became increasingly threatening, and finally led to the author sending a letter to the president before human intervention was achieved. Although this system had obvious weaknesses in terms of dealing with individuals, it is not atypical. Such experiences often mark the computer as the villain in a society in which systems are frequently designed to treat the individual as an object of automated processing rather than as someone for which processing is required.

Although the fears of computer surveillance have perhaps been overemphasized, there is little question but that the computer has introduced a new dimension in the conflict between the desire by segments of society to have information and the desire of individuals to have privacy and to restrict public information to a minimum. With many manual files, it was impossible from a practical standpoint to interchange data. Files degraded fairly quickly because of misfiling, etc. File access was limited by cost and speed of access. Computers, by contrast, make it possible for government and private organizations to interchange data about individuals quickly and cheaply.

Legislation defining the responsibilities of governmental agencies maintaining files on individuals and defining the rights and remedies of individuals with respect to such files has been passed by the federal government of the United States, by most states of the United States, and by many of the Western, industrialized nations. Legislation regulating nongovernmental data files is pending but has generally not been implemented.

Competitive Structure of Computer Industry

The computer industry presents a problem to the United States economic-social system. Unlike many countries which encourage monopolies, the United States views concentrations of economic power as inconsistent with the political system, and the policy of the government under the antitrust laws is to promote competition by "breaking up" giant companies which dominate an industry. The computer industry is under continuous scrutiny in this regard because IBM dominates, with about 70 percent of the market. Most of the remainder of the business is divided among five companies having United States market shares of from 3 to 7 percent (Honeywell Information Systems, Inc., Univac Division of Sperry Rand Corp., Burroughs Corp., The National Cash Register Co., and Control Data Corporation). There is then another set of companies with even smaller shares of the total market. The issue of competition is also found outside the United States. The number of independent computer mainframe manufacturers in Europe has declined to only two; Japanese computer manufacturers have flourished only through government intervention.

IBM has been very profitable; its competitors have not. This is not because of lack of economic power. The computer divisions of some large, powerful companies (General Electric Co. and RCA Corporation) were not able to obtain profitability. Yet IBM does not quote unduly low prices. In the industry, there is agreement that IBM provides a price umbrella under which the other companies have a chance of making a profit. The economics of scale in hardware and software favor IBM (to develop a compiler for one machine costs the same as for 10,000), but IBM's sales are usually made on the basis of marketing skill and level of support (such as software) rather than on the basis of hardware price. Should IBM be "broken up" into independent, smaller companies? The answer is not obvious, and the debate will likely continue for some time. An antitrust suit to legally decide the issue is in progress.

SUMMARY

Barring some dramatic new hardware change, there seems to be no major element which signals a change from third- to fourth-generation equipment. However, circuitry is becoming smaller, faster, and less expensive. More logic is being placed in peripheral units and terminals, circuitry is being used in place of software, and specialized processors are being used to handle specific functions in a processing system.

The changes in input devices are generally toward increase in "intelligence" in terminals. Some new devices such as voice recognition are coming into use. Relatively new devices to speed output are computer output microfilm and non-impact, electrostatic printers. Traditional storage devices continue to improve. New devices to watch are holographic optical storage and magnetic bubble memory. Data communications will continue to improve through the use of specialized data communication networks.

The trend in computer system configurations is toward either centralized multiprocessor systems or a distributed processing network of small computers. Developments in computer software suggest simplified user operation and improved performance for system software and greater use of leased or purchased application software.

One of the major areas of development in organizational use of computers is the design and implementation of management information systems which support management and decision-making functions in an organization. Because organizational information processing systems are difficult and time-consuming to design and implement, major research efforts are being devoted to the automation of at least part of the process of system design and building.

The computer is having a continuing and increasing impact on organizations and individuals. Although organization structure has not been dramatically changed, there are perceptible changes in organizational behavior. The quality of individual life is affected by changes in job content and by computer system responsiveness to human problems and to changes in privacy. This dominance of the computer industry is a matter of concern to those who believe in competition. The computer, like most technological innovations, can be both good and bad for individuals. On balance, there is probably little question that computers are beneficial to society. Yet, there is a need to improve the rules for those situations in which the individual deals with a computer-based system.

EXERCISES 1 Prepare a report on a hardware development. Examples are:
   (a) Microprocessor   (d) Use of laser beams in storage devices
   (b) Holographic memory   (e) Digital data communications networks
   (c) Bubble memory
2 Prepare a report on a computer use or computer industry development such as:
   (a) Privacy and the computer
   (b) Automated information processing system design
   (c) The IBM antitrust action
3 Investigate and report on the use of:
   (a) Microprocessors
   (b) Minicomputers in distributed processing networks serving remote locations
   (c) Specialized processors

4 What are the elements of an MIS? How does each support the management use of computers?

5 Why should an honest man need to worry about computer dossiers?

6 Assume that the price of a personal computer is in the same price range as a color television set.

    (*a*) What would it be useful for if it were a small unit the size of an adding machine with limited input, output, and storage?

    (*b*) What would it be useful for if it could be connected via the telephone to a large computer?

    (*c*) How would it change the usage if the home computer had a typewriter keyboard and alphanumeric input and output?

Appendix

1

The Certificate in Data Processing

One of the problems in data processing has been the lack of professional standards and of academic training to qualify persons to do programming and other data processing work. The formal academic programs directed toward employment in data processing are few, and most persons in the field have gained their training through computer manufacturer seminars and on-the-job experience. The heterogeneity of background and training makes it difficult to assess even minimum capabilities in the data processing area.

One method for achieving minimum standards of competence and professional orientation, a certification program, was initiated by the Data Processing Management Association (DPMA). A Certificate in Data Processing (CDP) was begun in 1962; a Registered Business Programmer (RBP) examination was first offered in 1970 (and suspended in 1974). In 1973, DPMA turned the CDP examination over to an independent organization sponsored by eight computer societies. The organization, the Institute for the Certification of Computer Professionals (ICCP), prepares and administers the business-oriented CDP examination. The ICCP has developed a code of ethics for data processing professionals and may develop other tests as well as the CDP. In 1977, it reinstated the programmer examination. In 1976 there were approximately 15,000 holders of the CDP. Another organization, The Society of Certified Data Processors (SCDP), a voluntary organization for CDP recipients, provides a program of assistance for those planning to take the CDP examination.

Requirements

The CDP certificate is awarded to individuals who meet the following qualifications:

1 Acquire 5 years of direct experience in data processing. Possible reduction for academic courses, based on an evaluation of the transcripts by ICCP.

2 Possess high character (as evidenced by references).

3 Pass the CDP examination. The examination may be taken prior to completing the experience requirement.

Persons who hold the certificate are entitled to use the designation "CDP" after their names.

The examination (as of 1976) consists of 300 multiple-choice questions divided into five 50-minute sections.

1 Data processing equipment
2 Computer programming and software
3 Principles of management
4 Quantitative methods
5 Systems analysis and design

The candidate need not take all sections. If a section is passed, it need not be taken again, except that all sections must be passed within 4 years, or the sections passed prior to 4 years must be retaken and repassed.

How to Apply

The CDP examination is offered annually (about the third Saturday in February). The application deadline has been about November 15. Cost in 1976 was $45 and $85, depending on the number of sections taken. Application blanks and study guides are available from:

Institute for Certification of Computer Professionals (ICCP)
304 East 45th Street
New York, N.Y. 10017

Information on a program for preparing for the examination is available from:

The Society of Certified Data Processors
500 12th Street
Washington, D.C. 20024

Appendix

2

Guide to United States Computer Organizations and Periodicals

There are a number of active computer organizations and journals in countries other than the United States, but this appendix surveys only those in the United States. The major world organization is the International Federation for Information Processing (IFIP), 3, Rue du Marche, 6H-1204 Geneva, Switzerland. It has constituent societies from 34 countries. IFIP includes an Administrative Data Processing Group (IAG) which is devoted to organizational data processing uses of computers.

Computer Organizations

American Federation of Information Processing Societies (AFIPS) 210 Summit Avenue, Montvale, N.J. 07645. This is a federation of societies representing the information processing community. AFIPS represents the United States in a similar international group (IFIP). A major activity of AFIPS is to sponsor the National Computer Conference (NCC). This consists of sessions at which papers are presented and a large equipment show at which manufacturers display their latest equipment. Proceedings of the conference are published. AFIPS has also sponsored research such as studies of the computing industry. A person receives AFIPS notices by being associated with one of its member societies—ACM, IEEE, AICPA, etc.

Association for Computing Machinery (ACM) 1133 Avenue of the Americas, New York, N.Y. 10036. This organization, founded to advance the science and arts of information processing, holds an annual meeting (usually in August), sponsors special-interest groups on various topics, organizes seminars, and publishes six journals—*Journal of the Association for Computing Machinery* (quarterly), *ACM Transactions on Database Systems* (quarterly), *ACM Transactions on Mathematical Software* (quarterly), *Communications of the ACM* (monthly), *Computing Reviews* (monthly), and *Computing Surveys* (quarterly). ACM tends to be oriented toward scientific problems, algorithms for solutions, etc. ACM chapters are active in many cities and on a number of college campuses. Annual dues include subscriptions to *Communications of the ACM* plus one other journal. There is a special student membership rate.

Association for Educational Data Systems (AEDS) 1201 16th Street N.W., Washington, D.C. Founded by professional educators, this association has a membership consisting of individuals interested in exchanging information about the impact of modern technology upon the educational process. The association provides a monthly publication, a quarterly journal, a national convention, regional chapters, etc., and operates the AEDS National Center for Educational Data Processing.

Association for Systems Management 7890 Brookside Drive, Cleveland, Ohio 44138. A national organization of persons interested in systems work. It has local chapters, publishes a journal (*Journal of Systems Management*), promotes educational programs, and holds an annual meeting with an accompanying equipment exposition.

Data Processing Management Association (DPMA)   505 Busse Highway, Park Ridge, Ill. 60068. The membership of this organization is concerned mainly with business methods and their mechanization. The association has local chapters, publishes a monthly journal, holds an annual conference and exposition, publishes the proceedings of this conference, and sponsors educational programs.

EDP Auditors Association   P.O. Box 15562, Los Angeles, Calif. 90015. This organization is concerned with control and audit of EDP systems. The association has local chapters, an annual meeting, and a quarterly journal (*The EDP Auditor*).

Society for Management Information Systems (SMIS)   One First National Plaza, Chicago, Ill. 60670. This society holds annual meeting, sponsors research, distributes papers, etc. It has student memberships. SMIS is cosponsor of a journal, *The MIS Quarterly.*

Interested organizations   A number of organizations have an active computer-interested constituency. As examples:

> IEEE (Institute of Electrical and Electronics Engineers)
> AIDS (Association for Decision Sciences)
> TIMS (The Institute of Management Science)

Selected Periodicals

Collected Algorithms from ACM Quarterly   Loose-leaf collection of algorithms for solving problems using the computer.

Communications of the ACM   A monthly journal of ACM. Reports ACM activities plus technical articles on a wide range of subjects.

Computer Decisions   New York, N.Y. Articles on administration and use of computers. Free to qualified individuals.

Computer Digest   Detroit, Mich. 48226. A monthly digest of articles from over 400 journals and other publications in computers.

Computers and the Humanities   Queens College Press, Flushing, N.Y. 11367. Monthly publication emphasizing applications in the humanities.

Computerworld   Chicago, Ill. A comprehensive weekly newspaper covering developments in the computer community.

Computing Newsletter for Schools of Business   University of Colorado, Colorado Springs, Col. 80907. Monthly newsletter of special interest to educators and students.

Computing Surveys A quarterly publication of ACM for tutorial and survey articles.

Computing Reviews A monthly publication of ACM devoted to reviews of books and papers in the computing field.

Data Base A quarterly publication of ACM Special Interest Group on Business Data Processing (SIGBDP).

Data Comm User Monthly. Deals with problems of users of data communications.

Datamation New York, N.Y. Circulated without charge to individuals (by name and title) who qualify. Also available on a subscription basis. It is a basic source of information on current and prospective developments in the computer field. Mixed technical and user material.

Data Processing Digest Los Angeles, Calif. A monthly service which reviews publications relevant to business data processing.

EDP Analyzer Vista, Calif. Monthly reports on specific topics. Highly regarded in the industry.

EDP Auditor Quarterly publication of EDP Auditors Association.

EDPACS Reston, Va. Monthly updating publication in the field of EDP audit, control, and security.

Electronic News Fairchild Publications, Inc., New York, N.Y. Weekly newspaper oriented toward hardware and technical developments.

IBM Systems Journal Armonk, N.Y. Quarterly journal of technical articles by IBM authors. Generally of high quality with a bias toward technical topics in hardware and software.

ICP Quarterly International Computer Programs, Inc., Indianapolis, Ind. Listing of available software programs. Very complete and valuable reference.

Infosystems Wheaton, Ill. Monthly publication oriented to data processing management and other management personnel. Free to subscribers who qualify.

Journal of the Association for Computing Machinery Baltimore, Md. A quarterly publication devoted to research papers.

Journal of Data Management Park Ridge, Ill. Published monthly by DPMA. Articles are oriented to business data processing.

Journal of Systems Management Cleveland, Ohio. Monthly publication of the Association for Systems Management. Contains articles on a variety of topics related to analysis and design of information and management systems.

MIS Quarterly Blegen 93 University of Minnesota, Minneapolis, Minn. 55455. Quarterly journal cosponsored by the Society for Management Information

Systems (SMIS) and the Management Information Systems Research Center at the University of Minnesota (MISRC). Contains both practitioner and academic articles of a scholarly nature.

Mini-Micro Systems   Hudson, Mass. Formerly *Modern Data.* Monthly user-oriented nontechnical publication emphasizing minicomputers and applications of microprocessors.

SIG Publications   Many of the special interest groups (SIGs) of the ACM have publications. Members of ACM may also join the SIGs.

Small Systems World   Canoga Park, Calif. Monthly publication covering problems of small business system computer users.

Transactions on Database Systems (*TODS*)   Published quarterly by ACM. Papers on database development and research.

Transactions on Mathematical Software (*TOMS*)   Published quarterly by ACM; significant research and development in fundamental algorithms and associated hardware.

Other publications   Other interested organizations have journals which contain articles of interest. Examples are *Decision Sciences* and *Management Sciences.*

Getting Started

The person who is starting a career in computers and information processing should maintain an awareness of the field by reading computer periodicals and by associating with computer organizations. It is difficult for the novice to know where to start. Each journal and each organization has a purpose, but there are logical places to begin. The beginner should start with a subscription to *Computerworld* and a general-coverage journal such as *Infosystems, Computer Decisions,* or *Datamation.* A student with a scholarly interest should consider the *MIS Quarterly* and *Computing Surveys.* In terms of computer organizations, the largest is ACM, but a student who has a business orientation will also want to consider DPMA and the Association for Systems Management.

Glossary

The glossary contains definitions for a selected list of terms used in the field of computers and data processing. The definitions are consistent with the two glossaries having official status.

International Federation for Information Processing, *IFIP Guide to Concepts and Terms in Data Processing,* Ian Gould, ed., North-Holland Publishing Company, Amsterdam, 1971. Distributed in the United States and Canada by AFIPS, Montvale, N.J.

American National Standards Institute, *American Standard Vocabulary for Information Processing,* USA Standard X3.12-1970, New York, 1970.

In preparing the selected glossary for the first edition of the text, the *Glossary of Automatic Data Processing,* published by the U.S. Bureau of the Budget, 1962, was used in choosing the terms to include and in preparing many of the definitions. Many terms have since been revised, and additional terms have been added to the second and third editions. Terms in the glossary appear in alphabetical order by the key word. Thus the term "double precision" appears under "precision, double."

A

absolute address See *address, absolute.*

access, direct Pertaining to the process of obtaining information from or placing data in storage where the access to the storage location is independent of the location most recently accessed. An example of direct access storage medium is disk storage. Direct access is in contrast to serial access, in which access is dependent on the position of the storage location in a set of storage locations that must be processed serially. An example of a serial access storage medium is magnetic tape.

access, random Same as *access, direct.*

access, serial See *access, direct.*

accumulator A register and associated equipment in the arithmetic unit of the computer where arithmetic and logical operations are performed.

acronym A word formed from the initial letter or letters in a name or phrase. An example is FORTRAN for FORmula TRANslator.

address A number, symbol, name, or label which identifies a register or location in storage.

address, absolute A machine-language address of a specific storage location.

address, base See *address, relative.*

address, immediate An instruction in which the address portion of the instruction is the operand itself rather than the address of the operand.

address, indirect An address which references a storage location containing the address of the operand needed. This is in contrast to direct addressing in which the address references the location of the operand.

address, relative An address which is translated into an absolute address by adding a base address to it. If, for example, a relative address were 390 and the base address were 4000, the absolute address would be 4390.

ADP Automatic Data Processing.

ALGOL An acronym for ALGOrithmic Language, an international algebraic, procedure-oriented language. Similar in concept and content to FORTRAN. Widely used in Europe.

alphanumeric (or alphameric) A contraction for alphabetic and numeric. A set of alphanumeric characters will usually include special characters such as the dollar sign and comma.

analog computer See *computer, analog.*

AND gate or AND circuit See *gate.*

application A specific task on which the computer is used. Examples are payroll, order entry, and inventory management.

arithmetic, fixed point Arithmetic in which the computer does not consider the location of the radix. For example, all numbers are considered to be integers. See *arithmetic, floating point,* for contrasting system.

arithmetic, floating point Arithmetic which automatically keeps track of the scaling for the results. In floating point operations, the numbers consist of two parts—a signed mantissa and an integral exponent. Arithmetic is performed on both the mantissas and the exponents in order to form a mantissa and exponent for the result. It is contrasted with fixed point arithmetic in which the programmer must keep track of the decimal point.

ASCII An acronym for American Standard Code for Information Interchange, a 7-bit (or 8-bit compatible) used when transmitting data between computers.

assembler Also called an "assembly program" or "assembly routine." A computer routine which translates computer instructions written in machine-oriented symbolic coding into machine-language instructions.

associative memory See *storage, associative.*

asynchronous Not synchronized. Operating independently.

auxiliary storage See *storage, secondary.*

B

background program See *multiprogramming.*

baud A unit of signaling speed equal to 1 bit per second. The Baudot code is a 5-bit code sometimes used in data communications. It has generally been replaced by the ASCII code.

binary-coded decimal code A system in which individual decimal digits are represented by a group of binary digits. A minimum of four binary digits is necessary to represent a decimal digit.

binary number system A number system having a radix of 2. Absolute values are 1 and 0; the positional values are powers of 2.

bit An abbreviation for binary digit.

bit, parity A bit added to a group of binary digits in order to detect the loss of a bit from the group during processing. Also called a *check bit.* In an odd-parity check, for example, a 1- or 0-bit is added to the group of digits to make the number of 1-bits odd.

bits, zone Two to four bits added to the four bits in a binary-coded decimal group in order for the group to represent alphabetic and special characters.

block A group of records, characters, or digits handled as a unit by input and output.

blocking Combining two or more records into a single physical block to reduce read or write time.

Boolean algebra An algebra for dealing with the truth of logical propositions. Operators are AND, OR, NOT, EXCEPT, IF . . . THEN. Named after George Boole, English mathematician (1815–1864).

branch Another name for a transfer-of-control instruction which causes the selection of one, two, or more possible program paths.

breakpoint A point in a program at which the program can be halted and the results to that point analyzed or preserved for a later continuation of the program. Used primarily in debugging.

buffer Storage used to compensate for differences in the rate of flow of data or to allow devices to operate asynchronously. For example, intermediate storage between an input or output device and the computer.

bug A mistake in a program or an equipment malfunction.

byte A group of adjacent binary digits operated upon as a unit. In many computers, it is an 8-bit set encoding one alphanumeric character or two decimal digits.

C

call A transfer to a subroutine.

central processing unit (CPU) The device containing the arithmetic unit, control unit, and main memory. Also referred to as the "main frame."

channel (1) A path along which information can flow, e.g., an input/output channel which connects input/output units to the central processor; (2) one of the parallel tracks on magnetic tape or bands on a magnetic drum.

charts, HIPO Hierarchy plus input-process-output charts. They are a method of planning and documenting a program. Associated with structured programming.

check, echo An error-control procedure in which information transmitted to an output device such as a printer is transmitted back to the computer for comparison with the original information.

clock In a synchronous computer, a circuit which emits pulses at equal intervals. The pulses are used to schedule the operation of the computer.

clock, realtime A clock which records the passage of time. It can be set and read by program instructions.

COBOL An acronym for COmmon Business Oriented Language, a high-level language oriented toward organizational data processing procedures.

collate To merge two or more sequenced files into a single sequenced file.

COM Computer-output microfilm.

compile To produce a machine-language program by translating a set of instructions written in a high-level language, such as FORTRAN or COBOL.

compiler A computer program to compile a high-level source language program into an object language.

computer, analog A computer which operates by using an electrical representation of the variables in the problem.

computer, asynchronous A computer in which an operation begins as a result of the signal that the previous operation is completed or that the part of the computer needed is available.

computer, synchronous A computer in which operations are performed in set intervals of time fixed by pulses from a clock.

console The control panel used by the computer operator. It typically contains a typewriter or visual display for operator communications and may contain register displays, switches, etc.

control card A punched card which is part of a set of job control cards which direct the execution of a job on the computer.

coupler, acoustic A modem which converts data into a sequence of tones that are sent over the telephone voice line.

CRT Cathode-ray tube display device.

D

DASD Direct access storage device.

data administrator Person responsible for defining, updating, and controlling access to a database.

database An integrated file of data used by many processing applications.

database management system Comprehensive

software system to build, maintain, and access a database.

data management system Software system to access files and prepare reports.

data set A set of data records (a file). Also used to refer to a modem.

DBMS Database management system.

debug To locate and correct errors in a program or malfunctions in equipment.

decimal, binary-coded See *binary-coded decimal code.*

decision table A description of decision rules in which sets of conditions are related to actions to be taken.

demodulator See *modem.*

density The number of characters which can be stored per unit of length, such as an inch of magnetic tape.

detail file See *file, detail.*

development, top-down An approach to program development in which high-level modules are coded first.

digit, check A redundant digit added to a group of digits to detect errors. When used in connection with an identification number, the check digit provides a means for detecting invalid numbers. Also used to refer to a check bit.

disk, magnetic A rotating metal disk having a magnetized surface on which data may be stored. Direct access storage. Also spelled disc.

double precision See *precision, double.*

drum, magnetic A rapidly revolving cylinder which stores information as small polarized spots on its surface. The data is stored or obtained by means of a read-write head. Provides direct access storage.

dump, storage A transfer of the contents of a storage device to another media, such as punching cards, printout, etc. Frequently used in debugging when the contents of memory need to be listed.

duplex (1) Pertaining to a pair or a two-in-one situation; (2) a channel which allows simultaneous transmission in both directions; (3) a stand-by unit to be used in the event of equipment failure.

E

EBCDIC Abbreviation for extended binary-coded decimal interchange code. An 8-bit code identified with IBM System/360 and 370.

echo check See *check, echo.*

edit To modify the form or format of data for output by inserting dollar signs, blanks, etc. To validate and rearrange input data.

emulator Stored logic that enables a computer to execute machine-language instructions for another computer of dissimilar design.

equipment, peripheral Auxiliary machines which may be placed under the control of the computer.

F

facilities management The use of an independent service organization to operate and manage a data processing installation.

factor, scale The coefficient in the scale factor method of scaling. A number is put into a given range of magnitude (such as between $+1$ and -1), and the scale factor is the coefficient necessary to convert the normalized number back to the original number.

field An assigned area in the storage defined for a record.

file An organized collection of records having a common feature or purpose.

file, detail A file containing transaction data. Frequently used to update a master file.

file, inverted A file organized so it can be accessed by characteristic rather than by record key.

file maintenance See *maintenance, file.*

file, master A file containing relatively permanent data.

fixed point arithmetic See *arithmetic, fixed point.*

fixed word length See *word.*

flag A program indicator which informs a part of the program about a condition that occurred earlier.

flip-flop A bistable device capable of storing a bit of information.

floating point arithmetic See *arithmetic, floating point.*

foreground See *multiprogramming.*

FORTRAN An acronym for FORmula TRANslator, a programming language designed for writing programs to solve problems which can be stated in terms of arithmetic procedures. This is the most popular of the algebraic procedure-oriented languages.

frame, main See *central processing unit.*

frontend See *processor, communications.*

full duplex See *duplex.*

G

gap (1) An interval of space or time which separates words, records, or files on a magnetic tape. For example, an interblock gap is a space between blocks of records which permits start-stop operations and keeps blocks separate; (2) a space between a read-write head and the recording medium.

gate A circuit which provides an output signal dependent on past or present input signals. An AND gate provides an output pulse only if there is an input pulse on all inputs. An OR circuit has the property that an input pulse on any input line will cause an output pulse.

generator, program A routine which writes a program based on a set of specifications. The specifications may be a set of parameters (such as the characteristics of a report to be prepared) or problem-oriented instructions. The generator program essentially puts together instructions from a library, making changes as necessary.

generator, report A routine to write a program to produce a specified report from a specified set of data.

H

half-adder A circuit which adds two binary digits but does not provide for a carry. Two circuits, plus a delay, form an adder, so that a half-adder is half of an adder.

half duplex See *duplex.*

hash total See *total, hash.*

header See *label.*

heuristic Serving to discover or invent. The term pertains to a guided trial-and-error method for problem solving.

hexadecimal number system A number system with the base 16. The 16 absolute values of the system are usually represented by the numbers 0 to 9 and the letters A to F.

Hollerith Refers to the 80-column punched card and related equipment originally designed by Herman Hollerith. Also character output in FORTRAN.

housekeeping In computer programming, the setup and initialization procedures (setting up constants, variables, and switches, and clearing locations, etc.) performed prior to the processing steps of the program.

I

immediate address See *address, immediate.*

index register See *register, index.*

index sequential Data organization in which records are organized in sequential order and also referenced directly via an index based on some characteristic.

indirect address See *address, indirect.*

informatics Theory and practice associated with analysis, design, and application of computer-based information systems in organizations. The term is popular in Europe.

input Reading of data from storage medium or entry of data from terminal.

input validation See *validation.*

instruction A set of characters which define an operation to be performed and the data or unit of equipment to be used.

instruction, macro An instruction which is translated into a set of object language instructions for performing the operation specified by the macro.

instruction, one-address An instruction with an operation code and the address for one operand.

instruction, symbolic An instruction using a symbolic operation code and symbolic addresses. It is usually translated into a single machine-language instruction.

instruction, two- or three-address A machine-oriented instruction with an operation code and two or three addresses which specify operands and/or the address where results are to be stored.

interblock gap See *gap.*

interface A common boundary or connection between computer systems or parts of a single system.

interpretative routine See *routine, interpretative.*

interrupt To stop the current operation to perform some other operation, after which control may be resumed at the point where it was stopped.

IOCS (Input/Output Control System) A standard set of routines which initiate and control input and output processes.

item A contiguous set of data treated as a unit. A part of a record.

K

key An item which identifies a record.

L

label (1) A name attached to or written alongside an entity to identify it; (2) a header label record at the beginning of a file to identify the file and selected characteristics and a trailer label at the end of the file to identify the number of records, hash totals, etc.

language, algorithmic A procedure-oriented language suited for stating numerical procedures.

language, business-oriented A procedure-oriented language especially suited for business file processing. Refers specifically to COBOL.

language, object The language which results from the translation of procedure-oriented language statements. These are typically machine-language instructions.

language, procedure-oriented A machine-independent language designed for ease in stating the procedures by which a problem is to be solved. Examples are FORTRAN, COBOL, and PL/1.

length, block The number of records, characters, or words contained in one block.

length, word The number of bits in a computer word.

library Organizational function which maintains custody of programs, disks, tapes, and documentation.

library routine See *routine, library.*

list Organization of data using indexes and pointers to allow for nonsequential retrieval.

loader A routine which loads programs into internal storage for execution.

loop A series of instructions which repeat a set of computations a number of times, modifying some variable each time. The looping is terminated when a test indicates that a termination condition is satisfied. Repetition program structure.

M

maintenance, file The updating of a file with corrections and nonperiodic changes.

maintenance, program The correction, modifying, and updating of a computer program.

Management Information System See *MIS.*

map A list of storage areas used by elements of a program.

mark sensing See *sensing, mark.*

masking Extracting a group of characters from a computer word or words.

merge To combine two separate sequenced files into a single sequenced file.

MICR Magnetic Ink Character Recognition. Coding using magnetically readable ink. Primarily for check processing.

micrologic The use of a permanent stored program to interpret instructions in a micro-program. Besides lower hardware cost, the advantage of micrologic is that it can be used when a computer needs to execute the instructions of another, possibly larger, computer. The same as stored logic.

microprocessor The basic logic and storage elements required to do processing. Generally on one or two chips containing integrated circuits.

microprogram A sequence of instructions which will be translated by micrologic hardware in the computer.

microsecond One millionth of a second.

millisecond One thousandth of a second.

minicomputer A small and inexpensive but typically fast computer with limited input and output capabilities.

MIS (Management Information System) An information processing system oriented toward providing information for management. The concept requires a data-base and substantial analysis and retrieval capabilities.

mnemonic As an aid to human memory. Use of codes which sound like the function, e.g., SUB for subtraction and DIV for division.

modem (modulator-demodulator) Device to interface between processing equipment and communications system.

monitor To supervise the operation of a program by a diagnostic routine.

monitor, communications A software system to supervise and manage data communications.

multiplex To make simultaneous use of a single communications channel to transmit a number of messages.

multiprocessor A computer system with more than one arithmetic and logic unit for simultaneous use.

multiprogramming A technique for running several programs simultaneously by interleaving their operations. If one of the programs must provide realtime response and therefore must have priority, it is frequently termed a "foreground program." The nonpriority program is then termed a "background program."

N

nanosecond One billionth of a second (i.e., one thousandth of a millionth of a second, or 10^{-9} second).

normalize In programming, to adjust the exponent and fraction of a floating point quantity so that the fraction is within a prescribed range.

O

OCR   Optical Character Recognition.

octal number system   A number system to use the base 8. Binary-coded octal represents octal numbers by groups of three binary digits.

offline   Not under the control of the central processing unit.

online   Under the control of, and connected to, the central processing unit.

operand   A unit of data in a storage location or an equipment unit which the instruction operation will use.

overflow   The loss of a digit when the results of an arithmetic operation exceed the capacity of the register or memory location where the result is to be stored.

overhead   The time and space for nonproductive operations in a computer system. Includes the time and space taken by the functions of the operating system.

overlay   The technique for putting a routine into memory when it is needed by a program and for using as storage location the positions occupied by a routine which is no longer needed. Used where the entire program cannot fit in memory at once.

P

pack   To put several data items into one fixed-length computer word.

packet-switching   Transmission of data over a communications network. Each group (packet) of data has destination identification so data to be sent to a variety of locations can be intermixed in transmission.

page   A segment of a program or data which can be moved in and out of storage in multiprogramming.

parallel   Handled simultaneously using separate facilities.

parity bit   See *bit, parity.*

pass   A processing cycle in which data is read, processed, and written out.

patch   To correct a program in a rough or expedient way.

PL/1 (Programming Language, Version 1)   A combined algebraic and business language introduced by IBM in connection with its System/360.

pointer   A data item associated with an index, a record, or other set of data which contains the address of a related data item or record. Allows data to be related and referenced.

precision, double   The use of twice as many digits to represent a quantity as the computer normally operates on. If the computer normally uses 32-bit words, double precision would use a pair of 32-bit words to represent a quantity, thus increasing the number of significant digits obtainable in processing.

processing, batch   Periodic processing of items after a number of like items have been gathered together.

processing, file   The periodic updating of a file with current data, such as transaction data.

processing, online   The processing of transactions when received—in contrast to batch processing where items must accumulate before processing. To accomplish online processing requires that all equipment be online and that data records be accessible directly.

processing, parallel   Concurrent running of two or more programs stored in the memory.

processing, realtime   The processing of information as received and in time for the result to be available for influencing the process being controlled.

processor   (1) A hardware unit—the CPU; (2) an assembler or compiler translator routine.

processor, communications   A small computer dedicated to handling data communications for a larger computer. Also called a "front-end."

processor, micro   See *microprocessor.*

program   (1) The set of instructions to solve a problem; (2) to plan the procedures for solving a problem.

program generator   See *generator, program.*

program, object   The coding which results from the translation by a compiler of a source program written in a source language, such as FORTRAN or COBOL.

programming, structured   A structured approach to coding of a computer program. Generally assumes top-down design and modular hierarchy of program.

programming, symbolic   Programming using symbolic addresses and mnemonic operation codes. The symbolic program is converted to a machine-language program by a symbolic assembly system.

protocol, communications   The coding and decoding of messages to/from terminals to obtain and provide all routing and control information.

R

radix   The base of a number system.

rate, clock The time rate at which pulses are emitted from the timing circuit. This rate governs all operations in a synchronous computer.

read-only storage See *micrologic.*

realtime system See *processing, realtime.*

record A collection of related items of data.

redundancy Added characters, bits, or operations not required for the message being sent or operation being performed but added for checking purposes.

reentrant Pertaining to a routine that can be used by two or more independent programs at the same time. Used in multiprogramming and timesharing.

register A hardware device for holding data (usually a computer word) to be operated upon.

register, index A register used to modify an instruction during the instruction cycle.

report generator See *generator, report.*

routine A set of instructions which direct the computer to perform a particular process.

routine, executive A routine to control the loading of programs, relocation of programs in memory, scheduling of runs, and other functions requiring manual intervention when an executive routine is not available. Also called a "monitor" or "supervisory" routine.

routine, interpretive A routine to decode and immediately execute instructions written in a high-level code.

routine, library A prewritten, standard routine for use in programs.

RPG Report Program Generator. See *generator, report.*

run A performance of a specific process on a file of data.

S

scale factor See *factor, scale.*

semiconductor As used in computer circuitry and storage, consists of circuits etched on a small silicon chip.

sensing, mark Using a pencil to mark a box on a punch card. The markings can be sensed by special equipment, translated, and punched as regular punches.

sequence, collating The sequence in which the computer will order the set of characters used by it.

serial Pertaining to the handling of arithmetic, data transmission, etc., a digit at a time.

simplex Transmission in only one direction at a time. Contrast with duplex.

software The programming aids available for a computer. These include library routines, assembly routines, utility routines, compilers, and applications programs. Contrasted to hardware.

storage, associative A content-addressable storage in which storage locations are identified by their contents rather than by name or position.

storage, auxiliary See *storage, secondary.*

storage, buffer See *buffer.*

storage protection Protection against one program writing in or reading from the storage assigned to another program.

storage, secondary A storage device providing storage in addition to the main storage of a computer. The secondary storage is typically less expensive and with slower access than the main memory. Examples are magnetic tape, disk files, cartridge files, and magnetic drums.

storage, virtual Use of storage segments in a hierarchy of storage devices which allow the programmer to ignore physical limits on main memory.

storage, working A portion of the internal storage set aside for data being operated upon.

subroutine A set of computer instructions to carry out a predefined computation. Subroutines are either open or closed. An open subroutine is put in as an integral part of the main program. A closed subroutine is arranged so that control may be transferred to it, and after computation control will return to the main program. A closed subroutine is used (1) to avoid repeating the coding for a set of computational steps applied more than once; (2) for modular programming.

switch (1) A hardware switch; (2) a program flag that causes a selection from among alternative sequences.

System, Management Information See *MIS.*

system, operating A set of routines for supervising the operations of a computer system. The routines provide for loading of programs, relocation of programs, sequencing of operations, assembly, compilation, accounting, diagnostics, etc. The operating system automatically brings in the proper routines and keeps the computer operating without the need for manual intervention.

T

table look-up The operation of obtaining a value from a table in computer storage, where the value obtained (value of the function) is dependent on the data (value of the argument).

telecommunications Data communications using communications facilities.

throughput The total amount of work during a given time period.

time, access The time required to locate data in storage and transfer it to the arithmetic unit for processing.

timesharing Carrying out two or more functions during the same time period by allocating small divisions of the total time to each function in turn. It allows many users to use the computer at the same time.

total, hash A sum of the numbers in one field of a batch of records. The numbers are not normally added, such as account numbers. The sum is used as a control total.

trace A diagnostic technique to provide an analysis of the results after each instruction (or a certain type of instruction) is executed.

track The recording paths on a recording medium.

trail, audit The means for identifying the processing performed. The audit trail may consist of transaction listings, batch references, input document references, terminal input transaction identification, etc. Provides processing trail so any input can be traced to output and any output traced back to constituent inputs.

U

unbundling Separate pricing of hardware and software.

unpack To separate parts of a tape record or computer word and store in separate locations.

update To incorporate changes in a program, master file, etc.

V

validation To test data for correctness, completeness, and readiness to be processed. Also termed input validation or input editing.

virtual memory See *storage, virtual*.

W

word An ordered set of characters handled as a unit by the computer. The word may be fixed or variable in length. In a fixed word-length computer, the number of characters in a word does not vary, and an address will typically refer to one set of characters. In a variable word-length computer, each character or byte has an address, and the word utilized by the computer can include a variable number of characters. The length of the variable word is generally specified by the instruction which calls for it.

Z

zone (1) On Hollerith punch cards, the top three positions, used for indicating alphabetic and special characters; (2) the part of a computer word or the bits in a byte used for alphabetic and special character representations.

INDEX

INDEX

A I I I
a   mnno